THE

MAGUS,

OR

CELESTIAL INTELLIGENCER;

BEING

A COMPLETE SYSTEM OF

OCCULT PHILOSOPHY.

First Published by
Lackington, Allen & Co in 1801
This Edition 2016

This facsimile edition has been carefully scanned
and reprinted in the traditional manner by
THE LOST LIBRARY
5 High Street,
Glastonbury UK BA6 9DP

The LOST LIBRARY is a publishing house based in
Glastonbury, UK, dedicated to the reproduction
of important rare esoteric and scholarly texts for
the discerning reader.

Cataloguing Information
The Magus
Francis Barret

ISBN 978 1 906621 08 7

Printed and bound in Great Britain by
Clays Ltd, St Ives plc

**THE LOST
LIBRARY**

THE

MAGUS,

OR

CELESTIAL INTELLIGENCER;

BEING

A COMPLETE SYSTEM OF

OCCULT PHILOSOPHY.

————◆◆◆————

IN THREE BOOKS:

Containing the Antient and Modern Practice of the Cabaliſtic Art, Natural and Celeſtial Magic, &c.; ſhewing the wonderful Effects that may be performed by a Knowledge of the

Celestial Influences, the occult Properties of Metals, Herbs, and Stones,

AND THE

APPLICATION OF ACTIVE TO PASSIVE PRINCIPLES.

EXHIBITING

THE SCIENCES OF NATURAL MAGIC;

Alchymy, or Hermetic Philosophy;

ALSO

THE NATURE, CREATION, AND FALL OF MAN;

His natural and ſupernatural Gifts; the magical Power inherent in the Soul, &c.; with a great Variety of rare Experiments in Natural Magic:

THE CONSTELLATORY PRACTICE, or TALISMANIC MAGIC;

The Nature of the Elements, Stars, Planets, Signs, &c.; the Conſtruction and Compoſition of all Sorts of Magic Seals, Images, Rings, Glaſſes, &c.;

The Virtue and Efficacy of Numbers, Characters, and Figures, of good and evil Spirits,

MAGNETISM,

AND CABALISTICAL OR CEREMONIAL MAGIC;

In which the ſecret Myſteries of the Cabala are explained; the Operations of good and evil Spirits; all Kinds of Cabaliſtic Figures, Tables, Seals, and Names, with their Uſe, &c.

THE TIMES, BONDS, OFFICES, AND CONJURATION OF SPIRITS.

TO WHICH IS ADDED

Biographia Antiqua, or the Lives of the most eminent Philosophers, Magi, &c.

The Whole illuſtrated with a great Variety of

CURIOUS ENGRAVINGS, MAGICAL AND CABALISTICAL FIGURES, &c.

————◆◆◆————

BY FRANCIS BARRETT, F.R.C.

Profeſſor of Chemistry, natural and occult Philoſophy, the Cabala, &c. &c.

PUBLISHED BY

THE LOST LIBRARY

GLASTONBURY, ENGLAND

Francis Barrett.
Student in Chemistry, Metaphysicks.
Natural & Occult Philosophy &c. &c.

PREFACE.

IN this Work, which we have written chiefly for the information of thofe who are curious and indefatigable in their enquiries into occult knowledge, we have, at a vaft labour and expence, both of time and charges, collected whatfoever can be deemed curious and rare, in regard to the fubject of our fpeculations in Natural Magic---the Cabala---Celeftial and Ceremonial Magic---Alchymy---and Magnetifm; and have divided it into two Books, fub-divided into Parts: to which we have added a third Book, containing a biographical account of the lives of thofe great men who were famous and renowned for their knowledge; fhewing upon whofe authority this Science of Magic is founded, and upon what principles. To which we have annexed a great variety of notes, wherein we have impartially examined the probability of the exiftence of *Magic*, both of the good and bad fpecies, in the earlieft, as well as in the latter, ages of the world. We have exhibited a vaft number of rare experiments in the courfe of this Treatife, many of which, delivered in the beginning, are founded upon the fimple application of actives to paffives; the others are of a higher fpeculation.

In our hiftory of the lives of Philofophers, &c. we have omitted nothing that can be called interefting or fatisfactory. We have taken our hiftorical characters from thofe authors moft deferving of credit; we have given an outline of the various reports tradition gives of them; to which are annexed notes, drawn from the moft probable appearance of truth, impartially defcribing their characters and actions; leaning neither to the fide of thofe who doubt every thing, nor to them whofe credulity takes in every report to be circumftantially true.

b

At

At this time, the abstruse sciences of Nature begin to be more investigated than for a century past, during which space they have been almost totally neglected; but men becoming more enlightened, they begin to consider the extraordinary effects that were wrought by antient philosophers, in ages that were called dark. Many, therefore, have thought that time, nature, causes, and effects, being the same, with the additional improvements of mechanical and liberal arts, we may, with *their knowledge of Nature*, surpass them in the producing of wonderful effects; for which cause many men are naturally impelled, without education or other advantage, to dive into the contemplation of Nature; but the study thereof being at first difficult, they have recourse to lay out a great deal of money in collecting various books : to remedy which inconvenience and expence, the Author undertook to compose The Magus, presuming that his labours herein will meet with the general approbation of either the novitiate or adept : for whose use and instruction it is now published.

But to return to the subject of our Book : we have, in the First Part, fully explained what Natural Magic is; and have shewn that, by the application of actives to passives, many wonderful effects are produced that are merely natural, and done by manual operations. We have procured every thing that was valuable and scarce respecting this department of our work, which we have introduced under the title of Natural Magic; and a variety of our own experiments likewise. In the possession of this work, the laborious and diligent student will find a complete and delectable companion; so that he who has been searching for years, for this author and the other, will in this book find the marrow of them all.

But I would advise, that we do not depend too much upon *our own wisdom* in the understanding of these mysteries; for all earthly wisdom is foolishness in the esteem of God---I mean all the wisdom of man, which he pretends to draw from any other source than God alone.

We come next to the Second Part of our First Book, treating of the art called the *Constellatory Practice*, or *Talismanic Magic*; in which we fully demonstrate the power and efficacy of *Talismans*, so much talked of, and so little understood,

understood, by most men : we therefore explain, in the clearest and most intelligible manner, how *Talismans* may be made, for the execution of various purposes, and by what means, and from what source they become vivified, and are visible instruments of great and wonderful effects. We likewise shew the proper and convenient times ; under what constellations and aspects of the planets they are to be formed, and the times when they are most powerful to act ; and, in the next place, we have taught that our own spirit is the vehicle of celestial attraction, transferring celestial and spiritual virtue into *Seals, Images, Amulets, Rings, Papers, Glasses, &c.* Also, we have not forgot to give the most clear and rational illustration of sympathy and antipathy---attraction and repulsion. We have likewise proved how cures are performed by virtue of sympathetic powers and medicines---by seals, rings, and amulets, even at unlimited distances, which we have been witnesses of, and are daily confirmed in the true and certain belief of. We know how to communicate with any person, and to give him intimation of our purpose, at a hundred or a thousand miles distance ; but then a preparation is necessary, and the parties should have their appointed seasons and hours for that purpose ; likewise, both should be of the same firm constancy of mind, and a disciple or brother in art. And we have given methods whereby a man may receive true and certain intimation of future things (by dreams), of whatsoever his mind has before meditated upon, himself being properly disposed. Likewise, we have recited the various methods used by the antients for the invocation of astral spirits, by *circles, crystals, &c. ;* their forms of exorcism, incantations, orations, bonds, conjurations ; and have given a general display of the instruments of their art ; all of which we have collected out of the works of the most famous magicians, such as Zoroaster, Hermes, Apollonius, Simon of the Temple, Trithemius, Agrippa, Porta (the Neapolitan), Dee, Paracelsus, Roger Bacon, and a great many others ; to which we have subjoined our own notes, endeavouring to point out the difference of these arts, so as to free the name of Magic from any scandalous imputation ; seeing it is a word originally significative not of any evil, but of every good and laudable science, such as a man might profit by, and become both wise and happy ; and the practice so far from

b 2

being

being offensive to God or man, that the very root or ground of all magic takes its rise from the Holy Scriptures, viz.---" The fear of God is the beginning of all wisdom ;"---and charity is the end: which fear of God is the beginning of Magic ; for Magic is wisdom, and on this account the wise men were called *Magi*. The magicians were the first Christians ; for, by their high and excellent knowledge, they knew that that Saviour which was promised, was now born man---that Christ was our Redeemer, Advocate, and Mediator ; they were the first to acknowledge his glory and majesty ; therefore let no one be offended at the venerable and sacred title of Magician---a title which every wise man merits while he pursues that path which Christ himself trod, viz. humility, charity, mercy, fasting, praying, &c. ; for the true magician is the truest Christian, and nearest disciple of our blessed Lord, who set the example we ought to follow ; for he says---" If ye have faith, &c. ;" and " This kind comes not by fasting and prayer, &c. ;" and " Ye shall tread upon scorpions, &c. ;" and again, " Be wise as serpents, and harmless as doves."---Such instructions as these are frequently named, and given in many places of the Holy Scriptures. Likewise, all the Apostles confess the power of working miracles through faith in the name of Christ Jesus, and that all wisdom is to be attained through him ; for he says, " I am the light of the world !"

We have thought it adviseable, likewise, to investigate the power of numbers, their sympathy with the divine names of God ; and, seeing the whole universe was created by number, weight, and measure, there is no small efficacy in numbers, because nothing more clearly represents the Divine Essence to human understanding than numbers ; seeing that in all the Divine holy names there is still a conformity of numbers, so that the conclusion of this our First Book, forms a complete system of mathematical magic ; in which I have collected a vast number of curious seals from that famous magician Agrippa, and likewise from Paracelsus, noting them particularly, as I have found them correspondent with true science on experiment.

The Second Book forms a complete treatise on the mysteries of the Cabala and Ceremonial Magic ; by the study of which, a man (who can separate himself from material objects, by the mortification of the sensual appetites---

abstinence

abftinence from drunkennefs, gluttony, and other beftial paffions, and who lives pure and temperate, free from thofe actions which degenerates a man to a brute) may become a recipient of Divine light and knowledge ; by which they may forefee things to come, whether to private families, or kingdoms, or ftates, empires, battles, victories, &c. ; and likewife be capable of doing much good to their fellow-creatures : fuch as the healing of all diforders, and affifting with the comforts of life the unfortunate and diftreffed.

We have fpoken largely of prophetic dreams and vifions in our Cabaliftic Magic, and have given the tables of the Cabala, fully fet down for the information of the wife ; fome few moft fecret things being referved by the Author for his pupils only, not to be taught by publication.

The Third Book forms a complete Magical Biography, being collected from moft antient authors, and fome fcarce and valuable manufcripts ; and which has been the refult of much labour in acquiring. Therefore, thofe who wifh to benefit in thofe ftudies, muft fhake off the drowfinefs of worldly vanity, all idle levity, floth, intemperance, and luft ; fo that they may be quiet, clean, pure, and free from every diftraction and perturbation of mind, and worthily ufe the knowledge he obtains from his labours.

Therefore, my good friend, whofoever thou art, that defireft to accomplifh thefe things, be but perfuaded firft to apply thyfelf to the ETERNAL WISDOM, entreating him to grant thee underftanding, then feeking knowledge with diligence, and thou fhalt never repent thy having taken fo laudable a refolution, but thou fhalt enjoy a fecret happinefs and ferenity of mind, which the world can never rob thee of.

Wifhing thee every fuccefs imaginable in thy ftudies and experiments, hoping that thou wilt ufe the benefits that thou mayeft receive to the honour of our Creator and for the profit of thy neighbour, in which exercife thou fhalt ever experience the fatisfaction of doing thy duty ; remember our inftructions---to be filent : talk only with thofe worthy of thy communication---do not give pearls to fwine ; be friendly to all, but not familiar with all ; for many are, as the Scriptures mention---wolves in fheep clothing.

FRANCIS BARRETT.

TABLE OF CONTENTS.

Ten

BOOK II.----PART I.

c   CHAP.

DIREC-

DIRECTIONS FOR PLACING THE PLATES.

BOOK I.

BOOK II.

INTRODUCTION

STUDY OF NATURAL MAGIC.

———————

OF THE INFLUENCES OF THE STARS.

IT has been a subject of ancient dispute whether or not the stars, as second causes, do so rule and influence man as to ingraft in his nature certain passions, virtues, propensities, &c., and this to take root in him at the very critical moment of his being born into this vale of misery and wretchedness; likewise, if their site and configuration at this time do shew forth his future passions and pursuits; and by their revolutions, transits, and directed aspects, they point out the particular accidents of the body, marriage, sickness, preferments, and such like; the which I have often revolved in my mind for many years past, having been at all times in all places a warm advocate for stellary divination or astrology: therefore in this place it is highly necessary that we examine how far this influence extends to man, seeing that I fully admit that man is endowed with a free-will from God, which the stars can in no wise counteract. And as there is in man the power and apprehension of all divination, and wonderful things, seeing that we have a complete system in ourselves, therefore are we called the microcosm, or little world; for we carry

A 2

a heaven

a heaven in ourfelves from our beginning, for God hath fealed in us the image of himfelf; and of all created beings we are the epitome, therefore we muft be careful, left we confound and mix one thing with another. Neverthelefs, man, as a pattern of the great world, fympathizes with it according to the ftars, which, agreeably to the Holy Scriptures, are fet for times and feafons, and not as caufes of this or that evil, which may pervade kingdoms or private families, although they do in fome meafure forefhew them, yet they are in no wife the caufe; therefore I conceive in a wide different fenfe to what is generally underftood that " Stars rule men, but a *wife man* rules the ftars :" to which I anfwer, that the ftars do not rule men, according to the vulgar and received opinion; as if the ftars fhould ftir up men to murders, feditions, broils, lufts, fornications, adulteries, drunkennefs, &c. which the common aftrologers hold forth as found and true doctrine; becaufe, they fay, Mars and Saturn, being conjunct, do this and much more, and many other configurations and afflictions of the two great infortunes, *(as they are termed)* when the benevolent planets Jupiter, Venus, and Sol, happen to be detrimented or afflicted; therefore, then, they fay men influenced by them are moft furely excited to the commiffion of the vices before named; yet a wife man may, by the liberty of his own free-will, make thofe affections and inclinations void, and this they call " To rule the ftars;" but let them know, according to the fenfe here underftood, firft, it is not in a wife man to refift evil inclinations, but of the grace of God, and we call none wife but fuch as are endued with grace; for, as we have faid before, all natural wifdom from the hands of man is foolifhnefs in the fight of God; which was not before underftood to be a wife man fenced with grace; for why fhould he rule the ftars, who has not any occafion to fear conquered inclinations?—therefore a natural wife man is as fubject to the flavery of fin as others more ignorant than himfelf, yet the ftars do not incline him to fin. God created the heavens without fpot, and pronounced them good, therefore it is the greateft abfurdity to fuppofe the ftars, by a continual inclining of us to this or that mifdeed, fhould be our tempters, which we eventually make them, if we admit they caufe inclinations; but know that it is not from without, but within, by fin, that evil inclinations do arife: according to the Scrip

tures,

tures, " Out of the heart of man proceeds evil cogitations, murmurs, adulteries, thefts, murders, &c." Becaufe, as the heavens and apprehenfion of all celeftial virtues are fealed by God in the foul and fpirit of man ; fo when man becomes depraved by fin and the indulgence of his grofs and carnal appetite, he then becomes the feat of the Infernal Powers, which may be juftly deemed a hell ; for then the bodily and flefhly fenfe obfcures the bright purity and thinnefs of the fpirit, and he becomes the inftrument of our fpiritual enemy in the exercife of all infernal lufts and paffions.

Therefore it is moft neceffary for us to know that we are to beware of granting or believing any effects from the influences of the ftars more than they have naturally ; becaufe there are many whom I have lately converfed with, and great men, too, in this nation, who readily affirm that the *ftars* are the caufes of any kinds of difeafes, inclinations, and fortunes ; likewife that they blame the ftars for all their mifconduct and misfortunes.

Neverthelefs, we do not by thefe difcourfes prohibit or deny all influence to the ftars ; on the contrary, we affirm there is a natural fympathy and antipathy amongft all things throughout the whole univerfe, and this we fhall fhew to be difplayed through a variety of effects ; and likewife that the ftars, as figns, do forefhew great mutations, revolutions, deaths of great men, governors of provinces, kings, and emperors ; likewife the weather, tempefts, earthquakes, deluges, &c. ; and this according to the law of Providence. The lots of all men do ftand in the hands of the Lord, for he is the end and beginning of all things ; he can remove crowns and fceptres, and difplace the moft cautious arrangements and councils of man, who, when he thinks himfelf moft fecure, tumbles headlong from the feat of power, and lies grovelling in the duft.

Therefore our aftrologers in moft of their fpeculations feek without a light, for they conceive every thing may be known or read in the ftars : if an odd filver fpoon is but loft, the innocent ftars are obliged to give an account of it ; if an old maiden lofes a favourite puppy, away fhe goes to an oracle of divination for information of the whelp. Oh ! vile credulity, to think that thofe celeftial bodies take cognizance of, and give in their configurations and afpects, continual information of the loweft and vileft tranfactions of dotards, the moft

trivial

trivial and frivolous queftions that are *pretended* to be refolved by an infpec-tion into the figure of the heavens. Well does our legiflature juftly condemn as juggling impoftors all thofe idle vagabonds who infeft various parts of this metropolis, and impofe upon the fimple and unfufpecting, by anfwering, for a fhilling or half-crown fee, whatever thing or circumftance may be propofed to them, as if they were God's vicegerents on earth, and his deputed privy counfellors.

They do not even fcruple ever to perfuade poor mortals of the lower clafs, that they fhew images in glaffes, as if they actually confederated with evil fpirits : a notable inftance I will here recite, that happened very lately in this city. Two penurious Frenchmen, taking advantage of the credulity of the common people, who are continually gaping after fuch toys, had fo contrived a telefcope or optic glafs as that various letters and figures fhould be reflected in an obfcure manner, fhewing the images of men and women, &c. ; fo that when any one came to confult thefe jugglers, after paying the ufual fee, they, according to the urgency of the query, produced anfwers by thofe figures or let-ters ; the which affrights the infpector into the glafs fo much, that he or fhe fup-pofes they have got fome devilifh thing or other in hand, by which they remain under the full conviction of having actually beheld the parties they wifhed to fee, though perhaps they may at the fame time be refiding many hundreds of miles diftance therefrom : they, having received this impreffion from a pre-con-ceived idea of feeing the image of their friend in this optical machine, go away, and anon report, with an addition of ten hundred lies, that they have been witnefs of a miracle. I fay this kind of deception is only to be acted with the vulgar, who, rather than have their imaginations balked, would fwallow the moft abominable lies and conceits. For inftance, who would fuppofe that any rational being could be perfuaded that a fellow-creature of proper fize and ftature fhould be able by any means to thruft his body into a quart bottle ?—the which thing was advertifed to the public by a merry knave (not thinking there were fuch fools in exiftence), to be done by him in a public theatre. Upwards of 600 perfons were affembled to behold the tranfaction, never doubting but the fellow meant to keep his word, when, to the great mortification

and

and difgrace of this long-headed audience, the conjuror came forth amidft a general ftir and buz of " Ay, now! fee! now! fee! he is juft going to jump in."—" Indeed," fays the conjuror, " ladies and gentlemen, I am not; for if you were fuch fools as to believe fuch an abfurdity, I am not wife enough to do it :"----- therefore, making his bow, he difappeared, to the great difcomfort of thefe wife-heads, who ftraightway withdrew in the beft manner they could.

As for the telefcope magicians, they were taken into cuftody by the gentle-men of the police office, in Bow Street; nor would their familiar do them the kind-nefs to attempt their refcue.

But to have done with thefe things that are unworthy our notice as philofo-phers, and to proceed to matters of a higher nature : it is to be noted what we have before faid, in refpeft of the influences of the ftars, that Ptolemy, in his qua-drapartite, in fpeaking of *generals*, comes pretty near our ideas on the fubjeft of planetary influence, of which we did not at any time doubt, but do not admit (nay, it is not neceffary, feeing there is an aftrology in Nature),—that each aftion of our life, our afflictions, fortunes, accidents, are deducible to the influential effefts of the planets : they proceed from ourfelves; but I admit that our thoughts, aftions, cogitations, fympathize with the ftars upon the principle of general fympathy. Again, there is a much ftronger fympathy between perfons of like conftitution and temperament, for each mortal creature poffeffes a Sun and fyftem within himfelf; therefore, according to univerfal fympathy, we are affefted by the general influence or univerfal fpirit of the world, as the vital princi-ple throughout the univerfe : therefore we are not to look into the configurations of the ftars for the caufe or incitement of men's beftial inclinations, for brutes have their fpecifical inclinations from the propagation of their principle by feed, not by the fign of the horofcope; therefore as man is oftentimes capable of the aftions and exceffes of brutes, they cannot happen to a man naturally from any other fource than the feminal being infufed in his compofition ; for, feeing likewife that the foul is immortal, and endued with free-will, which afts upon the body, the foul cannot be inclined by any configuration of the ftars either to good or evil ; but from its own immortal power of willingly being feduced by fin, it prompts to evil ; but enlightened by God, it fprings to good, on

either

either principle, according to its tendency, the foul feeds while in this frail body; but what further concerns the foul of man in this, and after this, we shall fully investigate the natural magic of the foul, in which we have fully treated every point of enquiry that has been suggested to us by our own imagination, and by scientific experiments have proved its divine virtue originally sealed therein by the Author of its being.

Sufficient it is to return to our subject relative to astrology, especially to know what part of it is necessary for our use, of which we will select that which is pure and to our purpose, for the understanding and effecting of various experiments in the course of our works, leaving the tedious calculation of nativities, the never-ceasing controversies and cavillations of its professors, the dissensions which arise from the various modes of practice; all which we leave to the figure-casting plodder, telling him, by-the-by, that whatever he thinks he can fore-shew by inspecting the horoscope of a nativity, by long, tedious, and night-wearied studies and contemplations; I say, whatever he can shew respecting personal or national mutations, changes, accidents, &c. &c. all this we know by a much easier and readier method; and can more comprehensively, clearly, and intelligibly, shew and point out, to the very letter, by our Cabal, which we know to be true, without deviation, juggling, fallacy, or collusion, or any kind of deceit or imposture whatsoever; which Cabal or spiritual astrology we draw from the Fountain of Knowledge, in all simplicity, humility, and truth; and we boast not of ourselves, but of Him who teaches us through his divine mercy, by the light of whose favour we see into things spiritual and divine: in the possession of which we are secure amidst the severest storms of hatred, malice, pride, envy, hypocrisy, levity, bonds, poverty, imprisonment, or any other outward circumstance; we should still be rich, want nothing, be fed with delicious meats, and enjoy plentifully all good things necessary for our support: all this we do not vainly boast of, as figurative, ideal, or chimerical; but real, solid, and everlasting, in the which we exult and delight, and praise his name for ever and ever: Amen.

All which we publicly declare to the world for the honour of our God, being at all times ready to do every kindness we can to our poor neighbour, and,

as

as far as in us lies, to comfort him, fick or afflicted; in doing which we afk no reward: it is fufficient to us that we can do it, and that we may be acceptable to Him who fays—" I am the light of the world; to whom with the Father, and Holy Spirit, be afcribed all power, might, majefty, and dominion: Amen."

To the faithful and difcreet Student of Wifdom.

Greeting:

TAKE our inftructions; in all things afk counfel of God, and he will give it; offer up the following prayer daily for the illumination of thy underftanding: depend for all things on God, the firft caufe; with whom, by whom, and in whom, are all things: fee thy firft care be to know thyfelf; and then in humility direct thy prayer as follows.

A Prayer or Oration to God.

ALMIGHTY and moft merciful God, we thy fervants approach with fear and trembling before thee, and in all humility do moft heartily befeech thee to pardon our manifold and blind tranfgreffions, by us committed at any time; and grant, O, moft merciful Father, for his fake who died upon the crofs, that our minds may be enlightened with the divine radiance of thy holy wifdom; for feeing, O, Lord of might, power, majefty, and dominion, that, by reafon of our grofs and material bodies, we are fcarce apt to receive thofe fpiritual inftructions that we fo earneftly and heartily defire. Open, O, bleffed Spirit, the fpiritual eye of our foul, that we may be releafed from this darknefs overfpreading us by the delufions of the outward fenfes, and may perceive and underftand thofe things which are fpiritual. We pray thee, oh, Lord, above all to ftrengthen our fouls and bodies againft our fpiritual

BOOK I.   B   enemies,

enemies, by the blood and righteoufnefs of our bleffed Redeemer, thy Son,
Jefus Chrift; and through him, and in his name, we befeech thee to illuminate
the faculties of our fouls, fo that we may clearly and comprehenfively hear
with our ears, and underftand with our hearts; and remove far from us all
hypocrify, deceitful dealing, profanenefs, inconftancy, and levity; fo that
we may, in word and act, become thy faithful fervants, and ftand firm and
unfhaken againft all the attacks of our bodily enemies, and likewife be proof
againft all illufions of evil fpirits, with whom we defire no communication or
intereft; but that we may be inftructed in the knowledge of things, natural
and celeftial: and as it pleafed thee to beftow on Solomon all wifdom, both
human and divine; in the defire of which knowledge he did fo pleafe thy
divine majefty, that in a dream, of one night, thou didft infpire him with all
wifdom and knowledge, which he did wifely prefer before the riches of this
life; fo may our defire and prayer be gracioufly accepted by thee; fo that,
by a firm dependence on thy word, we may not be led away by the vain and
ridiculous purfuits of worldly pleafures and delights, they not being durable,
nor of any account to our immortal happinefs. Grant us, Lord, power and
ftrength of intellect to carry on this work, for the honour and glory of thy
holy name, and to the comfort of our neighbour; and without defign of hurt
or detriment to any, we may proceed in our labours, through Jefus Chrift, our
Redeemer: Amen.

OF NATURAL MAGIC IN GENERAL.

BEFORE we proceed to particulars, it will not be amifs to
fpeak of general; therefore, as an elucidation, we fhall briefly fhew what
fciences we comprehend under the title of Natural Magic; and to haften
to the point, we fhall regularly proceed from theory to practice; therefore,
Natural Magic undoubtedly comprehends a knowledge of all Nature, which
we by no means can arrive at but by fearching deeply into her treafury,
which

which is inexhauftible; we therefore by long ftudy, labour, and practice, have found out many valuable fecrets and experiments, which are either unknown, or are buried in the ignorant knowledge of the prefent age. The wife ancients knew that in Nature the greateft fecrets lay hid, and wonderful active powers were dormant, unlefs excited by the vigorous faculty of the mind of man; but as, in thefe latter days, men give themfelves almoft wholly up to vice and luxury, fo their underftandings have become more and more depraved; 'till, being fwallowed up in the grofs fenfes, they become totally unfit for divine contemplations and deep fpeculations in Nature; their intellectual faculty being drowned in obfcurity and dulnefs, by reafon of their floth, intemperance, or fenfual appetites. The followers of Pythagoras enjoined filence, and forbade the eating of the flefh of animals; the firft, becaufe they were cautious, and aware of the vanity of vain babbling and fruitlefs cavillations: they ftudied the power of numbers to the higheft extent; they forbade the eating of flefh not fo much on the fcore of tranfmigration, as to keep the body in a healthful and temperate ftate, free from grofs humours: by thefe means they qualified themfelves for fpiritual matters, and attained unto great and excellent myfteries, and continued in the exercife of charitable arts, and the practice of all moral virtues: yet, feeing they were Heathens, they attained not unto the high and infpired lights of wifdom and knowledge that was beftowed on the Apoftles, and others, after the coming of Chrift; but they mortified their lufts, lived temperately, chafte, honeft, and virtuous; which government is fo contrary to the practice of modern Chriftians, that they live as if the bleffed word had come upon the earth to grant them privilege to fin. However, we will leave Pythagoras and his followers, to haften to our own work; whereof we will firft explain the foundation of Natural Magic, in as clear and intelligible a manner as the fame can be done.

THE

FIRST PRINCIPLES

of

NATURAL MAGIC.

BOOK THE FIRST.

==

CHAP. I.

NATURAL MAGIC DEFINED----OF MAN----HIS CREATION----DIVINE IMAGE-----AND OF THE
SPIRITUAL AND MAGICAL VIRTUE OF THE SOUL.

NATURAL MAGIC is, as we have faid, a comprehen-
five knowledge of all Nature, by which we fearch out her fecret and occult
operations throughout her vaft and fpacious elaboratory; whereby we come
to a knowledge of the component parts, qualities, virtues, and fecrets of
metals, ftones, plants, and animals; but feeing, in the regular order of the
creation, man was the work of the fixth day, every thing being prepared for
his vicegerency here on earth, and that it pleafed the omnipotent God, after
he had formed the great world, or macrocofm, and pronounced it good, fo he
created man the exprefs image of himfelf; and in man, likewife, an exact
model of the great world. We fhall defcribe the wonderful properties of man,
in which we may trace in miniature the exact refemblance or copy of the
univerfe; by which means we fhall come to the more eafy underftanding of
whatever we may have to declare concerning the knowledge of the inferior
nature, fuch as animals, plants, metals, and ftones; for, by our firft declaring
the occult qualities and properties that are hid in the little world, it will ferve
as a key to the opening of all the treafures and fecrets of the macrocofm, or

great

great world : therefore, we fhall haften to fpeak of the creation of man, and his divine image ; likewife of his fall, in confequence of his difobedience ; by which all the train of evils, plagues, difeafes, and miferies, were entailed upon his pofterity, through the curfe of our Creator, but deprecated by the mediation of our bleffed Lord, Chrift.

THE CREATION, DISOBEDIENCE, AND FALL OF MAN.

ACCORDING to the word of God, which we take in all things for our guide, in the 1ft chapter of Genefis, and the 26th verfe, it is faid—" God faid, let us make man in our image, after our likenefs ; and let them have dominion over the fifh of the fea, and over the fowl of the air, and over the cattle, and over *all* the earth, and over every creeping thing that creepeth upon the earth."—Here is the origin and beginning of.our frail human nature ; hence every foul was created by the very light itfelf, and Fountain of Life, after his own exprefs image, likewife immortal, in a beautiful and well-formed body, endued with a moft excellent mind, and dominion or unlimited monarchy over all Nature, every thing being fubjefted to his rule, or command ; one creature only being excepted, which was to remain untouched and confecrated, as it were, to the divine mandate : " Of every tree of the garden thou mayeft freely eat ;" " But of the tree of the knowledge of good and evil, thou fhalt not eat of it ; for in the day that thou eateft of it, thou fhalt furely die." Gen. ii. ver. 16. Therefore Adam was formed by the finger of God, which is the Holy Spirit ; whofe figure or outward form was beautiful and proportionate as an angel ; in whofe voice (before he finned) every found was the fweetnefs of harmony and mufic : had he remained in the ftate of innocency in which he was formed, the weaknefs of mortal man, in his depraved ftate, would not have been able to bear the virtue and celeftial fhrillnefs of his voice. But when the *deceiver* found that man, from the infpiration of God, had began to fing fo fhrilly, and to repeat the celeftial harmony of the heavenly country, he counterfeited the engines of craft : feeing his wrath
againft

againſt him was in vain, he was much tormented thereby, and began to think how he might entangle him into diſobedience of the command of his Creator, whereby he might, as it were, laugh him to ſcorn, in deriſion of his new creature, man.

Van Helmont, in his Oriatrike, chap. xcii. ſpeaking of the entrance of death into human nature, &c., finely touches the ſubjeçt of the creation, and man's diſobedience : indeed, his ideas ſo perfectly coincide with my own, that I have thought fit here to tranſcribe his philoſophy, which ſo clearly explains the text of Scripture, with ſo much of the light of truth on his ſide, that it carries along with it the ſureſt and moſt poſitive conviction.

" Man being eſſentially created after the image of God, after that, he raſhly preſumed to generate the image of God out of himſelf; not, indeed, by a certain monſter, but by ſomething which was ſhadowly like himſelf. With the raviſhment of Eve, he, indeed, generated not the image God like unto that which God would have inimitable, as being divine; but in the vital air of the ſeed he generated diſpoſitions; careful at ſome time to receive a ſenſitive, diſcurſive, and motive ſoul from the Father of Light, yet *mortal*, and *to periſh ;* yet, neverthelefs, he ordinarily inſpires, and of his own goodneſs, the ſubſtantial ſpirit of a mind ſhewing forth his own image: ſo that man, in this reſpect, endeavoured to generate his own image ; not after the manner of brute beaſts, but by the copulation of ſeeds, which at length ſhould obtain, by requeſt, a ſoulified light from the Creator ; and the which they call a ſenſitive ſoul.

" For, from thence hath proceeded another generation, conceived after a beaſtlike manner, mortal, and uncapable of eternal life, after the manner of beaſts ; and bringing forth with pains, and ſubject to diſeaſes, and death ; and ſo much the more ſorrowful, and full of miſery, by how much that very propagation in our firſt parents dared to invert the intent of God.

" Therefore the unutterable goodneſs forewarned them that they ſhould not taſte of that tree ; and otherwiſe he foretold, that the ſame day they ſhould die the death, and ſhould feel all the root of calamities which accompanies death."

Deſervedly, therefore, hath the Lord deprived both our parents of the benefit of immortality ; namely, death ſucceeded from a conjugal and brutal copulation :

neither

neither remained the fpirit of the Lord with man, after that he began to be flefh.

Further; becaufe that defilement of Eve fhall thenceforth be continued in the propagation of pofterity, even unto the end of the world, from hence the fin of the defpifed fatherly admonition, and natural deviation from the right way, is now among other fins for an impurity, from an inverted, carnal, and well nigh brutifh generation, and is truly called original fin; that is, man being fowed in the pleafure of the concupifcence of the flefh, fhall therefore always reap a neceffary death in the flefh of fin; but, the knowledge of good and evil, which God placed in the diffuaded apple, did contain in it a feminary virtue of the concupifcence of the flefh, that is, an occult forbidden conjunction, diametrically oppofite to the ftate of innocence, which ftate was not a ftate of ftupidity; becaufe He was he unto whom, before the corruption of Nature, the effences of all living creatures whatfoever were made known, according to which they were to be named from their property, and at their firft fight to be effentially diftinguifhed : *man*, therefore, though eating of the apple, attained a knowledge that he had loft his radical innocenty ; for, neither before the eating of the apple was he fo dull or ftupified that he knew not, or did not perceive himfelf naked ; but, with the effect of fhame and brutal concupifcence, he then firft declared he was naked.

For that the knowledge of good and evil fignifies nothing but the concupifcence of the flefh, the Apoftle teftifies ; calling it the law, and defire of fin. For it pleafed the Lord of heaven and earth to infert in the apple an incentive to concupifcence ; by which he was able fafely to abftain, by not eating of the apple, therefore diffuaded therefrom ; for otherwife he had never at any time been tempted, or ftirred up by his genital members. Therefore the apple being eaten, man, from an occult and natural property ingrafted in the fruit, conceived a luft, and fin became luxurious to him, and from thence was made an animal feed, which, haftening into the previous or foregoing difpofitions of a *fenfitive foul*, and undergoing the law of other *caufes*, reflected itfelf into the vital fpirit of Adam ; and, like an ignis-fatuus, prefently receiv-

ing

ing an archeus or ruling spirit, and animal idea, it presently conceived a power of propagating an animal and mortal seed, ending into life.

Furthermore, the sacred text hath in many places compelled me unto a perfect position, it making Eve an helper like unto Adam; not, indeed, that she should supply the *name*, and *room of a wife*, even as she is called, straightway after sin, for she was a virgin in the intent of the Creator, and afterwards filled with misery: but not, as long as the state of purity presided over innocency, did the will of man overcome her; for the translation of man into Paradise did foreshew another condition of living than that of a beast; and therefore the eating of the apple doth by a most chaste name cover the concupiscence of the *flesh*, while it contains the " knowledge of good and evil" in this name, and calls the ignorance thereof the state of innocence: for, surely, the attainment of that aforesaid knowledge did nourish a most hurtful death; and an irrevocable deprivation of eternal life: for if man had not tasted the apple, he had lived void of concupiscence, and offsprings had appeared out of Eve (a virgin) from the Holy Spirit.

But the apple being eaten, " presently their eyes were opened," and Adam began lustfully to covet copulation with the naked virgin, and defiled her, the which God had appointed for a naked help unto him. But man prevented the intention of God by a strange generation in the flesh of sin; whereupon there followed the corruption of the former nature, or the flesh of sin, accompanied by concupiscence: neither doth the text insinuate any other mark of " *the knowledge of good and evil*," than that they " *knew themselves to be naked*," or, speaking properly, of their virginity being corrupted, polluted with bestial lust, and defiled. Indeed, their whole " knowledge of good and evil" is included in their shame within their privy parts alone; and therefore in the 8th of Leviticus, and many places else in the Holy Scriptures, the privy parts themselves are called by no other etymology than that of shame; for from the copulation of the flesh their eyes were opened, because they then knew that the good being lost, had brought on them a degenerate nature, shamefulness, an intestine and inevitable obligation of death; sent also into their posterity.

Alas! too late, indeed they understood, by the unwonted novelty and shamefulness of their concupiscence, why God had so lovingly forbade the eating of the apple. Indeed, the truth being agreeable unto itself, doth attest the filthiness of impure Adamical generation; for the impurity which had received a contagion from any natural issues whatsoever of menstrues or seed, and that by its touching alone is reckoned equal to that which should by degrees creep on a person from a co-touching of dead carcases, and to be expiated by the same ceremonious rite that the text might agreeably denote, that death began by the concupiscence of the flesh lying hid in the fruit forbidden; therefore, also, the one only healing medicine, of so great an impurity contracted by touching, consisted in washing: under the similitude or likeness thereof, faith and hope, which in baptism are poured on us, are strengthened.

For as soon as Adam knew that by fratricide the first born of mortals, whom he had begotten in the concupiscence of the flesh, had killed his brother, guiltless and righteous as he was; and foreseeing the wicked errors of mortals that would come from thence, he likewise perceived his own miseries in himself; certainly knowing that all these calamities had happened unto him from the sin of concupiscence drawn from the apple, which were unavoidably issuing on his posterity, he thought within himself that the most discreet thing he could do, was hereafter wholly to abstain from his wife, whom he had violated; and therefore he mourned, in chastity and sorrow, a full hundred years; hoping that by the merit of that abstinence, and by an opposition to the concupiscence of the flesh, he should not only appease the wrath of the incensed Deity, but that he should again return into the former splendour and majesty of his primitive *innocence* and *purity*. But the repentance of one age being finished, it is most probable the mystery of Christ's incarnation was revealed unto him; neither that man ever could hope to return to the brightness of his ancient purity by his own strength, and much less that himself could reprieve his posterity from death; and that, therefore, marriage was well pleasing, and was after the fall indulged unto him by God because he had determined thus to satisfy his justice at the fulness of times, which should,

to

to the glory of his own *name*, and the confufion of Satan, elevate mankind to a more fublime and eminent ftate of bleffednefs.

From that time Adam began to know his wife, *viz.* after he was an hundred years old, and to fill the earth, by multiplying according to the bleffing once given him, and the law enjoined him---" Be fruitful and multiply."---Yet fo, neverthelefs, that although matrimony, by reafon of the great want of propagation, and otherwife impoffible courfary fucceffion of the primitive divine generation, be admitted as a facrament of the faithful.

If, therefore, both our firft parents,-after the eating of the apple, were afhamed, they covered only their privy parts ; therefore that fhame doth prefuppofe, and accufe of fomething committed againft juftice---againft the intent of the Creator---and againft their own proper nature : by confequence, therefore, that Adamical generation was not of the primitive conftitution of their nature, as neither of the original intent of the Creator ; therefore, when God foretels that the earth fhall bring forth thiftles and thorns, and that man fhall gain his bread by the fweat of his brow, they were not execrations, but admonitions, that thofe fort of things fhould be obvious in the earth : and, becaufe that beafts fhould bring forth in pain---fhould plow in fweat---fhould eat their food with labour and fear, that the earth fhould likewife bring forth very many things befides the intention of the hufbandman ; therefore, alfo, that they ought to be nourifhed like unto brute beafts, who had begun to generate after the manner of brute beafts.

It is likewife told Eve, after her tranfgreffion, that fhe fhould bring forth in pain. Therefore, what hath the pain of bringing forth common with the eating of the apple, unlefs the apple had operated about the concupifcence of the flefh, and by confequence ftirred up copulation ; and the Creator had intended to diffuade it, by dehorting from the eating of the apple. For, why are the genital members of women punifhed with pains at child-birth, if the eye in feeing the apple, the hands in cropping it, and the mouth in eating of it, have offended ? for was it not fufficient to have chaftifed the life with death, and the health with very many difeafes ?---Moreover, why is the womb afflicted, as in

brutes,

brutes, with the manner of bringing forth, if the conception granted to beafts were not forbidden to man ?

After their fall, therefore, *their eyes were opened, and they were. ashamed :* it denotes and fignifies that, from the filthinefs of concupifcence, they knew that the copulation of the flefh was forbidden in the moft pure innocent chaftity of nature ; and that they were overfpread with fhame, when, their eyes being opened, their underftandings faw that they had committed filthinefs moft deteftable.

But on the ferpent and evil fpirit alone was the top and fummit of the whole curfe, even as the privilege of the woman, and the myfterious prerogative of the blefling upon the earth, *viz.* That the woman's feed fhould bruife the head of the ferpent. So that it is not poffible that to *bring forth in pain* fhould be a curfe ; for truly with the fame voice of the Lord is pronounced the blefling of the woman, and victory over the infernal fpirit.

Therefore Adam was created in the poffeffion of immortality. God intended not that man fhould be an *animal* or *fenfitive* creature, nor be born, conceived, or live as an animal ; for of truth he was created unto a *living foul,* and that after the true image of God ; therefore he as far differed from the nature of an animal, as an immortal being from a mortal, and as a God-like creature from a brute.

I am forry that our fchool-men, many of them, wifh, by their arguments of noife and pride, to draw man into a total animal nature, (nothing more) drawing (by their logic) the effence of a man effentially from an animal nature : becaufe, although man afterwards procured death to himfelf and pofterity, and therefore may feem to be made nearer the nature of animal creatures, yet it ftood not in his power to be able to pervert the fpecies of the divine image : even fo as neither was the evil fpirit, of a fpirit, made an animal, although he became nearer unto the nature of an animal, by hatred and brutal vices. Therefore man remained in his own fpecies wherein he was created ; for as often as man is called an *animal,* or fenfitive living creature, and is in earneft thought to be fuch, fo many times the text is falfified which fays, " But the ferpent was more crafty than all the living creatures of the
earth,

earth, which the Lord God had made;" because he speaks of the natural craft and subtilty of that living and creeping animal. Again, if the position be true, man was not directed into the propagation of *seed* or *flesh*, neither did he aspire unto a sensitive soul; and therefore the sensible soul of Adamical generation is not of a brutal species, because it was raised up by a seed which wanted the original ordination and limitation of any species; and so that, as the *sensitive soul* in man arose, besides the intent of the Creator and Nature; so it is of no brutal species, neither can it subsist, unless it be continually tied to the *mind*, from whence it is supported in its life.

Wherefore, while man is of no brutal species, he cannot be an animal in respect to his mind, and much less in respect to his soul, which is of no species.

Therefore know, that neither evil spirit, nor whole nature also, can, by any means or any way whatever, change the essence given unto man from his Creator, and by his foreknowledge determined that he should remain continually such as he was created, although he, in the mean time, hath clothed himself with strange properties, as natural unto him from the vice of his own will; for as it is an absurdity to reckon man glorified among animals, because he is not without sense or feeling, so to be sensitive does not shew the inseparable essence of an animal.

Seeing, therefore, our first parents had both of them now felt the effect throughout their whole bodies of the eating of the apple, or concupiscence of the flesh in their members in Paradise, it shamed them; because their members, which, before, they could rule at their pleasure, were afterwards moved by a proper incentive to lust.

Therefore, on the same day, not only mortality entered through concupiscence, but it presently after entered into a conceived generation; for which they were, the same day, also driven out of Paradise: hence followed an adulterous, lascivious, beast-like, devilish generation, and plainly incapable of entering into the kingdom of God, diametrically opposite to God's ordination; by which means death, and the threatened punishment, *corruption*, became inseparable to man and his posterity.

Therefore,

Therefore, original fin was effectively bred from the concupifcence of the flefh, but occafioned only by the apple being eaten, and the admonition defpifed: but the ftimulative to concupifcence was placed in the diffuaded tree, and that occult luftful property radically inferted and implanted in it. But when Satan (befides his *hope*, and the deflowering of the virgin, nothing hindering of it) faw that man was not taken out of the way, according to the forewarning, (for he knew not that the *Son* of *God* had conftituted himfelf a furety, before the Father, for man) he, indeed, looked at the vile, corrupted, and degenerated nature of man, and faw that a power was withdrawn from him of uniting himfelf to the God of infinite majefty, and began greatly to rejoice. That joy was of fhort duration, for, by and by, he likewife knew that marriage was ratified by Heaven—that the divine goodnefs yet inclined to man—and that Satan's own fallacies and deceits were thus deceived: hence conjecturing that the Son of God was to reftore every defect of contagion, and, therefore, perhaps, to be incarnated. He then put himfelf to work how, or in what manner, he fhould defile the ftock that was to be raifed up by matrimony with a mortal foul, fo that he might render every conception of God in vain: therefore he ftirred up not only his fratricides, and notorioufly wicked perfons, that there might be evil abounding at all times; but he procured that Atheifm might arife, and that, together with Heathenifm, it might daily increafe, whereby indeed, if he could not hinder the co-knitting of the immortal mind with the fenfitive foul, he might, at leaft, by deftroying the law of Nature, bring man unto a level with himfelf under infernal punifhment: but his fpecial care and defire was to expunge totally the immortal mind out of the ftock of pofterity.

Therefore he *(the Devil)* ftirs up, to this day, deteftable copulations in Atheiftical libertines: but he faw from thence, that nothing but brutifh or favage monfters proceeded, to be abhorred by the very parents themfelves; and that the copulation with women was far more plaufible to men; and that by this method the generation of men fhould conftantly continue; for he endeavoured to prevent the hope of reftoring a remnant, that is, to hinder the incarnation of the Son of God; therefore he attempted, by an application of

active

active things, to frame the feed of man according to his own accurfed defire; which, when he had found vain and impoffible for him to do, he tried again whether an imp or witch might not be fructified by fodomy; and when this did not fully anfwer his intentions every way, and he faw that of an afs and a horfe a mule was bred, which was nearer a-kin to his mother than his father; likewife that of a coney and dormoufe being the father, a true coney was bred, being diftinct from his mother, only having a tail like the dormoufe; he declined thefe feats, and betook himfelf to others worthy, indeed, only of the fubtile craft of the *Prince of Darknefs.*

Therefore Satan inftituted a connexion of the feed of man with the feed and in the womb of a junior witch, or forcerefs, that he might exclude the difpofitions unto an immortal mind from fuch a new, polifhed conception: and afterwards came forth an adulterous and lafcivious generation of Faunii, Satyrs, Gnomes, Nymphs, Sylphs, Driades, Hamodriades, Neriads, Mermaids, Syrens, Sphynxes, Monfters, &c., ufing the conftellations, and difpofing the feed of man for fuch like monftrous prodigious generations.

And, feeing the Faunii and Nymphs of the woods were preferred before the others in beauty, they afterwards generated their offspring amongft themfelves, and at length began wedlocks with men, feigning that, by thefe copulations, they fhould obtain an immortal foul for them and their offspring; but this happened through the perfuafions and delufions of Satan to admit thefe monfters to carnal copulation, which the ignorant were eafily perfuaded to; and therefore thefe Nymphs are called Succubii: although Satan afterwards committed worfe, frequently tranfchanging himfelf, by affuming the perfons of both Incubii and Succubii, in both fexes; but they conceived not a true young by the males, except the Nymphs alone. The which, indeed, feeing the fons of God (that is, men) had now, without diftinction, and in many places, taken to be their wives, God was determined to blot out the whole race begotten by thefe infernal and deteftable marriages, through a deluge of waters, that the intent of the evil fpirit might be rendered fruftrate.

Of which monfters before mentioned, I will here give a ftriking example from Helmont: for he fays, a merchant of Ægina, a countryman of his,

failing

failing various times unto the Canaries, was afked by Helmont for his ferious judgment about certain creatures, which the mariners frequently brought home from the mountains, as often as they went, and called them Tude-fquils ;* for they were dried dead carcaffes, almoft three-footed, and fo fmall that a boy might eafily carry one of them upon the palm of his hand, and they were of an exact human fhape ; but their whole dead carcafs was clear or tranfparent as any parchment, and their bones flexible like griftles ; againft the fun, alfo, their bowels and inteftine were plainly to be feen ; which thing I, by Spaniards there born, knew to be true. I confidered that, to this day, the deftroyed race of the Pygmies were there ; for the Almighty would render the expectations of the evil fpirit, fupported by the abominable actions of mankind, void and vain ; and he has, therefore, manifoldly faved us from the craft and fubtilty of the Devil, unto whom eternal punifhments are due, to his extreme and perpetual confufion, unto the everlafting fanctifying of the Divine Name.

CHAP. II.

OF THE WONDERS OF NATURAL MAGIC, DISPLAYED IN A VARIETY OF SYMPATHETIC AND OCCULT OPERATIONS THROUGHOUT THE FAMILIES OF ANIMALS, PLANTS, METALS, AND STONES, TREATED OF MISCELLANEOUSLY.

THE wonders of Animal Magic we mean fully to difplay under the title of Magnetifm. But here we haften to inveftigate by what means, inftruments, and effects, we muft apply actives to paffives, to the producing of rare and uncommon effects; whether by *actions, amulets, alligations* and *fufpenfions*— or *rings, papers, unctions, fuffumigations, allurements, forceries, enchantments, images, lights, founds*, or the like. Therefore, to begin with things more fimple :—If any one fhall, with an entire new knife, cut afunder a lemon, ufing words expreffive of hatred, contumely, or diflike, againft any individual,

* Stude-quills, or Stew'd quills.

the

the abfent party, though at an unlimited diftance, feels a certain inexpref-
fible and cutting anguifh of the heart, together with a cold chillinefs and
failure throughout the body ;—likewife of living animals, if a live pigeon be
cut through the heart, it caufes the heart of the party intended to affect with
a fudden failure ;—likewife fear is induced by fufpending the magical image
of a man by a fingle thread ;—alfo death and deftruction by means fimilar to
thefe ; and all thefe from a fatal and magical fympathy.

Likewife of the virtues of fimple animals, as well as manual operations, of
which we fhall fpeak more anon :—The application of hare's fat pulls out a
thorn ;—likewife any one may cure the tooth-ache with the ftone that is in the
head of the toad ;—alfo, if any one fhall catch a living frog before fun-rife,
and he or fhe fpits in the mouth of the frog, will be cured of an afthmatic
confumption ;—likewife the right or left eye of the fame animal cures blindnefs ; and the fat of a viper cures a bite of the fame. Black hellebore eafeth
the head-ache, being applied to the head, or the powder fnuffed up the nofe
in a moderate quantity. Coral is a well-known prefervative againft witchcraft
and poifons, which if worn now, in this time, as much round children's necks
as ufual, would enable them to combat many difeafes which their tender years
are fubjected to, and to which, with fafcinations, they often fall a victim.
I know how to compofe coral amulets, or talifmans, which, if fufpended even
by a thread, fhall (God affifting) prevent all harms and accidents of violence
from fire, or water, or witchcraft, and help them to withftand all their difeafes.

Paracelfus and Helmont both agree, that in the toad, although fo irreverent
to the fight of man, and fo noxious to the touch, and of fuch ftrong violent
antipathy to the blood of man, I fay, out of this hatred Divine Providence
hath prepared us a remedy againft manifold difeafes moft inimical to man's
nature. The toad hath a natural averfion to man ; and this fealed image, or
idea of hatred, he carries in his head, eyes, and moft powerfully throughout his
whole body : now that the toad may be highly prepared for a fympathetic remedy
againft the plague or other diforders, fuch as the ague, falling, ficknefses, and
various others ; and that the terror of us, and natural inbred hatred may the more
ftrongly be imprinted and higher afcend in the toad, we muft hang him up aloft

BOOK I.　　　　　　　　D　　　　　　　　　　　in

in a chimney, by the legs, and set under him a dish of yellow wax, to receive whatsoever may come down, or fall from his mouth ; let him hang in this position, in our sight, for three or four days, at least till he is dead : now we must not omit frequently to be present in sight of the animal, so that his fears and inbred terror of us, with the ideas of strong hatred, may encrease even unto death.

So you have a most powerful remedy in this one toad, for the curing of forty thousand persons infected with the pest or plague.

Van Helmont's process for making a preservative amulet against the plague is as follows :—

" In the month of July, in the decrease of the moon, I took old toads, whose eyes abounded with white worms hanging forth into black heads, so that both his eyes were totally formed with worms, perhaps fifty in number, thickly compacted together, their heads hanging out ; and as oft as any one of them attempted to get out, the toad, by applying his fore-foot, forbade its utterance. These toads being hung up, and made to vomit in the manner before mentioned, I reduced the insects and other matters ejected from the toad, with the waxen dish being added thereto ; and, the dried carcass of the toad being reduced into powder, I formed the whole into troches, with gum-dragon ; which, being borne about the left breast, drove speedily away all contagion ; and being fast bound to the place affected, thoroughly drew out the poison : and these troches were more potent after they had returned into use divers times, than when new. I found them to be a most powerful amulet against the plague ; for if the serpent eateth dust all the days of his life, because he was the instrument of sinning ; so the toad eats earth, (which he vomits up) all the days of his life ; and, according to the Adeptical philosophy, the toad bears an hatred to man, so that he infects some herbs that are useful to man with his poison, in order for his death. But this difference note between the toad and the serpent : the toad, at the sight of man, from a natural quality sealed in him, called antipathy, conceives a great terror or astonishment ; which terror from man imprints on this animal a natural efficacy against the images of the affrighted archeus in man. For, truly, the terror of the toad kills and anni-

hilates

hilates the ideas of the affrighted archeus in man, because the terror in the toad is natural, therefore radical."

For the poison of the plague is subdued by the poison of the toad, not by an action primarily destructive, but by a secondary action; as the pestilent idea of hatred or terror extinguishes the ferment, by whose mediation the poison of the plague subsists, and proceeds to infect : for seeing the poison of the plague is the product of the image of the terrified archeus established in a fermental, putrified, odour, and mumial air, this coupling ferments the appropriate mean, and immediately the subject of the poison is taken away.

Therefore the opposition of the amulet formed from the body, &c., of the toad, takes away and prevents the baneful and most horrible effects of the pestilential poison and ferment of the plague.

Hence it is conjectured that he is an animal ordained by God, that the idea of his terror being poisonous indeed to himself, should be to us, and to our plague, a poison in terror. Since, therefore, the toad is most fearful at the beholding of man, which in himself, notwithstanding, forms the terror conceived from man, and also the hatred against man, into an image and active real being, and not consisting only in a confused apprehension ; hence it happens that a poison ariseth in the toad, which kills the pestilent poison of terror in man ; to wit, from whence the archeus waxeth strong, he not only perceiving the pestilent idea to be extinguished in himself ; but, moreover, because he knoweth that something inferior to himself is terrified, dismayed, and doth fly. Again, so great is the fear of the toad, that if he is placed directly before thee, and thou dost behold with an intentive furious look, so that he cannot avoid thee, for a quarter of an hour, he dies,* being fascinated with terror and astonishment.

* I have tried this experiment upon the toad, and other reptiles of his nature, and was satisfied of the truth of this affirmation.

OF THE SERPENT.

HIPPOCRATES, by the use of some parts of this animal, attained to himself divine honours ; for therewith he cured pestilence and contagion, consumptions, and very many other diseases ; for he cleansed the flesh of a viper. The utmost part of the tail and head being cut off, he stripped off the skin, casting away the bowels and gall ; he reserved of the intestines only the heart and liver ; he drew out all the blood, with the vein running down the back-bone ; he bruised the flesh and the aforesaid bowels with the bones, and dried them in a warm oven until they could be powdered, which powder he sprinkled on honey ; being clarified and boiled, until he knew that the fleshes in boiling had cast aside their virtue, as well in the broth as in the vapours ; he then added unto this electuary the spices of his country to cloak the secret. But this cure of diseases by the serpent contains a great mystery, viz. that as death crept in by the serpent of old, itself ought to be mitigated by the death of the serpent ; for Adam, being skilful in the properties of all beasts, was not ignorant also that the serpent was more crafty than other living creatures, and that the aforesaid balsam, the remedy of death, lay hid in the serpent ; wherefore the spirit of darkness could not more safely deceive our first parents than under the guileful serpent's form ; for they foolishly imagined they should escape the death, so sorely threatened by God, by the serpent's aid.

Amber is an amulet :—a piece of red amber worn about one, is a preservative against poisons and the pestilence.

Likewise, a sapphire stone is as effectual. Oil of amber, or amber dissolved in pure spirit of wine, comforts the womb being disordered : if a suffumigation of it be made with the warts of the shank of a horse, it will cure many disorders of that region.

The liver and gall of an eel, likewise, being gradually dried and reduced to powder, and taken in the quantity of a filbert-nut in a glass of warm wine, causes a speedy and safe delivery to women in labour. The liver of a serpent likewise effects the same.

Rhubarb,

Rhubarb, on account of its violent antipathy to choler, wonderfully purges the fame. Mufic is a well-known fpecific for curing the bite of a tarantula, or any venomous fpider; likewife, water cures the hydrophobia. Warts are cured by paring off the fame; or by burying as many pebbles, fecretly, as the party has warts. The king's-evil may be cured by the heart of a toad worn about the neck, firft being dried.—Hippomanes excites luft by the bare touch, or being fufpended on the party. If any one fhall fpit in the hand with which he ftruck, or hurt, another, fo fhall the wound be cured;—likewife, if any one fhall draw the halter wherewith a malefactor was flain acrofs the throat of one who hath the quinfey, it certainly cures him in three days;—alfo, the herb cinque-foil being gathered before fun-rife, one leaf thereof cures the ague of one day; three leaves, cures the tertian; and four, the quartan ague. Rape feeds, fown with curfings and imprecations, grows the fairer, and thrives; but if with praifes, the reverfe. The juice of deadly nightfhade, diftilled, and given in a proportionate quantity, makes the party imagine almoft whatever you chufe. The herb nip, being heated in the hand, and afterwards you hold in your hand the hand of any other party, they fhall never quit you, fo long as you retain that herb. The herbs arfemart, comfrey, flaxweed, dragon-wort, adder's-tongue, being fteeped in cold water, and if for fome time being applied on a wound, or ulcer, they grow warm, and are buried in a muddy place, cureth the wound, or fore, to which they were applied. Again, if any one pluck the leaves of afarabacca, drawing them upwards, they will purge another, who is ignorant of the drawing, by vomit only; but if they are wrefted downward to the earth, they purge by ftool. A fapphire, or a ftone that is of a deep blue colour, if it be rubbed on a tumour, wherein the plague difcovers itfelf, (before the party is too far gone) and by and by it be removed from the fick, the abfent jewel attracts all the poifon or contagion therefrom. And thus much is fufficient to be faid concerning natural occult virtues, whereof we fpeak in a mixed and mifcellaneous manner, coming to more diftinct heads anon.

CHAP.

CHAP. III.

OF AMULETS, CHARMS, AND ENCHANTMENTS.

THE inftrument of enchanters is a pure, living, breathing fpirit of the blood, whereby we bind, or attract, thofe things which we defire or delight in ; fo that, by an earneft intention of the mind, we take poffeffion of the faculties in a no lefs potent manner than ftrong wines beguile the reafon and fenfes of thofe who drink them ; therefore, to charm, is either to bind with words, in which there is great virtue, as the poet fings——

> " Words thrice fhe fpake, which caus'd, at will, fweet fleep ;
> " Appeas'd the troubled waves, and roaring deep."

Indeed, the virtue of man's words are fo great, that, when pronounced with a fervent conftancy of the mind, they are able to fubvert Nature, to caufe earthquakes, ftorms, and tempefts. I have, in the country, by only fpeaking a few words, and ufed fome other things, caufed terrible rains and claps of thunder. Almoft all charms are impotent without words, becaufe words are the fpeech of the fpeaker, and the image of the thing fignified or fpoken of ; therefore, whatever wonderful effect is intended, let the fame be performed with the addition of words fignificative of the *will or defire* of the operator ; for words are a kind of occult vehicle of the image conceived or begotten, and fent out of the body by the foul ; therefore, all the forcible power of the fpirit ought to be breathed out with vehemency, and an arduous and intent defire ; and I know how to fpeak, and convey words together, fo as they may be carried onward to the hearer at a vaft diftance, no other body intervening, which thing I have done often. Words are alfo oftentimes delivered to us, feemingly by others, in our fleep, whereby we feem to talk and converfe ; but then no vocal converfations are of any effect, except they proceed from fpiritual and occult caufes : fuch fpirits have often manifefted fingular things to me, while in fleep, the which, in waking, I have thought nought of, until conviction of the truth taught me credulity in fuch like matters.

In

In the late change of Adminiſtration, I knew, at leaſt five days before it actually terminated, that it would be as I deſcribed to a few of my friends. Theſe things are not alike manifeſted to every one ; only, I believe, to thoſe who have long ſeriouſly attended to contemplations of this abſtruſe nature ; but there are thoſe who will ſay it is not ſo, merely becauſe they themſelves cannot comprehend ſuch things.

However, not to loſe time, we proceed. There are various enchantments, which I have proved, relative to common occurrences of life, viz. a kind of binding to that effect which we deſire : as to love, or hatred ; or to thoſe things we love, or againſt thoſe things we hate, in all which there is a magical ſympathy above the power of reaſoning ; therefore, thoſe abſtruſe matters we feel, are convinced of, and reflect upon, and draw them into our uſe. I will here ſet down, while ſpeaking of theſe things, a very powerful amulet for the ſtopping, immediately, a bloody-flux ; for the which (with a faith) I dare lay down my life for the ſucceſs, and entire cure.

An Amulet for Flux of Blood.

" In the blood of Adam aroſe death---in the blood of Chriſt death is ex-
" tinguiſhed---in the ſame blood of Chriſt I command thee, O, blood, that
" thou ſtop fluxing !"*

In this one godly ſuperſtition there will be found a *ready*, cheap, eaſy remedy for that dreadful diſorder the bloody-flux, whereby a poor miſerable wretch will reap more real benefit than in a whole ſhop of an apothecary's drugs. Theſe four letters mrv are a powerful charm, or amulet, againſt the common ague ; likewiſe, let them be written upon a piece of clean and new vellum, at any time of the day or night, and they will be found a ſpeedy and certain cure, and much more efficacious than the word *Abracadabra :* how- ever, as that ancient charm is ſtill (amongſt ſome who pretend to cure agues, &c.) in ſome repute, I will here ſet down the form and manner of its being

---

* Let the party who pronounces theſe words hold the other's hand.

written

written ;* likewife it muft be pronounced, or fpoken, in the fame order as it is written, with the intent or will of the operator declared at the fame time of making it.

CHAP. IV.

OF UNCTIONS, PHILTERS, POTIONS, &c.---THEIR MAGICAL VIRTUES.

UNGUENTS, or unctions, collyries, philters, &c., conveying the virtues of things natural to our fpirits, do multiply, transform, transfigure, and tranfmute it accordingly ; they alfo tranfpofe *thofe* virtues, which are in *them*, into *it*, fo that it not only acts upon its *own body*, but alfo upon *that* which is *near it*, and affects that (by vifible rays, charms, and by touching it) ,with fome agreeable quality like to itfelf. For, becaufe our fpirit is the *pure, fubtil, lucid, airy*, and unctuous vapour of the blood, nothing, therefore, is better adapted for collyriums than the like *vapour*, which are more fuitable to our fpirit in fubftance ; for then, by reafon of their likenefs, they do more ftir up, attract, and transform the fpirit. The fame virtue have other ointments, and confections. Hence, by the touch, often plague, ficknefs, faintings, poifoning, and love, is induced, either by the hands or clothes being anointed ; and often by kiffing, things being held in the mouth, love is likewife excited.

---

* It is here to be particularly noticed by us, that, in forming of a charm, or amulet, it will be of no effect, except the very foul of the operator is ftrongly and intenfely exerted and impreffed, as it were, and the image of the idea fealed on the charm, or amulet ; for, without this, in vain will be all the obfervation of times, hours, and conftellations ; therefore, this I have thought fit to mention, once for all, that it may be almoft always uppermoft in the mind of the operator, for, without this one thing being obferved and noticed, many who form feals, &c., do fall fhort of the wifhed-for effect.

```
ABRACADABRA
 BRACADABRA
  RACADABRA
   ACADABRA
    CADABRA
     ADABRA
      DABRA
       ABRA
        BRA
         RA
          A
```

Now

Now the fight, as it perceives more purely and clearer than the other fenfes, feals in *us* the marks of things more acutely, and does, moft of all, and before all others, agree with our fantaftic fpirit; as is apparent in dreams, when things feen do more often prefent themfelves to us than things heard, or any thing coming under the other fenfes. Therefore, when collyriums transform the vifual fpirits, that fpirit eafily affects the imagination, which, being affected with divers fpecies and forms, tranfmits the fame, by the fame fpirit, unto the outward fenfe of fight, by which there is formed in it a perception of fuch fpecies and forms, in that manner, as if it were moved by external objects, that there appear to be feen terrible images, fpirits, and the like. There are fome *collyriums* which make us fee the *images of fpirits in the air*, or elfewhere ; which I can make of the *gall of a man*, and the *eyes of a black cat*, and fome other things. The fame is made, likewife, of the blood of a lapwing, bat, and a goat ; and if a fmooth fhining piece of fteel be fmeared over with the juice of mugwort, and be made to fume, it caufes invocated fpirits to appear. There are fome perfumes, or fuffumigations and unctions, which make men fpeak in their fleep, walk, and do thofe things that are done by men that are awake, and often what, when awake, they cannot, or dare not do ; others, again, make men hear horrid or delightful founds, noifes, and the like.

And, in fome meafure, this is the caufe why *mad* and melancholy men believe they hear and fee things equally falfe and improbable, falling into moft grofs and pitiful delufions, fearing where no fear is, and angry where there is none to contend. Such paffions as thefe *we* can induce by *magical vapours, confections, perfumes, collyries, unguents, potions, poifons, lamps, lights, &c.* ; likewife by *mirrors, images, enchantments, charms, founds* and *mufic* ; alfo by *divers rites, obfervations, ceremonies, religion,* &c.

CHAP. V.

OF MAGICAL SUSPENSIONS AND ALLIGATIONS----SHEWING HOW, AND BY WHAT POWER, THEY
RECEIVE VIRTUE, AND ARE EFFICACIOUS IN NATURAL MAGIC.

WHEN the foul of the world, by its virtue, doth make all things (that
are naturally generated, or artificially made) fruitful, by fealing and impreffing on them celeftial virtues for the working of fome wonderful effect, then
things themfelves not only applied by collyry, or fuffume, or ointment, or
any other fuch like way ; but when they are conveniently bound to, or wrapped
up, or fufpended about the neck, or any other way applied, although by ever
fo eafy a contact, they do imprefs their virtue upon us : by thefe alligations,
&c., therefore, the accidents of the body and mind are changed into ficknefs
or health, valour, fear, fadnefs or joy, and the like ; they render thofe that
carry them, gracious, terrible, acceptable, rejected, honoured, beloved, or
hateful and abominable.

Now thefe kinds of paffions are conceived to be infufed no otherwife than is
manifeft in the grafting of trees, where the vital life and virtue is communicated from the trunk to the twig engrafted into it, by way of contact and alligation : fo in the female palm-tree, when fhe comes near to the male, her
boughs bend to the male, which the gardener feeing, he binds them together
by ropes acrofs, but foon becomes ftraight, as if by the continuation of
the rope fhe had received a propagating virtue from the male. And it is faid,
if a woman takes a needle, and bewray it with dung, and put it up in earth in
which the carcafs of a man has been buried, and carry it about her in a piece
of cloth ufed at a funeral, no man can defile her as long as fhe carries that.

Now by thefe examples we fee how, by certain alligations of certain things,
alfo fufpenfions, or by the moft fimple contact or continuation of any thread,
we may be able to receive fome virtues thereby ; but it is neceffary to know
the certain rule of magical alligation and fufpenfion ; and the manner that the
art requires is this, viz. that they muft be done under a certain and fuitable
conftellation ; and they muft be done with wire, or filken threads, or finews

of

of certain animals ; and thofe things that are to be wrapped up, are to be done in the leaves of herbs, or fkins of animals, or membraneous parchments, &c. For, if you would procure the *folary* virtue of any thing, this is to be wrapped up in bay-leaves, or the fkin of a lion, hung round the neck with gold, filk, or purple or yellow thread : while the fun reigns in the heavens, fo fhalt thou be endued with the virtue of that thing. So if a faturnine quality or thing be defired, thou fhalt in like manner take that thing, while Saturn reigns, and wrap it up in the fkin of an afs, or in a cloth ufed at a funeral, efpecially if melancholy or fadnefs is to be induced, and with a fad, or afh, or leaden, or black filk or thread, hang it about thy neck ; and fo in the fame manner we muft proceed with the reft.

CHAP. VI.
OF ANTIPATHIES.

IT is neceffary, in this place, to fpeak of the *antipathies of natural things*, feeing it is requifite, as we go on, to have a thorough knowledge of that obftinate contrariety of Nature, where any thing fhuns its contrary, and drives it, as it were, out of its prefence. Such antipathy as this has the root rhubarb againft choler ; treacle againft poifon ; the *fapphire ftone againft hot biles*, feverifh heats, and difeafes of the eyes ; the *amethyft* againft drunkennefs ; the *jafper* againft the bloody-flux and offenfive imaginations ; the *emerald*, and *agnus caftus* againft luft ; *achates*, or *agates*, againft poifon ; piony againft the falling ficknefs ; *coral* againft the ebullition of black choler, and pains of the ftomach ; the *topaz* againft fpiritual heats, fuch as are covetoufnefs, luft, and all manner of love exceffes. The fame antipathy is there, alfo, of pif-mires againft the herb organ, and the wing of a bat, and the heart of a lap-wing, from the prefence of which they fly. Alfo, the organ is contrary to a certain poifonous fly which cannot refift the fun, and refifts falamanders, and loaths cabbage with fuch a deadly hatred that they cannot endure each other.

So they fay cucumbers hate oil. And the gall of a crow makes even men fearful, and drives them from the place wherein it is placed. *A diamond* difagrees with a *loadftone ;* that being prefent, it fuffers no iron to be drawn to it. Sheep avoid frog-parfley as a deadly thing ; and, what is more wonderful, Nature hath depictured the fign of this antipathy upon the livers of fheep, in which the very figure of frog-parfley doth naturally appear. Again, goats hate garden-bafil, as if there was nothing more pernicious. And, amongft animals, mice and weafels difagree ; fo a lizard is of a contrary nature to a fcorpion, and induces great terror to the fcorpion with its very fight, and they are therefore killed with the oil of them ; which oil will likewife cure the wounds made by fcorpions. There is a great enmity between fcorpions and mice ; therefore if a moufe be applied to the bite of a fcorpion, he cures it. Nothing is fo much an enemy to fnakes as crabs ; and if fwine be hurt by them, they are cured by crabs ; the fun, alfo, being in Cancer, ferpents are tormented. Alfo, the fcorpion and crocodile kill one another ; and if the bird ibis does but touch a crocodile with one of his feathers, he makes him unmoveable. The bird called a buftard flies away at the fight of a horfe ; and a hart at the fight of a ram, or a viper. An elephant trembles at the hearing of the grunting of a hog ; fo doth a lion at the crowing of a cock ; and a panther will not touch them that are anointed with the fat of a hen, efpecially if garlick has been put into it. There is alfo an enmity between foxes and fwans ; bulls and jackdaws. And fome birds are at a perpetual variance, as daws and owls ; kites and crows ; turtle and ring-tail ; egepis and eagles ; alfo, harts and dragons. Amongft water animals, there is a great antipathy between dolphins and whirlpools ; the mullet and pike ; lamprey and conger ; pourcontrel and lobfter, which latter, but feeing the former, is nearly ftruck dead with fear ; but the lobfter tears the conger. The civet-cat cannot refift the panther ; and if the fkins of both be hung up againft each other, the fkin or hairs of the panther will fall off. Apollo fays, in his hieroglyphics, if any one be girt about with the fkin of a civet-cat, he may pafs fafe through his enemies. The lamb flies from the wolf ; and if the tail, fkin, or head of lupus be hung up in the fheeps'-cot, they cannot eat their meat for very fear.
And

And Pliny mentions the bird called the marlin, that breaks the eggs of the crow, whofe young are annoyed by the fox ; that fhe alfo will pinch the whelps of the fox, and the fox likewife, which, when the crow fees, they help the fox againft her as againft a common enemy. The linnet lives in, and eats thiftles ; yet fhe hates the afs, becaufe he eats the thiftles and flowers of them. There is fo great an enmity between the little bird called efalon and the afs, that their blood will not mix ; and that, at the fimple braying of the afs, both the efalon's eggs and young perifh together. There is, alfo, a total antipathy of the olive-tree to the harlot ; that, if fhe plant it, it will neither thrive nor profper, but wither. A lion fears lighted torches, and is tamed by nothing fooner. The wolf fears not fword or fpear, but a ftone; by the throwing of which a wound being made, worms breed in the wolf. A horfe fears a camel fo much that he cannot endure the picture of that beaft. An elephant, when he rages, is quieted by feeing a cock. A fnake is afraid of a naked man, but purfues one clothed. A mad bull is tamed by being tied to a fig-tree. Amber attracts all things to it but garden-bafil, and things fmeared with oil, between which there is a natural antipathy.

CHAP. VII.

OF THE OCCULT VIRTUES OF THINGS WHICH ARE INHERENT IN THEM ONLY IN THEIR LIFE-TIME, AND SUCH AS REMAIN IN THEM EVEN AFTER DEATH.

IT is expedient for us to know that there are fome things which retain virtue only while they are living, others even after death. So in the cholic, if a live duck be applied to the belly, it takes away the pain, and the duck dies. If you take the heart out of any animal, and, while it is warm, bind it to one that has a quartan fever, it drives it away. So if any one fhall fwallow the heart of a lapwing, fwallow, weafel, or a mole, while it is yet living and warm with natural heat, it improves his intellect, and helps him to remember, underftand, and foretel things to come. Hence this general rule,---that whatever

ever

ever things are taken for magical ufes from animals, whether they are ftones, members, hair, excrements, nails, or any thing elfe, they muft be taken from thofe animals while they are yet alive, and, if it is poffible, that they may live afterwards. If you take the tongue of a frog, you put the frog into water again ;—and Democritus writes, that if any one fhall take out the tongue of a water-frog, no other part of the animal fticking to it, and lay it upon the place where the heart beats of a woman, fhe is compelled, againft her will, to anfwer whatfoever you fhall afk of her. Alfo, take the eyes of a frog, which muft be extracted before fun-rife, and bound to the fick party, and the frog to be let go again blind into the water, the party fhall be cured of a tertian ague ; alfo, the fame will, being bound with the flefh of a nightingale in the fkin of a hart, keep a perfon always wakeful without fleeping. Alfo, the roe of the fork fifh being bound to the navel, is faid to caufe women an eafy child-birth, if it be taken from it alive, and the fifh put into the fea again. So the right eye of a ferpent being applied to the forenefs of eyes, cures the fame, if the ferpent be let go alive. So, likewife, the tooth of a mole, being taken out alive, and afterwards let go, cures the tooth-ache ; and dogs will never bark at thofe who have the tail of a weafel that has efcaped. Democritus fays, that if the tongue of the cameleon be taken alive, it con- duces to good fuccefs in trials, and likewife to women in labour ; but it muft be hung up on fome part of the outfide of the houfe, otherwife, if brought into the houfe, it might be moft dangerous.

There are very many properties that remain after death ; and thefe are things in which the idea of the matter is lefs fwallowed up, *according to Plato*, in them : even after death, that which is immortal in them will work fome won- derful things :—as in the fkins we have mentioned of feveral wild beafts, which will corrode and eat one another after death ; alfo, a drum made of the rocket-fifh drives away all creeping things at what diftance foever the found of it is heard ; and the ftrings of an inftrument made of the guts of a wolf, and being ftrained upon a harp or lute, with ftrings made of fheep-guts, will make no harmony.

CHAP.

CHAP. VIII.

OF THE WONDERFUL VIRTUES OF SOME KINDS OF PRECIOUS STONES.

IT is a common opinion of magicians, that stones inherit great virtues, which they receive through the spheres and activity of the celestial influences, by the medium of the soul or spirit of the world. Authors very much disagree in respect of the probability of their actually having such virtues in potentia, some debating warmly against any occult or secret virtue lying hid in them; others, as warmly, shewing the causes and effects of these sympathetic properties. However, to leave these trifling arguments to those who love cavil and contentions better than I do, and, as I have neither leisure nor inclination to enter the lists with sophists, and tongue-philosophers; I say, that these occult virtues are disposed throughout the animal, vegetable, and mineral kingdoms, by seeds, or ideas originally emanating from the Divine mind, and through superceleftial spirits and intelligence always operating, according to their proper offices and governments allotted them; which virtues are infused, as we before said, through the medium of the Universal Spirit, as by a general and manifest sympathy and antipathy established in the law of Nature. Amongst a variety of examples, the loadstone is one most remarkable proof of the sympathy and antipathy we speak of. However to hasten to the point. Amongst stones, those which resemble the rays of the sun by their golden sparklings, (as does the glittering stone ætites) prevent the falling-sickness and poisons, if worn on the finger; so the stone which is called *oculis solis*, or eye of the sun, being in figure like to the apple of the eye, from which shines forth a ray, comforts the brain, and strengthens sight; the carbuncle, which shines by night, hath a virtue against all airy and vaporous poisons; the chrysolite stone, of a light green colour, when held against the sun, there shines in it a ray like a star of gold; this is singularly good for the lungs, and cures asthmatical complaints; and if it be bored through, and the hollow filled with the mane of an ass, and bound to the left arm, it chases away all foolish and idle imaginations and melancholy fears, and drives away folly.

The

The ftone called iris, which is like cryftal in colour, being found with fix corners, when held in the fhade, and the fun fuffered to fhine through it, reprefents a natural rainbow in the air. The ftone heliotropium, green, like a jafper or emerald, befet with red fpecks, makes the wearer conftant, renowned, and famous, and conduces to long life ; there is, likewife, another wonderful property in this ftone, and that is, that it fo dazzles the eyes of men, that it caufes the bearer to be invifible ; but then there muft be applied to it the herb bearing the fame name, viz. heliotropium, or the fun-flower ; and thefe kind of virtues Albertus Magnus, and William of Paris, mention in their writings. The jacinth alfo poffeffes virtue from the fun againft poifons, peftilences, and peftiferous vapours ; likewife it renders the bearer pleafant and acceptable ; conduces, alfo, to gain money ; being fimply held in the mouth, it wonderfully cheers the heart, and ftrengthens the mind. Then there is the pyrophilus, of a red mixture, which Albertus Magnus reports that Æfculapius makes mention of in one of his epiftles to Octavius Cæfar, faying, " There is a certain poifon, fo intenfely cold, which preferves the heart of man, being taken out, from burning ; fo that if it be put into the fire for any time, it is turned into a ftone, which ftone is called *pyrophilus :*" it poffeffes a wonderful virtue againft poifon ; and it infallibly renders the wearer thereof renowned and dreadful to his enemies. Apollonius is reported to have found a ftone called pantaura, (which will attract other ftones, as the loadftone does iron) moft powerful againft all poifons : it is fpotted like the panther, and therefore fome naturalifts have given this ftone the name of pantherus : Aaron calls it evanthum ; and fome, on account of its variety, call it pantochras.

CHAP.

CHAP. IX.

OF THE MIXTURES OF NATURAL THINGS ONE WITH ANOTHER, AND THE PRODUCING OF
MONSTROUS ANIMALS, BY THE APPLICATION OF NATURAL MAGIC.

MAGICIANS, ftudents, and obfervers of the operations of Nature, know
how, by the application of active forms to a matter fitly difpofed, and made,
as it were, a proper recipient, to effect many wonderful and uncommon things
that feem ftrange, and above Nature, by gathering this and that thing bene-
ficial and conducive to that effect which we defire ; however, it is evident that
all the powers and virtues of the inferior bodies are not found comprehended
in any one fingle thing, but are difperfed amongft many of the compounds
here amongft us ; wherefore it is neceffary, if there be a hundred virtues of
the fun difperfed through fo many animals, plants, metals, or ftones, we
fhould gather all thefe together, and bring them all into one form, in which
we fhall fee all the faid virtues, being united, contained. Now there is a
double virtue in commixing : one, viz. which was once planted in its parts,
and is *celeftial* ; the other is obtained by a certain artificial mixture of things,
mixed amongft themfelves, according to a due proportion, fuch as agree with
the heavens under a certain conftellation ; and this virtue defcends by a certain
fimilitude or likenefs that is in things amongft themfelves, by which they are
drawn or attracted towards their fuperiors, and as much as the following do by
degrees correfpond with them that go before, where the patient is fitly applied
to its agent. So from a certain compofition of *herbs, vapours*, and fuch like,
made according to the rules of Natural and Celeftial Magic, there refults a
certain common form ; of which we fhall deliver the true and infallible rules
and experiments in our Second Book, where we have written exprefsly on the
fame.

We ought, likewife, to underftand that by how much more noble and excellent the form of any thing is, by fo much the more it is prone, and apt to
receive, and powerful to act. Then the virtue of things do indeed become
wonderful ; viz. when they are applied to matters, mixed and prepared in fit

feafons to give them life, by procuring life for them from the ftars, our own fpirit powerfully co-operating therewith ; for there is fo great a power in pre-pared matters, which we fee do then receive life, when a perfect mixture of qualities do break the former contrariety ; for fo much the more perfect life things receive, by as much the temper and compofition is free from contrariety. Now the heavens, as a prevailing caufe, do, from the beginning of every thing, (to be generated by the concoction and perfect digeftion of the matter) together with life, beftow celeftial influences and wonderful gifts, according to the capacity that is in that life and fenfible foul to receive more noble and fublime virtues. For the celeftial virtue otherwife lies afleep, as fulphur kept from flame ; but in living bodies it doth always burn, as kindled fulphur, which, by its vapour, fills all the places that are near.

There is a book called, " A Book of the Laws of Pluto," which fpeaks of monftrous generations, which are not produced according to the laws of Nature. Of thefe things which follow we know to be true ; viz. of worms are generated gnats ; of a horfe, wafps ; of a calf and ox, bees. Take a living crab, his legs being broken off, and he buried under the earth, a fcorpion is produced. If a duck be dried into powder, and put into water, frogs are foon gene-rated ; but if he be baked in a pie, and cut into pieces, and be put in a moift place under ground, toads are generated. Of the herb garden-bafil, bruifed, and put between two ftones, are generated fcorpions. Of the hairs of a men-ftruous woman, put under dung, are bred ferpents ; and the hair of a horfe's tail, put into water, receives life, and is turned into a moft pernicious worm. And there is an art wherewith a hen, fitting upon eggs, may be generated the form of a man, which I myfelf know how to do, and which magicians call the mandrake, and it hath in it wonderful virtues.

You muft, therefore, know which and what kind of matters are either of art or nature, begun or perfected, or compounded of more things, and what celeftial influences they are able to receive. For a congruity of natural things is fufficient for the receiving of influence from celeftial ; becaufe, nothing hin-dering, the celeftials fend forth their light upon inferiors ; they fuffer no matter to be deftitute of their virtue. Wherefore as much matter as is *perfect* and
pure

pure is, as we before faid, fitted to receive celeftial influences ; for that is the binding and continuing of the matter of the foul to the world, which doth daily flow in upon things natural, and all things which *Nature hath prepared*, that it is impoffible that a prepared matter fhould not receive life, or a more noble form.

CHAP. X.

OF THE ART OF FASCINATION, BINDING, SORCERIES, MAGICAL CONFECTIONS, LIGHTS, CAN-
DLES, LAMPS, &c. &c. ; BEING THE CONCLUSION OF THE NATURAL MAGIC.*

WE have fo far fpoken concerning the great virtues, and wonderful efficacy, of natural things ; it remains now that we fpeak of a wonderful power and faculty of fafcination ; or, more properly, a magical and occult binding of men into love or hatred, ficknefs or health ;—alfo the binding of thieves, that they cannot fteal in any place ; or to bind them that they cannot remove, from whence they may be detected ;—the binding of merchants, that they cannot buy nor fell ;—the binding of an army, that they cannot pafs over any bounds ;—the binding of fhips, fo that no wind, though ever fo ftrong, fhall be able to carry them out of that harbour ;—the binding of a mill, that it cannot, by any means whatfoever, be turned to work ;—the binding of a ciftern, or fountain, that the water cannot be drawn up out of them ;—the binding of the ground, fo that nothing will bring forth fruit, or flourifh in it ; alfo, that nothing can be built upon it ;—the binding of fire, that, though it be ever fo ftrong, it fhall burn no combuftible thing that is put to it ;—alfo, the binding of lightnings and tempefts, that they fhall do no hurt ;—the binding of dogs, that they cannot bark ;—alfo, the binding of birds and wild beafts, that they fhall not be able to run or fly away ; and things fimilar to

* The latter part of this Chapter ferves as a rule to be obferved in the compofition of all kinds of mixed experiments ; and it is as appropriate to the materials collected for talifmans, feals, &c. treated of in our Celeftial Magic, Book II.　　　　*F. B.*

thefe,

thefe, which are hardly creditable, yet known by experience. Now how it is that thefe kind of bindings are made and brought to pafs, we muft know. They are thus done: by forceries, collyries, unguents, potions, binding to and hanging up of talifmans, by charms, incantations, ftrong imaginations, affections, paffions, images, characters, enchantments, imprecations, lights, and by founds, numbers, words, names, invocations, fwearings, conjurations, confecrations, and the like.

OF SORCERIES.

THE force of forceries are, no doubt, very powerful ; indeed they are able to confound, fubvert, confume, and change all inferior things ; likewife there are forceries by which we can fufpend the faculties of men and beafts. Now, as we have promifed, we will fhew what fome of thefe kind of forceries are, that, by the example of thefe, there may be a way opened for the whole fubject of them. Of thefe, the firft is menftruous blood, which, how much power it has in forcery, we will now confider :—Firft, if it comes over new wine, it will turn it four ; and if it does but touch a vine, it will fpoil it for ever ; and, by its very touch, it renders all plants and trees barren, and thofe newly fet, die ; it burns up all the herbs in the garden, and makes fruit fall from trees ; it makes dim the brightnefs of a looking-glafs, dulls the edges of knives and razors, dims the beauty of polifhed ivory, and makes iron rufty ; it likewife makes brafs rufty, and to fmell very ftrong ; by the tafte, it makes dogs run mad, and, being thus mad, if they once bite any one, that wound is incurable ; it deftroys whole hives of bees, and drives them away, if it does but touch them ; it makes linen black that is boiled with it ; it makes mares caft their foals by touching them with it, and women mifcarry ; it makes affes barren if they eat of the corn touched by it. The afhes of menftruous clothes caft upon purple garments, that are to be wafhed, change their colour, and likewife take away the colour of flowers. It alfo drives away tertian and quartan agues, if it be put into the wool of a black ram, and tied up in a
                                                                        filver

silver bracelet ; as alſo if the ſoles of the patient's feet be anointed therewith, and eſpecially if it be done by the woman herſelf, the patient not knowing what ſhe uſes. It likewiſe cures the falling ſickneſs ; but moſt eſpecially it cures them that are afraid of water or drink after they are bitten by a mad dog, if only a menſtruous cloth be put under the cup. Likewiſe, if a menſtruous woman ſhall walk naked, before ſun-riſe, in a field of ſtanding corn, all hurtful things periſh ; but if after ſun-riſe, the corn withers ; alſo, they are able to expel hail, rain, thunders, and lightnings ; more of which Pliny mentions. Know this, that if they happen at the decreaſe of the moon, they are a much greater poiſon than in the increaſe, and yet much greater if they happen between the decreaſe and change ; but if they happen in the eclipſe of the ſun or moon, they are a moſt incurable and violent poiſon. But they are of the greateſt force when they happen in the firſt years of the virginity, for then if they but touch the door-poſts of a houſe, no miſchief can take effect in it. And ſome ſay that the threads of any garment touched therewith cannot be burnt, and if they are caſt into a fire, it will ſpread no farther. Alſo it is noted, that the root of piony being given with caſtor, and ſmeared over with a menſtruous cloth, it certainly cureth the falling ſickneſs.

Again, let the ſtomach of a hart be roaſted, and to it be put a perfume made with a menſtruous cloth ; it will make croſs-bows uſeleſs for the killing of any game. The hairs of a menſtruous woman, put under dung, breeds ſerpents ; and if they are burnt, will drive away ſerpents with the fume. So great and powerful a poiſon is in them, that they are a poiſon to poiſonous creatures.

We next come to ſpeak of hippomanes, which, amongſt ſorceries, are not accounted the leaſt : and this is a little venomous piece of fleſh, the ſize of a fig, and black, which is in the forehead of a colt newly foaled, which, unleſs the mare herſelf doth preſently eat, ſhe will hardly ever love her foles, or let them ſuck ; and this is a moſt powerful philter to cauſe love, if it be pow-dered, and drank in a cup with the blood of him that is in love : ſuch a potion was given by Medea to Jaſon.

There is another ſorcery which is called hippomanes, viz. a venomous liquor iſſuing out of the ſhare of a mare at the time ſhe luſts after the horſe. The
                                                                                                civet

civet-cat, alſo, abounds with ſorceries; for the poſts of a door being touched with her blood, the arts of jugglers and ſorcerers are ſo invalid that evil ſpirits can by no means be called up, or compelled to talk with them:---this is Pliny's report. Alſo, thoſe that are anointed with the oil of her left foot, being boiled with the aſhes of the ancle bone of the ſame and the blood of a weaſel, ſhall become odious to all. The ſame, alſo, is to be done with the eye being decocted. If any one hath a little of the ſtrait-gut of this animal about him, and it is bound to the left arm, it is a charm; that if he does but look upon a woman, it will cauſe her to follow him at all opportunities; and the ſkin of this animal's forehead withſtands witchcraft.

We next come to ſpeak of the blood of a baſiliſk, which magicians call the blood of Saturn.---This procures (by its virtue) for him that carries it about him, good ſucceſs of petitions from great men; likewiſe makes him amazingly ſucceſsful in the cure of diſeaſes, and the grant of any privilege. They ſay, alſo, that a tike, if it be taken out of the left ear of a dog, and it be altogether black, if the ſick perſon ſhall anſwer him that brought it in, and who, ſtanding at his feet, ſhall aſk him concerning his diſeaſe, there is certain hope of life; and that he ſhall die if he make him no anſwer. They ſay, alſo, that a ſtone bitten by a mad dog cauſes diſcord, if it be put into drinks; and if any one ſhall put the tongue of a dog, dried, into his ſhoe, or ſome of the powder, no dog is able to bark at him who hath it; and more powerful this, if the herb hound's-tongue be put with it. And the membrane of the ſecundine of a bitch does the ſame; likewiſe, dogs will not bark at him who hath the heart of a dog in his pocket.

The red toad (Pliny ſays) living in briers and brambles, is full of ſorceries, and is capable of wonderful things: there is a little bone in his left ſide, which being caſt into cold water, makes it preſently hot; by which, alſo, the rage of dogs are reſtrained, and their love procured, if it be put in their drink, making them faithful and ſerviceable; if it be bound to a woman, it ſtirs up luſt. On the contrary, the bone which is on the right ſide makes hot water cold, and it binds it ſo that no heat can make it hot while it there remains. It is a certain cure for quartans, if it be bound to the ſick in a ſnake's ſkin; and like-

wiſe

wife cures all fevers, the St. Anthony's fire, and reftrains love and luft. And the fpleen and heart are effectual antidotes againft the poifons of the faid toad. Thus much Pliny writes.

Alfo it is faid, that the fword with which a man is flain hath wonderful power; for if the fnaffle of a bridle, or bit, or fpurs, be made of it, with thefe a horfe ever fo wild is tamed, and made gentle and obedient. They fay, if we dip a fword, with which any one was beheaded, in wine, that it cures the quartan, the fick being given to drink of it. There is a liquor made, by which men are made as raging and furious as a bear, imagining themfelves in every refpect to be changed into one; and this is done by diffolving or boiling the brains and heart of that animal in new wine, and giving any one to drink out of a fkull, and, while the force of the draught operates, he will fancy every living creature to be a bear like to himfelf; neither can any thing divert or cure him till the fumes and virtue of the liquor are entirely expended, no other diftemper being perceivable in him.

The moft certain cure of a violent head-ache, is to take any herb growing upon the top of the head of an image; the fame being bound, or hung about one with a red thread, it will foon allay the violent pain thereof.

OF MAGICAL LIGHTS, CANDLES, LAMPS, &c.

THERE are made, artificially, fome kinds of lamps, torches, candles, and the like, of fome certain and appropriate materials and liquors opportunely gathered and collected for this purpofe, which, when they are lighted and fhine alone, produce fome wonderful effects. There is a *poifon* from mares, after copulation, which, being lighted in torches compofed of their fat and marrow, doth reprefent on the walls a monftrous deformity of horfes' heads, which thing is both eafy and pleafant to do: the like may be done of affes and flies. And the fkin of a ferpent or fnake, lighted in a green lamp, makes the images of the fame to appear; and grapes produce the fame effect, if, when they are

in.

in their flowers, you shall take a phial, and bind it to them, filled with oil, and shall let that remain so till they are ripe, and then the oil be lighted in a lamp, you shall see a prodigious quantity of grapes; and the same in other fruits. If centaury be mixed with honey and the blood of a lapwing, and be put in a lamp, they that stand about will be of a gigantic stature; and if it be lighted in a clear evening, the stars will seem scattered about.

The ink of the cuttle-fish being put into a lamp, makes Blackamoors appear. So, also, a candle made of some saturnine things, such as man's fat and marrow, the fat of a black cat, with the brains of a crow or raven, which being extinguished in the mouth of a man lately dead, will afterwards, as often as it shines alone, bring great horror and fear upon the spectators about it.

Of such like *torches, candles, lamps,* &c., (of which we shall speak further in our Book of *Magnetism and Mummies*) Hermes speaks largely of; also Plato and Chyrannides; and, of the later writers, Albertus Magnus makes particular mention of the truth and efficacy of these, in a treatise on these particular things relative to lights, &c.

OF THE ART OF FASCINATION, OR BINDING BY THE LOOK OR SIGHT.

WE call fascination a binding, because it is effected by a look, glance, or observation, in which we take possession of the spirit, and overpower the same, of those we mean to fascinate or suspend; for it comes through the eyes, and the instrument by which we fascinate or bind is a certain, pure, lucid, subtil spirit, generated out of the ferment of the purer blood by the heat of the heart, and the firm, determined, and ardent will of the soul which directs it to the object previously disposed to be fascinated. This doth always send forth by the eyes rays or beams, carrying with them a pure subtil spirit or vapour into the eye or blood of him or her that is opposite. So the eye, being opened and intent upon any one with a strong imagination, doth dart its beams, which are the
vehicle

vehicle of the fpirit, into whatever we will affect or bind, which fpirit ftriking the eye of them who are fafcinated, being ftirred up in the heart and foul of him that fends them forth, and poffeffing the breaft of them who are ftruck, wounds their hearts, infects their fpirits, and overpowers them.

Know, likewife, that in witches, thofe are moft bewitched, who, with often looking, direct the edge of their fight to the edge of the fight of thofe who bewitch or fafcinate them ; whence arofe the faying of " Evil eyes, &c." For when their eyes are reciprocally bent one upon the other, and are joined beams to beams, and lights to lights, then the fpirit of the one is joined to the fpirit of the other, and then are ftrong ligations made ; and moft violent love is ftirred up, only with a fudden looking on, as it were, with the darting a look, or piercing into the very inmoft of the heart, whence the fpirit and amorous blood, being thus wounded, are carried forth upon the lover and enchanter ; no otherwife than the fpirit and the blood of him that is murdered is upon the murderer, who, if ftanding near the body killed, the blood flows afrefh, which thing has been tried by repeated experiments.

So great power is there in fafcination that many uncommon and wonderful things are thereby effected, efpecially when the vapours of the eyes are fub-fervient to the affection ; therefore collyries, ointments, alligations, &c. are ufed to affect and corroborate the fpirit in this or that manner : to induce love, they ufe venereal collyriums, as hippomanes, blood of doves, &c. To induce fear, they ufe martial collyriums, as the eyes of wolves, bear's fat, and the civet-cat. To procure mifery, or ficknefs, they ufe faturnine, and fo on.

Thus much we have thought proper to fpeak concerning Natural Magic, in which we have, as it may be faid, only opened the firft chamber of Nature's ftorehoufe ; *indeed we fhould have inferted many more things here*, but as they fall more properly under the heads of *Magnetifm, Mummy*, &c., to which we refer the reader, we fhall take our leave of the reader for the prefent, that we may give him time to breathe, likewife to digeft what he has here feafted upon ; and, while he is preparing to enter the unlocked chambers

Book I.   G   of

of Magic and Nature, we will procure him a rich fervice of moſt delicious meats, fit for the hungry and thirſty traveller through the vaſt labyrinths of wiſdom and true ſcience.

END OF THE NATURAL MAGIC.

THE Author having, under the title of Natural Magic, collected and arranged every thing that was curious, ſcarce, and valuable, as well his own experiments, as thoſe in which he has been indefatigable in gathering from thê ſcience and practice of Magical Authors, and thoſe the moſt ancient and abſtruſe, as may be ſeen in the liſt at the end of the Book, where he has put down the names of the authors, from which he has tranſlated many things that were never yet publiſhed in the Engliſh language, particularly *Hermes, Tritemius, Paracelſus, Bacon, Dee, Porta, Agrippa,* &c. &c. &c. ; from whom he has not been aſhamed to borrow what he thought and knew would be valuable and gratifying to the ſons of Wiſdom, in addition to many other rare and uncommon experiments relative to this art.

THE

THE

TRUE SECRET OF THE PHILOSOPHERS' STONE;

OR,

JEWEL OF ALCHYMY.

WHEREIN

THE PROCESS OF MAKING THE GREAT ELIXIR

is discovered;

BY WHICH BASE METALS MAY BE TURNED INTO PURE GOLD; CONTAINING THE MOST
EXCELLENT AND PROFITABLE INSTRUCTIONS IN THE

HERMETIC ART;

DISCOVERING THAT VALUABLE AND SECRET

MEDICINE OF THE PHILOSOPHERS,

To make Men Healthy, Wise, and Happy.

BY F. BARRETT,

STUDENT OF CHEMISTRY, NATURAL PHILOSOPHY, &c.

1801.

EPISTLE TO MUSEUS.

> " Thou, O, Mufeus! whofe mind is high,
> " Obferve my words, and read them with thine eye ;
> " Thefe fecrets in thy facred breaft repone,
> " And in thy journey think of God alone ;
> " The Author of all things, that cannot die ;
> " Of whom we now fhall fpeak———"

I TELL thee here, Mufeus, to obferve our words, and read them with thine eye, that is, the eye of thine underftanding ; for, know, there are many that hear us fpeak, that read not the meaning of our words. Wherefore fhouldft thou contemplate thefe myfteries with fo much conftancy of mind, if thou didft not perceive in them fome great good moft defirable ?— Liften, then, O, young man, and hear our words ! We will fhew thee the dangerous precipice of vanity and head-long defire—we will defcribe to thee the ftubborn and fatal will of our paffions, even with tears of contrition, and heart-felt compaffion for thy inexperience—we will lead thee, as it were, by the hand, through thofe labyrinths of vice, wherewith thou art daily furrounded ; and, however prejudiced thou mighteft be againft the receiving of our doctrine, yet, be affured, we have in our poffeffion the magical virtue and power of binding thee to our principles, and making thee happy, in fpite of thyfelf. Here is a great fecret ! thou fhalt fay---every man wifhes to be happy—which I grant ; but my anfwer is—moft men prevent their own happinefs ; they deftroy it, by fuffering themfelves to be governed by the outward principle of the flefh, thinking the *greateft good* to be in the fatisfying of their carnal appetites, or in the amaffing together heaps of wealth, whereby they thruft down the meek and poor, raifing up the ftandards of Pride, Envy, and Oppreffion. Thefe things every day's experience confirms ; nay, there are fome fo blind, that, in the poffeffion of much wealth, they think there is nothing

beyond

beyond it ; infomuch, that they triumph in *luft*, *oppreffion*, *revenge*, and *con-tumely*. But how is it, thou wilt fay, that, feeing man is a reafonable being, he can poffibly give up his government fo eafily ?—I fay, when man fuffers the unreafonable and beftial part to deprave him, then he immediately be-comes a flave, (and the vileft of flavery is that which deprives man of his focial virtues ;) for then, although in the poffeffion of great wordly things, fuch as houfes, eftates, and all other temporal gifts, yet he becomes an immediate inftrument to the Prince of this World and the Powers of Darknefs, feeing that thofe riches he inherits are merely given him in this life, to beftow upon others thofe neceffaries and comforts which he himfelf does not feel the want of, and by which he might, if not blinded by his paffions and lufts, fecure himfelf an eternal and incorruptible treafure. But he who poffeffes treafures without mercy, liberality, bounty, charity, &c., robs the Eternal Author of all good, of the honour due unto him, and, in fhort, is working deftruction to his own foul ; his riches, inftead of benefitting himfelf and others, eventually and finally terminates as a curfe : while he lives here, he is a fcourge to fociety ; and, after he leaves this, it is plain enough pointed out in the New Teftament what will be his fituation and condition.

Therefore, thou young man, that haft but a few years to live, ftudy how to attain the ftone we teach of : it will protract the beauty of thy youth, though thou fhouldft live for centuries—it will ever fupply thee with the means of comforting the afflicted ; infomuch, that when thou haft attained this truly defirable and moft perfect talifman, thy life will become foft and plea-fant ; no cares, nor corroding pangs—no felf-torment will ever invade thy mind ; neither fhalt thou want the means to be happy, in refpect of the pof-feffion of the goods of this life, but fhalt have abundantly. But how, and from what fource, all this is to proceed---out of what *thing* or *matter* thou fhalt attain thy wifhed-for end,---the ftudying of the enfuing Treatife will fufficiently fhew.

Thy Friend,

F. B.

TO

TO THE READER.

ALTHOUGH we do not, in any point of fcience, arrogate perfection to ourfelves, yet fomething we have attained by dear experience, by diligent labour, and by ftudy, worthy of being communicated for the inftruction of either the licentious libertine, or the grave ftudent----the obferver of Nature ; and this, our Work, we concentrated into a *focus :* it is, as it were, a fpiritual effence drawn from a large quantity of matter ; for we can fay, with propriety, that this little Treatife is truly fpiritual, and effential to the happinefs of man : therefore, to thofe who wifh to be happy, with every good intention we commend this Work to be their conftant companion and ftudy, in which, if they perfevere, they fhall not fail of their defires in the attainment of the true Philofophers' Stone.

PART

PART THE FIRST.

IT is not neceffary here to enter into a long detail of the merits of Alchymical Authors and Philofophers ; fuffice it to fay, that Alchymy, the grand touch-ftone of natural wifdom, is of Divine origin : it was brought down from Heaven by the Angel Uriel. Zoroafter, the firft philofopher by fire, made pure gold from all the feven metals ; he brought the fun ten times brighter from the bed of Saturn, and fixed it with the moon, who thereby copulating, begot a numerous offspring of an immortal nature, a pure living fpiritual fun, burning in the refulgency of its own divine light, a feed of a fublime and fiery nature, a vigorous progenitor. This Zoroafter was the father of alchymy, illumined divinely from above ; he knew every thing, yet feemed to know nothing ; his precepts of art were left in hieroglyphics, yet in fuch fort that none but the favourites of Heaven ever reaped benefit thereby. He was the firft who engraved the pure Cabala in moft pure gold, and, when he died, refigned it to his Father who liveth eternally, yet begot him not : that Father gives it to his fons, who follow the precepts of Wifdom with vigilance, ingenuity, and induftry, and with a pure, chafte, and free mind.

Hermes Trifmegiftus, Geber, Artephius, Bacon, Helmont, Lully, and Bafil Valentine, have written moft profoundly, yet abftrufely, and all declare not the thing fought for. Some fay they were forbid ; others, that they declared it obvioufly and intelligibly, yet fome few little points they kept to themfelves.

themfelves. However far off the main point they lead us, of this be fure,---that fomething valuable is to be drained, as it were, out of each.

Geber is good---Artephius is better---but Flammel is beft of all ;---and better ftill than thefe is the inftructions we give ; for with them a man (following our directions) fhall never want gold ; therefore to be an adept is poffible, but firft " feek the kingdom of God, and all thefe things fhall be added unto you." This is truth incontrovertible, and herein lies a vaft fecret---" feek, and ye fhall find ;"---but remember, whatfoever ye afk, that fhall ye receive.

The cabala, in its utmoft purity, is contained in the many precepts given in this book. The cabala enables us to underftand---to bring our underftandings to act, and, by that means, to attain knowledge ;---knowledge makes us the children of God---God makes whom he pleafes adepts in wifdom. To be an adept, according to God's will, is no contemptible calling.

The noble and virtuous Brethren of the Rofy Crofs hold this truth facred,---that " Virtue flies from no man ;" therefore how defirable a thing is Virtue. She teaches us, firft, wifdom, then charity, love, mercy, faith, and conftancy : all thefe appertain to Virtue ; therefore it is phyfically poffible for any well-inclined man to become an adept, provided he lays afide his pride of reafoning, all obftinacy, blindnefs, hypocrify, incredulity, fuperftition, deceit, &c.

An adept, therefore, is one who not only ftudies to do God's will upon earth, in refpect of his moral and religious duties ; but who ftudies, and ardently prays to his benevolent Creator to beftow on him wifdom and knowledge from the fulnefs of his treafury ; and he meditates, day and night, how he may attain the true *aqua vita*---how he may be filled with the grace of God ; which, when he is made fo happy, his fpiritual or internal eye is open to a glorious profpect of mortal and immortal riches :---he wants not *food*, *raiment*, joy, or any other thing---he is filled with the celeftial fpiritual manna---he enjoys the marrow and fat things of the earth---he treads the wine-prefs, not of the *wrath*, but of the *mercy* of God---he *lives* to the glory of God, *and dies* faying " Holy, holy, holy Lord of Sabaoth ! bleffed is thy name, now and for evermore ! Amen."

Boox I.   H   Therefore,

'Therefore, to be an adept, as we have before hinted, is to know thyfelf, fear God, and love thy neighbour as thyfelf ; and by this thou fhalt come to the fulfilment of thy defires, O, man ; but by no other means under the fcope of Heaven.

When thy foul fhall be made drunk by the divine ambrofial nectar, then fhall thy underftanding be more clear than the noontide fun ;---then, by thy ftrong and fpiritualized intellectual eye, fhalt thou fee into the great treafury of Nature, and thou fhalt praife God with thy whole heart ;---then wilt thou fee the folly of the world ; and thou fhalt unerringly accomplifh thy defire, and fhalt poffefs the true Philofophers' ftone, to the profit of thy neighbour. I fay, thou fhalt vifibly and fenfibly, according to thy corporal faculties ; not imaginary, not delufively, but real.

Helmont, an author of no mean repute, avouches that he had actually feen the ftone which converts bafe metals into gold ; that he had feen it with his eyes, and handled it with his fingers : taken from his own relation of the fact ; notwithftanding Kircher's declamation againft the poffibility of obtaining it, noting them all who profeffed alchymy to be a fet of impoftors and jugglers, giving no better an expofition of their procefs of tranfmutation than this---" An Alchymift," fays Kircher, " procures or defires a crucible to be brought, wherein is put lead or any other bafe metal, which, while in fufion, he (the Alchymift) ftirs about with an iron rod, and then," he fays, " he drops in, from between his fingers, a bit of gold ; and after ftirring up for fome time, and effay being made, gold is found." This is, indeed, a very lame method of exploding alchymy ; but, however, to leave Kircher as much in the dark as he was, we fhall give you Van Helmont's declaration, a philofopher of much greater note than this pfeudo-chemift Kircher. Van Helmont fays---" I have divers times handled that ftone with my hands, and have feen a real tranfmutation of faleable quickfilver with mine eyes, which, in proportion, did exceed the powder which made the gold in fome thoufand degrees.

" It was of the colour that is in faffron, being weighty in its powder, and fhining like bruifed glafs, when it fhould be the lefs exactly beaten. But there was once given unto me the fourth part of one grain, (I call, alfo, a
grain

grain the fix hundredth part of an ounce). This powder I involved in wax, fcraped off a certain letter, left, in cafting it into the crucible, it fhould be difperfed, through the fmoak of the coals; which pellet of wax I afterwards caft into the three-cornered veffel of a crucible upon a pound of quickfilver, hot and newly bought; and prefently the whole quickfilver, with fome little noife, ftood ftill from flowing, and refided like a lump; but the heat of that *argent vive* was as much as might forbid melted lead from recoagulating. The fire being ftraightway after increafed under the bellows, the metal was melted; the which, the veffel of fufion being broken, I found to weigh eight ounces of the moft pure gold.

" Therefore, a computation being made, a grain of that powder doth convert nineteen thoufand two hundred grains of impure and volatile metal, which is obliterable by the fire, into true gold.

" For that powder, by uniting the aforefaid quickfilver unto itfelf, preferved the fame, at one inftant, from an eternal ruft, putrefaction, death, and torture of the fire, howfoever moft violent it was, and made it as an immortal thing, againft any vigour or induftry of art and fire, and tranfchanged it into the virgin purity of gold; at leaftwife one only fire of coals is required herein."

By which we fee, that fo learned and profound a philofopher as Van Helmont could not fo eafily have been made to believe that there exifted a poffibility of tranfmutation of bafe metals into pure gold, without he had actually proved the fame by experiment.

Again, let the ftanding monuments of Flammel's liberal bounty to the poor, through this mean, to be feen at Paris every day, ftand as a teftimony to the truth of the exifting poffibility of tranfmutation. Likewife, Helmont mentions a ftone that he faw, and had in his poffeffion, which cured all diforders, the plague not excepted. I fhall relate the circumftance in his own words, which are as follow :—

" There was a certain Irifhman, whofe name was Butler, being fome time great with James, King of England, he being detained in the prifon of the Caftle of Vilvord; and taking pity on one Baillius, a certain Francifcan Monk, a moft famous preacher of Gallo-Britain, who was alfo imprifoned, having an crifipelas in his arm ; on a certain evening, when the Monk did almoft defpair, he fwiftly tinged a certain little ftone in a fpoonful of almond-milk, and prefently withdrew it thence. So he fays to the keeper---' Reach this fupping to that Monk ; and how much foever he fhall take thereupon, he fhall be whole, at leaft within a fhort hour's fpace.'---Which thing even fo came to pafs, to the great admiration of the keeper and the fick man, not knowing from whence fo fudden health fhone upon him, feeing that he was ignorant that he had taken any thing : for his left arm, being before hugely fwollen, fell down as that it could fcarcely be difcerned from the other. On the morning following, I, being entreated by fome great men, came to Vilvord, as a witnefs of his deeds ; therefore I contracted a friendfhip with Butler.

" Soon afterwards, I faw a poor old woman, a laundrefs, who, from the age of fixteen years, had laboured with an intolerable megrim, cured in my prefence. Indeed he, by the way, lightly dipped the fame little ftone in a fpoonful of oil of olives, and prefently cleanfed the fame ftone by licking it with his tongue, and laid it up into his fnuff-box ; but that fpoonful of oil he poured into a fmall bottle of oil, whereof one only drop he commanded to be anointed over the head of the aforefaid old woman, who was thereby ftraightway cured, and remained whole ; which I atteft I was amazed, as if he was become another Midas ; but he, fmiling, faid---

' My moft dear friend, unlefs thou come hitherto, fo as to be able, by one only remedy, to cure *every difeafe*, thou fhalt remain in thy *young beginnings*, however *old* thou fhalt become.'---I eafily affented to this, becaufe I had learned that from the fecrets of Paracelfus ; and being now more confirmed by fight and hope. But I willingly confefs, that that new mode of curing was unaccuftomed and unknown to me : I therefore faid, that a young Prince of our Court, Vifcount of Gaunt, brother to the Prince of Epifuoy, of a very great Houfe, was fo wholly proftrated by the gout, that he thenceforth lay only on one fide, being wretched, and deformed with many knots : he, therefore, taking hold of my right hand, faid---' Wilt thou that I cure the young man ? I will cure him for thy fake.'---' But,' I replied, ' he is of that obftinacy, that he had rather die, than drink one only medicinal potion.'

Be

' Be it fo,' faid Butler ; ' for neither do I require any other thing, than that he do, every morning, touch this little ftone, thou feeft, with the top of his tongue ; for after three weeks from thence, let him wafh the painful and unpainful knots with his own urine, and thou fhalt foon afterwards fee him cured, and foundly walking. Go thy ways, and tell him, with joy, what I have faid.'

" I, therefore, being glad, returned to Bruffels, and told him what Butler had faid.

" But the Potentate anfwered---' Go, tell Butler that if he fhall reftore me as thou haft faid; I will give him as much as he fhall require ;---demand the price, and I will willingly fequefter that which is depofited for his fecurity.'--- And when I declared that thing to Butler, on the day following, he was very wrath, and faid---' That Prince is mad, or witlefs and miferable, and there-fore will I never help him : for neither do I ftand in need of his money--- neither do I yield---nor am I inferior to him.'---Nor could I ever induce him, afterwards, to perform what before he had promifed ; wherefore I began to doubt whether the things I had before feen were dreams.

" It happened, in the mean time, that a friend, overfeer and mafter of the glafs-furnace at Antwerp, being exceeding fat, moft earneftly requefted of Butler that he might be freed from his fatnefs ; unto whom Butler offered a fmall piece of that little ftone, that he might once every morning lick, or fpeedily touch it with the top of his tongue : and, within three weeks, I faw his breaft made more ftrait, or narrow, by-one fpan, and him to have lived no lefs whole afterwards. Wherefore I began again to believe that the afore-faid gouty Prince might have been cured, according to the manner Butler had promifed.

" In the mean time, I fent to Vilvord, to Butler, for a remedy, in the cafe of poifon given me by a fecret enemy ; for I miferably languifhed---all my joints were pained ; and my pulfe, vehement, being at length become an in-termitting one, did accompany the faintings of my mind, and extinguifh-ment of my ftrength.

" Butler,

" Butler, being still detained in prison, commanded my household-servant, whom I had sent, that forthwith he should bring unto him a small bottle of oil of olives; and his little stone, aforesaid, being tinged therein, as at other times, he sent that oil unto me ; and told the servant, that with one only small drop of the oil, I should anoint only one place of the pain, or all the places, if I would ; the which I did, and yet felt no help thereby. In the mean time, my enemy, according to his lot, being about to die, bade that pardon should be craved of me for his sin ; and so I knew that I had taken poison, the which I suspected ; and therefore, also, I procured with all care to extinguish the slow venom, which, through the grace of God favouring me, I escaped.

" Seeing that, afterwards, many other cures were performed upon certain gentlewomen, I asked Butler why so many women should be cured, but that I (while that I sharply conflicted with death itself, being also environed with pains of all my joints and organs) should not feel any ease ?---But he asked with what disease I had laboured ?---And when he understood that poison had given a beginning to the disease, he said,---that, as the cause had come from within to without, the oil ought to be taken into the body, or the stone to be touched with the tongue ; because the grief being cherished within, it was not local or external ; and also observed, that the oil did, by degrees, uncloath itself with the efficacy of healing, because the little stone being lightly tinged in it, it had not pithily charged the oil throughout its whole body, but had only ennobled it with a delible or obliterable besprinkling of its odour : for truly that stone did present, in the eyes and tongue, sea-salt spread abroad, or rarified ; and it is sufficiently known that salt is not to be very intimately mixed with oil.

" This same man, also, cured an Abbess, who, for eighteen years, had had her right arm swelled, with an entire deprivation of motion, and the fingers thereof stiff and unmoveable, only by the touching of her tongue with this admirable stone.

" But very many being present witnesses of these same wonders, did suspect some hidden sorcery, or diabolical craft ; for the common people have it for an ancient custom, that whatsoever honest thing their ignorance has determined

not

not to comprehend, they do, for a privy fhift of their ignorance, refer the fame to be the juggling of an evil fpirit. But I could never decline fo far, becaufe the remedy was fuppofed to be natural ; for neither words, ceremonies, nor any other fufpected thing, was required. For neither is it lawful, according to man's power of underftanding, to refer the glory of God, fhewn forth in Nature, unto the devil. For none of thofe people had required aid of Butler, as from necromancy any way fufpected ; yea the thing was at firft made trial of with fmiling, and without faith and confidence ; yet this eafy method of curing fhall long remain fufpected by many ; for the wit of the vulgar being inconftant and idle, they do more readily confecrate fo great a bounty of reftitution unto diabolical contrivance, than to Divine goodnefs, the framer, lover, faviour, refrefher of human nature, and the father of the poor. And thefe vile prejudices are not only inherent in the common people, but alfo in thofe that are learned, who rafhly fearch into the beginning of healing, being not yet inftructed, or obferving the common and blockifh rules ; becaufe they are always wife as children, who have never gone over their mother's threfhold, being afraid of every fable. For they who have not hitherto known the whole circuit of difeafes to be included within the fpirit of life, which maketh the affault ; or if they hereafter, reading my ftudies by the way, fhall imprint on themfelves this moment or concernment of healing ; neverthelefs, becaufe they have been already before accuftomed, from the very beginnings of their ftudies, to the precepts of the humorifts, they will eafily, at length, depart from me, and leap back to the favourite bigotry and ancient opinions of the fchools."

But now we will haften to the manner of preparation neceffary to qualify a man for the attainment of thefe fublime gifts.

Of the Preparation of a Man to qualify him for the Search of this Treasure;
and of the first Matter (prima materia) of the Stone.

LESSON I.

THE preparation for this work is simply this:—Learn to cast away from
thee all vile affections—all levity and inconstancy of mind; let all thy dealings be free from deceit and hypocrisy; avoid the company of vain young
men; hate all profligacy, and profane speaking.

LESSON II.

Keep thy own, and thy neighbours' secrets; court not the favours of the
rich; despise not the poor, for he who does will be poorer than the poorest.

LESSON III.

Give to the needy and unfortunate what little thou canst spare; for he that
has but little, whatever he spares to the miserable, God shall amply reward him.

LESSON IV.

Be merciful to those who offend thee, or who have injured thee; for what
must that man's heart be, who would take heavy vengeance on a slight offence?
Thou shalt forgive thy brother until seventy times seven.

LESSON V.

Be not hasty to condemn the actions of others, lest thou shouldst, the
next hour, fall into the very same error; despise scandal and tattling; let thy
words be few.

LESSON

LESSON VI.

Study day and night, and supplicate thy Creator that he would be pleased to grant thee knowledge and understanding; and that the pure spirits may have communication with, and influence, in thee.

LESSON VII.

Be not overcome with drunkenness; for, be assured, that half the evils that befall mankind originate in drunkenness: for too great a quantity of strong liquors deprive men of their reason; then, having lost the use of the faculty of their judgment, they immediately become the recipient of all evil influences, and are justly compared to weathercocks, that are driven hither and thither by every gust of wind; so those who drown the reasonable power, are easily persuaded to the lightest and most frivolous pursuits, and, from these, to vices more gross and reprobate; for the ministers of darkness have never so favourable an opportunity of insinuating themselves into the minds and hearts of men, as when they are lost in intoxication. I pray you to avoid this dreadful vice.

LESSON VIII.

Avoid gluttony, and all excess---it is very pernicious, and from the Devil: these are the things that constantly tempt man, and by which he falls a prey to his spiritual adversary; for he is rendered incapable of receiving any good or divine gift. Besides, the divine and angelic powers or essences delight not to be conversant about a man who is defiled, and stinking with debauchery and excess.

LESSON IX.

Covet not much gold, but learn to be satisfied with enough; for to desire more than enough, is to offend the Deity.

Book I. I

LESSON X.

Read often thefe ten preparatory Leffons to fit thee for the great work, and for the receiving of higher things ; for the more pure thou art in heart and mind, by fo much quicker fhall you perceive thofe high fecrets we teach, and which are entirely hid from the difcernment of the vicious and depraved, becaufe it never can happen that fuch a fource of treafure can be attained merely to fatisfy our more grofs, earthly, and vain defires and inclinations ; becaufe here nothing muft be thought to be grafped, or wrefted out of this book, but to the fulfilling of a good end and purpofe. When thou fhalt have fo far purified thy heart, as we have fpoken is indifpenfably neceffary for the receiving of every good thing, thou fhalt then fee with other eyes than thou doft at prefent---thy fpiritual eye will be opened, and thou fhalt read man as plain as thou wilt our books ; but, for all this, depend not on the ftrength of thy own wifdom, for even then, when we think our hearts fecure, if we do not watch them that they fleep not, the Devil, or his minifters, immediately take us at this unguarded moment, and tempts us into the actual commiffion of fome fin or other : either he excites our appetite for luft and concupifcence, or any other deadly fin ; therefore, ufing our bleffed Redeemer's words---" What I fay unto you, I fay unto you all---watch !"

Perhaps, I do not doubt but, there are fome that will fay, when they look at our works, this fellow is all rant, all preaching---he tells us what we knew before as well as himfelf. To fuch I fay, let them read our book but twice ; if they do not gather fomething that they will acknowledge precious, (nay, be *convinced* that it is precious, to their own fatisfaction) I will burn thefe writings, and they fhall be no more remembered by me.

To conclude this Part : we fay that the Firft Matter (*Prima Materia*) Adam brought with him out of Paradife, and left it, as an inheritance, to us his fucceffors ; had he remained in his original purity, he would have been permitted to have ufed it himfelf ; but the eternal fiat was paffed, that he was to " earn his bread by the fweat of his brow ;" therefore he could not effect what was afterwards performed by fome of his offspring.

Hermes

Hermes Trifmegiftus, that ancient philofopher, wrote touching the attainment of this ftone, which he pronounced to be of all benefit to man, and one of the greateft bleffings he could poffefs ; and although his writings contain much of the excellency of truth, being wrapped up in fuch fymbolical figures, it renders them exceedingly difficult to be underftood, yet, if comprehended, they, no doubt, contain fome very great fecrets by which mortal man may profit.

Now it belongs to our purpofe to know *what it is* from which we muft extract the firft matter of this ftone, to go on with our procefs, becaufe we muft have materials to work upon ; for all philofophers agree that, the firft matter being found, we may proceed without much difficulty. *For the firft matter,* (I fhall fpeak as plainly as poffible) firft, the grand queftion in debate is--- Where is it to be found ?---I fay it is to be found in ourfelves. We all poffefs this firft matter, from the beggar to the king ; every mothers' fon carries it about him ; and, could our ingenious chemifts but find a procefs for the extracting, how well would all their labours be repaid. The next queftion naturally comes thus---How are we to draw, or attract the fecret matter of the ftone out of ourfelves ?---Not by any common means ; and yet it is to be drawn into very action, and that by the moft fimple means, and in a manner that the attaining of the philofophers' ftone would very foon follow it. I pray you, my friend, look into thyfelf, and endeavour to find out in what part of thy compofition is the *prima materia* of the *lapis philofophorum,* or out of what part of thy fubftance can the firft matter of our ftone be drawn out. Thou fayeft, it muft either be in the *hair, fweat,* or *excrement.* I fay in none of thefe thou fhalt ever be able to find it, and yet thou fhalt find it in thyfelf.

Many great philofophers and chemifts, whom I have the pleafure to know, affirm that, admitting of the poffibility of tranfmutation, it (*i. e.* the *firft matter*) muft be taken from the pureft gold. To this I fay it muft not ; neither has it any thing at all to do with extrinfical gold. They will fay then that the pure ens of gold may be drawn from gold itfelf. True, it may fo ; but then I would afk if they could ever produce more gold than

that

that out of which the foul or effence was extracted ; if they have, they have indeed found out a fecret beyond the powers of our comprehenfion ; becaufe it is againft reafon to fuppofe that if a pound of gold yields a drachm of the foul or effence, that that only will tinge any more than a pound of purified lead, or ☿ ; becaufe we have tried various experiments, and I have, in some of my firft effays, turned both lead and mercury into good gold ; but no more than that out of which the foul was extracted. But, however, not to lofe our time in vain and ridiculous difputation, know that whatever prodigious things or experiments have been tried with refpect to the firft matter, by external fubjects, either in the mineral, animal, or vegetable kingdoms, as they are called, I fay in us is the power of all wonderful things, which the fupreme Creator has, of his infinite mercy, implanted in our fouls ; out of her is to be extracted the firft matter, the true *argent vive*, the ☿ of the philofophers, the true ens of ☉, viz. a fpiritual living gold, or waterifh mercury, or firft matter, which, by being maturated, is capable of tranfmuting a thoufand pts. of impure metal into good and perfect gold, which endure fire, teft, or cupel.

PART II.

OF THE MANNER OF EXTRACTING THE FIRST MATTER OF THE PHILOSOPHERS' STONE, AND THE USE IT IS PUT TO IN PURIFYING THE IMPERFECT METALS, AND TRANSMUTING THEM INTO GOOD GOLD.

LESSON XI.

TAKE the foregoing inftructions as thy principal inftrument, and know that our foul has the power, when the body is free, as we before faid, of any pollution, the heart void of malice and offence ; I fay the foul is then a free agent, and has the power, fpiritually and magically, to act upon any matter whatfoever ; therefore I faid the firft matter is in the foul ; and the extracting of it, is to bring the dormant power of the pure, living, breathing fpirit and eternal foul into act. Note well that every agent has its power of acting upon

its

its patient. Every effence that is diftilled forth is received into a recipient, but that recipient muft firft be made clean. Even fo muft the foul and heart of man : the vile affections muft be thrown away, and trampled under foot ; then fhalt thou be able to proceed in thy work, which do in the manner following.

LESSON XII.

The expence thou muft be at will be but a trifle : all the inftruments neceffary are but three, viz. a crucible, an egg philofophical, and a retort with its receiver. Put your fine gold, in weight about 5 dwts., file it up, put it into your philofophic egg, pour upon it the twice of its weight of the beft Hungarian ☿ , clofe up the egg with an Hermetic feal, put it for three months in horfe-dung, take it out at the end of that time, and fee what kind of form thy gold and ☿ has affumed ; take it out, pour on it half its weight of good fpirit of fal ammon., fet them in a pot full of fand over the fire in the retort, let them diftil into a pure effence, add to one pt. of this ☿ two pts. of thy water of life, or *prima materia*, put them into thy philofophical egg, and

LESSON XIII.

fet them into horfe-dung for another three months ; then take them out, and fee what thou haft---a pure etherial effence, which is the living gold ; pour this pure fpiritual liquor upon a drachm of molten fine gold, and you will find that which will fatisfy thy hunger and thirfting after this fecret ; for the increafe of thy gold will feem to thee miraculous, as indeed it is. Take it to a jeweller's, or goldfmith's ; let him try it in thy prefence, and thou wilt have reafon to blefs God for his mercy to thee. Do thy duty as he hath commanded thee, and ufe all the benefit thou fhalt receive, in actions worthy of thy nature.

LESSON XIV.

When thy fpiritual eye is opened, and thou fhalt begin to fee to what end thou wert created, thou fhalt want no neceffary thing either for thy comfort or
                                                                                    fupport ;

support ; only keep in the rules we have prescribed in the beginning of this little treatise---Fear God, and love thy neighbour as thyself ; be not hasty to reveal any secrets thou mayest learn, for the good spirits, both day and night, will be thy instructors, and will continually reveal thee many secrets. Think not that thou canst either profit or benefit so much by the instruction of those who profess great advantages in classical education and high schooling ; be assured they are, in spiritual knowledge, much in the dark : for he who desires not spiritual knowledge cannot attain it by any means, but by, first, coming to God ; secondly, by purifying his own heart ; thirdly, by submitting himself to the will of the Holy Spirit, to guide and direct him in all truth, to the attaining of all knowledge, both human and divine ; and by arrogating no-thing to our own power or strength, but by referring all to the mercy and goodness of God.---*Amen.*

THE

THE

MAGUS;

OR,

CELESTIAL INTELLIGENCER.

CONTAINING

THE CONSTELLATORY PRACTICE,

OR

TALISMANIC MAGIC.

SHEWING

The true Properties of the Elements, Meteors, Stars, Planets, &c. &c. ; likewife the Nature of Intelligences, Spirits, Dæmons, and Devils ; the Conftruction and Compofition of all Sorts of Magic Seals, Images, Rings, Glaffes, Pictures, &c. &c. ; the Power and Compofition of Numbers, Mathematical Figures, and Characters of Spirits both good and evil.

THE WHOLE OF THE ABOVE ILLUSTRATED BY A GREAT VARIETY OF

Beautiful Figures, Types, Letters, Seals, Images, Magic Characters, &c.

FORMING A COMPLETE SYSTEM OF

DELIGHTFUL KNOWLEDGE AND ABSTRUSE SCIENCE;

Such as is warranted never before to have been published in the English Language.

BY FRANCIS BARRETT,

STUDENT OF CHEMISTRY, OCCULT PHILOSOPHY, THE CABALA, &c. &c. &c.

1801.

PART THE SECOND.

CHAP. I.

OF THE FOUR ELEMENTS, AND THEIR NATURAL QUALITIES.

IT is neceffary that we fhould know and underftand the nature and quality of the four elements, in order to our being perfect in the principles and ground-work of our ftudies in the Talifmanic, or Magical Art.

Therefore, there are four elements, the original grounds of all corporeal things, viz. fire, earth, water, and air, of which elements all inferior bodies are compounded ; not by way of being heaped up together, but by tranfmutation and union ; and when they are deftroyed, they are refolved into elements. But there are none of the fenfible elements that are pure ; but they are, more or lefs, mixed, and apt to be changed the one into the other : even as earth, being moiftened and diffolved, becomes *water*, but the fame being made thick and hard, becomes earth again ; and being evaporated through heat it paffes into air, and that being kindled into fire, and this being extinguifhed, into air again, but being cooled after burning, becomes earth again, or elfe ftone, or fulphur ; and this is clearly demonftrated by lightning. Now every one of thefe elements have two fpecifical properties : the former whereof it retains as proper to itfelf ; in the other, as a mean, it agrees with that which comes directly after it. For fire is hot and dry---earth, cold and dry ;---water, cold and moift---and air, hot and moift. And fo in this manner the elements, according to two contrary qualities, are oppofite one to the other : as fire to water, and earth to air. Likewife, the elements are contrary one to the other on another account : two are heavy, as earth and water---and the others are light, as fire and air ; therefore the Stoics called the former, paffives---but the latter, actives. And Plato diftinguifhes them after another manner, and

BOOK I.   K   affigns

affigns to each of them three qualities, viz. to the fire, brightnefs, thinnefs, and motion----to the earth, darknefs, thicknefs, and quietnefs ; and, according to thefe qualities, the elements of fire and earth are contrary.   Now the other elements borrow their qualities from thefe, fo that the air receives two qualities from the fire,----thinnefs, and motion ; and the earth one, viz. darknefs.   In like manner water receives two qualities of the earth,----darknefs and thicknefs ; and the fire one, viz. motion.   But fire is twice as thin as air, thrice more move-able, and four times brighter ; the air is twice more bright, thrice more thin, and four times more moveable.   Therefore, as fire is to air, fo is air to water, and water to the earth ; and again, as the earth is to the water, fo is water to air, and air to fire.   And this is the root and foundation of all bodies, natures, and wonderful works ; and he who can know, and thoroughly underftand thefe qualities of the elements, and their mixtures, fhall bring to pafs wonderful and aftonifhing things in magic.

Now each of thefe elements have a threefold confideration, fo that the num-ber of four may make up the number of twelve ; and, by paffing by the num-ber of feven into ten, there may be a progrefs to the fupreme unity, upon which all virtue and wonderful things do depend.   Of the firft order are the pure elements, which are neither compounded, changed, or mixed, but are incorruptible ; and not or which, but THROUGH which, the virtues of all natural things are brought forth to act.   No man is able fully to declare their vir-tues, becaufe they can do all things upon all things.   He who remains igno-rant of thefe, fhall never be able to bring to pafs any wonderful matter.

Of the fecond order are elements that are compounded, changeable, and impure ; yet fuch as may, by art, be reduced to their pure fimplicity ; whofe virtue, when they are thus reduced, doth, above all things, perfect all occult and common operations of Nature ; and thefe are the foundation of the whole of Natural Magic.

Of the third order, are thofe elements which originally and of themfelves are not elements, but are twice compounded, various and changeable into another.   Thefe are the infallible *medium*, and are called the *middle nature*, or foul of the middle nature ; very few there are that underftand the deep myfteries

teries thereof. In them is, by means of certain numbers, degrees, and orders, the perfection of every effect in what thing foever, whether *natural, celeſtial*, or fuperceleſtial : they are full of wonders and myſteries, and are operative as in Magic natural, fo divine. For from thefe, through them, proceeds the binding, loofing, and tranfmutation of all things---the knowledge and foretelling of things to come---alfo, the expelling of evil, and the gaining of good fpirits. Let no one, therefore, without thefe three forts of elements, and the true knowledge thereof, be confident that he can work any thing in the Occult Sciences of Magic and Nature.

But whofoever fhall know how to reduce thofe of one order into another, impure into pure, compounded into fimple, and fhall underſtand diſtinctly the *nature, virtue*, and power of them, in number, degrees, and order, without dividing the fubſtance, he fhall eafily attain to the knowledge and perfect operation of all natural things, and celeſtial fecrets likewife ; and this is the perfection of the Cabala, which teaches all thefe before mentioned ; and, by a perfect knowledge thereof, we perform many rare aud wonderful experiments.

CHAP. II.

OF THE PROPERTIES AND WONDERFUL NATURE OF FIRE AND EARTH.

THERE are two things, (fays Hermes) viz. fire and earth, which are fufficient for the operation of all wonderful things : the former is active, and the latter paffive. Fire, in all things and through all things, comes and goes away bright ; it is in all things bright, and at the fame time occult, and unknown. When it is by itfelf (no other matter coming to it, in which it fhould manifeſt its proper action) it is boundlefs and invifible ; of itfelf fufficient for every action that is proper to it ;---itfelf is one, and penetrates through all things ; alfo fpread abroad in the heavens, and fhining. But in the infernal place, ſtraitened, dark, and tormenting ; and in the midway it partakes of both. It is in ſtones, and is drawn out by the ſtroke of the ſteel ; it is in earth, and

　　　caufes

caufes it, after digging up, to fmoak ; it is in water, and heats fprings and wells ; it is in the depths of the fea, and caufes it, being toffed with the winds, to be hot ; it is in the air, and makes it (as we often fee) to burn. And all animals, and all living things whatfoever, as alfo vegetables, are preferved by heat ;---and every thing that lives, lives by reafon of the inclofed heat. The properties of the fire that is above, are heat, making all things fruitful ; and a celeftial light, giving life to all things. The properties of the infernal fire are a parching heat, confuming all things ; and darknefs ; making all things barren. The celeftial and bright fire drives away fpirits of darknefs ;---alfo, this our fire, made with wood, drives away the fame, in as much as it hath an analogy with, and is the *vehiculum* of, that fuperior light ; as alfo of him who faith, " I am the light of the world," which is true fire--- the Father of lights, from whom every good thing that is given comes ;--- fending forth the light of his fire, and communicating it firft to the fun and the reft of the celeftial bodies, and by thefe, as by mediating inftruments, conveying that light into our fire. As, therefore, the fpirits of darknefs are ftronger in the dark----fo good fpirits, which are angels of light, are augmented not only by that light (which is divine, of the fun, and celeftial), but alfo by the light of our common fire. Hence it was that the firft and moft wife inftitutors of religions and ceremonies, ordained that prayers, fingings, and all manner of divine worfhips whatfoever, fhould not be performed without lighted candles or torches : hence, alfo, was that fignificant faying of Pythagoras---" Do not fpeak of God without a light !"---And they commanded that, for the driving away of wicked fpirits, lights and fires fhould be kindled by the carcaffes of the dead, and that they fhould not be removed until the expiations were, after a holy manner, performed, and then buried. And the great Jehovah himfelf, in the old law, commanded that all his facrifices fhould be offered with fire, and that fire fhould always be burning upon the altar, which cuftom the Priefts of the Altar did always obferve and keep amongft the Romans. Now the bafis and foundation of all the elements is the earth ; for that is the objeft, fubjeft, and receptacle of all celeftial rays and influences : in it are contained the feeds, and feminal virtues of all things ; and, therefore, it is faid to be
animal,

animal, vegetable, and mineral. It, being made fruitful by the other elements and the heavens, brings forth all things of itself. It receives the abundance of all things, and is, as it were, the first fountain from whence all
things spring ;—it is the centre, foundation, and mother of all things. Take
as much of it as you please, separated, washed, depurated, and subtilized, and,
if you let it lie in the open air a little while, it will, being full and abounding
with heavenly virtues, of itself bring forth plants, worms, and other living
things ; also stones, and bright sparks of *metals*. In it are great secrets : if,
at any time, it shall be purified, by the help of fire,* and reduced into its
simple nature by a convenient washing, it is the first matter of our creation,
and the truest medicine that can restore and preserve us.

CHAP. III.
OF THE WATER AND AIR.

THE other two elements, viz. water and air, are not less efficacious than
the former ; neither is Nature wanting to work wonderful things in them.
There is so great a necessity of water, that without it nothing can live
—no herb nor plant whatsoever without the moistening of water, can bring
forth ; in it is the seminary virtue of all things, especially of animals, whose
seed is manifestly waterish. The seeds, also, of trees and plants, although
they are earthy, must, notwithstanding, of necessity be rotted in water before
they can be fruitful ; whether they be imbibed with the moisture of the earth,
or with dew, or rain, or any other water that is on purpose put to them.—
For Moses writes, that only earth and water can bring forth a living soul ;
but he ascribes a two-fold production of things to water, viz. of things swim-
ming in the water, and of things flying in the air above the earth ; and

* Agrippa here, speaking of the element of earth being reduced to its utmost simplicity, by being purified
by fire and a convenient washing, means, that it is the first and principal ingredient necessary to the production of the Philosopher's stone, either of animals or metals.

that

that thofe productions that are made in and upon the earth are partly attributed to the very water the fame fcripture teftifies, where it faith, that the
plants and the herbs did not grow, becaufe God had not caufed it to rain upon
the earth. Such is the efficacy of this element of water, that fpiritual rege-
neration cannot be done without it, as Chrift himfelf teftified to Nicodemus.
Very great, alfo, is the virtue of it in the religious worfhip of God, in expiations and purifications ; indeed the neceffity of it is no lefs than
that of fire. Infinite are the benefits, and divers are the ufes, thereof ; as being
that, by virtue of which all things fubfift, are generated, nourifhed, and increafed. Hence it was that Thales of Miletus, and Hefiod, concluded that
water was the beginning of all things ; and faid it was the firft of all the
elements, and the moft potent ; and that, becaufe it hath the maftery over all
the reft. For, as Pliny faith----" Waters fwallow up the earth----extinguifh
flames----afcend on high----and, by the ftretching forth of the clouds, challenge
the heavens for their own ; the fame, falling down, becomes the caufe of all
things that grow in the earth." Very many are the wonders that are done by
waters, according to the writings of Pliny Solinus, and many other hiftorians.

Jofephus alfo makes relation of the wonderful nature of a certain river betwixt Arcea and Raphanea, cities of Syria, which runs with a full channel
all the Sabbath-day, and then on a fudden ftops, as if the fprings were
ftopped, and all the fix days you may pafs over it dry-fhod ; but again, on
the feventh day, no man knowing the reafon of it, the waters return again in
abundance as before ! wherefore the inhabitants thereabout called it the Sabbath-day River, becaufe of the feventh day, which was holy to the Jews.----
The Gofpel, alfo, teftifies of a fheep-pool, into which whofoever ftepped firft,
after the water was troubled by the Angel, was made whole of whatfoever
difeafe he had. The fame virtue and efficacy, we read, was in a fpring of the
Ionian Nymphs, which was in the territories belonging to the town of Elis,
at a village called Heradea, near the river Citheron, which whofoever ftepped
into, being difeafed, came forth whole, and cured of all his difeafes. Pau-
fanias alfo reports, that in Lyceus, a mountain of Arcadia, there was a
                                                                    fpring

spring called Agria, to which, as often as the dryneſs of the region threatened the deſtruction of fruits, Jupiter, Prieſt of Lyceus, went ; and, after the offering of ſacrifices, devoutly praying to the waters of the ſpring, holding a bough of an oak in his hand, put it down to the bottom of the hallowed ſpring ; then, the waters being troubled, a vapour aſcending from thence into the air, was blown into clouds, which being joined together, the whole heaven was overſpread ; which being, a little after, diſſolved into rain, watered all the country moſt wholeſomely.----Moreover, Ruffus, a phyſician of Epheſus, beſides many other authors, wrote ſtrange things concerning the wonders of waters, which, for aught I know, are found in no other author.

It remains, that I ſpeak of the air.----This is a vital ſpirit paſſing through all beings---giving life and ſubſiſtence to all things---moving and filling all things. Hence it is that the Hebrew doctors reckon it not amongſt the elements ; but count it as a medium, or glue, joining things together ; and as the reſounding ſpirit of the world's inſtrument. It immediately receives into itſelf the influence of all celeſtial bodies, and then communicates them to the other elements, as alſo to all mixed bodies. Alſo, it receives into itſelf, as if it were a divine looking-glaſs, the ſpecies of all things, as well natural as artificial ; as alſo of all manner of ſpeeches, and retains them ; and carrying them with it, and entering into the bodies of men, and other animals, through their pores, makes an impreſſion upon them, as well when they are aſleep as when they are awake, and affords matter for divers ſtrange dreams and divinations.----Hence, they ſay, it is that a man, paſſing by a place where a man was ſlain, or the carcaſs newly hid, is moved with fear and dread ; becauſe the air, in that place, being full of the dreadful ſpecies of man-ſlaughter, doth, being breathed in, move and trouble the ſpirit of the man with the like ſpecies ; whence it is that he becomes afraid. For every thing that makes a ſudden impreſſion aſtoniſhes Nature. Whence it is that many philoſophers were of opinion, that air is the cauſe of dreams, and of many other impreſſions of the mind, through the prolonging of images, or ſimilitudes, or ſpecies (which proceed from things and ſpeeches, multiplied in the very air), until they come to the ſenſes, and then to the phantaſy and ſoul of him that receives them ;

them ; which, being freed from cares, and no way hindered, expecting to meet such kind of species, is informed by them. For the species of things, although of their own proper nature they are carried to the senses of men, and other animals in general, may, notwithstanding, get some impression from the heavens whilst they are in the air ; by reason of which, together with the aptness and disposition of him that receives them, they may be carried to the sense of one, rather than of another. And hence it is possible, naturally, and far from all manner of superstition (no other spirit coming between), that a man should be able, in a very small time, to signify his mind unto another man, abiding at a very long and unknown distance from him--- although he cannot precisely give an estimate of the time when it is, yet, of necessity, it must be within twenty-four hours ;---and I, myself, know how to do it, and have often done it. The same also, in time past, did the Abbot Tritemius both know and do.---Also, when certain appearances (not only spiritual, but also natural) do flow forth from things, that is to say, by a certain kind of flowings forth of bodies from bodies, and do gather strength in the air, they shew themselves to us as well through light as motion---as well to the sight as to other senses---and sometimes work wonderful things upon us, as Platonius proves and teacheth.' And we see how, by the south-wind, the air is condensed into thin clouds, in which, as in a looking-glass, are reflected representations, at a great distance, of castles, mountains, horses, men, and other things, which, when the clouds are gone, presently vanish.---And Aristotle, in his Meteors, shews that a rainbow is conceived in a cloud of the air, as in a looking-glass.---And Albertus says, that the effigies of bodies may, by the strength of Nature, in a moist air, be easily represented ; in the same manner as the representations of things are in things.---And Aristotle tells of a man, to whom it happened, by reason of the weakness of his sight, that the air that was near to him became, as it were, a looking-glass to him, and the optic-beam did reflect back upon himself, and could not penetrate the air, so that, whithersoever he went, he thought he saw his own image, with his face towards him, go before him.---In like manner, by the artificialness of some certain looking-glasses, may be produced at a distance, in the air, besides the

looking-

looking-glaffes, what images we pleafe ; which, when ignorant men fee, they think they fee the appearances of fpirits or fouls——when, indeed, they are nothing elfe but femblances a-kin to themfelves, and without life. And it is well-known, if in a dark place, where there is no light but by the coming in of a beam of the fun fome where through a little hole, a white paper or plain looking-glafs be fet up againft the light, that there may be feen upon them whatfoever things are done without, being fhined upon by the fun. And there is another flight or trick yet more wonderful :——if any one fhall take images, artificially painted, or written letters, and, in a clear night, fet them againft the beams of the full moon, thofe refemblances being multiplied in the air, and caught upward, and reflected back together with the beams of the moon, another man, that is privy to the thing, at a long diftance, fees, reads, and knows them in the very compafs and circle of the moon ; which art of declaring fecrets is, indeed, very profitable for towns and cities that are befieged, being a thing which Pythagoras long fince did, and which is not unknown to fome in thefe days ; I will not except myfelf. And all thefe things, and many more, and much greater than thefe, are grounded in the very nature of the air, and have their reafons and caufes declared in mathematics and optics. And as thefe refemblances are reflected back to the fight, fo alfo are they, fometimes, to the hearing, as is manifeft in echo. But there are many more fecret arts than thefe, and fuch whereby any one may, at a remarkable diftance, hear, and underftand diftinctly, what another fpeaks or whifpers.

CHAP. IV.

OF COMPOUND, OR MIXED BODIES——IN WHAT MANNER THEY RELATE TO THE ELEMENTS ——AND HOW THE ELEMENTS RELATE TO THE SOULS, SENSES, AND DISPOSITIONS OF MEN.

THE next in order, after the four fimple elements, are the four kinds of perfect bodies compounded of them, viz. metals, ftones, plants, and animals ; and although in the generation of each of thefe, all the elements combine to-

BOOK I.　　　　　　　　L　　　　　　　　gether

gether in the composition, yet every one of them follows and resembles one of the elements which is most predominant : for all stones, being earthy, are naturally heavy, and are so hardened with dryness that they cannot be melted ;---but metals are watery, and may be melted, which naturalists and chemists find to be true, viz. that they are composed or generated of a viscous water, or watery *argent vive*. Plants have such an affinity with the air, that unless they are out in it, and receive its benefit, they neither flourish nor increase. So also animals, as the Poet finely expresses it----

> " Have, in their natures, a most fiery force,
> " And also spring from a celestial source:"

and fire is so natural to them that, being extinguished, they soon die.

Now, amongst stones, those that are dark and heavy, are called *earthy*---those which are transparent, of the *watery element*, as crystal, beryl, and pearls---those which swim upon the water and are spongious, as the pumice-stone, sponge, and sophus, are called airy---and those are attributed to the element of fire, out of which fire is extracted, or which are resolved into fire ; as thunder-stones, fire-stones, asbestos. Also, amongst metals ;---lead and silver are earthy ; quicksilver is watery ; copper and tin, airy ; gold and iron, fiery. In plants, also, the roots resemble earth---the leaves, water---flowers, the air---and seed, the fire, by reason of their multiplying spirit. Besides, some are hot, some cold, some moist, others dry, borrowing their names from the qualities of the elements. Amongst animals, also, some are, in comparison of others, earthy, because they live in the very bowels of the earth, as worms, moles, and many other reptiles ; others watery, as fish ; others which always abide in the air, therefore airy ; others, again, fiery, as salamanders, crickets ; and such as are of a fiery heat, as pigeons, ostriches, eagles, lions, panthers, &c. &c.

Now, in animals, the bones resemble earth---vital spirit, the fire---flesh, the air---and humours, the water ; and these humours also resemble the elements, viz. yellow choler, the fire---the blood, the air---phlegm, the water---and

black

black choler, or melancholy, the earth. And, laftly, in the foul itfelf, the underftanding refembles the fire---reafon, the air---imagination, the water--- and the fenfes the earth. And thefe fenfes again are divided amongft themfelves, according to the elements : for the fight is fiery, becaufe it cannot perceive without the help of fire and light---the hearing is airy, for a found is made by the ftriking of the air---the fmell and tafte refemble water, without the moifture of which there is neither fmell nor tafte---and, laftly, the feeling is wholly earthly, becaufe it takes grofs bodies for its object. The actions, alfo, and operations of man are governed by the elements : for the earth fignifies a flow and firm motion ; the water, fearfulnefs, fluggifhnefs, and remiffnefs in working ; air fignifies cheerfulnefs, and an amiable difpofition ; but fire, a fierce, working, quick, fufceptible difpofition. The elements are, therefore, the firft and original matter of all things ; and all things are of and according to them ; and they in and through all things diffufe their virtues.

CHAP. V.

THAT THE ELEMENTS ARE IN THE HEAVENS, IN THE STARS, IN DEVILS, ANGELS, INTELLIGENCES, AND, LASTLY, IN GOD HIMSELF.

IN the original and exemplary world, all things are all in all ; fo alfo in this corporeal world. And the elements are not only in thefe inferior things ; but are in the heavens, in ftars, in devils, in angels, and likewife in God himfelf, the maker and original example of all things.

Now it muft be underftood that in thefe inferior bodies the elements are grofs and corruptible ; but in the heavens they are, with their natures and virtues, after a celeftial and more excellent manner than in fublunary things : for the firmnefs of the celeftial earth is there without the groffnefs of water ; and the agility of air without exceeding its bounds ; the heat of fire without burning, only fhining, giving light and life to all things by its celeftial heat.---Now

L 2   amongft amongst the stars, or planets, some are fiery, as Mars, and the Sun---airy, as Jupiter, and Venus---watery, as Saturn, and Mercury---and earthy, such as inhabit the eighth orb, and the Moon (which by many is accounted watery), seeing that, as if it were earth, it attracts to itself the celestial waters, with which being imbibed it does, on account of its proximity to us, pour forth and communicate to our globe.

There are, likewise, amongst the signs, some fiery, some airy, some watery, and some earthy. The elements rule *them*, also, in the heavens, distributing to them these four threefold considerations of every element, according to their triplicities, viz. the beginning, middle, and end.

Likewise, devils are distinguished according to the elements: for some are called earthy devils, others fiery, some airy, and others watery. Hence, also, those four infernal rivers: fiery Phlegethon, airy Cocytus, watery Styx, earthy Acheron. Also, in the Gospel, we read of comparisons of the elements: as hell fire, and eternal fire, into which the cursed shall be commanded to go ;--- and in Revelations, of a lake of fire ;---and Isaiah, speaking of the damned, says that the Lord will smite them with corrupt air ;---and in Job, they shall skip from the waters of the snow to the extremity of heat ; and, in the same, we read, that the earth is dark, and covered with the darkness of death, and *miserable* darkness.

And these elements are placed in the angels of heaven, and the blessed intelligences: there is in them a stability of their essence, which is an earthy virtue, in which is the stedfast seat of God. By the Psalmist they are called waters, where he says---" Who ruleft the waters that are higher than the heavens ;"---also, in them their subtile breath is air, and their love is shining fire ; hence they are called in Scripture, the wings of the wind ; and, in another place, the Psalmist speaks of them thus---" Who makest angels thy spirits, and thy ministers a flaming fire !"---Also, according to the different orders of spirits or angels, some are fiery, as seraphims, authorities, and powers--- earthy, as cherubim---watery, as thrones and archangels---airy, as dominions and principalities.

And

And do we not read of the original Maker of all things, that the earth fhall be opened and bring forth a Saviour?---Likewife it is fpoken of the fame, that he fhall be a fountain of living water, cleanfing and regenerating; and the fame fpirit breathing the breath of life; and the fame, according to Mofes' and Paul's teftimony---*a confuming fire.*

That the elements are, therefore, to be found every where, and in all things, after their manner, no man will dare to deny: firft, in thefe inferior bodies, feculent and grofs; and in celeftials, more pure and clear; but in fuper-celeftials, living, and in all refpects bleffed. Elements, therefore, in the exemplary world, are ideas of things to be produced; in intelligences, they are diftributed powers; in the heavens, they are virtues; and in inferior bodies, are grofs forms.

CHAP. VI.

THAT THE WISDOM OF GOD WORKS BY THE MEDIUM OF SECOND CAUSES (I. E. BY THE INTELLIGENCES, BY THE HEAVENS, ELEMENTS, AND CELESTIAL BODIES) IS PROVED BEYOND DISPUTE IN THIS CHAPTER.

IT is to be noted, that God, in the firft place, is the end and beginning of all virtues: he gives the *feal* of the *ideas* to his fervants, *the intelligences,* who, as faithful officers, *fign* all things entrufted to them with an *ideal virtue;* the heavens and ftars, as inftruments, difpofing the matter, in the mean while, for the receiving of thofe forms which refide in Divine Majefty, and to be conveyed by ftars. And the Giver of forms diftributes them by the miniftry of his intelligences, which he has ordained as rulers and comptrollers over his works; to whom fuch a power is entrufted, in things committed to them, that fo all virtue in ftones, herbs, metals, and all other things, may come from the intelligences, the governors. Therefore the form and virtue of things come firft from the *ideas*---then from the ruling and governing intelligences---then from the afpects of the heavens difpofing---and, laftly, from the tempers of

the

the elements difpofed, anfwering the influences of the heavens, by which the elements themfelves are ordered or difpofed. Thefe kinds of operations, therefore, are performed in thefe inferior things by exprefs forms ; and in the heavens, by difpofing virtues ; in intelligences, by mediating rules ; in the original caufe, by *ideas* and exemplary forms ; all which muft of neceffity agree in the execution of the effect and virtue of every thing.

There is, therefore, a wonderful virtue and operation in every herb and ftone, but greater in a ftar ; beyond which, even from the governing intelligences, every thing receives and obtains many things for itfelf, efpecially from the Supreme Caufe, with whom all things mutually and exactly correfpond, agreeing in an harmonious confent.

Therefore there is *no other caufe* of the neceffity of effects, than the connection of all things with the Firft Caufe, and their correfpondency with thofe divine patterns and eternal ideas, whence every thing hath its determinate and particular place in the exemplary world, from whence it lives and receives its original being ; and every virtue of herbs, ftones, metals, animals, words, fpeeches, and all things that are of God, are placed there.

Now the Firft Caufe (which is God), although he doth, by intelligences and the heavens, work upon thefe inferior things, does fometimes (thefe mediums being laid afide, or their officiating being fufpended) work thofe things immediately by himfelf—which works are then called miracles. But whereas fecondary caufes do, by the command and appointment of the Firft Caufe, neceffarily act, and are neceffitated to produce their effects ; if God fhall, notwithstanding, according to his pleafure, fo difcharge and fufpend them that they fhall wholly defift from the neceffity of that command, then they are called the greateft miracles of God. For inftance : the fire of the Chaldean furnace did not burn the children ; the fun ftood ftill at the command of Jofhua, and became retrograde one whole day ; alfo, at the prayer of Hezekiah, it went back ten degrees ; and when our Saviour Chrift was crucified, it became darkened, though at full moon.

And

And the reason of these operations can by no rational difcourfe, no magic or fcience, occult or profound foever, be found out or underftood ; but are to be learned by Divine oracles only.*

CHAP. VII.

OF THE SPIRIT OF THE WORLD.

NOW feeing that the foul is the effential form, intelligible and incorruptible, and is the firft mover of the body, and is moved of itfelf ; but that the body, or matter, is of itfelf unable and unfit for motion, and does very much degenerate from the foul, it appears that there is need of a more excellent medium :—now fuch a medium is conceived to be the fpirit of the world, or that which fome call a quinteffence ; becaufe it is not from the four elements, but a certain *firft thing*, having its being above and befide them.　There is, therefore, fuch a kind of medium required to be, by which celeftial fouls may be joined to grofs bodies, and beftow upon them wonderful gifts.　This fpirit is, in the fame manner, in the body of the world, as our fpirit is in our bodies ; for as the powers of our foul are communicated to the members of the body by the medium of the fpirit, fo alfo the virtue of the foul of the world is diffufed, throughout all things, by the medium of the univerfal fpirit ; for there is nothing to be found in the whole world that hath not a fpark of the virtue thereof.　Now this fpirit is received into things, more or lefs, by the rays of the ftars, fo far as things are difpofed, or made fit recipients of it.　By this fpirit, therefore, every occult property is conveyed into herbs, ftones, metals, and animals, through the fun, moon, planets, and through ftars higher than the planets.　Now this fpirit may be more advantageous to us if we knew how to feparate it from the elements ; or, at leaft, to ufe thofe things chiefly

* The foregoing Chapter, if well confidered, will open the intellect to a more eafy comprehenfion of the Magical Science of Nature, &c. ; and will facilitate, in a wonderful degree, our ftudies in thefe fublime myfteries.

which

which are most abounding with this spirit. For those things in which the spirit is less drowned in a body, and less checked by matter, do much more powerfully and perfectly act, and also more readily generate their like; for in it are all *generative* and *seminal virtues*. For which cause the alchymist endeavours to separate this spirit from gold and silver, which, being rightly separated and extracted, if it shall be afterwards projected upon any metal, turns it into gold or silver; which is no way impossible or improbable, when we consider that by art that may be done in a short time, what Nature, in the bowels of the earth (as in a matrix), perfects in a very long space of time.

CHAP VIII.

OF THE SEALS AND CHARACTERS IMPRESSED BY CELESTIALS UPON NATURAL THINGS.

ALL stars have their peculiar natures, properties, and conditions, the seals and characters whereof they produce through their rays even in these inferior things, viz. in elements, in stones, in plants, in animals, and their members; whence every thing receives from an harmonious disposition, and from its star shining upon it, some particular seal or character stamped upon it, which is the significator of that star or harmony, containing in it a peculiar virtue, different from other virtues of the same matter, both generically, specifically, and numerically. Every thing, therefore, hath its *character* impressed upon it by its *star* for some peculiar effect, especially by that star which doth principally govern it; and these characters contain in them the particular natures, virtues, and roots of their stars, and produce the like operations upon other things on which they are reflected; and stir up and help the influences of their stars, whether they be planets, or fixed stars and figures, or celestial constellations, viz. as often as they shall be made in a fit matter, and in their due and accustomed times; which the ancient wise men (considering such as laboured much in finding out occult properties of things) did set down, in writing, the images of the stars, their figures, seals, marks, characters, such as Nature herself did describe by the rays of the stars in these inferior bodies: some in
stones,

ftones, fome in plants, fome in joints and knots of trees and their boughs, and fome in various members of animals. For the bay-tree, lote-tree, and marigold, are folary herbs, and, their roots and knots being cut, they fhew the chara&ters of the fun ; and in ftones the chara&ters and images of celeftial things are often found. But there being fo great a diverfity of things, there is only a traditional knowledge of a few things which human underftanding is able to reach ; therefore very few of thofe things are known to us, which the ancient philofophers and chiromancers attained to, partly by reafon and partly by experience ; and there yet lie hid many things in the treafury of Nature, which the diligent ftudent and wife fearcher fhall contemplate and difcover.

CHAP IX.

TREATING OF THE VIRTUE AND EFFICACY OF PERFUMES, OR SUFFUMIGATIONS, AND VA-
POURS ; AND TO WHAT PLANETS THEY ARE PROPERLY AND RIGHTLY ATTRIBUTED

IT is neceffary, before we come to the operative or pra&tical part of Talifmanic Magic, to fhew the compofitions of fumes or vapours, that are proper to the ftars, and are of great force for the opportunely receiving of celeftial gifts, under the rays of the ftars—inafmuch as they ftrongly work upon the air and breath ; for our breath is very much changed by fuch kind of vapours, if both vapours be of the other like. The air being alfo, through the faid vapours, eafily moved, or infe&ted with the qualities of inferiors, or celeftial (daily quickly penetrating our breaft and vitals), does wonderfully reduce us to the like qualities. Let no man wonder how great things fuffumigations can do in the air; efpecially when they fhall, with Porphyry, confider that, by certain vapours exhaled from proper fuffumigations, ærial fpirits are raifed ; alfo thunder and lightnings, and the like : as the liver of a cameleon, being burnt on the houfe top, will raife fhowers and lightnings ; the fame effe&t has the head and throat, if they are burnt with oaken wood. There are fome fuffumigations under the influences of the ftars, that caufe

Book I.   M   images,

images of fpirits to appear in the air, or elfewhere : for if coriander, fmallage, henbane, and hemlock be made to fume, by invocations fpirits will foon come together, being attracted by the vapours which are moft congruous to their own natures ; hence they are called the herbs of the fpirits. Alfo it is faid, that if a fume be made of the root of the reedy herb fagapen, with the juice of hemlock and henbane, and the herb tapfus barbatus, red fanders, and black poppy, it will likewife make ftrange fhapes appear ; but if a fuffume be made of fmallage, it chafes them away, and deftroys their vifions. Again, if a perfume be made of calamint, piony, mint, and palma chrifti, it drives away all evil fpirits and vain imaginations. Likewife, by certain fumes, animals are gathered together, and put to flight. Pliny mentions concerning the ftone liparis, that, with the fume thereof, all beafts are attracted together. The bones in the upper part of the throat of a hart, being burnt, bring ferpents together ; but the horn of the hart, being burnt, chafes away the fame ; like-wife, a fume of peacock's feathers does the fame. Alfo, the lungs of an afs, being burnt, puts all poifonous things to flight ; and the fume of the burnt hoof of a horfe drives away mice ; the fame does the hoof of a mule ; and with the hoof of the left-foot flies are driven away. And if a houfe, or any place, be fmoaked with the *gall* of a *cuttle-fifh*, made into a confection with red ftorax, rofes, and lignum aloes, and then there be fome fea-water or blood caft into that place, the whole houfe will feem to be full of water or blood.

Now fuch kind of vapours as thefe, we muft conceive, do infect a body, and infufe a virtue into it which continues long, even as the poifonous vapour of the peftilence, being kept for two years in the walls of a houfe, infects the inha-bitants ; and as the contagion of peft or leprofy lying hid in a garment, will, long after, infect him that wears it.

Now there are certain fuffumigations ufed to almoft all our inftruments of magic (of which hereafter), fuch as images, rings, &c. For fome of the magicians fay, that if any one fhall hide gold, or filver, or any other fuch like precious thing (the moon being in conjunction with the fun), and fhall perfume the place with *coriander*, *faffron*, *henbane*, fmallage, and black poppy, of each the fame quantity and bruifed together, and tempered with
                                                                    the

the juice of hemlock, that thing which is so hid shall never be taken away therefrom, but that spirits shall continually keep it ; and if any one shall endeavour to take it away by force, they shall be hurt, or struck with a frenzy. And *Hermes* says, there is nothing like the fume of spermaceti for the raising up of spirits ; therefore, if a fume be made of that, lignum aloes, pepperwort, musk, saffron, and red storax, tempered together with the blood of a lapwing or bat, it will quickly gather airy spirits to the place where it is used ; and if it be used about the graves of the dead, it will attract spirits and ghosts thither.

Now the use of suffumigations is this : that whenever we set about making any talisman, image, or the like, under the rule or dominion of any star or planet, we should by no means omit the making of a suffumigation appropriate to that planet or constellation under which we desire to work any effect or wonderful operation ; as for instance :---when we direct any work to the sun, we must suffume with solary things ; if to the moon, with lunary things ; and so of the rest. And we must be careful to observe, that as there is a contrariety, or antipathy, in the natures of the stars and planets and their spirits, so there is also in suffumigations :---for there is an antipathy between lignum aloes and sulphur frankincense and quicksilver ; and spirits that are raised by the fume of lignum aloes, are laid by the burning of sulphur. For the learned Proclus gives an example of a spirit that appeared in the form of a lion, furious and raging : by setting a white cock before the apparition it soon vanished away ; because there is so great a contrariety between a cock and a lion ;---and let this suffice for a general observation in these kind of things. We shall proceed with shewing distinctly the composition of the several fumes appropriated to the seven planets.

CHAP.

CHAP. X.

OF THE COMPOSITION OF SOME PERFUMES APPROPRIATED TO THE SEVEN PLANETS.

THE SUN. ☉

WE make a fuffumigation for the fun in this manner :——

Take of faffron, ambergris, mufk, lignum aloes, lignum balfam, the fruit of the laurel, cloves, myrrh, and frankincenfe, of each a like quantity ; all of which being bruifed, and mixed together, fo as to make a fweet odour, muft be incorporated with the brain of an eagle, or the blood of a white cock, after the manner of pills, or troches.

THE MOON. ☽

For the moon, we make a fuffume of the head of a frog dried, the eyes of a bull, the feed of white poppies, frankincenfe, and camphire, which muft be incorporated with menftruous blood, or the blood of a goofe.

SATURN. ♄

For faturn, take the feed of black poppies, henbane, mandrake root, loadftone, and myrrh, and mix them up with the brain of a cat and the blood of a bat.

JUPITER. ♃

Take the feed of afh, lignum aloes, ftorax, the gum Benjamin, the lapis lazuli, the tops of peacocks' feathers, and incorporate with the blood of a ftork, or fwallow, or the brain of a hart.

MARS. ♂

Take uphorbium, bdellium, gum armoniac, the roots of both hellebores, the loadftone, and a little fulphur, and incorporate them altogether with the brain of a hart, the blood of a man, and the blood of a black cat.

VENUS.

VENUS. ♀

Take musk, ambergris, lignum aloes, red roses, and red coral, and make them up with sparrow's brains and pigeon's blood.

MERCURY. ☿

Take mastich, frankincense, cloves, and the herb cinquefoil, and the agate stone, and incorporate them all with the brain of a fox, or weasel, and the blood of a magpie.

GENERAL FUMES OF THE PLANETS.

To Saturn are appropriated for fumes, odoriferous roots : as pepper-wort root, &c., and the frankincense tree. To *Jupiter*, all odoriferous fruits : as nutmegs, cloves, &c. To *Mars*, all odoriferous woods : as sanders, cyprus, lignum balsam, and lignum aloes. To the *Sun*, all gums : as frankincense, mastich benjamin, storax, laudanum, ambergris, and musk. To *Venus*, flowers : as roses, violets, saffron, and the like. To Mercury, all the parings of wood or fruit : as cinnamon, lignum caffia, mace, citron peel, and bay-berries, and whatever seeds are odoriferous. To the Moon, the leaves of all vegetables : as the leaf indum, the leaf of the myrtle, and bay tree. Know, also, that, according to the opinion of all magicians, in every good matter (as love, good-will, &c.), there must be a good perfume, odoriferous and pre-cious ;---and in evil matters (as hatred, anger, misery, and the like), there must be made a stinking fume that is of no worth.

The twelve Signs of the Zodiac also have their proper suffumigations viz., Aries, *myrrh ;* Taurus, *pepper-wort ;* Gemini, *mastich ;* Cancer, *camphire ;* Leo, *frankincense ;* Virgo, *sanders ;* Libra, *galbanum ;* Scorpio, *oppoponax ;* Sagittarius, *lignum aloes ;* Capricorn, *benjamin ;* Aquarius, *euphorbium ;* Pisces, *red storax*. But Hermes describes the most powerful fume to be, that which is compounded of the seven aromatics, according to the powers of the seven planets : for it receives from *Saturn*, pepper-wort ; from *Jupiter*, nut-meg ;

meg ; from *Mars*, lignum-aloes ; from the *Sun*, maftich ; from *Venus*, faffron ; from *Mercury*, cinnamon ; and from the *Moon*, myrtle.

By a clofe obfervation of the above order of fuffumigations, conjoined with
other things, of which we fhall fpeak hereafter (neceffary to the full accomplifhment of Talifmanic Magic), many wonderful effects may be caufed, efpecially if
we keep in eye what was delivered in the firft part of our Magic, viz. that the
foul of the operator muft go along with this ; otherwife, in vain is *fuffumiga-*
tion, feal, ring, image, picture, glafs, or any other inftrument of magic :
feeing that it is not merely the difpofition, but the act of the difpofition, and
firm and powerful intent or imagination, that gives the effect.----We fhall now
haften to fpeak, generally, of the conftruction of rings magical, and their
wonderful and potent virtues and operations.

CHAP. XI.

OF THE COMPOSITION AND MAGIC VIRTUE OF RINGS.

RINGS, when they are opportunely made, imprefs their virtues upon us,
infomuch that they affect the fpirit of him that carries them with gladnefs or fadnefs ; and render him bold or fearful, courteous or terrible, amiable or hateful ;
inafmuch, alfo, as they fortify us againft * ficknefs, poifons, enemies, evil fpirits,
and all manner of hurtful things ; and often, where the law has no effect, thefe
little trifles greatly affift and corroborate the troubled fpirit of the wearer, and
help him, in a wonderful manner, to overcome his adverfaries, while they do wonder how it is that they cannot effect any hurtful undertaking againft him.
Thefe things, I fay, are great helps againft wrathful, vicious, wordly-minded
men, inafmuch as they do terrify, hurt, and render invalid the machinations of
thofe who would otherwife work our mifery or deftruction.   All which we are
neither afraid nor afhamed to declare, well knowing that thefe things will be
hid from the wicked and profane, fo as that they cannot draw the fame into

---

* The Author will engage to teach any that are curious in thofe ftudies, the particular compofition of
Talifmanic Rings ; whereby they may be enabled to judge themfelves of the effects that are to be produced
by them.

any

any abufe, or privy mifchief toward their neighbour; we having referved fome few things in this art to ourfelves---not willing to throw pearls before fwine. And however fimple and plain we may defcribe fome certain experiments and operations (fo as that the great-mouthed fchool philofophers may mutter or fcoff thereat), yet there is nothing delivered in this book but what may be, by an underftanding thereof, brought into effect, and, likewife, out of which fome good may be derived. But to proceed.

The manner of making of thefe rings is thus :---when any ftar afcends in the horofcope (fortunately), with a fortunate afpect or conjunction of the moon, we proceed to take a *ftone* and herb, that is under that ftar, and like-wife make a ring of the metal that is correfponding to the ftar; and in the ring, under the ftone, put the herb or root, not forgetting to infcribe the *effect*, *image*, *name*, and *character*, as alfo the proper fuffume. But I fhall fpeak more of thefe in another place, where I fpeak of images and characters. Therefore, in making of rings magical, thefe things are unerringly to be ob-ferved as we have ordered ;---if any one is willing to work any effect or expe-riment in magic, he muft by no means neglect the neceffary circumftances which we have fo uniformly delivered. I have read, in Philoftratus Jarchus, that a Prince of the Indians beftowed feven rings, marked with the virtues and names of the feven planets, to Appollonius, of which he wore one every day, diftinguifhing according to the names of the days; by the benefit of which he lived above one hundred and thirty years, as alfo always retained the beauty of his youth. In like manner, Mofes, the Lawgiver and Ruler of the He-brews, being fkilled in the Egyptian Magic, is faid, by Jofephus, to have made rings of love and oblivion. There was alfo, as faith Ariftotle, among the Cireneans, a ring of Battas, which could procure love and honour. We read, alfo, that Eudamus, a certain philofopher, made rings againft the bites of ferpents, bewitchings, and evil fpirits. The fame doth Jofephus relate of Solomon. Alfo we read, in Plato, that Gygus, King of Lydia, had a ring of wonderful and ftrange virtues; the feal of which, when he turned it towards the palm of his hand, no body could fee him, but he could fee all things; by the opportunity of which ring, he ravifhed the Queen, and flew the

the King his mafter, and killed whomfoever he thought ftood in his way ; and in thefe villanies nobody could fee him ; and at length, by the benefit of this ring, he became King of Lydia.*

CHAP. XII.

THAT THE PASSIONS OF THE MIND ARE ASSISTED BY CELESTIALS----AND THAT CONSTANCY OF MIND IS IN EVERY WORK NECESSARY.

THE paffions of the mind are much helped, and are helpful, and become moft powerful, by virtue of the heaven, as they agree with the heaven---either by any natural agreement, or voluntary election ; for, as Ptolemy fays, he who chufeth that which is the better, feems to differ nothing from him who hath this of Nature. It conduceth, therefore, very much for the receiving the benefit of the heavens, in any work, if we fhall, by the heaven, make ourfelves fuitable to it in our thoughts, affections, imaginations, elections, deliberations, contemplations, and the like. For fuch like paffions vehemently ftir up our fpirit to their likenefs, and fuddenly expofe us, and our's, to the fuperior fignificators of fuch like paffions ; and alfo, by reafon of their dignity and nearnefs to the fuperiors, do partake more of the celeftials than any material things ; for our mind can, through imaginations or reafon by a kind of imitation, be fo conformed to any ftar, as fuddenly to be filled with the virtues of that ftar, as if we were a proper receptacle of the influence thereof. Now the contemplating mind, as it withdraws itfelf from all *fenfe, imagination, nature,* and *deliberation,* and calls itfelf back to things feparated, effects divers things by faith, which is a firm adhefion, a fixed intention, and vehement application of the worker or receiver to him that co-operates in any thing, and gives power to the work which we intend to do. So that there is

* We have above fhewn the power and virtue of magical rings; but the particular characters, infcriptions, and images to be made in, or upon them, we refer the ftudent to that chapter treating of " The Compofition of various Talifmans ;" in which we have defcribed exactly the exprefs methods of perfecting them.

made,

made, as it were, in us the image of the virtue to be received, and the thing
to be done in us, or by us. We muſt, therefore, in every work and application of things, *affect vehemently*, imagine, hope, and believe ſtrongly, for
that will be a great help. And it is verified amongſt phyſicians, that a ſtrong
belief, and an undoubted hope, and love towards the phyſician, conduce much
to health, yea more ſometimes than the medicine itſelf ; for the ſame that the
efficacy and virtue of the medicine works, the ſame doth the ſtrong imagination of the phyſician work, being able to change the qualities of the body of
the ſick, eſpecially when the patient places much confidence in the phyſician,
by that means diſpoſing himſelf for the receiving the virtue of the phyſician
and phyſic. Therefore, he that works in magic muſt be of a conſtant belief,
be credulous, and not at all doubt of the obtaining of the effect ; for as a firm
and ſtrong belief doth work wonderful things, although it be in falſe works---
ſo diſtruſt and doubting doth diſſipate and break the virtue of the mind of the
worker, which is the medium betwixt both extremes ; whence it happens that
he is fruſtrated of the deſired influence of the ſuperiors, which could not be
enjoined and united to our labours without a firm and ſolid virtue of our
mind.

CHAP. XIII.

HOW MAN'S MIND MAY BE JOINED WITH THE MIND OF INTELLIGENCES AND CELESTIALS,
AND, TOGETHER WITH THEM, IMPRESS CERTAIN WONDERFUL VIRTUES UPON INFERIOR
THINGS.

THE philoſophers, eſpecially the Arabians, ſay, that man's mind, when
it is moſt intent upon any work, through its paſſion and effects, is joined with
the mind of the ſtars and intelligences, and, being ſo joined, is the cauſe that
ſome wonderful virtue be infuſed into our works and things ; and this, as becauſe there is in it an apprehenſion and power of all things, ſo becauſe all
things have a natural obedience to it, and of neceſſity an efficacy, and more

to that which defired them with a ftrong defire. And according to this is
verified the art of characters, images, enchantments, and fome fpeeches, and
many other wonderful experiments, to every thing which the mind affects.
By this means, whatfoever the mind of him that is in vehement love affects,
hath an efficacy to caufe love; and whatfoever the mind of him that ftrongly
hates, dictates, hath an efficacy to hurt and deftroy. The like is in other
things which the mind affects with a ftrong defire; for all thofe things which
the mind acts, and dictates by *characters, figures, words, fpeeches, geftures,
and the like*, help the appetite of the 'foul, and acquire certain wonderful
virtues from the foul of the operator, in that hour when fuch a like appetite
doth invade it; fo from the opportunity and celeftial influence, moving the
mind in this or that manner: for our mind, when it is carried upon the great
excefs of any paffion or virtue, oftentimes takes to itfelf a ftrong, better and
more convenient hour or opportunity; which Thomas Aquinas, in his third
book againft the Gentiles, allows. So, many wonderful virtues both caufe
and follow certain admirable operations by great affections, in thofe things
which the foul doth dictate in that hour to them. But know, that fuch kind
of things confer nothing, or very little, but to the author of them, and to
him who is inclined to them, as if he were the author of them; and this is
the manner by which their efficacy is found out. And it is a general rule in
them, that every mind, that is more excellent in its defire and affection, makes
fuch like things more fit for itfelf, as alfo efficacious to that which it defires.
Every one, therefore, that is willing to work in magic, muft know the
virtue, meafure, order, and degree of his own foul in the power of the
univerfe.

CHAP.

CHAP. XIV.

THE doctrines of mathematics are so necessary to and have such an affinity with magic, that they who profess it without them are quite out of the way, and labour in vain, and shall in no wise obtain their desired effect. For whatsoever things are, and are done in these inferior natural virtues, are all done and governed by *number, weight, measure, harmony, motion,* and *light :* and all things which we see in these inferiors have root and foundation in them ; yet, nevertheless, without natural virtues of mathematical doctrines, only works like to naturals can be produced : as Plato saith---a thing not partaking of truth or divinity, but certain images akin to them (as bodies going, or speaking, which yet want the animal faculty), such as were those which, amongst the ancients, were called Dedalus's images, and αυτοματα, of which Aristotle makes mention, viz. the three-footed images of Vulcan and Dedalus moving themselves ; which, Homer saith, came out of their own accord to the exercise ; and which, we read, moved themselves at the feast of Hiarba, the philosophical exerciser. So there are made glasses (some concave, others of the form of a column) making the representation of things in the air seem like shadows at a distance ; of which sort Apollonius and Vitellius, in their books, " De Prospectiva," and " Speculis," taught the making and the use. And we read that Magnus Pompeius brought a certain glass, amongst the spoils from the East, to Rome, in which were seen armies of armed men. And there are made certain transparent glasses, which (being dipped in some certain juices of herbs, and irradiated with an artificial light) fill the whole air round about with visions. And we know how to make reciprocal glasses, in which the sun shining, all things which were illustrated by the rays thereof are apparently seen many miles off. Hence a magician (expert in natural philosophy and mathematics, and knowing the middle sciences, consisting of both these, viz. arithmetic, music, geometry, optics, astronomy, and such sciences that are of

weights,

weights, meafures, proportions, articles, and joints ; knowing, alfo, mechanical arts refulting from thefe) may, without any wonder, if he excel other
men in the art and wit, do many wonderful things, which men may much
admire.   There are fome relics now extant of the antients, viz. Hercules ahd
Alexander's pillars ; the gate of Cafpia, made of brafs, and fhut with iron
beams, that it could by no art be broken ; and the pyramis of Julius Cæfar,
erected at Rome, near the hill Vaticanus ; and mountains built by art in
the middle of the fea ; and towers, and heaps of ftones, fuch as I have feen
in England, put together by incredible art.   But the vulgar feeing any wonderful fight, impute it to the Devil as. his work ; or think that a miracle
which, indeed, is a work of natural or mathematical philofophy.   But here it is
convenient that you know, that, as by natural virtues we collect natural virtues,
fo by abftracted, mathematical, and celeftial, we receive celeftial virtues : as motion, fenfe, life, fpeech, foothfaying, and divination, even in matter lefs difpofed,
as that which is not made by nature, but only by art.   And fo images that
fpeak, and foretel things to come, are faid to be made : as William of Paris
relates of a brazen-head, made under the rifing of Saturn, which, they fay,
fpake with a man's voice.   But he that will chufe a difpofed matter, and moft
fit to receive, and a moft powerful agent, fhall undoubtedly produce more
powerful effects.   For it is a general opinion of the Pythagoreans, that, as
mathematical are more formal than natural, fo alfo they are more efficacious ;
as they have lefs dependance in their being, fo alfo in their operation.   But
amongft all mathematical things, *numbers*, as they have more of form in
them, fo alfo are more efficacious, as well to effect what is good as what is
bad.   All things, which were firft made by the nature of things in its firft age,
feem to be formed by the proportion of numbers ; for this was the principal
pattern in the mind of the Creator.   Hence is borrowed the number of the
elements---hence the courfes of times---hence the motion of the ftars, and the
revolution of the heavens, and the ftate of all things fubfift by the uniting
together of numbers.   Numbers, therefore, are endowed with great and fublime virtues.   For it is no wonder, feeing there are fo many occult virtues in
natural things, although of manifeft operations, that there fhould be in num-
                                                                          bers

bers much greater and more occult, and alfo more wonderful and efficacious ; for as much as they are more formal, more perfect, and naturally in the celef- tials, not mixed with feparated fubftances ; and, laftly, having the greateft and moft fimple commixion with the ideas in the mind of God, from which they receive their proper and moft efficacious virtues ; wherefore they alfo are of moft force, and conduce moft to the obtaining of fpiritual and divine gifts--- as, in natural things, elementary qualities are powerful in the tranfmuting of any elementary thing.   Again, all things that are, and are made, fubfift by and receive their virtue from numbers :---for time confifts of numbers---and all motion and action, and all things which are fubject to time and motion. Harmony, alfo, and voices have their power by and confift of numbers and their proportions ; and the proportion arifing from numbers do, by lines and points, make characters and figures ; and thefe are proper to magical opera- tions---the middle, which is betwixt both, being appropriated by declining to the extremes, as in the ufe of letters.   And laftly, all fpecies of natural things, and of thofe which are above Nature, are joined together by certain numbers ; which Pythagoras feeing, fays, that number is that by which all things fub- fift, and diftributes each virtue to each number.   And Proclus fays, number hath always a being : yet there is one in voice---another in proportion of them---another in the foul and reafon---and another in divine things.   But Themiftius, Boetius, and Averrois (the Babylonian), together with Plato, do fo extol numbers, that they think no man can be a true philofopher without them.   By them there is a way made for the fearching out and underftanding of all things knowable ;---by them the next accefs to natural prophecying is had--- and the Abbot Joachim proceeded no other way in his prophecies, but by formal numbers.

CHAP. XV.

THAT there lies wonderful efficacy and virtue in numbers, as well to good as to bad, the moſt eminent philoſophers unanimouſly teach ; eſpecially Hierom, Auſtin, Origen, Ambroſe, Gregory of Nazianzen, Athanaſius, Baſilius, Hilarius, Rubanas, Bedè, and many more conform.   Hence Hilarius, in his commentaries upon the Pſalms, teſtifies that the ſeventy elders, according to the efficacy of numbers, brought the Pſalms into order.   The *natural number* is not here conſidered ; but the *formal* conſideration that is in the number ;---and let that which we ſpoke before always be kept in mind, viz. that theſe powers are not in vocal numbers of merchants buying and ſelling ; but in rational, formal, and natural ;---theſe are the diſtinct myſteries of God and Nature. But he who knows how to join together the vocal numbers and natural with divine, and order them into the ſame harmony, ſhall be able to work and know wonderful things by numbers ; in which, unleſs there was a great myſtery, John had not ſaid, in the Revelation---" He that hath underſtanding, let him compute the number of the name of the beaſt, which is the number of a man ;"---and this is the moſt famous manner of computing amongſt the Hebrews and Cabaliſts, as we ſhall ſhew afterwards.   But this you muſt know, that ſimple numbers ſignify divine things, numbers of ten ; celeſtial numbers of an hundred ; terreſtrial numbers of a thouſand---thoſe things that ſhall be in a future age.   Beſides, ſeeing the parts of the mind are according to an arithmetical mediocrity, by reaſon of the identity, or equality of exceſs, coupled together ; but the body, whoſe parts differ in their greatneſs, is, according to a geometrical mediocrity, compounded ; but an animal conſiſts of both, viz. ſoul and body, according to that mediocrity which is ſuitable to harmony. Hence it is that *numbers* work very much upon the *ſoul*, *figures* upon the *body*, and *harmony* upon the *whole animal*.

CHAP. XVI.
OF THE SCALE OF UNITY.

NOW let us treat particularly of numbers themfelves ; and, becaufe number is nothing elfe but a repetition of unity, let us firft confider unity itfelf ; for unity doth moft fimply go through every number, and is the common meafure, fountain, and original of all numbers ; contains every number joined together in itfelf entirely ; the beginner of every multitude, always the fame, and unchangeable ; whence, alfo, being multiplied into itfelf, produceth nothing but itfelf : it is indivifible, void of all parts. Nothing is before one, nothing is after one, and beyond it is nothing ; and all things which are, defire that one, becaufe all things proceed from one ; and that all things may be the fame, it is neceffary that they partake of that one : and as all things proceed of one into many things, fo all things endeavour to return to that one, from which they proceeded ; it is neceffary that they fhould put off multitude. One, therefore, is referred to the moft high God, who, feeing he is one and innumerable, yet creates innumerable things of himfelf, and contains them within himfelf. There is, therefore, one God---one world of the one God--- one fun of the one world---alfo one phœnix in the world---one king amongft bees---one leader amongft flocks of cattle---one ruler amongft herds of beafts--- and cranes follow one, and many other animals honour unity. Amongft the members of the body there is one principal, by which all the reft are guided ; whether it be the head, or (as fome will) the heart. There is one element, overcoming and penetrating all things, viz. fire. There is one thing created of God, the fubject of *all wondering* which is in earth or in heaven---it is actually animal, vegetable, and mineral ; every where found, known by few, called by none by its proper name, but covered with figures and riddles, without which neither Alchymy, nor Natural Magic can attain to their complete end or perfection. From one man, Adam, all men proceeded---from that one, all became mortal---from that one, *Jefus Chrift*, they are regenerated ; and, as faith St. Paul, one Lord, one faith, one baptifm, one God and Father of all, one

Mediator

Mediator betwixt God and man, one moſt high Creator, who is over all, by all, and in us all. For there is one Father, God, from whence all, and we in him; one Lord Jeſus Chriſt, by whom all, and we by him; one God Holy Ghoſt, into whom all, and we into him.

THE SCALE OF UNITY.

In the Exemplary World,	Jod.	One Divine Eſſence, the fountain of all virtues and power, whoſe name is expreſſed with one moſt ſimple letter.
In the Intellectual World,	The Soul of the World.	One Supreme Intelligence, the firſt creature, the fountain of life.
In the Celeſtial World,	The Sun.	One King of Stars, fountain of life.
In the Elemental World,	The Philoſophers' Stone.	One ſubject, and inſtrument of all virtues, natural and ſupernatural.
In the Leſſer World,	The Heart.	One firſt living and laſt dying.
In the Infernal World,	Lucifer.	One Prince of Rebellion, of Angels, and Darkneſs.

CHAP XVII.
OF THE NUMBER TWO, AND SCALE.

THE firſt number is two, becauſe it is the firſt multitude; it can be meaſured by no number beſides unity alone, the common meaſure of all numbers; it is not compounded of numbers, but of one unity only; neither is it called a number uncompounded, but more properly not compounded. The number three, is called the firſt number uncompounded. But the number two is the firſt branch of unity, and the firſt procreation; and it is called the number of ſcience, and memory, and of light, and the number of man, who is called

another

another, and the leffer world : it is alfo called the number of charity, and of mutual love ; of marriage, and fociety : as it is faid by the Lord---" Two fhall be one flefh."---And Solomon faith, " It is better that two be together than one, for they have a benèfit by their mutual fociety : if one fhall fall, he fhall be fupported by the other. Woe to him that is alone ; becaufe, when he falls, he hath not another to help him. And if two fleep together, they fhall warm one another : how fhall one be hot alone ?---And if any prevail againft him, two refift him." And it is called the number of wedlock, and fex ; for there are two fexes---mafculine and feminine. And two doves bring forth two eggs ; out of the firft of which is hatched the male, out of the fecond the female. It is alfo called the middle, that is capable, that is good and bad, partaking ; and the beginning of divifion, of multitude, and diftinction ; and fignifies mat- ter. This is alfo, fometimes, the number of difcord, of confufion, of mis- fortune, and uncleannefs ; whence St. Hierom, againft Jovianus, faith---" that therefore it was not fpoken in the fecond day of the creation of the world."--- " And God faid, that it was good ;"---becaufe the number of two is evil. Hence alfo it was, that God commanded that all unclean animals fhould go into the ark by couples ; becaufe, as I faid, the number of two is a number of uncleannefs. Pythagorus, as Eufebius reports, faid, that unity was God, and a good intellect ; but that duality was a devil, and an evil intellect, in which is a material multitude : wherefore the Pythagorians fay, that two is not a number, but a certain confufion of unities. And Plutarch writes, that the Pythagorians called unity, Apollo ; and two, ftrife and boldnefs ; and three, juftice, which is the higheft perfection, and is not without many myfteries. Hence there were two tables of the law in Sinai---two chefubims looking to the propitiatory in Mofes---two olives dropping oil, in Zachariah---two natures in Chrift, divine and human : hence Mofes faw two appearances of God, viz. his face, and back parts ;---alfo two Teftaments---two commands of love---two firft dignities---two firft people---two kinds of fpirits, good and bad---two in- tellectual creatures, an angel and foul---two great lights---two folftitia---two equinoctials---two poles---two elements, producing a living foul, viz. earth and water.

Book I.   O   THE

THE SCALE OF THE NUMBER TWO.

In the Exemplary World,	יְהֹ Jah אֵל El		The Names of God, expressed with two Letters.
In the Intellectual World,	An Angel,	The Soul;	Two Intelligible Substances.
In the Celestial World,	The Sun,	The Moon;	Two great Lights.
In the Elementary World,	The Earth,	The Water;	Two Elements producing a living Soul.
In the Lesser World,	The Heart,	The Brain;	Two principal Seats of the Soul.
In the Infernal World,	Beemoth, weeping,	Leviathan, gnashing of Teeth;	Two Chiefs of the Devils. Two things Christ threatens to the damned.

CHAP. XVIII.

OF THE NUMBER THREE, AND SCALE.

THE number Three, is an uncompounded number, a holy number, a number of perfection, a most powerful number :---for there are three persons in God ; there are three theological virtues in religion.   Hence it is that this number conduceth to the ceremonies of God and religion, that by the solemnity of which, prayers and sacrifices are thrice repeated ; for corporeal and spiritual things consist of three things, viz. beginning, middle, and end. By three, as Trismegistus saith, the world is perfected---harmony, necessity, and order, i. e. concurrence of causes (which many call fate), and the execution of them to the fruit, or increase, or a due distribution of the increase. The whole measure of time is concluded in three, viz. past, present, and to come ;---all magnitude is contained in three---line, superfices, and body ;---
                                                                                    every

every body confifts of three intervals,---length, breadth, and thickneſs. Harmony contains three confents in time---diapafon, hemiolion, diateſſeron. There are alfo three kinds of fouls---vegetatiye, fenfitive, and intelleⅽ̆tual. And as fuch, faith the Prophet, God orders the world by number, weight, and meafure ; and the number three is deputed to the ideal forms thereof, as the number two is the procreating matter, and unity to God the maker of it.---Magicians do conftitute three Princes of the world---Oromafis, Mithris, Araminis ; *i. e.* God, the mind, and the fpirit. By the three-fquare or folid, the three numbers of nine, of things produced, are diftributed, viz.' of the fuperceleftial into nine orders of intelligences ; of celeftial, into nine orbs ; of inferiors, into nine kinds of generable and corruptible things. Laftly, into this eternal orb, viz. twenty-feven, all mufical proportions are included, as Plato and Proclus do at large difcourfe ; and the number three hath, in a harmony of five, the grace of the firft voice. Alfo, in intelligences, there are three hierarchies of angelical fpirits. There are three powers of intelleⅽ̆tual creatures---memory, mind, and will. There are three orders of the bleffed, viz. martyrs, confeffors, and innocents. There are three quaternions of celeftial figns, viz. of fixed, moveable, and common ; as alfo of houfes, viz. centres, fucceeding, and falling. There are, alfo, three faces and heads in every fign, and three Lords of each triplicity. There are three fortunes amongft the planets. In the infernal crew, three judges, three furies, three-headed Cerberus : we read, alfo, of a thrice-double Hecate. Three months of the Virgin Diana. Three perfons in the fuper-fubftantial Divinity. Three times---of nature, law, and grace. Three theological virtues---faith, hope, and charity. Jonah was three days in the whale's belly ; and fo many was Chrift in the grave.

THE

THE SCALE OF THE NUMBER THREE.

In the Original World,	The Father,	Adai, The Son,	The Holy Ghost;	The Name of God with three Letters.
In the Intellectual World,	Supreme Innocents,	Middle Martyrs,	Lowest of all Confessors ;	Three hierarchies of Angels. Three degrees of the Blessed.
In the Celestial World,	Moveable, Corners, Of the Day,	Fixed, Succeeding, Nocturnal,	Common; Falling; Partaking;	Three quaternions of Signs. Three quaternions of houses. Three Lords of triplicities.
In the Elementary World,	Simple,	Compounded,	Thrice compounded;	Three degree of elements.
In the Lesser World,	The head, in which the intellect grows, answering to the intellectual world,	The breast, where is the heart, the seat of life, answering to the celestial world,	The belly, where the faculty of generation is, and the genital members, answering the elemental world;	Three parts, answering to the threefold world.
In the Infernal World,	Alecto, Minos, Wicked,	Megera, Acacus, Apostates,	Ctesiphone ; Rhadamantus; Infidels;	Three infernal Furies. Three infernal Judges. Three degrees of the damned.

CHAP. XIX.

OF THE NUMBER FOUR, AND SCALE.

THE Pythagorians call the number Four, Tectractis, and prefer it before all the virtues of numbers, because it is the foundation and root of all other numbers ; whence, also, all foundations, as well in artificial things, as natural and divine, are four square, as we shall shew afterwards ; and it signifies solidity, which also is demonstrated by a four-square figure ; for the number four, is the first

four-

four-square plane, which confifts of two proportions, whereof the firft is of one to two, the latter of two to four ; and it proceeds by a double proceffion and proportion, viz. of one to one, and of two to two---beginning at a unity, and ending at a quaternity : which proportions differ in this, that, according to Arithmetic, they are unequal to one another ; but, according to Geometry, are equal. Therefore a four-fquare is afcribed to God the Father ; and alfo contains the myftery of the whole Trinity : for by its fingle proportion, viz. by the firft of one to one, the unity of the paternal fubftance is fignified, from which proceeds one Son, equal to Him ;---by the next proceffion, alfo fimple, viz. of two to two, is fignified (by the fecond proceffion) the Holy Ghoft ; from both---that the Son be equal to the Father, by the firft proceffion ; and the Holy Ghoft be equal to both, by the fecond proceffion. Hence that fuperexcellent and great name of the Divine Trinity in God is written with four letters, viz. *Jod*, *He*, and *Van*. He, where it is the afpiration He, fignifies the proceeding of the Spirit from both ; for He, being duplicated, terminates both fyllables, and the whole name, but is pronounced Jova, as fome will, whence that Jove of the heathen, which the antients did picture with four ears ; whence the number four, is the fountain and head of the whole Divinity. And the Pythagorians call it the perpetual fountain of Nature : for there are four degrees in the fcale of Nature, viz. *to be*, *to live*, *to be fenfible*, *to underftand*. There are four motions in Nature, viz. afcendant, defcendant, going forward, circular. There are four corners in Heaven, viz. rifing, falling, the middle of the Heaven, the bottom of it. There are four elements under Heaven, viz. fire, air, water, and earth ; according to thefe there are four triplicities in Heaven. There are four firft qualities under Heaven, viz. cold, heat, drynefs, and moifture ; from thefe are the four humours---blood, phlegm, choler, melancholy. Alfo, the year is divided into four parts, which are the fpring, fummer, autumn, and winter :---alfo the wind is divided into eaftern, weftern, northern, and fouthern. There are, alfo, four rivers in Paradife ; and fo many infernal. Alfo, the number four makes

up

up all knowledge : firſt, it fills up every ſimple progreſs of numbers with four
terms, viz. with one, two, three, and four, conſtituting the number ten. It
fills up every difference of numbers : the firſt even, and containing the firſt odd
in it. It hath in muſic, diateſſeron---the grace of the fourth voice ; alſo it
contains the inſtrument of four ſtrings ; and a Pythagorian diagram, whereby
are found out firſt of all muſical tunes, and all harmony of muſic : for double,
treble, four times doublè, one and a half, one and a third part, a concord of
all, a double concord of all, of five, of four, and all conſonancy is limited
within the bounds of the number four. It doth alſo contain the whole of
Mathematics in four terms, viz. *point, line, ſuperſices,* and *profundity.* It
comprehends all Nature in four terms, viz. ſubſtance, quality, quantity, and
motion ; alſo all natural philoſophy, in which are the ſeminary virtues of
Nature, the natural ſpringing, the growing form, and the *compoſitum.* Alſo
metaphyſics is comprehended in four bounds, viz. *being, eſſence, virtue,* and
action. Moral philoſophy is comprehended with four virtues, viz. *prudence,
juſtice, fortitude,* and *temperance.* It hath alſo the power of juſtice : hence a
four-fold law---of *providence,* from God ; *fatal,* from the ſoul of the world ; of
Nature, from Heaven ; of *prudence,* from man. There are alſo four judiciary
powers in all things being, viz. the intellect, diſcipline, opinion, and ſenſe.
Alſo, there are four rivers of Paradiſe. Four Goſpels, received from four
Evangeliſts, throughout the whole Church. The Hebrews received the chiefeſt
name of God written with four letters. Alſo, the Egyptians, Arabians, Perſians, Magicians, Mahometans, Grecians, Tuſcans, and Latins, write the
name of God with four letters, viz. thus---Thet, Alla, Sire, Orſi, Abdi, θεὸς,
Eſar, Deus. Hence the Lacedemonians were wont to paint Jupiter with four
wings. Hence, alſo, in Orpheus's Divinity, it is ſaid that Neptune's cha-
riots are drawn with four horſes. There are alſo four kinds of divine furies,
proceeding from ſeveral deities, viz. from the Muſes, Dionyſius, Apollo, and
Venus. Alſo, the Prophet Ezekiel ſaw four beaſts by the river Chobar, and
four cherubims in four wheels. Alſo, in Daniel, four great beaſts did aſcend
from

from the sea ; and four winds did fight. And in the Revelations, four beasts
were full of eyes, before and behind, standing round about the throne of God ;
and four angels, to whom was given power to hurt the earth and the sea, did
stand upon the four corners of the earth, holding the four winds, that they
should not blow upon the earth, nor upon the sea, nor upon any tree.

THE

THE SCALE OF

The Name of God with four letters,	יהוה				In the original world, whence the law of Providence.
Four triplicities, or intelligible hierarchies,	Seraphim, Cherubim, Thrones,	Dominations, Powers, Virtues,	Principalities, Archangels, Angels,	Innocents, Martyrs, Confessors.	In the intellectual world, whence the fatal law.
Four angels ruling over the four corners of the world,	מיכאל Michael,	רפאל Raphael,	גבריאל Gabriel,	אוריאל Uriel.	
Four rulers of the elements,	שרף Seraph,	כרוב Cherub,	תרשיש Tharsis,	אריאל Ariel.	
Four consecrated animals,	The Lion,	The Eagle,	Man,	A Calf.	
Four triplicities of the tribes of Israel,	Dan, Asser, Naphthalin,	Jehuda, Isachar, Zebulun,	Manasse, Benjamin, Ephraim,	Reuben, Simeon, Gad.	
Four triplicities of the Apostles,	Matthias, Peter, Jacob the elder,	Simon, Bartholomew, Matthew,	John, Philip, James the younger	Thaddeus, Andrew, Thomas.	
Four Evangelists,	Mark,	John,	Matthew,	Luke.	
Four triplicities of signs,	Aries, Leo, Sagittarius,	Gemini, Libra, Aquarius,	Cancer, Scorpion, Pisces,	Taurus, Virgo, Capricornus.	In the celestial world, where is the law of Nature.
The stars and planets related to the elements,	Mars, and the Sun,	Jupiter, and Venus,	Saturn, and Mercury,	The fixed Stars, and the Moon.	
Four qualities of the celestial elements,	Light,	Diaphanousness,	Agility,	Solidity.	
Four elements,	אש Fire,	ריח Air,	מים Water,	עפר Earth.	In the elementary, where the law of generation and corruption is.
Four qualities,	Heat,	Moisture,	Cold,	Dryness.	
Four seasons,	Summer,	Spring,	Winter,	Autumn.	
Four corners of the world,	East,	West,	North,	South.	
Four perfect kinds of mixed bodies,	Animals,	Plants,	Metals.	Stones.	
Four kinds of animals,	Walking,	Flying,	Swimming,	Creeping.	

THE NUMBER FOUR.

What anſwers the elements in plants,	Seeds,	Flowers,	Leaves,	Roots.	
What in metals,	Gold and iron,	Copper and tin,	Quickſilver,	Lead and ſilver.	
What in ſtones,	Bright and burning,	Light and tranſparent,	Clear and congealed,	Heavy and dark.	
Four elements of man,	The Mind,	Spirit,	Soul,	Body.	In the leſſer world, viz. man, from whom is the law of prudence.
Four powers of the ſoul,	The Intellect,	Reaſon,	Phantaſy,	Senſe.	
Four judiciary powers,	Faith,	Science,	Opinion,	Experience.	
Four moral virtues,	Juſtice,	Temperance,	Prudence,	Fortitude.	
The ſenſes anſwering to the elements,	Sight,	Hearing,	Taſte and ſmell,	Touch.	
Four elements of man's body,	Spirit,	Fleſh,	Humours,	Bones.	
A fourfold ſpirit,	Animal,	Vital,	Generative,	Natural.	
Four humours,	Choler,	Blood,	Phlegm,	Melancholy.	
Four manners of complexion,	Violence,	Nimbleneſs,	Dulneſs,	Slowneſs.	
Four princes of devils, offenſive in the elements,	סמאל Samael,	עזאזל Azazel,	עזאל Azael,	מאזאל Mahazael.	In the infernal world, where is the law of wrath and puniſhment.
Four infernal rivers,	Phlegethon,	Cocytus,	Styx,	Acheron.	
Four princes of ſpirits, upon the four angles of the world,	Oriens,	Paymon,	Egyn,	Amaymon.	

CHAP. XX.
OF THE NUMBER FIVE, AND ITS SCALE.

THE number Five is of no fmall force; for it confifts of the firft even, and the firft odd; as of a female and male: for an odd number is the male, and the even the female; whence arithmeticians call that the father, and this the mother. Therefore the number five is of no fmall perfection or virtue, which proceeds from the mixtion of thefe numbers; it is, alfo, the juft middle of the univerfal number, viz. ten: for if you divide the number ten, there will be nine and one, or eight and two, and feven and three, or fix and four, and every collection makes the number ten, and the exact middle is always the number five, and its equa-diftant; and therefore it is called, by the Pythagorians, the number of wedlock, as alfo of juftice, becaufe it divides the number ten in an even fcale. There are five fenfes in man—fight, hearing, fmelling, tafting, and feeling; five powers in the foul—vegetative, fenfitive, concupifcible, irafcible, and rational; five fingers on the hand; five wandering planets in the heavens, according to which there are fivefold terms in every fign. In elements there are five kinds of mixed bodies, viz. ftones, metals, plants, plant-animals, animals; and fo many kinds of animals—as men, four-footed beafts, creeping, fwimming, and flying. And there are five kinds by which all things are made of God, viz. effence, the fame, another, fenfe, and motion. The fwallow brings forth but five young, which fhe feeds with equity, beginning with the eldeft, and fo the reft according to their age. For in this number the father Noah found favour with God, and was preferved in the flood of waters. In the virtue of this number, Abraham, being an hundred years old, begat a fon of Sarah (Sarah being ninety years old, and a barren woman, and paft child-bearing), and grew up to be a great people. Hence, in time of grace, the name of Divine Omnipotency is called upon in five letters; in time of nature, the name of God was called upon with three letters שדי Sadai; in time of the law, the ineffable name of God was expreffed with four letters יהוה, inftead of which the Hebrews exprefs אדני Adonai; in time of grace, the ineffable name

name of God was written with five letters יהשוה Jhesu, which is called upon
with no less mystery than that of three letters שי.

THE SCALE OF THE NUMBER FIVE.

The Names of God with five letters. . The Name of Christ with five letters,		אליה אלדים יהשוה	Eloim, Elohi, Jhesu,			In the exemplary world.
Five intelligible substances,	Spirits of the first hierarchy, called Gods, or the sons of God,	Spirits of the second hierarchy, called Intelligences,	Spirits of the third hierarchy, called Angels which are sent,	Souls of celestial bodies,	Heroes and blessed souls.	In the intellectual world,
Five wandering stars, lords of the terms,	Saturn,	Jupiter,	Mars,	Venus,	Mercury.	In the celestial world.
Five kinds of corruptible things,	Water,	Air,	Fire,	Earth,	A mixed body.	In the elementary world.
Five kinds of mixed bodies,	Animal,	Plant,	Metal,	Stone,	Plant-animal.	
Five senses,	Taste,	Hearing,	Seeing,	Touching,	Smelling.	In the lesser world.
Five corporeal torments,	Deadly bitterness,	Horrible howling,	Terrible darkness,	Unquenchable heat,	A piercing stink.	In the infernal world.

CHAP. XXI.
OF THE NUMBER SIX, AND THE SCALE.

SIX is a number of perfection, because it is the most perfect in nature, in
the whole course of numbers, from one to ten ; and it alone is so perfect that
in the collection of its parts, it results the same, neither wanting nor abound-

P 2   ing

ing; for if the parts thereof, viz. the middle, third, and sixth part, which are three, two, one, be gathered together, they perfectly fill up the whole body of six, which perfection all the other numbers want. Hence, by the Pythagorians, it is said to be altogether to be applied to generation and marriage, and is called the scale of the world; for the world is made of the number six---neither doth it abound, nor is defective: hence that is, because the world was finished by God the sixth day; for the sixth day God saw all things which he had made, and they were * *very good;* therefore the heaven, and the earth, and all the host thereof, were finished. It is also called the number of man, because the sixth day † man was created. And it is also the number of our redemption; for on the sixth day Christ suffered for our redemption: whence there is a great affinity between the number six and the cross, labour, and servitude. Hence it is commanded in the law, that in six days the manna is to be gathered, and work to be done. Six years the ground was to be sown; and that the Hebrew servant was to serve his master six years. Six days the glory of the Lord appeared upon Mount Sinai, covering it with a cloud. The Cherubims had six wings. Six circles in the firmament: Artic, Antartic, two Tropics, Equinoctial, and Ecliptical. Six wandering planets: Saturn, Jupiter, Mars, Venus, Mercury, the Moon, running through the latitude of the Zodiac on both sides the Ecliptic. There are six substantial qualities in the elements, viz. sharpness, thinness, motion; and the contrary to these---dulness, thickness, and rest. There are six differences of position: upwards, downwards, before, behind, on the right side, and on the left side. There are six natural offices, without which nothing can be, viz. magnitude, colour, figure, interval, standing, motion. Also, a solid figure of any four-square thing hath six superfices. There are six tones of all harmony, viz. five tones, and two half tones which make one tone, which is the sixth.

---

* The sixth day, the Eternal Wisdom pronounced all things created by his divine hand to be " *very good.*"

† Hence arose the mystery of the number of the beast, six hundred three score and six, being the number of a man---DCLXVI.

SCALE

THE SCALE OF THE NUMBER SIX.

In the Exemplary World,	אל גבוד־אלותים						Names of six letters.
In the Intelligible World,	Seraphim,	Cherubim,	Thrones,	Domina-tions,	Powers,	Virtues;	Six orders of Angels, which are not fent to inferiors.
In the Celestial World.	Saturn,	Jupiter,	Mars,	Venus,	Mercury,	The Moon;	Six planets wan-dering through the latitude of the Zodiac from the Ecliptic.
In the Elemental World,	Reft,	Thinnefs,	Sharpnefs,	Dulnefs,	Thicknefs,	Motion;	Six fubftantial qualities of the elements.
In the Leffer World.	The Intellect,	Memory,	Senfe,	Motion,	Life,	Effence;	Six degrees of the mind.
In the Infernal World,	Acteus,	Megalefius,	Ormenus,	Lycus,	Nicon,	Mimon;	Six Devils, the authors of all calamities.

CHAP XXII.
OF THE NUMBER SEVEN, AND THE SCALE.

THE number Seven is of various and manifold power; for it confifts of one and fix, or of two and five, or of three and four; and it hath a unity, as it were the coupling together of two threes: whence if we confider the feveral parts thereof, and the joining together of them, without doubt we fhall confefs that it is, as well by the joining together of the parts thereof as by its fulnefs apart, moft full of all majefty. And the Pythagorians call it the *vehiculum* of man's life, which it doth not receive from its parts fo, as it perfects by its

proper

proper right of its whole---for it contains body and soul ; for the body consists of four elements, and is endowed with four qualities : also, the number three respects the soul, by reason of its threefold power, viz. rational, irascible, and concupiscible. The number seven, therefore, because it consists of three and four, joins the soul to the body ; and the virtue of this number relates to the generation of men, and it causes man to be received, formed, brought forth, nourished, live, and indeed altogether to subsist : for when the genital feed is received in the womb of the woman, if it remains there seven hours after the effusion of it, it is certain that it will abide there for good ; then the first seven days it is coagulated, and is fit to receive the shape of a man ; then it produces mature infants, which are called infants of the seventh month, *i. e.* because they are born the seventh month ; after the birth, the seventh hour tries whether it will live or no---for that which will bear the breath of the air after that hour, is conceived will live ; after seven days, it casts off the relics of the navel ; after twice seven days, its sight begins to move after the light ; in the third seventh, it turns its eyes and whole face freely ; after seven months, it breeds teeth ; after the second seventh month, it sits without fear of falling ; after the third seventh month, it begins to speak ; after the fourth seventh month, it stands strongly and walks ; after the fifth seventh month, it begins to refrain sucking its nurse ; after seven years, its first teeth fall, and new are bred, fitter for harder meat, and its speech is perfected ; after the second seventh year, boys wax ripe, and then it is a beginning of generation ; at the third seventh year, they grow to men in stature, and begin to be hairy, and become able and strong for generation ; at the fourth seventh year, they cease to grow taller ; in the fifth seventh year, they attain to the perfection of their strength ; the sixth seventh year, they keep their strength ; the seventh seventh year, they attain to their utmost discretion and wisdom, and the perfect age of men ; but when they come to the tenth seventh year, where the number seven is taken for a complete number, then they come to the common term of life--- the Prophet saying, our age is seventy years. The utmost height of a man's body is seven feet. There are, also, seven degrees in the body, which complete the dimension of its altitude from the bottom to the top, viz. marrow, bone, nerve, vein, artery, flesh, and skin. There are seven, which, by the

Greeks,

Greeks, are called black members: the tongue, heart, lungs, liver, fpleen, and the two kidnies. There are, alfo, feven principal parts of the body : the head, breaft, hands, feet, and the privy members. It is manifeft, concerning breath and meat, that, without drawing of the breath, the life doth not remain above feven hours ; and they that are ftarved with famine, live not above feven days.* The veins, alfo, and arteries, as phyficians fay, are moved by the feventh number. Alfo, judgments in difeafes are made with greater manifeftation upon the feventh day, which phyficians call critical, *i. e.* judicial. Alfo, of feven portions God creates the foul ;---the foul, alfo, receives the body by feven degrees. All difference of voices proceeds to the feventh degree, after which there is the fame revolution. Again, there are feven modulations of the voices : ditonus, femiditonus, diatefferon, diapente with a tone, diapente with a half tone, and diapafon. There are alfo, in celeftials, a moft potent power of the number feven ; for feeing there are four corners of the Heaven diametrically looking one towards the other, which indeed is accounted a moft full and powerful afpect, and confifts of the number feven ; for it is made with the feventh fign, and makes a crofs, the moft powerful figure of all, of which we fhall fpeak in its due place ;---but this you muft not be ignorant of, that the number feven hath a great communion with the crofs. By the fame radiation and number the folftice is diftant from winter, and the winter equinoctium from the fummer, all which are done by feven figns. There are alfo feven circles in the Heavens, according to the longitudes of the axle-tree. There are feven ftars about the Artic Pole, greater and leffer, called Charles Wain ; alfo feven ftars called the Pleiades ; and feven planets, according to thofe feven days conftituting a week. The Moon is the feventh of the planets, and next to us, obferving this number more than thereft, this number difpenfing the motion and light thereof ; for in twenty-eight days it runs round the compafs of the whole Zodiac ; which number of days, the number feven with its feven terms, viz. from one to feven, doth make and fill up as much as the

* There have been fome exceptions to this affirmation, one of which fell under my notice of late years : Doctor Edward Spry, of Plymouth Dock, Philofopher, Cabalift, and Phyfician, lived upwards of two years upon a goofeberry a day in fummer, and an oat cake and three glaffes of white wine the reft of the feafon, per day : this gentleman was particularly abftemious in his diet.

feveral

feveral numbers, by adding to the antecedents, and makes four times feven days, in which the Moon runs through and about all the longitude and latitude of the Zodiac, by meafuring and meafuring again : with the like feven days it difpenfes its light, by changing it ; for the firft feven days, unto the middle as it were of the divided world, it increafes ; the fecond feven days it fills its whole orb with light ; the third, by decreafing, is again contracted into a divided orb ; but, after the fourth feven days, it is renewed with the laft diminution of. its light ; and by the fame feven days, it difpofes the increafe and decreafe of the fea : for in the firft feven of the increafe of the moon, it is by little and little leffened ; in the fecond, by degrees increafed ; but the third is like the firft, and the fourth does the fame as the fecond. It is alfo applied to Saturn, which afcending from the lower, is the feventh planet, which betokens reft ; to which the feventh day is afcribed, which fignifies the feven thoufandth, wherein, as St. John fays, the dragon (which is the devil) and fatan being bound, men fhall be quiet, and lead a peaceable life. And the leprous perfon that was to be cleanfed, was fprinkled feven times with the blood of a fparrow ; and Elifha the Prophet, as it is written in the fecond book of Kings, faith unto the leprous perfon---" Go, and wafh thyfelf feven times in Jordan, and thy flefh fhall be made whole, and thou fhalt be cleanfed."--- Alfo, it is a number of repentance and remiffion. And Chrift, with feven petitions, finifhed his fpeech of our fatisfaction. It is called the number of liberty, becaufe the feventh year the Hebrew fervant did challenge liberty for himfelf. It is alfo moft fuitable to divine praifes ; whence the Prophet faith--- " Seven times a day do I praife thee, becaufe of thy righteous judgments."--- It is moreover called the number of revenge, as fays the Scripture---" And Cain fhall be revenged fevenfold."---And the Pfalmift fays---" Render unto our neighbours fevenfold into their bofom their reproach."---Hence there are feven wickedneffes, as faith Solomon ; and feven wicked fpirits taken, are read of in the Gofpel. It fignifies, alfo, the time of the prefent circle, becaufe it is finifhed in the fpace of feven days. Alfo it is confecrated to the Holy Ghoft, which the Prophet Ifaiah defcribes to be fevenfold, according to his gift, viz. the fpirit of wifdom and underftanding, the fpirit of counfel and ftrength, the fpirit of knowledge and holinefs, the fpirit of fear of the Lord, which

which we read in Zachariah to be the *seven eyes of God*. There are alfo feven
angels, fpirits ftanding in the prefence of God, as is read in Tobias, and in the
Revelation : feven lamps did burn before the throne of God, and feven golden
candlefticks, and in the middle thereof was one like unto the Son of Man, and
he had in his right hand feven ftars. Alfo, there were feven fpirits before the
throne of God, and feven angels ftood before the throne, and there were given
to them feven trumpets. And he faw a Lamb, having feven horns and feven
eyes ; and he faw the book fealed with feven feals ; and when the feventh feal
was opened, there was made filence in Heaven.

Now, by all that has been faid, it is apparent that the number feven, amongft the
other numbers, may be defervedly faid to be moft full of efficacy. Moreover, the
number feven hath great conformity with the number twelve ; for as three and four
make feven, fo thrice four makes twelve, which are the numbers of the celeftial
planets and figns refulting from the fame root ; and by the number three partaking of the Divinity, and by the number four of the nature of inferior things.
There is in facred writ a very great obfervance of this number before all others,
and many, and very great are the myfteries thereof : many we have decreed
to reckon up here, repeating them out of holy writ, by which it will eafily
appear that the number feven doth fignify a certain fulnefs of facred myfteries ;
for we read, in Genefis, that the feventh was the day of reft of the Lord ;
that Enoch, a pious holy man, was the feventh from Adam ; and that there
was another feventh man from Adam, a wicked man, by name Lamech, that
had two wives; and that the fin of Cain fhould be abolifhed the feventh generation, as it is written---Cain fhall be punifhed fevenfold ; and that he who fhall
flay Cain, fhall be revenged fevenfold ; to which the mafter of the hiftory col-
lects that there were feven fins of Cain. Alfo, of all clean beafts feven, and
feven were brought into the ark, as alfo of fowls ; and after feven days the
Lord rained upon the earth ; and upon the feventh day the fountains of the
deep were broken up, and the waters covered the earth. Alfo, Abraham gave
to Abimelech feven ewe lambs ; and Jacob ferved feven years for Leah, and

Book I.   Q   feven

seven more for Rachel ; and seven days the people of Israel bewailed the death
of Jacob. Moreover we read, in the same place, of seven kine ; and seven
years of corn ; seven years of plenty, and seven years of scarcity. And in
Exodus, the Sabbath of Sabbaths, the holy rest to the Lord, is commanded
to be on the seventh day ; also, on the seventh day Moses ceased to pray. On
the seventh day there shall be a solemnity of the Lord ; the seventh year
the servant shall go out free ; seven days let the calf and the lamb be with
its dam ; the seventh year, let the ground that hath been sown six years
be at rest ; the seventh day shall be a holy Sabbath, and a rest ; the
seventh day, because it is the Sabbath, shall be called holy. In Leviticus, the
seventh day also shall be more observed, and be more holy ; and the first day
of the seventh month shall be a Sabbath of memorial ; seven days shall the
sacrifices be offered to the Lord ; seven days shall the holy days of the Lord
be celebrated ; seven days in a year everlastingly in the generations. In the
seventh month you shall celebrate feasts, and shall dwell in tabernacles seven
days ; seven times he shall sprinkle himself before the Lord that hath dipped
his finger in blood ; he that is cleansed from the leprosy, shall dip seven times
in the blood of a sparrow ; seven days shall she be washed with running water
that is menstruous ; seven times he shall dip his finger in the blood of a bul-
lock ; seven times I will smite you for your sins. In Deuteronomy, seven
people possessed the Land of Promise. There is also read, a seventh year of
remission ; and seven candles set up on the south side of the candlesticks.
And in Numbers it is read, that the sons of Israel offered up seven ewe lambs
without spot ; and that seven days they did eat unleavened bread ; and that sin
was expiated with seven lambs and a goat ; and that the seventh day was celebrated, and holy ; and the first day of the seventh month was observed, and
kept holy ; and the seventh month of the Feast of Tabernacles ; and seven
calves were offered on the seventh day ; and Baalam erected seven altars ; seven
days Mary, the sister of Aaron, went forth leprous out of the camp ; seven
days he that touched a dead carcass was unclean. And in Joshua, seven
priests carried the ark of the covenant before the host : and seven days they
                                                                              went

went round the cities ; and feven trumpets were carried by the feven priefts ; and on the feventh day, the feven priefts founded the trumpets. And in the book of Judges, Abeffa reigned in Ifrael feven years ; Sampfon kept his nuptials feven days, and the feventh day he put forth a riddle to his wife ; he was bound with feven green withes ; feven locks of his head were fhaved off ; feven years were the children of Ifrael oppreffed by the King of Maden. And in the books of the Kings, Elias prayed feven times, and at the feventh time beheld a little cloud ; feven days the children of Ifrael pitched over againft the Syrians, and in the feventh day of the battle were joined ; feven years' famine was threatened to David, for the people's murmuring ; and feven times the child fneezed that was raifed by Elifha ; and feven men were crucified together, in the days of the firft harveft ; Naaman was made clean with feven wafhings, by Elifha ; the feventh month Goliah was flain. And in Hefter we read, that the King of Perfia had feven eunuchs. And in Tobias, feven men were coupled with Sarah, the daughter of Raguel. And, in Daniel, Nebuchadnezzar's furnace was heated feven times hotter than it was ufed to be ; and feven lions were in the den, and the feventh day came Nebuchadnezzar. In the book of Job, there is mention of feven fons of Job ; and feven days and nights Job's friends fat with him on the earth ; and, in the fame place—" In feven troubles no evil fhall come near thee." In Ezra, we read of Artaxerxes's feven counfellors ; and in the fame place, the trumpet founded ; the feventh month of the Feaft of Tabernacles was, in Ezra's time, whilft the children of Ifrael were in the cities ; and on the firft day of the feventh month, Efdras read the law to the people. And, in the Pfalms, David praifed the Lord feven times in the day ; filver is tried feven times ; and he renders to his neighbours fevenfold into their bofoms. And Solomon faith, that Wifdom hath hewn herfelf feven pillars ; feven men that can render a reafon ; feven abominations which the Lord abhors ; feven abominations in the heart of an enemy ; feven overfeers ; feven eyes beholding. Ifaiah numbers up feven gifts of the Holy Ghoft ; and feven women fhall take hold on a man. And in Jeremiah, if fhe that hath

borne

borne feven, languifhes, fhe has given up the ghoft. In Ezekiel, the Prophet continued fad for feven days. In Zachariah, feven lamps, and feven pipes to thofe feven lamps; and feven eyes running to and fro through the whole earth; and feven eyes on one ftone; and the faft of the feventh day is turned into joy. And in Micah, feven fhepherds are raifed againft the Affyrians. Alfo, in the Gofpel, we read of feven bleffings; and feven virtues, to which feven vices are oppofed; feven petitions of the Lord's Prayer; feven words of Chrift upon the crofs; feven words of the bleffed Virgin Mary; feven loaves diftributed by the Lord; feven bafkets of fragments; feven brothers having one wife; feven difciples of the Lord who were fifhers; feven water pots in Cana of Galilee; feven woes which the Lord threatens to hypocrites; feven devils caft out of the unclean woman, and feven wickeder devils taken in after that which was caft out; alfo, feven years Chrift was fled into Egypt; and the feventh hour the fever left the governor's fon. And in the canonical epiftles, James defcribes feven degrees of wifdom; and Peter, feven degrees of virtues. And in the Acts, we reckon feven deacons, and feven difciples chofen by the Apoftles. Alfo, in the Revelation, there are many myfteries relating to this number; for there we read of feven candlefticks, feven ftars, feven crowns, feven churches, feven fpirits before the throne, feven rivers of Egypt, feven feals, feven marks, feven horns, feven eyes, feven fpirits of God, feven angels with feven trumpets, feven horns of the dragon, feven heads of the dragon which had feven diadems, alfo feven plagues, and feven vials which were given to every one of the feven angels, feven heads of the fcarlet beaft, feven mountains and feven kings fitting upon them, and feven thunders uttered their voices.

Moreover, this number hath much power; as in natural fo in facred ceromonial, and alfo in other things; therefore the feven days are related hither; alfo the feven planets, the feven ftars called Pleiades, the feven ages of the world, the feven changes of man, the feven liberal arts, and as many mechanic, and fo many forbidden; feven colours, feven metals, feven holes

in

in the head of a man, feven pair of nerves, feven mountains in the city of
Rome, feven Roman kings, feven civil wars, feven wife men in the time of
Jeremiah, feven wife men of Greece; alfo Rome did burn feven days by
Nero; by feven kings were flain ten thoufand martyrs: there were feven
fleepers; and feven principal churches of Rome.

THE

THE SCALE OF

In the Original World,	Ararita,	אראריתא		
In the Intelligible World,	צפקאיל Zaphiel,	צדקיאל Zadkiel,	כמאל Camael,	דפאל Raphael,
In the Celeftial World,	שבתאי Saturn,	צרק Jupiter,	מאדיים Mars,	שמש The Sun,
In the Elementary World,	The lapwing, The cuttle fith, The mole, Lead, The onyx,	The eagle, The dolphin, The hart, Tin, The faphire,	The vulture, The pike, The wolf, Iron, The diamond,	The fwan, The fea calf, The lion, Gold, The carbuncle,
In the Leffer World,	The right foot, The right ear,	The head, The left ear,	The right hand, The right noftril,	The heart, The right eye,
In the Infernal World,	Hell, גיהבם	The gates of death, רצלמוח	The fhadow of death, ירעשוריס	The pit of deftruction, באךשהת

THE NUMBER SEVEN.

Affer Eheie,	אשר אהיה		The name of God with seven letters.
דאביאל Haniel,	מיכאל Michael,	צבדיאל Gabriel ;	Seven angels which stand in the presence of God.
כונה Venus,	כוכב Mercury,	לבכה The Moon ;	Seven planets.
The dove, Thimallus, The goat, Copper, The emerald,	The stork, The mullet, The ape, Quickfilver, The achates,	The owl ; The fea cat ; Cat; Silver ; Chryftal ;	Seven birds of the planets. Seven fish of the planets. Seven animals of the planets. Seven metals of the planets. Seven ftones of the planets.
The privy members, The left noftril,	The left hand, The mouth,	The left foot ; The left eye ;	Seven integral members diftributed to the planets. Seven holes of the head diftributed to the planets.
The Clay of death, סימחיה	Perdition, אבח	The depth of the earth; שאול	Seven habitations of infernals, which Rabbi Jofeph of Caftilia, the Cabalift, defcribes in the garden of nuts.

CHAP.

CHAP. XXIII.
OF THE NUMBER EIGHT, AND THE SCALE.

THE Pythagorians call Eight the number of juftice, and fulnefs : firft, be-caufe it is firft of all divided into numbers equally even, viz. into four; and that divifion is, by the fame reafon, made into twice two, viz. twice two twice ; and by reafon of this equality of divifion it took to itfelf the name of juftice. But the other received the name of fulnefs, by reafon of the contex-ture of the corporeal folidity, fince the firft makes a folid body. Hence that cuftom of Orpheus fwearing by the eight deities, if at any time he would be-feech Divine juftice, whofe names are thefe :—Fire, Water, Earth, the Heaven, Moon, Sun, Phanes, and the Night. There are only eight vifible fpheres of the heavens. Alfo, by it the property of corporeal nature is figni-fied, which Orpheus comprehends in eight of his fea fongs : this is alfo called the covenant, or circumcifion, which was commanded to be done by the Jews the eighth day.

There were alfo, in the old law, eight ornaments of the prieft, viz. a breaft-plate, a coat, a girdle, a mitre, a robe, an ephod, a girdle of the ephod, and a golden plate. Hither belongs the number to eternity, and the end of the world, becaufe it follows the number feven, which is the myftery of time. Hence, alfo, the number of bleffednefs, as you may fee in Matthew. It is alfo called the number of fafety, and confervation ; for there were fo many fouls of the fons of Jeffe, from which David was the eighth.

THE

THE SCALE OF THE NUMBER EIGHT.

The name of God with eight letters,	Eloa Vadaath אלוה רדעת Jehova Vedaath יהוה רהעת								In the original world.
Eight rewards of the bleſſed,	Inheritance,	Incorruption,	Power,	Victory,	The viſion of God,	Grace,	A kingdom,	Joy;	In the intelligible world.
Eight viſible heavens,	The ſtarry heaven,	The heaven of Saturn,	The heaven of Jupiter,	The heaven of Mars,	The heaven of the Sun,	The heaven of Venus,	The heaven of Mercury,	The heaven of the Moon;	In the celeſtial world.
Eight particular qualities,	The dryneſs of the earth,	The coldneſs of water,	The moiſture of air,	The heat of fire,	The heat of air,	The moiſture of water,	The dryneſs of fire,	The coldneſs of earth;	In the elementary world.
Eight kinds of bleſſed men,	The peacemakers,	They that hunger and thirſt after righteouſneſs,	The meek,	They which are perſecuted for righteouſneſs ſake,	Pure in heart,	Merciful,	Poor in ſpirit,	Mourners;	In the leſſer world.
Eight puniſhments of the damned.	Priſon,	Death,	Judgment,	The wrath of God,	Darkneſs,	Indignation,	Tribulation,	Anguiſh;	In the infernal world.

CHAP. XXIV.

OF THE NUMBER NINE, AND THE SCALE.

THERE are nine orders of bleſſed angels, viz. Seraphim, Cherubim, Thrones, Dominations, Powers, Virtues, Principalities, Archangels, and Angels, which Ezekiel figures out by nine ſtones, which are the ſapphire, emerald, carbuncle, beryl, onyx, chryſolite, jaſper, topaz, and ſardis. This number hath alſo a great and occult myſtery of the croſs ; for the ninth hour our Lord Jeſus Chriſt breathed out his ſpirit. The aſtrologers alſo take notice of the number nine in the ages of men, no otherwiſe than they do of ſeven, which they call climacterical years, which are eminent for ſome remarkable change. Yet ſometimes it ſignifies imperfeĉtneſs and incompleteneſs, becauſe it does not attain to the perfeĉtion of the number ten, but is leſs by one, without which it is deficient, as Auſtin interprets it of the ten lepers. Neither is the longitude of nine cubits of Og, King of Baſan, who is a type of the devil without a myſtery.

THE

THE SCALE OF THE NUMBER NINE.

The name of God with nine letters,	Jehovah Sabboath, יהוה צבאוה			Jehovah Zidkenu, יהוהצרקבו			Elohim Gibor, אלוחים גיפוך			In the original world.
Nine quires of angels,	Sera-phim,	Che-rubim,	Thrones,	Domina-tions,	Powers	Virtues,	Principa-lities,	Arch-angels,	Angels;	In the intelligible world.
Nine angels ruling the heavens,	Merat-tron,	Opha-niel,	Zaphkiel,	Zadkiel,	Camael	Ra-phael,	Haniel,	Michael,	Gabriel;	
Nine moveable spheres,	The primum mobile,	The starry heaven,	The sphere of Saturn,	The sphere of Jupiter,	The sphere of Mars,	The sphere of the Sun,	The sphere of Venus,	The sphere of Mercury,	The sphere of the Moon;	In the celestial world.
Nine stones representing the nine quires of angels,	Saphire	Eme-rald,	Carbun-cle,	Beryl,	Onyx,	Chryso-lite,	Jasper,	Topaz,	Sardis;	In the elementary world.
Nine senses, inward and outward together,	Memo-ry,	Cogita-tive,	Imagina-tive,	Common sense,	Hear-ing,	Seeing,	Smelling,	Tasting,	Touch-ing;	In the lesser world.
Nine orders of devils,	False Spirits,	Spirits of lying,	Vessels of iniquity,	Avengers of wickedness,	Jug-glers,	Airy Powers	Furies sowing mischief,	Sifters or triers,	Tempters, or ensnarers;	In the infernal world.

CHAP. XXV.
OF THE NUMBER TEN, AND THE SCALE.

THE number Ten is called every number, or an univerfal number, complete, fignifying the full courfe of life ; for beyond that we cannot number but by replication ; and it either implies all numbers within itfelf, or explains them by itfelf, and its own, by multiplying them ; wherefore it is accounted to be of manifold religion and power, and is applied to the purging of fouls. Hence the antients called ceremonies Denary, becaufe they were to be expiated and to offer facrifices, and were to abftain from fome certain things for ten days.

There are ten fanguine parts of man : the menftrues, the fperm, the plafonatic fpirit, the mafs, the humours, the organical body, the vegetative part, the fenfitive part, reafon, and the mind. There are, alfo, ten fimple integral parts conftituting man : the bone, cartilage, nerve, fibre, ligament, artery, vein, membrane, flefh, and fkin. There are, alfo, ten parts of which a man confifts intrinfically : the fpirit, the brain, the lungs, the heart, the liver, the gall, the fpleen, the kidnies, the tefticles, and the matrix. There are ten curtains in the temple, ten ftrings in the pfaltery, ten mufical inftruments with which the pfalms were fung, the names whereof were—*neza*, on which their odes were fung ; *nablum*, the fame as organs ; *mizmor*, on which the Pfalms ; *fir*, on which the Canticles ; *tehila*, on which orations ; *beracha*, on which benedictions ; *halel*, on which praifes ; *hodaia*, on which thanks ; *afre*, on which the felicity of any one ; *hallelujah*, on which the praifes of God only, and contemplations. There were alfo ten fingers of pfalms, viz. *Adam*, *Abraham*, *Melchifedech*, *Mofes*, *Afaph*, *David*, *Solomon*, and *the three fons of Chora*. There are, alfo, ten commandments. And the tenth day after the afcenfion of Chrift, the Holy Ghoft came down. Laftly, this is the number, in which Jacob, wreftling with the Angel all night, overcame, and, at the rifing of the fun, was bleffed, and called by the name of Ifrael. In this number, Jofhua overcame thirty-one kings ; and David overcame Goliah and the Philiftines ; and Daniel efcaped the danger of the lions. This number is alfo circular, as unity ; becaufe, being heaped together, returns into a unity, from whence it had its beginning ; and it is the end and perfection of all numbers, and the

begin-

beginning of tens. As the number ten flows back into a unity, from whence it proceeded, fo every thing that is flowing is returned back to that from which it had the beginning of its flux : fo water returns to the fea, from whence it had its beginning ; the body returns to the earth, from whence it was taken ; time returns into eternity, from whence it flowed ; the fpirit fhall return to God, who gave it ; and, laftly, every creature returns to nothing, from whence it was created.* Neither is it fupported but by the word of God, in whom all things are hid, and all things with the number ten, and by the number ten, make a round, as Proclus fays, taking their beginning from God, and ending in him. God, therefore (that firft unity, or one thing), before he communicated himfelf to inferiors, diffufed himfelf firft into the firft of numbers, viz. the number three ; then into the number ten, as into ten ideas and meafures of making all numbers and all things, which the Hebrews call ten attributes, and account ten divine names ; from which caufe there cannot be a further number. Hence all tens have fome divine thing in them, and in the law are required as his own, together with the firft fruits, as the original of all things and beginning of numbers, and every tenth is as the end given to him, who is the beginning and end of all things.

SCALE OF THE NUMBER TEN.

---

* At the laft, the elements give up what they have ever received; the fea gives up her dead, the fire gives up its fuel ; the earth gives up the feminal virtue, &c. ; and the air gives up whatever voice, found, or impreffion it has received, fo that not an oath, lie, or fecret blafphemy, but what will appear as clear as noon-day light at the great day of God.

THE

THE SCALE OF

In the original,	יהוה יהוה יהוה The name of Jehovah of ten letters collected,			ואו הא The name of Jehovah of ten letters,	
	אהיה Eheie, כתר Kether,	ויהוה Jod Jehovah, הכמה Hochmah,	יהוהאלהים Jehovah Elohim, בינה Binah,	אל El, הכד Hesed,	אלהימגיבר Elohim Gibor, גבורה Geburah,
In the intelligible world,	Seraphim, Hajothhakados, Merattron,	Cherubim, Orphanim, Jophiel,	Thrones, Aralim, Zaphkiel,	Dominations, Hafmallim, Zadkiel,	Powers, Seraphim, Camael,
In the celeftial world,	Refchith hagallalim, the primum mobile,	Mafloth, the fphere of the Zodiac,	Sabbathi, the fphere of Saturn,	Zedeck, the fphere of Jupiter,	Madim, the fphere of Mars,
In the elementary world,	A dove,	A lizard,	A dragon,	An eagle,	A horfe,
In the leffer world,	Spirit,	Brain,	Spleen,	Liver,	Gall,
In the infernal world,	Falfe gods,	Lying fpirits,	Veffels of iniquity,	Revengers of wickednefs,	Jugglers,

THE NUMBER TEN.

יוד הא Extended,		אלהימצבאות The name Elohim Sabaoth ;			The name of God with ten letters.
אליה Eloha, תפארת Tiphereth,	יהוהצבאות Jehovah Sabaoth, נצח Nezah,	אלהימצבאות Elohim Sabaoth, הוד Hod,	שדי Sadai, יסוד Jesod,	אדני Adonai melech ; מלכות Malchuth ;	Ten names of God. Ten Sephiroth.
Virtues,	Principalities,	Archangels,	Angels,	Blessed souls ;	Ten orders of the blessed, according to Dionysius.
Malachim,	Elohim,	Ben Elohim,	Cherubim,	Issim ;	Ten orders of the blessed, according to the traditions of men.
Raphael,	Haniel,	Michael,	Gabriel,	The soul of Messiah ;	Ten angels ruling.
Schemes, the sphere of the Sun,	Noga, the sphere of Venus,	Cochab, the sphere of Mercury,	Levanah, the sphere of the Moon,	Holom Jesodoth, the sphere of the elements ;	Ten spheres of the world.
Lion,	Man,	The fox,	Bull,	Lamb ;	Ten animals consecrated to the gods.
Heart,	Kidnies,	Lungs,	Genitals,	Matrix ;	Ten parts intrinsical of man.
Airy powers,	Furies, the seminaries of evil,	Sifters, or triers,	Tempters, or ensnarers,	Wicked souls bearing rule ;	Ten orders of the damned.

CHAP.

CHAP. XXVI.

OF THE NUMBERS ELEVEN AND TWELVE, WITH THE CABALISTICAL SCALE.

THE number Eleven, as it exceeds number ten, which is the number of the commandments, fo it falls fhort of the number Twelve, which is of grace and perfection ; therefore it is called the number of fins, and the penitent. Now the number twelve is divine, and that whereby the celeftials are meafured ;* it is, alfo, the number of figns in the Zodiac, over which there are

twelve

* The ufe of thefe Scales, in the compofition of Talifmans, Seals, Rings, &c., muft be obvious to every ftudent upon infpection, and are indifpenfably neceffary to the producing of any effect whatever that the artift may propofe to himfelf ; for, as we have before obferved, all things were formed according to the proportion of numbers, this feeming to be the principal pattern in the mind of the Creator ; therefore, when at any time we fet about any work or experiment in Celeftial Magic, we are to have efpecial regard to the rule of numbers and proportions. For example, if we would obtain the celeftial influence of any ftar, we are, firft of all, to obferve at what time that ftar is powerful in the heavens, I mean in good afpect with the benefices, and ruling in the day and hour appropriated to the planet, and in fortunate places of the figure ; then we are to obferve what divine names are ruling the intelligences, or fpirits, to which the faid planets are fubject with their characters (which you may fee at large in the Magical Tables of Numbers) ; then, by referring to the above Tables of the Scales, we may fee, by infpection, to what numbers are attributed divine names, and, under them, the orders of the intelligences—the heavenly fpheres—elements and their properties—animals, metals, and ftones—powers of the foul—fenfes of man—virtues—the princes of the evil fpirits—places of punifhment—degrees of the damned fouls—degrees of torments hereafter—and every thing that is either in heaven, or earth, or hell ;—all our fenfes, motions, qualities, virtues, words, or works, are fubmitted to the proportions of numbers, as you may fee fully exemplified in the different Scales of the Numbers ; and all things that are knowable are demonftrable by them, and are attributed to them ; therefore great is the knowledge and wifdom to be derived from numbers. Therefore the artift muft be well acquainted with their virtues and properties—by them there is a way open for the knowing and underftanding of all things ; therefore let him diligently contemplate thefe Scales, and likewife what we have fet down in our fourteenth and fifteenth Chapters preceding the Scales, where we have, upon good authority, explained fufficiently the extent and force of formal numbers, which ought to be well underftood and attentively confidered, as the ground and foundation of all our operations in this fcience, without which we are defrauded of the defired effect : therefore whenever we intend to fet about any experiment, whether it be an image, or ring, or tablet, or mirror, or amulet, or any other inftrument, we are to note firft the fite, order, number, and government of the intelligence and his planet, his meafure of time, revolution in the heavens, &c. ; likewife we are to engrave or write upon it its number, intelligence, or fpirit, either for a good or bad effect, with the fuitable characters and tables ; likewife the effect defired, with the divine names congruent thereto ; fo that our operations may be ftrong, powerful, and fuitable to the conftellation and ftar, both in time, number, and proportion ; with a due and attentive obfervation of all that we have written con-

cerning

twelve angels as chief, fupported by the irrigation of the great name of God. In twelve years, alfo, Jupiter perfeﬅs his courfe ; and the Moon daily runs through twelve degrees. There are, alfo, twelve chief joints in the body of man, viz. in hands, elbows, ﬔoulders, thighs, knees, and vertebræ of the feet. There is, alfo, a great power of the number twelve in divine myﬅeries. God chofe twelve families of Ifrael, and fet over them twelve princes ; fo many ﬅones were placed in the midﬅ of Jordan ; and God commanded that fo many ﬓould be fet on the breaﬅ of the prieﬅ. Twelve lions did bear the brazen fea that was made by Solomon ; there were fo many fountains in Helim ; and fo many Apoﬅles of Chriﬅ fet over the twelve tribes ; and twelve thoufand people were fet apart and chofen.

cerning this, without which all our operations could never be brought to have the effeﬅ defired ; and we are to mind that whenever fuch an inﬅrument is perfeﬅed, that it is the more powerful when the planet or con-ﬅellation (under which it was conﬅruﬅed) is ruling and potent in the Heavens ; for at that time, whatever we defire to bring to perfeﬅion by the faid Talifman, as a medium and inﬅrument, ﬓall by no means be pre-vented or hindered. Therefore take this as a general rule, that all magical inﬅruments whatfoever have no power in themfelves, further than as they are formed under the influences, and according to the times and numbers of their proper ﬅars and conﬅellations ; hence is derived the title we give this Book, viz. the *Conﬅellatory Art*, or *Talifmanic Magic*. Thofe who would further confider the power, virtue, extent, and harmony of numbers, let them read Pythagoras, Plato, Averroena, Averroës, &c. who all agree in the virtues lying hid in numbers ; and without the knowledge of which, no man can be a true philofopher.

THE SCALE OF

The names of God with twelve letters,			הוא Holy,	ברור Bleffed,	הקדש He,	
The great name returned back into twelve banners,	יהוה	יההו	יוהה	הוהי	הויה	ההיו
Twelve orders of bleffed spirits,	Seraphim,	Cherubim,	Thrones,	Dominations,	Powers,	Virtues,
Twelve angels ruling over the twelve figns,	Malchidial,	Afmodel,	Ambriel,	Muriel,	Verchiel,	Hamaliel,
Twelve tribes,	Dan,	Ruben,	Judah,	Manaffeh,	Afher,	Simeon,
Twelve prophets,	Malachi,	Haggai,	Zachariah,	Amos,	Hofea,	Micha,
Twelve apoftles,	Matthias,	Thaddeus,	Simon,	John,	Peter,	Andrew,
Twelve figns of the Zodiac,	Aries,	Taurus,	Gemini,	Cancer,	Leo,	Virgo,
Twelve months	March,	April,	May,	June,	July,	Auguft,
Twelve plants,	Sang,	Upright vervain,	Bending vervain,	Comfrey,	Ladies' feal,	Calamint,
Twelve ftones,	Sardonius,	A cornelian,	Topaz,	Calcedony,	Jafper,	Emerald,
Twelve principal members,	Head,	Neck,	Arms,	Breaft,	Heart,	Belly,
Twelve degrees of the damned, and of devils.	Falfe gods,	Lying fpirits,	Veffels of iniquity,	Revengers of wickednefs,	Jugglers,	Airy powers,

THE NUMBER TWELVE.

		אבבזוורותהקרש Father, Son, Holy Ghoft.				In the original world.
וחזי	יוהה	יהיה	היהו	היוה	החוי	
Principalities,	Archangels,	Angels,	Innocents,	Martyrs,	Confeffors.	In the intelligible world.
Zuriel,	Barbiel,	Adnachiel,	Hanael,	Gabriel,	Barchiel.	
Iffachar,	Benjamin,	Naphthalin,	Gad,	Zabulon,	Ephraim.	
Jonah,	Obadiah,	Zephaniah,	Nahum,	Habakkuk,	Joel.	
Bartholomew,	Philip,	James the elder,	Thomas,	Matthew,	James the younger.	
Libra,	Scorpius,	Sagittarius,	Capricorn,	Aquarius,	Pifces.	In the celeftial world.
September,	October,	November,	December,	January,	February.	In the elemental world.
Scorpion grafs,	Mugwort,	Pimpernel,	Dock,	Dragonwort,	Ariftolochy.	
Beryl,	Amethyft,	Hyacinth,	Chryfophrafus,	Chryftal,	Sapphire.	
Kidnies,	Genitals,	Hams,	Knees,	Legs,	Feet.	In the elementary world.
Furies, the fowers of evil,	Sifters, or triers,	Tempters, or enfnarers,	Witches,	Apoftates,	Infidels.	In the infernal world.

CHAP.

CHAP. XXVII.

OF THE NOTES OF THE HEBREWS AND CHALDEANS, AND OTHER NOTES OF MAGICIANS.

THE Hebrew characters have marks of numbers attributed to them far more excellent than any other language, since the greatest mysteries lie in the Hebrew letters, as is handled concerning these in that part of Cabala which we call Notariacon. Now the principal Hebrew letters are in number twenty-two, whereof five have various other certain figures in the end of a' word, which, therefore, they call the five ending letters, which, being added to them afore-said, make twenty-seven; which being then divided into three degrees, signify units, which are in the first degree---tens, which are in the second---and hundreds, which are in the third degree. Now every one, if they are marked with a great character, signifies so many thousands, as here----

3000	2000	1000
ג	ב	א

The classes of the Hebrew numbers are these which follow :----

9	8	7	6	5	4	3	2	1
ט	ח	ז	ו	ה	ד	ג	ב	א
90	80	70	60	50	40	30	20	10.
צ	פ	ע	ס	נ	מ	ל	כ	י
900	800	700	600	500	400	300	200	100
ץ	ף	ן	ם	ך	ת	ש	ר	ק

Sometimes the final letters are not used, but we write thus :----

1000	900	800	700	600	500
א	קתת	תת	שת	רת	קת

And by those simple figures, and by the joining them together, they describe all other compound numbers: as eleven, twelve, an hundred and ten, an
hundred

hundred and eleven, by adding to the number ten thofe which are units; and in the like manner to the reft, after their manner; yet we defcribe the fifteenth number not by ten and five, but by nine and fix, viz. ⅏; and that out of honour to the Divine name יה, which fignifies fifteen, left that facred name fhould be abufed to profane things. Likewife the Egyptians, Æthiopians, Chaldeans, and Arabians, have their marks of numbers, which ferve for the making of magical charaɛters; but the Chaldeans mark their numbers with the letters of their alphabet, after the manner of the Hebrews. I found, in a very antient book of Magic, fome very elegant charaɛters, which I have figured in the following manner :----

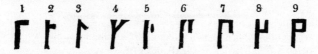

Now of thefe charaɛters, turned towards the left hand, are made tens.

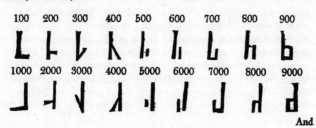

And thofe marks being downwards, to the right hand, make hundreds; to the left, thoufands, viz..

And

And by the compofition and mixture of thefe characters, other compound numbers are moft elegantly made, as you may perceive by thefe few :—

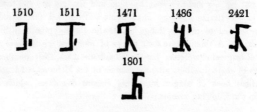

CHAP. XXVIII.

THE MAGIC TABLES OF THE PLANETS—THEIR FORM AND VIRTUE—WHAT DIVINE NAMES,
INTELLIGENCES, AND SPIRITS, ARE SET OVER THEM.

THERE are certain magic tables of numbers diftributed to the feven planets, which they call the facred tables of the planets ; becaufe, being rightly formed, they are endued with many great virtues of the heavens, infomuch that they reprefent the divine order of the celeftial numbers, impreffed upon them by the *ideas* of the divine mind, by means of the foul of the world, and the fweet harmony of thofe celeftial rays ; fignifying, according to proportion, fuperceleftial intelligences, which can no other way be expreffed than by the marks of numbers, letters, and characters ; for *material* numbers and figures can do nothing in the myfteries of hidden things, but reprefentatively by *formal* numbers and figures, as they are governed and informed by intelligences and divine enumerations, which unite the extremes of the matter and fpirit to the will of the elevated foul, receiving (through great affection, by the celeftial power of the operator) a virtue and power from God, applied through the foul of the univerfe ; and the obfervation of celeftial conftellations

to

Plate 1.

The Magic Tables Seals & Characters of the Planets their Intelligences Spirits.

The Table of Saturn in his Compass

4	9	2
3	5	7
8	1	6

The same Table in Hebrew

כ	ט	ב
ג	ה	ז
ח	א	י

The Seal of Saturn

Of the Intelligence of ♄

Of the Spirit of ♄

The Table of Jupiter

4	14	15	1
9	7	6	12
5	11	10	8
16	2	3	13

In Hebrew

א	שׁ	יד	ר
יט	ז	ו	יב
ח	יא	ה	ח
יו	כ	ג	יג

The Seal of Jupiter

Of the Intelligence of ♃

Of the Spirit of ♃

The Table of Mars

11	24	7	20	3
4	12	25	8	16
17	5	13	21	9
10	18	1	14	22
23	6	19	2	15

In Hebrew

יא	כד	ז	כ	ג
ר	יח	מה	יב	יו
יז	ח	יג	כא	ט
י	יח	א	יד	כב
כג	ו	יט	ב	יה

The Seal of Mars

Of his Intelligence

Of his Spirit

Designed by F. Barrett.   Pub. by Lackington Allen & Co.   Engraved by R. Griffith.

to a *matter* fit for a form, the mediums being difpofed by the fkill and induftry of the magician.

But now we will haften to explain each particular table.* The firft table
is affigned to the planet Saturn, and confifts of a fquare of three, containing
the particular numbers of nine, and in every line three every way, and through
each diameter making fifteen----the whole fum of numbers forty-five ; over this
are fet fuch divine names as fill up the numbers with an intelligence, to what is
good, and a fpirit to bad ; and out of the fame numbers are drawn the feal
and chara¿ter of Saturn, and of the fpirits thereof, fuch as is beneath afcribed
to the table.

Now this table being with a fortunate Saturn, engraven on a plate of lead,
helps child-birth ; and to make any man fafe or powerful ; and to caufe fuccefs of petitions with princes and powers ; but if it be done, Saturn being unfortunate, it hinders buildings, planting, and the like, and cafts a man from
honours and dignities, caufes difcord, quarrelling, and difperfes an army.

The fecond is the table of Jupiter, which confifts of a fquare drawn into
itfelf ; it contains fixteen particular numbers, and in every line and diameter
four, making thirty-four ; the fum of all is one hundred and thirty-fix.   There
are over it divine names, with an intelligence to that which is good, and a
fpirit to bad ; and out of it is drawn the chara¿ter of Jupiter and the fpirits
thereof ; if this is engraven on a plate of filver, with Jupiter being powerful
and ruling in the heavens, it conduces to gain riches and favour, love, peace,
and concord, and to appeafe enemies, and to confirm honours, dignities, and
counfels ; and diffolves enchantments if engraven on a coral.

The third table belongs to Mars, which is made of a fquare of five, containing twenty-five numbers, and of thefe, in every fide and diameter, five,
which makes fixty-five, and the fum of all is three hundred and twenty-five ;
and there are over it divine names with an intelligence to good, and a fpirit to
evil, and out of it is drawn the chara¿ters of Mars and of his fpirits.   Thefe,
with *Mars* fortunate, being engraven on an iron plate, or fword, makes

* For tho figure of the Tables, Seals, Chara¿ters, &c. of the feven Planets, fee the following Plates.

a man

a man potent in war and judgment, and petitions, and terrible to his enemies, and victorious over them ; and if engraven upon the stone correola, it stops blood, and the menstrues ; but if it be engraven, with *Mars* being unfortunate, on a plate of red brass, it prevents and hinders buildings---it casts down the powerful from dignities, honours, and riches---causes discord and hatred amongst men and beasts---drives away bees, pigeons, and fish---and hinders mills from working, *i. e.* binds them ;---it likewise renders hunters and fighters unfortunate---causes barrenness in men and women---and strikes a terror into our enemies, and compels them to submit.

The fourth table is of the *Sun*, and is made of a square of six, and contains thirty-six particular numbers, whereof six in every side and diameter produce one hundred and eleven, and the sum of all is six hundred and sixty-six ; there are over it divine names, with an intelligence to what is good, and a spirit to what is evil, and out of it is drawn the character of the Sun and of his spirits. This being engraven on a plate of pure gold, Sol being fortunate, renders him that wears it renowned, amiable, acceptable, potent in all his works, and equals him to a king, elevating his fortunes, and enabling him to do whatever he will. But with an unfortunate Sun, it makes one a tyrant, proud, ambitious, insatiable, and finally to come to an ill ending.

The fifth table is of Venus ; consisting of a square of seven, drawn into itself, viz. of forty-nine numbers, whereof seven on each side and diameter make one hundred and seventy-five, and the sum of all is one thousand two hundred and twenty-five ; there are, likewise, over it divine names, with an intelligence to good, and a spirit to evil ; and there is drawn out of it the character of Venus, and her spirits. This being engraven on a plate of silver, Venus being fortunate, promotes concord, ends strife, procures the love of women, helps conception, is good against barrenness, gives ability for gene- ration, dissolves enchantments, causes peace between man and woman, and makes all kinds of animals fruitful, and likewise cattle ; and being put into a dove or pigeon house, causes an increase ; it likewise drives away melancholy distempers, and causes joyfulness ; and this being carried about travellers,

makes

The Table of the Sun in his Compass

6	32	3	34	35	1
7	11	27	28	8	30
19	14	16	15	23	24
18	20	22	21	17	13
25	29	10	9	26	12
36	5	33	4	2	31

The same in Hebrew

The Character of the Seal of the Sun.

His Intellegence.

His Spirit

The Table of Venus in her Compass

22	47	16	41	10	35	4
5	23	43	17	42	11	29
30	6	24	49	21	36	12
13	31	7	25	43	19	37
38	14	32	1	26	44	20
21	39	8	33	2	27	45
46	15	40	9	34	3	28

in Hebrew

The Seal of Venus

Her Intelligence

Her Spirit

Her Intelligences

Barrett Del.   Pub. by Lackington & Allen   R. Griffith Sculp.

Plate 3.

The Magick Tables, Seals & Characters, of the Planets, their Intelligences & Spirits.

The Table of Mercury in his Compass.

8	58	59	5	4	62	63	1
49	15	14	52	53	11	10	56
41	23	22	44	48	19	18	45
32	34	38	29	25	35	39	28
40	26	27	37	36	30	31	33
17	47	46	20	21	43	42	24
9	55	54	12	13	51	50	16
64	2	3	61	60	6	7	57

The same in Hebrew

ח	נח	נש	ה	ד	סג	סב	סא
מש	יה	יד	גב	גג	יא	י	נר
סא	לב	כב	מר	מה	יש	יח	מה
לב	לר	לח	כש	כה	לח	לש	כה
לג	כז	כז	לז	לו	ר	לא	לג
יז	מב	מג	כא	כא	מ	מב	לר
יד	נה	ירר	כג	כב	יב	נד	יד
סד	ב	ג	סא	ם	ו	ז	נז

$☿$

The Seal or Character of Mercury

The Character of the Intelligence of Mercury

$☿$

The Character of the Spirit of Mercury

$☿$

Designed by F. Barrett 1801.　　Pub. by Lackington Allen & Co.　　Engraved by J Scott 1801.

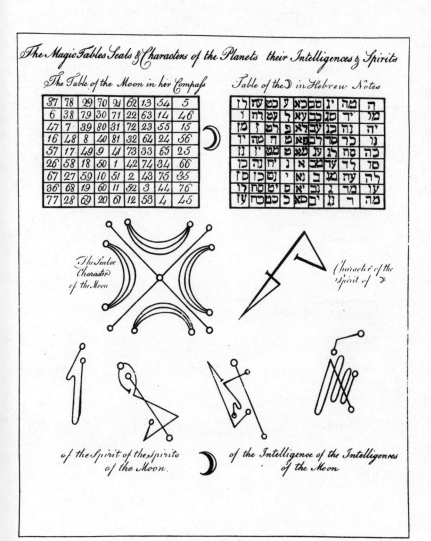

The Magic Tables Seals & Characters of the Planets their Intelligences & Spirits

The Table of the Moon in her Compass

37	78	29	70	21	62	13	34	5
6	38	79	30	71	22	63	14	46
47	7	39	80	31	72	23	55	15
16	48	8	40	81	32	64	24	56
57	17	49	9	41	73	33	65	25
26	58	18	50	1	42	74	34	66
67	27	59	10	51	2	43	75	35
36	68	19	60	11	52	3	44	76
77	28	69	20	61	12	53	4	45

Table of the ☽ in Hebrew Notes

The Seal or Character of the Moon

Character of the Spirit of ☽

of the Spirit of the Spirits of the Moon.

of the Intelligence of the Intelligences of the Moon

...rrett Del.   Pub. by Lackington & Allen.   R. Griffith

makes them fortunàte.   But if it be formed upon brafs, Venus being unfortunate, it acts contrary to all that has been faid.

The fixth table is of Mercury, refulting from a fquare of eight drawn into
itfelf, containing fixty-four numbers, whereof eight on every fide and by both
diameters make two hundred and fixty, and the fum of all is two thoufand and
eighty ; and over it are fet divine names, with an intelligence to good, with a
fpirit to bad, and from it is drawn a character of Mercury, and the fpirits
thereof ; and if, with Mercury being fortunate, you engrave it upon filver,
tin, or yellow brafs, or write it upon virgin parchment, it renders the bearer
thereof grateful, acceptable, and fortunate to do what he pleafes : it brings gain,
and prevents poverty ; helps the memory, underftanding, and divination, and
to the underftanding of occult things by dreams ; but with an unfortunate
Mercury does every thing contrary to this.

The feventh and laft table is of the Moon : it confifts of a fquare of nine,
having eighty-one numbers in every fide, and diameter nine, producing three
hundred and fixty-nine ; and the fum of all is three thoufand three hundred
and twenty-one.   There are over it divine names, with an intelligence to what
is good, and a fpirit to evil ; and from it are drawn the characters of the Moon
and the fpirits thereof.   This, the Moon being fortunate, engraven on filver,
makes the bearer amiable, pleafant, cheerful, and honoured, removing all
malice and ill-will ; it caufes fecurity in a journey, increafe of riches, and
health of body ; drives away enemies, and other evil things from what place
foever thou fhalt wifh them to be expelled.   But if the Moon be unfortunate,
and it be engraved on a plate of lead, wherever it fhall be buried it makes that
place unfortunate, and the inhabitants thereabouts, as alfo fhips, rivers, fountains, and mills ; and it makes every man unfortunate againft whom it fhall be
directly done, making him fly his place of abode (and even his country)
where it fhall be buried ; and it hinders phyficians and orators, and all men
whatfoever in their office, againft whom it fhall be made.

Now how the feals and characters of the planets are drawn from thefe tables,
the wife fearcher, and he who fhall underftand the verifying of thefe tables,
fhall eafily find out.

Book I.   T   Here

Here follow the divine names correfponding with the numbers of the planets, with the names of the intelligences and dæmons, or fpirits, fubject to thofe names.

It is to be underftood that the intelligences are the prefiding good angels that are fet over the planets; but that the fpirits or dæmons, with their names, feals, or characters, are never infcribed upon any Talifman, except to execute any evil effect, and that they are fubject to the intelligences, or good fpirits; and again, when the fpirits and their characters are ufed, it will be more conducive to the effect to add fome divine name appropriate to that effect which we defire.

Names anfwering to the Numbers of Saturn.

ה

Numbers.	Divine Names.	Divine Names in Hebrew.
3	Ab	אב
9	Hod	הד
15	Jah	יה
15	Hod	הוד
45	Jehovah extended	יודהאואהא
45	Agiel, the Intelligence of Saturn	אגיאל
45	Zazel, the Spirit of Saturn	זאזל

Names anfwering to the Numbers of Jupiter.

ч

4	Aba	אבא
16		הוה
16		אחי
34	El Ab	אלאב
136	Johphiel, the Intelligence of Jupiter	יהפיאל
136	Hifmæl, the Spirit of Jupiter	חסמאל

Names anfwering to the Numbers of Mars.

♂

5	He, the letter of the holy name	ה
25		יהי
65	Adonai	אדני
		Numbers.

Numbers.	Divine Names.	Divine Names in Hebrew:
325	Graphiel, the Intelligence of Mars	גראפיאל
325	Barzabel, the Spirit of Mars	בראצאבאל

Names answering to the Numbers of the Sun.

☉

6	Vau, the letter of the holy name	י
6	He extended, the letter of the holy name	הא
36	Eloh	אלה
111	Nachiel, the Intelligence of the Sun	נכיאל
666	Sorath, the Spirit of the Sun	סורה

Names answering to the Numbers of Venus.

♀

7	Aha	אהא
49	Hagiel, the Intelligence of Venus	הגיאל
175	Kedemel, the Spirit of Venus	קדמאל
1225	Bne Seraphim, the Intelligence of Venus	בני שרפים

Names answering to the Numbers of Mercury.

☿

8	Asboga, eight extended	אזבגה
64	Din	דין
64	Doni	דיני
260	Tiriel, the Intelligence of Mercury	טיריאל
2080	Tapthartharath, the Spirit of Mercury	תפתרתרת

Names answering to the Numbers of the Moon.

☽

9	Hod	הד
81	Elim	אלים
369	Hasmodai, the Spirit of the Moon	השמודאי
3321	Schedbarschemoth Schartathan, the Spirit of the Spirits of the Moon	שדברשהמעחשרתתו
3321	Malcha betharsisim hed beruah achehalim, the Intelligence of the Intelligences of the Moon	קלכאבתרשיסיסערברוהשוהקיס

CHAP.

CHAP. XXIX.

OF THE OBSERVATION OF THE CELESTIALS NECESSARY IN EVERY MAGICAL WORK.

EVERY natural virtue works things far more wonderful when it is not only compounded of a natural proportion, but also is informed by a choice observation of the celestials opportune to this (viz. when the celestial power is most strong to that effect which we desire, and also helped by many celestials), by subjecting inferiors to the celestials, as proper females, to be made fruitful by their males. Also, in every work there are to be observed the situation, motion, and aspect of the stars and planets, in signs and degrees, and how all these stand in reference to the length and latitude of the climate; for by this are varied the qualities of the angles, which the rays of the celestial bodies upon the figure of the thing describe, according to which celestial virtues are infused. So when you are working any thing which belongs to any planet, you must place it in its dignities, fortunate, and powerful, and ruling in the day hour, and in the figure of the heavens. Neither must you expect the signification of the work to be powerful, but you must observe the Moon opportunely directed to this; for you shall do nothing without the assistance of the Moon. And if you have more patterns of your work, observe them all, being most powerful, and looking upon one another with a friendly aspect; and if you cannot have such aspects, it will be convenient at least that you take them angular. But you shall take the Moon either when she looks upon both, or is joined to one, and looks upon the other, or when when she passes from the conjunction or aspect of one, to the conjunction or aspect of the other; for that, I conceive, must in no wise be omitted. Also, you shall in every work observe Mercury, for he is a messenger between the higher gods and the infernal gods: when he goes to the good, he increases their goodness—when to the bad, he hath influence on their wickedness. We call it an unfortunate sign or planet, when it is, by the aspect of Saturn or Mars especially, opposite or quadrant, for these are the aspects of enmity; but a conjunction, a trine, and a sextile aspect, are of friendship; between these there is a greater conjunction; but yet if you do already

behold

behold it through a trine, and the planet be received, it is accounted as already conjoined. Now all planets are afraid of the conjunction of the Sun, rejoicing in the trine, and fextile afpect thereof.

CHAP. XXX.

WHEN THE PLANETS ARE OF MOST POWERFUL INFLUENCE.

NOW we fhall have the planets powerful when they are ruling in a houfe, or in exaltation, or triplicity, or term, or face, without combuftion of what is direct in the figure of the heavens, viz. when they are in angles, efpecially of the rifing, or tenth, or in houfes prefently fucceeding, or in their delights ; but we muft take heed that they are not in the bounds or under the dominion of Saturn or Mars, left they be in dark degrees, in pits, or vacuities. You fhall obferve that the angles of the afcendant, and tenth, and feventh, be fortunate ; as alfo the lord of the afcendant, and place of the Sun and Moon, and place of the part of fortune, and the lord thereof, the lord of the foregoing conjunction and prevention. But that they of the malignant planet fall unfortunate ; unlefs happily they be fignificators of thy work, or can be of any advantage to thee, or in thy revolution or birth they had the predominance, for then they are not at all to be depreffed. Now we fhall have the Moon powerful if fhe be in her houfe, or exaltation, or triplicity, or face, or in degree convenient for the defired work ; and if it hath a manfion of thefe twenty-eight, fuitable to itfelf and the work, let her not in the way be burnt up,* nor flow in courfe---let her not be in the eclipfe, or burnt by the Sun, unlefs fhe be in unity with the Sun---let her not defcend in the fouthern latitude, when fhe goeth out of the burning---neither let her be oppofite to the Sun, nor deprived of light---let her not be hindered by Mars or Saturn.

* Via Combufta.

CHAP.

CHAP. XXXI.

OBSERVATIONS ON THE FIXED STARS, AND THEIR NAMES AND NATURES.

THERE is the like confideration to be had in all things concerning the fixed ftars. Know this, that all the fixed ftars are of the fignification and nature of the feven planets ; but fome are of the nature of one planet, and fome of two. Hence, as often as any planet is joined with any of the fixed ftars of its own nature, the fignification of that ftar is made more powerful, and the nature of the planet augmented ; but if it be a ftar of two natures, the nature of that which fhall be the ftronger with it, fhall overcome in fignification : as for ex- ample, if it be of the nature of Mars and Venus, if Mars fhall be the ftronger with it, the nature of Mars fhall overcome ; but if Venus, the nature of Venus fhall overcome. Now the natures of fixed ftars are difcovered by their colours, as they agree with certain planets, and are afcribed to them. Now the colours of the planets are thefe :----of Saturn, blue, and leaden, and fhining with this ; of Jupiter, citrine, near to a palenefs, and clear with this ; of Mars, red and fiery ; of the Sun, yellow, and when it rifes red, afterwards glittering ; of Venus, white and fhining---white in the morning, and reddifh in the evening ; of Mercury, glittering ; of the Moon, fair. Know, alfo, that of the fixed ftars, by how much the greater, and brighter, and apparent they are, fo much the greater and ftronger is the fignification : fuch are thofe ftars called by the aftrologers of the firft and fecond magnitude. I will tell thee fome of thefe which are more potent to this faculty, viz. the navel of Andromeda, in the twenty-fecond degree of Aries, of the nature of Venus and Mercury---fome call it jovial and faturnine ; the head of Algol, in the eighteenth degree of Taurus, of the nature of Saturn and Jupiter ; the Pleiades are alfo in the twenty-fecond degree, a lunary ftar by nature, and complexion martial ; alfo Aldeboram, in the third degree of Gemini, is of the nature of Mars, and complexion of Venus---but Hermes places this in the twenty-fifth degree of Aries ; the Goat ftar, in the thirteenth degree of Gemini, is of the nature of Jupiter and Saturn ; the Great Dog ftar is in the feventh degree of Cancer and Venereal ;

                                                                        the

the Little Dog ftar is in the feventeenth degree of the fame, and is of the na-
ture of Mercury, and complexion of Mars ; the King ftar, which is called the
Heart of the Lion, is in the twenty-firft degree of Leo, and of the nature of
Jupiter and Mars ; the tail of the Great Bear is in the nineteenth degree of
Virgo, and is venereal and lunary. The ftar which is called the Right Wing
of the Crow, is in the feventh degree of Libra ; and in the thirteenth degree
of the fame, is the left wing of the fame, and both of the nature of Saturn and
Mars. The ftar called Spica, is in the fixteenth degree of the fame, and is
venereal and mercurial. In the feventeenth degree of the fame is Alcameth,
of the nature of Mars and Jupiter ; but of this, when the Sun's afpeét is full
towards it----of that, when on the contrary. Elepheia, in the fourth degree of
Scorpio, of the nature of Venus and Mars. The Heart of the Scorpion is in
the third degree of Sagittarius, of the nature of Mars and Jupiter. The falling Vulture is in the feventh degree of Capricorn, temperate, mercurial, and
venereal. The tail of Capricorn is in the fixteenth degree of Aquarius, of the
nature of Saturn and Mercury. The ftar called the Shoulder of the Horfe, is
in the third degree of Pifces, of the nature of Jupiter and Mars.----And it fhall
be a general rule for you to expeét the proper gifts of the ftars, whilft they
rule---to be prevented of them, they being unfortunate, as is above fhewed ;
for celeftial bodies, inafmuch as they are affeéted fortunately or unfortunately,
fo much do they affeét us, our works, and thofe things which we ufe, fortunately or unhappily. And although many effeéts proceed from the fixed
ftars, yet they are attributed to the planets ; as becaufe being more near to us,
and more diftinét and known, fo becaufe they execute whatever the fuperior
ftars communicate to them.

CHAP.

CHAP. XXXII.

OF THE SUN AND MOON, AND THEIR MAGICAL CONSIDERATIONS.

THE Sun and Moon have obtained the administration of ruling the heavens, and all bodies under the heavens.   The Sun is the lord of all elementary
virtues ; and the Moon, by virtue of the Sun, is mistress of generation, increase
or decrease.   Albumfar says, that by the Sun and Moon, life is infused into
all things ; which Orpheus calls the enlivening eyes of Heaven.   The Sun
giveth light to all things of itself, and gives it plentifully, not only to all things
in heaven and air, but earth and deep.   Whatever good we have, Jamblicus
says, we have it from the Sun alone ; or from it through other things.   Hera-
clitus calls the Sun, the fountain of celestial light ; and many of the Platonists
placed the soul of the world chiefly in the Sun, as that which, filling the whole
globe of the Sun, doth send forth its rays on all sides, as it were a spirit through
all things, distributing life, sense, and motion to the universe.   Hence the
antient naturalists called the Sun the very heart of Heaven ; and the Chaldeans
put it as the middle of the Planets.   The Egyptians also placed it in the middle
of the world, viz. between the two fives of the world ; i. e. above the Sun they
place five planets, and under him, the Moon and four elements.   For it is,
amongst the other stars, the image and statue of the great Prince of both
worlds, viz. terrestrial and celestial ; the true light, and the most exact image
of God himself : whose essence resembles the Father---light, the Son---heat,
the Holy Ghost.   So that the Platonists have nothing to hold forth the divine
essence more manifestly by than this.   The Sun disposes even the very spirit
and mind of man, which Homer says, and is approved by Aristotle, that
there are in the mind such like motions as the Sun, the prince and moderator
of the planets, brings to us every day ; but the Moon, the nearest to the earth,
the receptacle of all the heavenly influences, by the swiftness of her course, is
joined to the Sun, and the other planets and stars, every month ; and receiving the beams and influences of all the other planets and stars, as a conception,
bringing them forth to the inferior world, as being next to itself ; for all the

stars

stars have influence on it, being the last receiver, which afterwards communicates the influence of all the superiors to these inferiors, and pours them forth on the earth; and it more manifestly disposes these inferiors than others. Therefore her motion is to be observed before the others, as the parent of all conceptions, which it diversely issues forth in these inferiors, according to the diverse complexion, motion, situation, and different aspects to the planets and other stars; and though it receives powers from all the stars, yet especially from the Sun, as oft as it is in conjunction with the same, it is replenished with vivifying virtue; and, according to the aspect thereof, it borrows its complexion. From it the heavenly bodies begin that series of things which Plato calls the golden chain; by which every thing and cause, being linked one to another, do depend on the superior, even until it may be brought unto the supreme cause of all, from which all things depend; hence it is, that, without the Moon intermediating, we cannot at any time attract the power of the superiors; therefore, to obtain the virtue of any star, take the stone and herb of that planet, when the Moon fortunately comes under, or has a good aspect on, that star.

CHAP XXXIII.

OF THE TWENTY-EIGHT MANSIONS OF THE MOON, AND THEIR VIRTUES.

AND seeing the Moon measures the whole space of the Zodiac in the time of twenty-eight days, hence it is that the wise men of the *Indians*, and most of the antient astrologers have granted twenty-eight mansions to the Moon, which, being fixed in the eighth sphere, do enjoy (as *Alpharus* says) divers names and properties, from the various signs and stars which are contained in them; through which, while the Moon wanders, it obtains many other powers and virtues; but every one of these mansions, according to the opinion of *Abraham*, contained twelve degrees, and fifty-one minutes, and almost twenty-

Book I.   U   fix

fix feconds, whofe names, and alfo their beginnings in the Zodiac, of the
eighth fphere, are thefe :---The firft is called *Alnath*; that is, the horns of
Aries : his beginning is from the head of Aries, of the eighth fphere ; it
caufes difcords and journies. The fecond is called *Allothaim*, or *Albochan*;
that is, the belly of Aries ; and his beginning is from the twelfth degree of the
fame fign, fifty-one minutes, twenty-two feconds complete : it conduces to the
finding of treafures, and to the retaining captives. The third is called
Achaomazon, or *Athoray*; that is, fhowering, or Pleiades : his beginning is from
the twenty-fifth degree of Aries complete, forty-two minutes, and fifty-one
feconds ; it is profitable to failors, huntfmen, and alchymifts. The fourth
manfion is called *Aldebaram*, or *Aldelamen*; that is, the eye or head of Taurus :
his beginning is from the eighth degree of Taurus, thirty-four minutes and
feventeen feconds of the fame, Taurus being excluded : it caufes the deftruction and hindrances of buildings, fountains, wells, gold mines, the flight of
creeping things, and begets difcord. The fifth is called *Alchatay*, or *Albachay*;
the beginning of it is after the twenty-firft degree of Taurus, twenty-five minutes, forty feconds : it helps to the return from a journey, to the inftruction
of fcholars ; it confirms edifices, it gives health and good-will. The fixth is
called *Athanna*, or *Alchaya*; that is, the little ftar of great light : his beginning is after the fourth degree of Gemini, feventeen minutes, and nine feconds ; it conduces to hunting and befieging towns, and revenge of princes :
it deftroys harvefts and fruits, and hinders the operation of the phyfician. The
feventh is called *Aldimiach*, or *Alarzach*; that is, the arm of Gemini, and begins from the feventeenth degree of Gemini, eight minutes, and thirty-four
feconds, and lafts even to the end of the fign ; it confirms gain and friendfhip ;
it is profitable to lovers, and deftroys magiftracies : and fo is one quarter of
the heaven completed in thefe feven manfions, and in the like order and number of degrees, minutes, and feconds ; the remaining manfions, in every
quarter, have their feveral beginnings ; namely, fo that in the firft fign of
this quarter three manfions take their beginnings ; in the other two figns, two
manfions in each ; therefore the feven following manfions begin with Cancer,
whofe names are *Alnaza Anatrachya*; that is, mifty or cloudy, viz. the eighth
                                                                    manfion

manfion; it caufes love, friendfhip, and fociety of fellow travellers : it drives away mice, and afflicts captives, confirming their imprifonment. After this is the ninth, called *Archaam*, or *Arcaph*; that is, the eye of the Lion : it hinders harveft and travellers, and puts difcord between men. The tenth is called *Algelioche*, or *Albgebh*; that is, the neck or forehead of Leo : it ftrengthens buildings, promotes love, benevolence, and help againft enemies. The eleventh is called *Azobra*, or *Ardaf*; that is, the hair of the lion's head : it is good for voyages, and gain by merchandife, and for redemption of captives. The twelfth is called *Alzarpha*, or *Azarpha*; that is, the tail of Leo : it gives profperity to harveft and plantations, but hinders feamen, and is good for the bettering of fervants, captives, and companions. The thirteenth is named *Alhaire*; that is, Dog ftars, or the wings of Virgo : it is prevalent for benevolence, gain, voyages, harvefts, and freedom of captives. The fourteenth is called *Achureth*, or *Arimet*; by others, *Azimeth*, or *Athumech*, or *Alcheymech*; that is, the fpike of Virgo, or flying fpike : it caufes the love of married folks ; it cures the fick, is profitable to failors, but hinders journies by land ; and in thefe the fecond quarter of the heaven is completed. The other feven follow : the firft of which begins in the head of Libra, viz. the fifteenth manfion, and its name is *Agrapha*, or *Algrapha*; that is, covered, or covered flying : it is profitable for extracting treafures, for digging of pits ; it affifts divorce, difcord, and deftruction of houfes and enemies, and hinders travellers. The fixteenth is called *Azubene*, or *Ahubene*; that is, the horns of Scorpio : it hinders journies and wedlock, harveft and merchandife ; it prevails for redemption of captives. The feventeenth is called *Alchil*; that is, the crown of Scorpio : it betters a bad fortune, makes love durable, ftrengthens buildings, and helps feamen. The eighteenth is called *Alchas*, or *Altob*; that is, the heart of Scorpio : it caufes difcord, fedition, confpiracy againft princes and mighty ones, and revenge from enemies ; but it frees captives, and helps edifices. The nineteenth is called *Allatha*, or *Achala*; by others, *Hycula*, or *Axala*; that is, the tail of Scorpio : it helps in befieging of cities, and taking of towns, and in the driving of men from their places, and for the deftruction of feamen, and perdition of captives. The twentieth is called *Abnahaya*; that is, a beam :

it

it helps for the taming of wild beasts, for strengthening of prisons; it destroys the wealth of societies; it compels a man to come to a certain place. The twenty-first is called *Abeda*, or *Albeldach*, which is a desert : it is good for harvest, gain, buildings, and travellers, and causes divorce; and in this is the third quarter of heaven completed. There remains the seven last mansions, completing the last quarter of Heaven : the first of which, being in order to the twenty-second, beginning from the head of Capricorn, called *Sadahacha*, or *Zodeboluch*, or *Zandeldena;* that is, a pastor : it promotes the flight of servants and captives, that they may escape, and helps the curing of diseases. The twenty-third is called *Zabadola*, or *Zobrach;* that is, swallowing : it is for divorce, liberty of captives, and health to the sick. The twenty-fourth is called *Sadabath*, or *Chadezoad;* that is, the star of fortune : it is prevalent for the benevolence of married people, for the victory of soldiers; it hurts the execution of government, and prevents its being exercised. The twenty-fifth is called *Sadalabra*, or *Sadalachia;* that is, a butter-fly, or a spreading forth : it favours besieging and revenge; it destroys enemies, and causes divorce; confirms prisons and buildings, hastens messengers ; it conduces to spells against copulation, and so binds every member of man that it cannot perform its duty. The twenty-sixth is called *Alpharg*, or *Phragal Mocadeu;* that is, the first drawing : it causes union, health of captives, destroys buildings and prisons. The twenty-seventh is called *Alchara Alyhalgalmoad*, or the second drawing : it increases harvest, revenues, gain, and heals infirmities ; but hinders buildings, prolongs prisons, causes danger to seamen, and helps to infer mischiefs on whom you shall please. The twenty-eighth and last is called *Albotham*, or *Alchalcy;* that is, Pisces : it increases harvest and merchandise; it secures travellers through dangerous places ; it makes for the joy of married people ; but it strengthens prisons, and causes loss of treasures. And in these twenty-eight mansions lie hid many secrets of the wisdom of the antients, by which they wrought wonders on all things which are under the circle of the Moon ; and they attributed to every mansion his resemblances, images, and seals, and his president intelligences, and worked by the virtue of them after different manners.

CHAP.

CHAP. XXXIV.

HOW SOME ARTIFICIAL THINGS (AS IMAGES, SEALS, AND SUCH LIKE) MAY OBTAIN SOME
VIRTUE FROM THE CELESTIAL BODIES.

SO great is the extent, power, and efficacy of the celeftial bodies, that not
only natural things, but alfo artificial, when they are rightly expofed to thofe
above, do prefently fuffer by that moft potent agent, and obtain a wonderful
life. The magicians affirm, that not only by the mixture and application of
natural things, but alfo in images, feals, rings, glaffes, and fome other inftruments, being opportunely framed under a certain conftellation, fome celeftial illuftration may be taken, and fome wonderful thing may be received ;
for the beams of the celeftial bodies being animated, living, fenfual, and
bringing along with them admirable gifts, and a moft violent power, do,
even in a moment, and at the firft touch, imprint wonderful powers in the
images, though their matter be lefs capable. Yet they beftow more powerful
virtues on the images if they be framed not of any, but of a certain matter,
namely, whofe natural, and alfo fpecifical virtue is agreeable with the work,
and the figure of the image is like to the celeftial ; for fuch an image, both in
regard to the matter naturally congruous to the operation and celeftial influence, and alfo for its figure being like to the heavenly one, is beft prepared
to receive the operations and powers of the celeftial bodies and figures, and
inftantly receives the heavenly gift into itfelf ; though it conftantly worketh
on another thing, and other things yield obedience to it.

CHAP.

CHAP. XXXV.

OF THE IMAGES OF THE ZODIAC----WHAT VIRTUES, THEY BEING ENGRAVEN, RECEIVE
FROM THE STARS.

BUT the celeftial images, according to whofe likenefs images of this kind
are framed, are many in the heavens; fome vifible and confpicuous, others
only imaginary, conceived and fet down by the *Egyptians*, *Indians*, and
Chaldeans; and their parts are fo ordered, that even the figures of fome of
them are diftinguifhed from others; for this reafon they place in the circle
of the Zodiac twelve general images, according to the number of the figns;
of thefe, they conftituting Aries, Leo, and Sagittarius, for the fiery and oriental
triplicity, report that it is profitable againft fevers, palfy, dropfy, gout, and
all cold and phlegmatic infirmities; and that it makes him who carries it to
be acceptable, eloquent, ingenious, and honourable; becaufe they are the
houfes of Mars, Sol, and Jupiter. They made, alfo, the image of a lion
againft melancholy phantafies, dropfy, plague, and fevers, and to expel
difeafes, at the hour of the Sun, the firft degree of the fign Leo afcending,
which is the face and decanate of Jupiter; but againft the ftone, and difeafes
of the reins, and againft hurts of beafts, they made the fame image when Sol,
in the heart of the lion, obtained the midft of heaven. And again, becaufe
Gemini, Libra, and Aquarius, do conftitute the ærial and occidental triplicity,
and are the houfes of Mercury, Venus, and Saturn, they are faid to put to
flight difeafes, to conduce to friendfhip and concord, to prevail againft melancholy, and to caufe health; and they report that Aquarius efpecially frees
from the quartan. Alfo, that Cancer, Scorpio, and Pifces, becaufe they conftitute the watery and northern triplicity, do prevail againft hot and dry fevers,
alfo againft the hectic, and all choleric paffions; but Scorpio, becaufe among
the members it refpects the privy parts, doth provoke to luft; but thefe did
frame it for this purpofe, his third face afcending, which belongs to Venus;
and they made the fame, againft ferpents and fcorpions, poifons and evil fpirits, his fecond face afcending, which is the face of the Sun, and decanate of
                                                                    Jupiter;

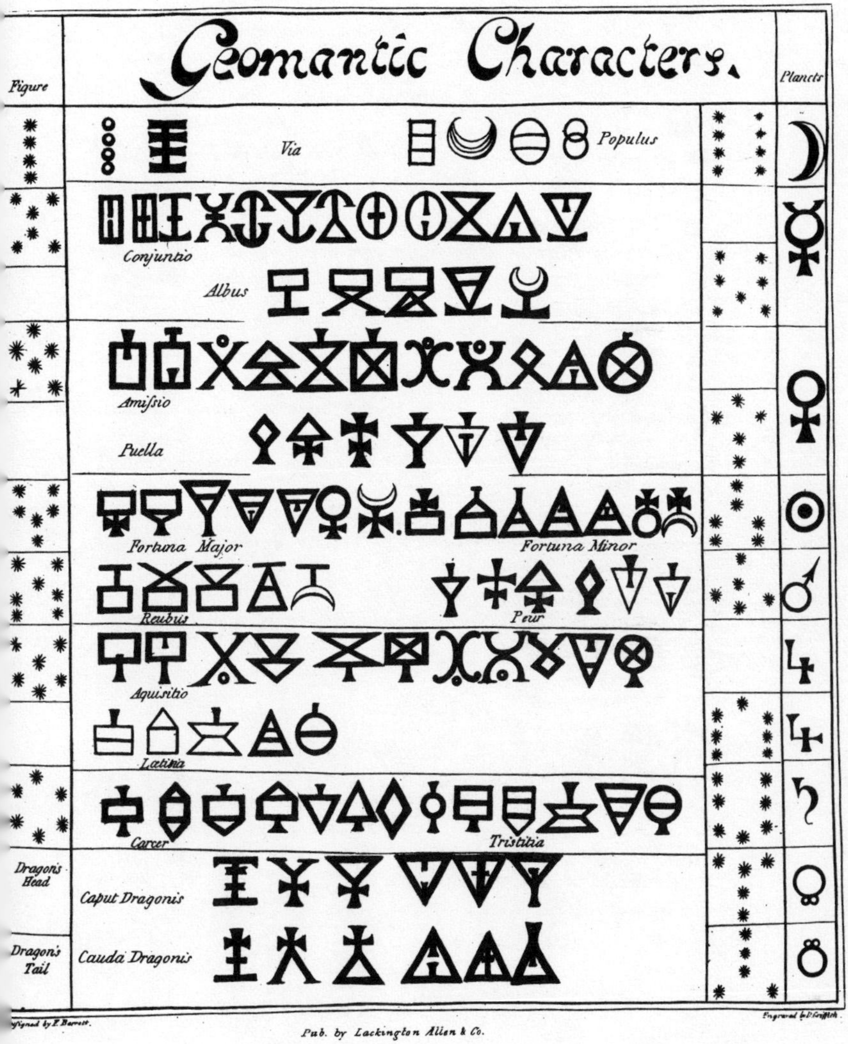
Geomantic Characters.
Figure
Planets
Via
Populus
Conjuntio
Albus
Amissio
Puella
Fortuna Major
Fortuna Minor
Reubus
Peur
Aquisitio
Lætitia
Carcer
Tristitia
Dragon's Head
Caput Dragonis
Dragon's Tail
Cauda Dragonis

signed by F. Barrett. Engraved by D. Griffith.

Pub. by Lackington Allen & Co.

Jupiter ; and they report that it maketh him who carries it wise, of a good colour ; and they say that the image of Cancer is most efficacious against serpents and poison, when Sol and Luna are in conjunction in it, and ascend in the first and third face ; for this is the face of Venus, and the decanate of Luna ; but the second face of Luna the decanate of Jupiter.   They report, also, that serpents are tormented when the Sun is in Cancer ; also, that Taurus, Virgo, and Capricorn, because they constitute the earthly and southern triplicity, do cure hot infirmities, and prevail against the synocal fever ; it makes those who carry it grateful, acceptable, eloquent, devout, and religious ; because they are the houses of Venus, Mars, and Saturn.   Capricorn also is reported to keep men in safety, and also places in security, because it is the exaltation of Mars.

CHAP. XXXVI.
OF THE IMAGES OF SATURN.

BUT now what images they did attribute to the planets. Although of these things very large volumes have been written by the antient wise men, so that there is no need to declare them here, notwithstanding I will recite a few of them ; for they made, from the operations of Saturn, *Saturn* ascending in a stone, which is called the load-stone, the image of a man, having the countenance of a hart, and camel's feet, and sitting upon a chair or else a dragon, holding in his right hand a scythe, in his left a dart, which image they hoped would be profitable for prolongation of life ; for Albumasar, in his book *Sadar*, proves that Saturn conduces to the prolongation of life ; where, also, he says that certain regions of India being subject to Saturn, there men are of a very long life, and die not unless by extreme old age. They made, also, an image of Saturn, for length of days, in a sapphire, at the hour of Saturn, *Saturn* ascending or fortunately constituted ; whose figure was an old man sitting upon a high chair, having his hands lifted up above his head, and

and in them holding a fish or fickle, and under his feet a bunch of grapes, his head covered with a black or dufky coloured cloth, and all his garments black or dark. They alfo make this fame image againft the ftone, and difeafes of the kidnies, viz. in the hour of Saturn, *Saturn* afcending with the third face of Aquarius. They made alfo, from the operations of Saturn, an image for the increafing of power, Saturn afcending in Capricorn ; the form of which was an old man leaning on a ftaff, having in his hand a crooked fickle, and clothed in black. They alfo made an image of melted copper, Saturn afcending in his rifing, viz. in the firft degree of Aries, or the firft degree of Capricorn ; which image they affirm to fpeak with a man's voice. They made alfo, from the operations of Saturn, and alfo Mercury, an image of caft metal, like a beautiful man, which, they faid, would foretel things to come ; and made it on the day of Mercury, on the third hour of Saturn, the fign of Gemini afcending, being the houfe of Mercury, fignifying prophets ; Saturn and Mercury being in conjunction in Aquarius, in the ninth houfe of heaven, which is alfo called God. Moreover, let Saturn have a trine afpect on the afcendant, and the Moon in like manner, and the Sun have an afpect on the place of conjunction ; Venus, obtaining fome angle, may be powerful and occidental ; let Mars be combuft by the Sun, but let it not have an afpect on Saturn and Mercury ; for they faid that the fplendour of the powers of thefe ftars was diffufed upon this image, and it did fpeak with men, and declare thofe things which are profitable for them.

CHAP. XXXVII.
OF THE IMAGES OF JUPITER.

FROM the operations of Jupiter they made, for prolongation of life, an image in the hour of Jupiter, Jupiter being in his exaltation fortunately afcending, in a clear and white ftone ; whofe figure was a man crowned,
clothed

clothed with garments of a faffron colour, riding upon an eagle or dragon, having in his right hand a dart, about, as it were, to ftrike it into the head of the fame eagle or dragon. They made, alfo, another image of Jupiter, at the fame convenient feafon, in a white and clear ftone, efpecially in cryftal ; and it was a naked man crowned, having both his hands joined together and lifted up, as it were, deprecating fomething fitting in a four-footed chair, which is carried by four winged boys ; and they affirm that this image increafes felicity, riches, honours, and confers benevolence and profperity, and frees from enemies. They made, alfo, another image of Jupiter, for a religious and glorious life, and advancement of fortune ; whofe figure was a man, having the head of a lion or a ram, and eagle's feet, and clothed in faffron coloured clothes.

CHAP. XXXVIII.
OF THE IMAGES OF MARS.

FROM the operations of Mars, they made an image in the hour of Mars (Mars afcending in the fecond face of Aries), in a martial ftone, efpecially in a diamond ; the form of which was a man armed, riding upon a lion, having in his right hand a naked fword erect, carrying in his left hand the head of a man. They report that an image of this kind renders a man powerful in good and evil, fo that he fhall be feared by all ; and whoever carries it, they give him the power of enchantment, fo that he fhall terrify men by his looks when he is angry, and ftupify them. They made another image of Mars, for obtaining boldnefs, courage, and good fortune, in wars and contentions ; the form of which was a foldier, armed and crowned, girt with a fword, carrying in his right hand a long lance ; and they made this at the hour of Mars, the firft face of Scorpio afcending with it.

CHAP. XXXIX.
OF THE IMAGES OF THE SUN.

FROM the operations of the Sun they made an image at the hour of the Sun, the first face of Leo afcending with the Sun ; the form of which was a king crowned, fitting in a chair, having a raven in his bofom, and under his feet a globe : he is clothed in faffron coloured clothes. They fay that this image renders men invincible and honourable, and helps to bring their bufinefs to a good end, and to drive away vain dreams ; alfo to be prevalent againft fevers, and the plague ; and they made it in a balanite ftone, or a ruby, at the hour of the Sun, when he, in his exaltation, fortunately afcends. They made another image of the Sun in a diamond, at the hour of the Sun afcending in his exaltation ; the figure of which was a woman crowned, with the gefture of one, dancing and laughing, ftanding in a chariot drawn by four horfes, having in her right hand a looking-glafs or buckler, in the left a ftaff, leaning on her breaft, carrying a flame of fire on her head. They fay that this image renders a man fortunate, and rich, and beloved of all ; and they made this image on a cornelian ftone, at the hour of the Sun afcending in the firft face of Leo, againft lunatic paffions, which proceed from the combuftion of the Moon.

CHAP. XL.
OF THE IMAGES OF VENUS.

FROM the operations of Venus they made an image, which was available for favour and benevolence, at the very hour it afcended into Pifces ; the form of which was the image of a woman, having the head of a bird, the feet of an eagle, and holding a dart in her hand. They made another image of Venus,
to

to obtain the love of women, in the lapis lazuli, at the hour of Venus, *Venus* ascending in *Taurus;* the figure of which was a naked maid, with her hair spread abroad, having a looking-glass in her hand, and a chain tied about her neck---and near her a handsome young man, holding her with his left hand by the chain, but with his right hand doing up her hair, and both looking lovingly on one another---and about them is a little winged boy, holding a sword or dart. They made another image of Venus, the first face of *Taurus*, *Libra*, or *Pisces*, ascending with Venus ; the figure of which was a little maid, with her hair spread abroad, clothed in long and white garments, holding a laurel apple, or flowers, in her right hand, in her left a comb : it is said to make men pleasant, jocund, strong, cheerful, and to give beauty.

CHAP. XLI.
OF THE IMAGES OF MERCURY.

FROM the operations of Mercury they made an image of Mercury, Mercury ascending in Gemini ; the form of which was a handsome young man, bearded, having in his left hand a rod, round which a serpent was entwined---in the right he carried a dart ; having his feet winged. They say that this image confers knowledge, eloquence, diligence in merchandise, and gain ; moreover, to obtain peace and concord, and cure fevers. They made another image of Mercury, ascending in Virgo, for good will, wit, and memory ; the form of which was a man sitting upon a chair, or riding on a peacock, having eagle's feet, and on his head a crest, and in his left hand holding a cock of fire.

X 2   CHAP.

CHAP. XLII.

OF THE IMAGES OF THE MOON,

FROM the operations of the Moon they made an image for travellers againſt wearineſs, at the hour of the Moon, the *Moon* aſcending in its exaltation ; the figure of which was a man leaning on a ſtaff, having a bird on his head, and a flouriſhing tree before him. They made another image of the Moon for the increaſe of the fruits of the earth, and againſt poiſons, and infirmities of children, at the hour of the Moon, it aſcending in the firſt face of Cancer ; the figure of which was a woman cornuted, riding on a bull, or a dragon with ſeven heads, or a crab, and ſhe hath in her right hand a dart, in her left a looking glaſs, clothed with white or green, and having on her head two ſerpents with horns twined together, and to each arm a ſerpent twined about, and to each foot one in like manner. And thus much ſpoken concerning the figures of the planets, may ſuffice.

CHAP. XLIII.

OF THE IMAGES OF THE HEAD AND TAIL OF THE DRAGON OF THE MOON.

THEY made, alſo, the image of the head and tail of the Dragon of the Moon, namely, between an ærial and fiery circle, the likeneſs of a ſerpent, with the head of a hawk, tied about them after the manner of the great letter Theta ; they made it when Jupiter, with the head, obtained the mid heaven ; which image they affirm to avail much for the ſucceſs of petitions, and would ſignify by this image a good and fortunate genius, which they would repreſent by this image of the ſerpent ; for the Egyptians and Phœnicians do extol this creature above all others, and ſay it is a divine creature, and hath a divine nature ; for in this is a more acute ſpirit, and a greater fire than in any other, which thing is manifeſt both by his ſwift motion without feet, hands,

or

or any other inſtruments ; and alſo that it often renews its age with his ſkin, and becomes young again ; but they made the image of the tail like as when the Moon was eclipſed in the tail, or ill affeĉted by Saturn or Mars, and they made it to introduce anguiſh, infirmity, and misfortune : we call it an evil genius.

THE TALISMAN OF THE DRAGON's HEAD.

CHAP. XLIV.
OF THE IMAGES OF THE MANSIONS OF THE MOON.

THEY made, alſo, images for every manſion of the Moon as follows :——

In the firſt, for the deſtruĉtion of ſome one, they made, in an iron ring, the image of a black man, in a garment of hair, and girdled round, caſting a ſmall lance with his right hand : they ſealed this in black wax, and perfumed it with liquid ſtorax, and wiſhed ſome evil to come.

In the ſecond, againſt the wrath of the prince, and for reconciliation with him, they ſealed, in white wax and maſtich, the image of a king crowned, and perfumed it with lignum aloes.

In the third, they made an image in a ſilver ring, whoſe table was ſquare ; the figure of which was a woman, well clothed, ſitting in a chair, her right hand being lifted up on her head ; they ſealed it, and perfumed it with muſk, camphire, and calamus aromaticus. They affirmed that this gives happy fortune, and every good thing.

In the fourth, for revenge, ſeparation, enmity, and ill-will, they ſealed, in red wax, the image of a ſoldier ſitting on a horſe, holding a ſerpent in his right hand : they perfumed it with red myrrh and ſtorax

In

In the fifth, for the favour of kings and officers, and good entertainment, they fealed, in filver, the head of a man, and perfumed it with red fanders.

In the fixth, to procure love between two, they fealed, in white wax, two images embracing one another, and perfumed them with lignum aloes and amber.

In the feventh, to obtain every good thing, they fealed, in filver, the image of a man, well clothed, holding up his hands to Heaven, as it were, praying and fupplicating, and perfumed it with good odours.

In the eighth, for victory in war, they made a feal in tin, being an image of an eagle, having the face of a man, and perfumed it with brimftone.

In the ninth, to caufe infirmities, they made a feal of lead, being the image of a man wanting his privy parts, covering his eyes with his hands ; and they perfumed it with rofin of the pine.

In the tenth, to facilitate child bearing, and to cure the fick, they made a feal of gold, being the head of a lion, and perfumed it with amber.

In the eleventh, for fear, reverence, and worfhip, they made a feal of a plate of gold, being the image of a man riding on a lion, holding the ear thereof in his left hand, and in his right holding forth a bracelet of gold ; and they perfumed it with good odours and faffron.

In the twelfth, for the feparation of lovers, they made a feal of black lead, being the image of a dragon fighting with a man ; and they perfumed it with the hairs of a lion, and affafœtida.

In the thirteenth, for the agreement of married people, and for diffolving of all the charms againft copulation, they made a feal of the images of both (of the man in red wax, and the woman in white), and caufed them to embrace one another ; perfuming it with lignum aloes and amber.

In the fourteenth, for divorce and feparation of the man from the woman, they made a feal of red copper, being the image of a dog biting his tail ; and they perfumed it with the hair of a black dog and a black cat.

In the fifteenth, to obtain friendfhip and good will, they made the image of a man fitting, and inditing letters, and perfumed it with frankincenfe and nutmegs.

In

In the fixteenth, for gaining much merchandifing, they made a feal of filver, being the image of a man, fitting on a chair, holding a balance in his hand ; and they perfumed it with well fmelling fpices.

In the feventeenth, againſt thieves and robbers, they fealed with an iron feal the image of an ape, and perfumed it with the hair of an ape.

In the eighteenth, againſt fevers and pains of the belly, they made a feal of copper, being the image of a fnake with his tail above his head ; and they perfumed it with hartſhorn ; and faid this fame feal to put to flight ferpents, and all venomous creatures, from the place where it is buried.

In the nineteenth, for facilitating birth, and provoking the menſtrues, they made a feal of copper, being the image of a woman holding her hands upon her face ; and they perfumed it with liquid ſtorax.

In the twentieth, for hunting, they made a feal of tin, being the image of Sagittary, half a man and half a horfe ; and they perfumed it with the head of a wolf.

In the twenty-firſt, for the deſtruction of fome body, they made the image of a man, with a double countenance before and behind ; and they perfumed it with brimſtone and jet, and put it in a box of brafs, and with it brimſtone and jet, and the hair of him whom they would hurt.

In the twenty-fecond, for the fecurity of runaways, they made a feal of iron, being the image of a man, with wings on his feet, bearing a helmet on his head ; and they perfumed it with *argent vive*.

In the twenty-third, for deſtruction and waſting, they made a feal of iron, being the image of a cat, having a dog's head ; and they perfumed it with dog's hair taken from the head, and buried it in the place where they intended the hurt.

In the twenty-fourth, for multiplying herds of cattle, they took the horn of a ram, bull, or goat, or of that fort of cattle they would increafe, and fealed in it, burning, with an iron feal, the image of a woman giving fuck to her fon ; and they hanged it on the neck of that cattle who was the leader of the flock, or they fealed it in his horn.

In

In the twenty-fifth, for the prefervation of trees and harveft, they fealed, in the wood of a fig tree, the image of a man planting ; and they perfumed it with the flowers of the fig tree, and hung it on the tree.

In the twenty-fixth, for love and favour, they fealed, in white wax and maftich, the figure of a woman wafhing and combing her hair ; and they perfumed it with good odours.

In the twenty-feventh, to deftroy fountains, pits, medicinal waters, and baths, they made, of red earth, the image of a man winged, holding in his hand an empty veffel, and perforated ; and the image being burnt, they put in the veffel affafœtida and liquid ftorax, and they buried it in the pond or fountain which they would deftroy.

In the twenty-eighth, for getting fifh together, they made a feal of copper, being the image of a fifh ; and they perfumed it with the fkin of a fea fifh, and caft it into the water where they would have the fifh gathered.

Moreover, together with the aforefaid images, they wrote down alfo the names of the fpirits, and their charaƈters, and invocated and prayed for thofe things which they pretended to obtain.

CHAP. XLV.

THAT HUMAN IMPRECATIONS NATURALLY IMPRESS THEIR POWERS UPON EXTERNAL THINGS---AND HOW MAN'S MIND, THROUGH A DEGREE OF DEPENDENCIES, ASCENDS INTO THE INTELLIGIBLE WORLD, AND BECOMES LIKE TO THE MORE SUBLIME SPIRITS AND INTELLIGENCES.

THE celeftial fouls fend forth their virtues to the celeftial bodies, which tranfmit them to this fenfible world ; for the virtues of the terrene orb proceed from no other caufe than celeftial. Hence the magician, that will work by them, ufes a cunning invocation of the fuperiors, with myfterious words and a certain kind of ingenious fpeech, drawing the one to the other ; yet by a natural force, through a certain mutual agreement between them, whereby
things

things follow of their own accord, or fometimes are drawn unwillingly. Hence fays Ariſtotle, in his fixth book of his Myſtical Philoſophy, " that when any one, by binding or bewitching, calls upon the Sun or other ſtars, praying them to aſſiſt the work defired, the Sun and other ſtars do not hear his words ; but are moved, after a certain manner, by a certain conjunction and mutual feries, whereby the parts of the world are mutually ſubordinate the one to the other, and have a mutual confent, by reaſon of their great union : as in a man's body, one member is moved by perceiving the motion of another ; and in a harp, one ſtring is moved by the motion of another. So when any one moves any part of the world, other parts are moved by the perceiving of that motion."---The knowledge, therefore, of the dependency of things following one the other, is the foundation of all wonderful operation, which is neceſſarily required to the exerciſing the power of attracting ſuperior virtues. Now the words of men are certain natural things ; and becauſe the parts of the world mutually draw one the other ; therefore a magician invocating by words, works by powers fitted to Nature, by leading ſome by the love of one to the other ; or drawing others, by reaſon of the one following after the other ; or by repelling, by reaſon of the enmity of one to the other, from the contrariety and difference of things, and multitude of virtues ; which, although they are contrary and different, yet perfect one part. Sometimes, alfo, he compels things by way of authority, by the celeſtial virtue, becauſe he is not a ſtranger to the heavens. A man, therefore, if he receives the impreſſion of a ligation, or faſcination, doth not receive it according to the rational ſoul, but ſenſual ; and if he ſuffers in any part, he ſuffers according to the animal part ; for they cannot draw a knowing and intelligent man by reaſon, but by receiving that impreſſion and force by ſenſe ; inaſmuch as the animal ſpirit of man is, by the influence of the celeſtials, and co-operation of the things of the world, affected beyond his former and natural diſpoſition. As the ſon moves the father to labour, although unwilling, to keep and maintain him, although he be wearied ; and the deſire to rule, is moved by anger and other labours to get the dominion ; and the indigency of nature, and fear of poverty, moves a man to defire riches ; and the ornaments and beauty of women, is an incitement to concupifcence ; and the harmony of a wife mufician moves his hearers with various paffions, whereof fome do voluntary follow the confonancy of art, others conform themfelves by gefture, although unwilling, becaufe their fenfe is captivated, their reafon not being intent to thefe things. Hence they fall into errors, who think thofe things to be above nature, or contrary to nature---which indeed are by nature, and according to nature. We muft know, therefore, that evey fuperior moves its next inferior, in its degree and order, not only in bodies, but alfo in fpirits : fo the univerfal foul moves the particular foul ; the rational acts upon the fenfual, and that upon the vegetable ; and every part of the world acts upon another, and every part is apt to be moved by another. And every part of this inferior world fuffers from the heavens, according to their nature and aptitude, as one part of the animal body fuffers for another. And the fuperior intellectual world moves all things below itfelf ; and, after a manner, contains all the fame beings, from the firft to the laft, which are in the inferior world. Celeftial bodies, therefore, move the bodies of the elementary world, compounded, generable, fenfible (from the circumference to the center), by fuperior, perpetual, and fpiritual effences, depending on the primary intellect, which is the acting intellect ; but upon the virtue put in by the word of God ; which word the wife Chaldeans of Babylon call, the Caufe of Caufes ; becaufe from it are produced all beings : the acting intellect, which is the fecond, from it depends ; and that by reafon of the union of this word with the Firft Author, from whom all things being are truly produced : the word, therefore, is the image of God---the acting intellect, the image of the word---the foul is the image of this intellect---and our word is the image of the foul, by which it acts upon natural things naturally, becaufe nature is the work thereof. And every one of thofe perfects his fubfequent : as a father his fon ; and none of the latter exifts without the former ; for they are depending among themfelves by a kind of ordinate dependency---fo that when the latter is corrupted, it is returned into that which was next before it, until it come to the heavens ; then to the univerfal foul ; and, laftly, into the acting intellect, by which all other creatures exift ; and itfelf exifts in the principal author, which is the creating word of God, to which, at length, all things are returned.

returned. Our foul, therefore, if it will work any wonderful thing in thefe inferiors, muft have refpect to their beginning, that it may be ftrengthened and illuftrated by that, and receive power of acting through each degree, from the very firft Author. Therefore we muft be more diligent in contemplating the fouls of the ftars---then their bodies, and the fuper-celeftial and intellectual world---then the celeftial, corporeal, becaufe that is more noble ; although, alfo, this be excellent, and the way to that, and without which medium the influence of the fuperior cannot be attained to. As for example : the Sun is the king of ftars, moft full of light ; but receives it from the intelligible world, above all other ftars, becaufe the foul thereof is more capable of intelligible fplendour. Wherefore he that defires to attract the influence of the Sun, muft contemplate upon the Sun ; not only by the fpeculation of the exterior light, but alfo of the interior. And no man can do this, unlefs he return to the foul of the Sun, and become like to it, and comprehend the intelligible light thereof with an intellectual fight, as the fenfible light with the corporeal eye ; for this man fhall be filled with the light thereof, and the light whereof, which is an under type impreffed by the fupernal orb, it receives into itfelf ; with the illuftration whereof his intellect being endowed, and truly like to it, and being affifted by it, fhall at length attain to that fupreme brightnefs, and to all forms that partake thereof ; and when he hath received the light of the fupreme degree, then his foul fhall come to perfection, and be made like to fpirits of the Sun, and fhall attain to the virtues and illuftrations of the fupernatural virtue, and fhall enjoy the power of them, if he has obtained faith in the Firft Author. In the firft place, therefore, we muft implore affiftance from the Firft Author ; and praying, not only with mouth, but a religious gefture and fupplicant foul, alfo abundantly, inceffantly, and fincerely, that he would enlighten our mind, and remove darknefs, growing upon our fouls by reafon of our bodies.

CHAP.

CHAP. XLVI.

THE CONCLUSION OF THE CONSTELLATORY PRACTICE, OR TALISMANIC MAGIC; IN WHICH
IS INCLUDED THE KEY OF ALL THAT HAS BEEN WRITTEN UPON THIS SUBJECT; SHEW-
ING THE PRACTICE OF IMAGES, &c. BY WAY OF EXAMPLE, AND LIKEWISE THE NECES-
SARY OBSERVATIONS OF THE CELESTIALS, TOWARDS THE PERFECTION OF TALISMANICAL
OPERATIONS.

WE will now shew thee the observations of celestial bodies, which are required for the practice of these things, which are briefly as follow :----

To make any one fortunate, we make an image at that time in which the
significator of life, the giver of life, or *Hylech, the signs and planets,*
are fortunate: let the ascendant and mid-heaven, and the lords thereof be fortunate ; and also the place of the Sun and Moon ; part of fortune and lord of
conjunction or prevention, made before their nativity, by depressing the malignant planets, *i. e.* taking the times when they are depressed. But if we
would make an image to procure misery, we must do contrary to this ; and
those which we before placed fortunate, we must now make unfortunate, by
taking the malignant stars when they rule. And the same means we must take
to make any place, region, city, or house unfortunate. But if you would
make any one unfortunate who hath injured you, let there be an image made
under the ascension of that man whom thou wouldst make unfortunate ; and
thou shalt take, when unfortunate, the lord of the house of his life, the lord of
the ascendant and the Moon, the lord of the house of the Moon, the lord of the
house of the lord ascending, and the tenth house and the lord thereof. Now,
for the building, success, or fitting of any place, place fortunes in the ascendant
thereof ; and in the first and tenth, and second and eighth house, thou shalt
make the lord of the ascendant, and the lord of the house of the Moon, fortunate. But to chase away certain animals (from any place) that are noxious
to thee, that they may not generate or abide there, make an image under the
ascension of that animal which thou wouldst chase away or destroy, and after
the likeness thereof ; for instance, now, suppose thou wouldst wish to chase away
scorpions from any place : let an image of a scorpion be made, the sign
                                                                    Scorpio

Scorpio afcending with the Moon; then thou fhalt make unfortunate the afcendant, and the lord thereof, and the lord of the houfe of *Mars;* and thou fhalt make unfortunate the lord of the afcendant in the eighth houfe; and let them be joined with an afpect malignant, as oppofite or fquare, and write upon the image the name of the afcendant, and of the lord thereof, and the Moon, the lord of the day and hour; and let there be a pit made in the middle of the place from which thou wouldft drive them, and put into it fome earth taken out of the four corners of the fame place, then bury the image there, with the head downwards, faying---" This is the burying of the *Scorpions,* that they may be forced to leave, and come no more into this place."---And fo do by the reft.

Now for gain, make an image under the afcendant of that man to whom thou wouldft appoint the gain; and thou fhalt make the lord of the fecond houfe, which is the houfe of fubftance, to be joined with the lord of the afcendant, in a trine or fextile afpect, and let there be a reception amongft them; thou fhalt make fortunate the eleventh, and the lord thereof, and the eighth; and, if thou canft, put part of fortune in the afcendant or fecond; and let the image be buried in that place, or from that place, to which thou wouldft appoint the gain or fortune. Likewife, for agreement or love, let be made an image in the day of Jupiter, under the afcendant of the nativity of him whom you would wifh to be beloved; make fortunate the afcendant and the tenth, and hide the evil from the afcendant; and you muft have the lords of the tenth, and planets of the eleventh, fortunate, joined to the lord of the afcendant, from the trine or fextile, with reception; then proceed to make another image, for him whom thou wouldft ftir up to love; whether it be a friend, or female, or brother, or relation, or companion of him whom thou wouldft have favoured or beloved, if fo, make an image under the afcenfion of the eleventh houfe from the afcendant of the firft image; but if the party be a wife, or a hufband, let it be made under the afcenfion of the feventh; if a brother, fifter, or coufin, under the afcenfion of the third houfe; if a mother, of the tenth, and fo on :---now let the fignificator of the afcendant of the fecond image be joined to the fignificator of the afcendant of the firft, and let there be be between them a reception, and let the reſt be fortunate, as in the firſt image ; afterwards join both the images together in a mutual embrace, or put the face of the ſecond to the back of the firſt, and let them be wrapped up in ſilk, and caſt away or ſpoiled.

Alſo, for the ſuccefs of petitions, and obtaining of a thing denied, or taken, or poſſeſſed by another, make an image under the aſcendant of him who petitions for the thing ; and cauſe the lord of the ſecond houſe to be joined with the lord of the aſcendant, from a trine or ſextile aſpeĉt, and let there be a reception betwixt them ; and, if it can be ſo, let the lord of the ſecond be in the obeying ſigns, and the lord of aſcendant in the ruling : make fortunate the aſcendant and the lord thereof ; and beware that the lord of the aſcendant be not retrograde, or combuſt, or cadent, or in the houſe of oppoſition, *i. e.* in the ſeventh from his own houſe ; let him not be hindered by the malignant planets, but let him be ſtrong and in an angle ; thou ſhalt make fortunate the aſcendant, and the lord of the ſecond, and the Moon : and make another image for him that is petitioned to, and begin it under the aſcendant belonging to him : as if he is a king, or prince, &c. begin it under the aſcendant of the tenth houſe from the aſcendant of the firſt image ; if a father, under the fourth ; if a ſon, under the fifth, and ſo of the like ; then put the ſignificator of the ſecond image, joined with the lord of the aſcendant of the firſt image from a trine or ſextile, and let him receive it ; and put them both ſtrong and fortunate, without any hinderance ; make all evil fall from them ; thou ſhalt make fortunate the tenth and the fourth, if thou canſt, or any of them ; and when the ſecond image ſhall be perfeĉt, join it with the firſt, face to face, and wrap them in clean linen, and bury them in the middle of his houſe who is the petitioner, under a fortunate ſignificator, *the fortune being ſtrong ;* and let the face of the firſt image be towards the north, or rather towards that place where the thing petitioned for doth remain ; or, if it happens that the petitioner goes forward to obtain the thing deſired or petitioned for, let him carry the ſaid images with him. Thus we have given, in a few examples, the key of all Taliſmanical operations whatſoever, by which wonderful effeĉts may be wrought either by images, by rings, by glaſſes, by ſeals, by tables, or any

other

Magick Seals or Talismans.

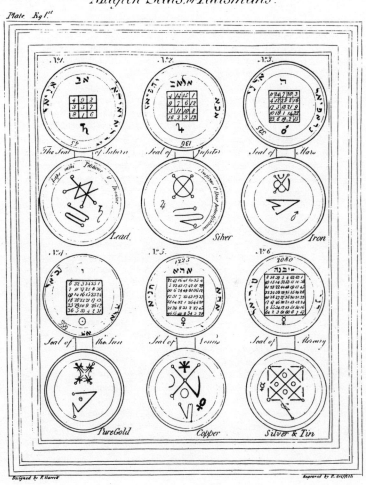

The Seal of Saturn.

Seal of Jupiter.

Seal of Mars.

Lead.

Silver.

Iron.

Seal of the Sun.

Seal of Venus.

Seal of Mercury.

Pure Gold.

Copper.

Silver & Tin.

Designed by P. Harrell.

Engraved by R. Griffith.

Pub. by Lackington Allen & Co.

other magical inftruments whatfoever ; but as thefe have their chief grounds
in the true knowledge of the effects of the planets, and the rifing of the conftellations, we recommend an earneft attention to that part of Aftrology * which
teaches of the power, influences, and effects of the celeftial bodies amongft
themfelves generally ; likewife, we would recommend the artift to be expert
in the afpects, motions, declinations, rifings, &c. &c. of the feven planets, and
perfectly to underftand their natures, either mixed or fimple ; alfo, to be ready
and correct in the erecting of a figure, at any time, to fhew the true pofition
of the heavens ; there being fo great a fympathy between the celeftials and
ourfelves ; and to obferve all the other rules which we have plentifully recited :
and, without doubt, the induftrious ftudent fhall receive the fatisfaction of
bringing his operations and experiments to effect that which he ardently defires.
With which, wifhing all fuccefs to the contemplator of the creature and the
Creator, we will here clofe up this Second Part of our Work, and the conclufion of our Book of Talifmanical Magic.

* Thofe who would be perfect in the neceffary knowledge of Aftrology, ought to ftudy from Coley, his
book, called Clavis Aftrologiæ Elimata, or his Key new filed—Salmon's Soul of Aftrology—Lilley's, or
Partridge's, Vade Mecum—or Middleton's Aftrology.

THE END OF THE FIRST BOOK.

Knight and Compton, Typ., Middle Street,
Cloth Fair.

THE MAGUS;

OR,

CELESTIAL INTELLIGENCER.

BOOK II. PART I.

CONTAINING

MAGNETISM,

AND

CABALISTICAL MAGIC;

DISCOVERING

THE SECRET MYSTERIES

OF

CELESTIAL MAGIC.

With the Art of calculating by the divine Names of God; shewing the Rule, Order, and Government of
ANGELS, INTELLIGENCES, AND BLESSED SPIRITS, HOLY TABLES AND
SEALS, TABLES OF THE CABALA, &c.

Likewise treating of Ceremonial Magic, Invocation of Spirits, Consecrations, Circles, &c.
Also of Dreams, Phophecy, Miracles, &c.

By FRANCIS BARRETT,
STUDENT OF CHEMISTRY, NATURAL AND OCCULT PHILOSOPHY, THE CABALA, &c.

TO WHICH IS ADDED,

A Translation of the Works of TRITEMIUS of SPANHEIM, *viz.*
His Book of Secret Things, and of Spirits.

BOOK II.   B

W. Blackader, Printer, Took's Court, Chancery Lane,

THE MAGUS.

CONTAINING

MAGNETISM,

AND

CABALISTICAL MAGIC.

TO WHICH IS ADDED

A TREATISE

ON

PROPHECY, PROPHETIC DREAMS AND INSPIRATION.

BOOK II. PART I.

MAGNETISM.

IN our following Treatise of Magnetifm we have collected and arranged in order fome valuable and fecret things out of the writings of that moft learned chemift and philofopher Paracelfus, who was the ornament of Germany and the age he lived in. Likewife we have extracted the very marrow of the fcience of Magnetifm out of the copious and elaborate works of that moft celebrated philofopher (by fire) Van Helmont, who, together with Paracelfus, induftrioufly promulgated all kinds of magnetic and fympathetic cures, which, through the drowfinefs, ignorance, unbelief, and obftinacy of

B 2

the

the prefent age, have been fo much and fo totally neglected and condemned ; yet, however impudent in their affertions, and bigotted to their own falfe opinions, fome of our modern philofophers may be, yet we have feen two or three individuals, who, by dint of perfeverance, have proved the truth and poffibility of Magnetifm, by repeated and public experiments. Indeed the ingenious invention of the Magnetic Tractors prove at once that fcience fhould never be impeded by public flander or mifreprefentation of facts that have proved to be of general utility. And we do not doubt but that we fhall be able to fhew, by the theory and practice delivered in the fequel, that many excellent cures may be performed by a due confideration and attentive obfervance of the principles upon which fympathy, antipathy, magnetic attraction, &c. are founded; and which will be fully illuftrated in the following compendium :

We fhall haften to explain the firft principles of Magnetifm, by examining the magnetic or attractive power.

CHAP. I.

* THE MAGNETIC, OR ATTRACTIVE POWER OR FACULTY.

AS concerning an action locally at a diftance, wines do fuggeft a demonftration unto us : for, every kind of wine, although it be bred out of co-bordering provinces, and likewife more timely bloffoming elfewhere, yet it is troubled while our country vine flowereth ; neither doth fuch a difturbance ceafe as long as the flower fhall not fall off from our vine ; which thing furely happens, either from a common motive-caufe of the vine and wine, or from a particular difpofition of the vine, the which indeed troubles the wine, and doth fhake it up and down with a confufed tempeft : or likewife, becaufe the wine itfelf doth thus trouble itfelf of its own free accord,

* Van Helmont.

by

by reason of the flowers of the vine : of both the which latter, if there be a fore-touched conformity, consent, co-grieving, or congratulation ; at least, that cannot but be done by an action at a distance : to wit, if the wine be troubled in a cellar under ground, whereunto no vine perhaps is near for some miles, neither is there any discourse of the air under the earth, with the flower of the absent vine ; but, if they will accuse a common cause for such an effect, they must either run back to the stars, which cannot be controuled by our pleasures and liberties of boldness ; or, I say, we return to a confession of an action at a distance : to wit, that some one and the same, and as yet unknown spirit, the mover, doth govern the absent wine, and the vine which is at a far distance, and makes them to talk and suffer together. But, as to what concerns the power of the stars, I am unwilling, as neither dare I, according to my own liberty, to extend the forces, powers, or bounds of the stars beyond or besides the authority of the sacred text, which saith (it being pronounced from a divine testimony) that the stars shall be unto us for signs, seasons, days, and years : by which rule, a power is never attributed to the stars, that wine bred in a foreign soil, and brought unto us from far, doth disturb, move, or render itself confused : for, the vine had at some time received a power of encreasing and multiplying itself before the stars were born : and vegetables were before the stars, and the imagined influx of these : wherefore also, they cannot be things conjoined in essence, one whereof could consist without the other. Yea, the vine in some places flowereth more timely ; and, in rainy, or the more cold years, our vine flowereth more slowly, whose flower and stages of flourishing the wine doth, notwithstanding, imitate ; and so neither doth it respect the stars, that it should disturb itself at their beck.

In the next place, neither doth the wine hearken unto the flourishing or blossoming of any kind of capers, but of the wine alone : and therefore we must not flee unto an universal cause, the general or universal ruling air of worldly successive change ; to wit, we may rather run back unto impossibilities and absurdities, than unto the most near commerces of resemblance and unity, although hitherto unpassable by the schools.

Moreover,

Moreover, that thing doth as yet far more manifeſtly appear in ale or beer: when, in times paſt, our anceſtors had ſeen that of barley, after whatſoever manner it was boiled, nothing but an empty ptiſana or barley-broth, or alſo a pulp was cooked; they meditated, that the barley firſt ought to bud (which then they called malt) and next, they nakedly boiled their ales, imitating wines: wherein, firſt of all, ſome remarkable things do meet in one; to wit, there is ſtirred up in barley, a vegetable bud, the which when the barley is dried, doth afterwards die, and loſeth the hope of growing, and ſo much the more by its changing into meal, and afterwards by an after-boiling, it deſpairs of a growing virtue; yet theſe things nothing hindering, it retains the winey and intoxicating ſpirit of aqua vitæ, the which notwithſtanding it doth not yet actually poſſeſs: but at length, in number of days, it attaineth it by virtue of a ferment: to wit, in the one only boſom of one grain one only ſpirit is made famous with diverſe powers, and one power is gelded, another being left: which thing indeed, doth as yet more wonderfully ſhine forth; when as the ale or beer of malt diſturbs itſelf while the barley flowereth, no otherwiſe than as wine is elſewhere wont to do: and ſo a power at a far abſent diſtance is from hence plain to be ſeen: for truly there are cities from whom pleaſant meadows do expel the growing of barley for many miles; and by ſo much the more powerfully do ales prove their agreement with the abſent flowering barley; in as much as the gelding of their power hath withdrawn the hopes of budding and increaſing: and at length the aqua vitæ being detained and ſhut up within the ale, hogſhead, and priſon of the cellar, cannot with the ſafety of the ale or beer wandering for ſome leagues unto the flowering ear of barley, that thereby, as a ſtormy returner, it may trouble the remaining ale with much confuſion. Certainly there is a far more quiet paſſage for a magnetical or attractive agreement among ſome agents at a far diſtance from each other, than there is to dream an aqua vitæ wandering out of the ale of a cellar, unto the flowering barley, and from thence to return unto the former receptacles of its pen-caſe, and ale: But the ſign imprinted by the appetite of a woman great with child, on her young, doth fitly, and alike clearly confirm a magnetiſm or attractive faculty and its operation at a diſtance: to wit, let there be a woman great with child,
                                                                                which

which defires another cherry, let her but touch her forehead or any other place with her finger ; without doubt, the young is figned in its forehead with the image of the cherry, which afterwards doth every year wax green, white, yellow, and at length looks red, according to the tenor of the trees : and it much more wonderfully expreffes the fame fucceffive alteration of maturities in Spain than in Germany : and fo hereby an *action at a diftance* is not only confirmed, but alfo a conformity or agreement of the effences of the cherry tree, in its wooden and flefhly trunk ; a confanguinity or near affinity of a *being* impreffed upon the part by an inftantaneous imagination, and by a fucceffive courfe of the years of its kernel ; furely the more learned ought not to impute thofe things unto evil fpirits, which, through their own weaknefs, they are ignorant of ; for thefe things do on all fides occur in nature, the which, through our flendernefs, we are not able to unfold ; for to refer whatfoever gifts of God are in nature (becaufe our dull capacity does not comprehend the fame rightly) to the devil, fhews both ignorance and rafhnefs, efpecially when, as all demonftration of *caufes* from a former thing or caufe is banifhed from us, and efpecially from Ariftotle, who was ignorant of all nature, and deprived of the good gifts which defcends from the Father of Lights ; unto whom be all honour and glory.

━━━━━━━━━

Note. We may, by the aforefaid chapter, fee the wonderful working power of the attractive or univerfal fpirit, which can by no other means be fo clearly demonftrated as by the fympathies in natural things, which are inherent throughout all nature ; and, upon this principle of fympathy and antipathy, we fay is founded that fpiritual power which tends to things and objects remote one from the other, *i. e.* a magnetic attraction, which does actually exift, as we fhall clearly prove by experiment, where we fully fhew the action and paffion that is between natural fpirits, by which means wonderful effects are produced, which have ignorantly been attributed to divers fuperftitions, as *Sorcery, Inchantment, Nigromancy,* or *the Black Art,* &c.

CHAP.

CHAP. II.

OF SYMPATHETIC MEDICINES.

IN the year 1639, a little book came forth, whose title was, ‘ The Sympathetical Powder of Edricius Mohynus, of Eburo,’ whereby wounds are cured without application of the medicine unto the part afflicted, and without superstition ; it being sifted by the sieve of the reasons of Galen and Aristotle ; wherein it is Aristotetically, sufficiently, proved, whatsoever the title of it promises ; but it hath neglected the *directive faculty*, or *virtue*, which may bring the virtues of the sympathetical powder, received in the bloody towel or napkin, unto the distant wound.

Truly, from a wound, the venal blood, or corrupt pus, or sanies, from an ulcer, being received in the towel, do receive, indeed, a balsam from a sanative or healing being ; I say, from the power of the vitriol, a medicinal power connected and limited in the aforesaid mean ; but the virtues of the balsam received are directed unto the wounded object, not indeed by an influential virtue of the stars, and much less do they fly forth of their own accord unto the object at a distance : therefore the ideas of him that applieth the sympathetical remedy are connected in the mean, and are made directresses of the balsam unto the object of his desire : even as we have above also minded by injections concerning ideas of the desire. Mohyns supposed that the power of sympathy depends upon the stars, because it is an imitator of influences : but I draw it out of a much nearer subject : to wit, out of directing ideas, begotten by their mother Charity, or a desire of goodwill : for, from hence does that sympathetic powder operate more successfully, being applied by the hand of one than another : therefore I have always observed the best process where the remedy is instituted by a desire of charity ; but, that it doth succeed, with small success, if the operator be a careless or drunken person : and, from hence, I have more esteemed the stars of

the

the mind, in fympathetical remedies, than the ftars of heaven : but that images, being conceived, are brought unto an object at a diftance, a pregnant woman is an example of, becaufe fhe is fhe who prefently transfers all the ideas of her conception on her young, which dependeth no otherwife on the mother than from a communion of univerfal nourifhment. Truly, feeing fuch a direction of defire is plainly natural, it is no wonder that the evil fpirit doth require the ideas of the defires of his imps to be annexed unto a mean offered by him. Indeed, the ideas of the defire are after the manner of the influences of heaven caft into a proper object how locally re- mote foever; that is, they are directed by the defire, efpecially pointing out an object for itfelf, even as the fight of the bafilifk, or touch of the torpedo, is reflected on their willed object; for I have already fhewn in its place, that the devil doth not attribute fo much as any thing in the directions of things injected; but that he hath need of a free, directing, and operative power or faculty. But I will not difgrace fympathetical remedies becaufe the devil operates fomething about things injected into the body: for what have fympathetical remedies in common ? Although Satan doth co-operate in injections by wicked natural means required from his bond flaves ; for every thing fhall be judged guilty, or good, from its ends and intents : and it is fufficient that fympathetical remedies do agree with things injected in *natural means*, or medicines.

C H A P. III.

OF THE MAGNETIC OR SYMPATHETIC UNGUENT, THE POWDER OF SYMPATHY, ARMARY UN-
GUENT, CURING OF WOUNDS, ECSTASIES, WITCHCRAFT, MUMMIES, &c.

WE fhall now fhow fome remarkable operations that are effected by magnetifm, and founded upon natural fympathy and antipathy, likewife how by thefe means fome extraordinary cures may be performed.

Book II.   C   The

The goodnefs of the Creator every where extended, created every thing for the ufe of ungrateful man; neither did he admit any of the theologifts, or divines, as affiftants in council, how many or how great virtues he fhould infufe into things natural. But there are thofe who venture to meafure the wonderful works of God by their own fharpened and refined wit, whereby they deny God to have given fuch virtue to things; as though man (a worm) was able, by his narrow and limited capacity, to comprehend Omnifcience; he therefore meafures the minds of all men by his own, who think that cannot be done, which they cannot underftand. *They* therefore can only develope the myfteries of nature, who being verfed in the art of Cabala, Fire, and Magic, examined the properties of things, and draw, from darknefs into light, the lurking powers of *Man, Animals, Vegetables, Minerals,* and *Stones*; and, feparating the crudities, dregs, poifons, heterogenities, that are the thorns implanted in virgin nature from the curfe. For an obferver of nature fees daily fhe doth *diftil, fublime, calcine, ferment, diffolve, coagulate, fix,* &c. therefore we who are the minifters of nature do feparate, &c. finding out the caufes and effects of every phænomena fhe produces.

Now, as magnetifm is ordained for the ufe of man, and for the curing of the various diforders incident to human nature, we fhall firft touch upon the grand fubject of magnetifm, known to poffefs wonderful properties, and which are not only evident to every eye, but fhew us fufficient grounds for our admitting the poffibility and reality of magnetifm in general.

The loadftone poffeffes an eminent medicinal faculty againft many violent and implacable diforders. Helmont fays, that the back of the loadftone, as it repulfes iron, fo alfo it removes gout, fwellings, rheum, &c. that is of the nature or quality of iron. The iron-attracting faculty, if it be joined to the mummy of a woman, and the back of the loadftone be put within her thigh, and the belly of the loadftone on her loins, it fafely prevents a mifcarriage, already threatened; but the belly of the loadftone applied within the thigh and the back to her loins, it doth wonderfully facilitate her delivery.

Likewife the wearing the loadftone eafes and prevents the cramp, and fuch like diforders and pains.

Uldericus

Uldericus Balk, a dominican friar, publifhed a book at Frankfort in the year 1611, concerning the lamp of life; in which we fhall find (taken from Paracelfus) the true magnetical cure of many difeafes, *viz.* the dropfy, gout, jaundice, &c. For if thou fhalt enclofe the warm blood of the fick in the fhell and white of an egg, which is expofed to a nourifhing warmth, and this blood, being mixed with a piece of flefh, thou fhalt give to a hungry dog, the diforder departs from thee into the dog; no otherwife than the leprofy of Naaman paffed over into Gehazi through the execration of the prophet.

If women, weaning their infants, fhall milk out their milk upon hot burning coals, the breaft foon dries.

If any one happens to commit nuifance at thy door, and thou wilt prevent that beaftly trick in future, take the poker red-hot, and put it into the excrement, and, by magnetifm, his pofteriors fhall become much fcorched and inflamed.

Make a fmall table of the lighteft, whiteft, and bafeft kind of lead; and at one end put a piece of amber, and, three fpans from it, lay a piece of green vitriol; this vitriol will foon lofe its colour and acid: both which effects are found in the preparation of amber. The root of the Caroline thiftle being plucked up when full of juice and virtue, and tempered with the mummy of a man, will exhauft the powers and natural ftrength out of a man, on whofe fhadow thou fhalt ftand, into thyfelf.

CHAP. IV.

OF THE ARMARY UNGUENT, OR WEAPON SALVE, &c.

THE principal ingredient in this confection, is the mofs of a dead man's fkull, which Van Helmont calls the excrefcencies or fuperfluities of the ftars. Now the mofs growing on the fkull of a dead man, feeing it has received its feed from the heavens, but its increafe from the mummial marrow of the fkull of man, or tower of the microcofm, has obtained excellent aftral and magnetic powers beyond the common condition of vegetables, although herbs, as they are herbs, want not their own magnetifm.

Now, the magnetifm of this unguent draws out that ftrange difpofition from the wound (which otherwife, by a difunion of the parts that held together, and by which, I fay, ftrange difpofition and foreign quality is produced) from whence it flips, not being overburdened or opprefled by any accident, fuddenly grow together ; and this is effected by the armary unguent, or weapon falve. From this it appears that the unguent, or weapon falve, its property is to heal fuddenly and perfectly without pain, cofts, peril, or lofs of ftrength ; hence it is manifeft that the magnetical virtue is from God.

It is now feafonable to difcover the immediate caufe of magnetifm in the unguent.

Firft of all, by the confent of myftical divines, we divide man into the external and internal man, affigning to both the powers of a certain mind, or intelligence : for fo there doth a will belong to flefh and blood, which may not be either the will of man or the will of God ; and the heavenly Father alfo reveals fome things unto the more inward man, and fome things flefh and blood reveals, that is, the outward and fenfitive, or animal man. For, how could the fervice of idols, envy, &c. be rightly numbered among the works of the flefh, feeing they confift only in the imagination, if the flefh had not alfo its own imagination and elective will ?

Furthermore, that there are miraculous ecftafies belonging to the more inward man, is beyond difpute. That there are alfo ecftafies in the animal man, by reason of an intense, or heightend imagination, is, without doubt. Martin del Ris, an elder of the society of Jesus, in his Magical Disquisitions or Enquiries, makes mention of a certain young man in the city Insulis, that was transported with so violent a desire of seeing his mother, that through the same intense desire, as if being rapt up by an ecstasy, he saw her perfectly, although many miles absent from thence; and, returning again to himself, being mindful of all that he had seen, gave many true signs of his true presence with his mother.

Now that desire arose from the more outward man, *viz.* from blood and sense, or flesh, is certain; for, otherwise, the soul being once dislodged, or loosened from the bonds of the body, cannot, except by miracle, be reunited to it; there is therefore in the blood a certain ecstatical or transporting power, which, if at any time shall be excited or stirred up by an ardent desire and most strong imagination, it is able to conduct the spirit of the more outward man even to some absent and far distant object, but then that power lies hid in the more outward man, as it were, in *potentia*, or by way of possibility; neither is it brought into act, unless it be roused up by the imagination, inflamed and agitated by a most fervent and violent desire.

C H A P V.

OF THE IMAGINATIVE POWER AND THE MAGNETISM OF THE NATURAL SPIRITS, MUMMIAL ATTRACTION, SYMPATHIES OF ASTRAL SPIRITS, WITH THEIR BODIES, UPON WHICH THE WHOLE ART OF NECROMANCY IS FOUNDED.

MOREOVER, when as the blood is after some sort corrupted, then indeed all the powers thereof which, without a foregoing excitation of the imagination, were before in possibility, are of their own accord, drawn forth into action; for, through corruption of the grain, the seminal virtue, otherwise drowsy, and barren, breaks forth into act; because, that seeing the essences of things, and
their

their vital spirits, know not how to putrify by the dissolution of the inferior harmony, they sprung up as surviving afresh. For, from thence it is that every occult property, the compact of their bodies being by foregoing digestion, (which we call putrifaction) now dissolved, comes forth free to hand, dispatched, and manifest for action.

Therefore when a wound, through the entrance of air, hath admitted of an adverse quality, from whence the blood forthwith swells with heat or rage in its lips, and otherwise becomes mattery, it happens, that the blood in the wound just made, by reason of the said foreign quality, doth now enter into the beginning of some kind of corruption (which blood being also then received on the weapon or splinter thereof, is besmeared with the magnetic ungent) the which entrance of corruption, mediating the ecstatical power lurking potentially in the blood, is brought forth into action; which power, because it is an exiled returner unto its own body, by reason of the hidden ecstasy; hence that blood bears an individual respect unto the blood of its whole body. Then indeed the magnetic or attractive faculty is busied in operating in the unguent, and through the mediation of the ecstatical power (for so I call it for want of an etymology) sucks out the hurtful quality from the lips of the wound, and at length, through the mummial, balsamical, and attractive virtue, attained in the unguent, the magnetism is perfected.

So thou hast now the positive reason of the natural magnetism in the unguent, drawn from natural magic, whereunto the light of truth assents; saying, " where the treasure is there is the heart also."

For if the treasure be in heaven, then the heart, that is, the spirit of the internal man is in God, who is the paradise, who alone is eternal life.

But if the treasure be fixed or laid up in frail and mortal things, then also the heart and spirit of the external man is in fading things; neither is there any cause of bringing in a mystical sense, by taking not the spirit, but the cogitation and naked desire, for the heart; for that would contain a frivolous thing, that wheresoever a man should place his treasure in his thought or cogitation, there his cogitation would be.

Also truth itself doth not interpret the present text mystically, and also by an example adjoined, shews a local and real presence of the eagles with the dead

carcass,

carcafs, fo alfo that the fpirit of the inward man is locally in-the kingdom of God in us, which is God himfelf; and that the heart or fpirit of the animal or outward fenfitive man is locally about its treafure.

What wonder is it, that the aftral fpirits of carnal or animal men fhould, as yet, after their funerals, fhew themfelves as in a bravery, wandering about their buried treafure, whereunto the whole of Necromancy (or art of divination by the calling of fpirits) of the antients hath enflaved itfelf?

I fay, therefore, that the internal man is an animal or living creature, making ufe of the reafon and will of blood: but, in the mean time, not barely an animal, but moreover the image of God.

Logicians therefore may fee how defectively they define a man from the power of rational difcourfe. But of thefe things more elfewhere.

I will therefore adjoin the magnetifm of eagles to carcaffes; for neither are flying fowls endowed with fuch an acute fmelling, that they can, with a mutual confent, go from Italy into Africa unto carcaffes.

For neither is an odour fo largely and widely fpread; for the ample latitude of the interpofed fea hinders it, and alfo a certain elementary property of confuming it; nor is there any ground that thou fhouldeft think thefe birds do perceive the dead carcaffes at fo far a diftance, with there fight, efpecially if thofe birds fhall lie fouthwards behind a mountain.

But what need is there to enforce the magnetifm of fowls by many arguments, fince God himfelf, who is the beginning and end of philofophy, doth exprefsly determine the fame procefs to be of the heart and treafure, with thefe birds and the carcafs, and fo interchangeably between thefe and them?

For if the eagles were led to their food, the carcaffes, with the fame appetite whereby four-footed beafts are brought on to their paftures, certainly he had faid, in one word, that living creatures flock to their food even as the heart of man to his treafure; which would contain a falfehood: for neither doth the heart of man proceed unto its treafure, that he may be filled therewith, as living creatures do to their meat; and therefore the comparifon of the heart of man and of the eagle lies not in the end for which they tend or incline to a defire, but in the manner of tendency; namely that they are allured and carried on by magnetifm, really and locally.

Therefore

Therefore the spirit and will of the blood fetched out of the wound, having intruded itself into the ointment by the weapon being anointed therewith, do tend towards their treasure, that is, the rest of the blood as yet enjoying the life of the more inward man : but he saith by a peculiar testimony, that the eagle is drawn to the carcass, because she is called thereunto by an implanted and mummial spirit of the carcass, but not by the odour of the putrifying body : for indeed that animal, in assimilating, appropritates to himself only this mummial spirit : for from thence it is said of the eagle, in a peculiar manner, "my youth shall be renewed as the eagle's."

For truly the renewing of her youth proceeds from an essential extraction of the mummial spirit being well refined by a certain singular digestion proper to that fowl, and not from a bare eating of the flesh of the carcass ; otherwise dogs also and pies would be renewed, which is false.

Thou wilt say, that it is a reason far-fetched in behalf of magnetism ; but what wilt thou then infer hereupon ? If that which thou confesseth to be far remote for thy capacity of understanding, that shall also with thee be accounted to be fetched from far. Truly the book of Genesis avoucheth, that in the blood of all living creatures doth their soul exist.

For there are in the blood certain vital powers *, the which, as if they were soulified or enlivened, do demand revenge from Heaven, yea, and judicial punishment from earthly judges on the murderer ; which powers, seeing they cannot be denied to inhabit naturally in the blood, I see not why they can

* This singular property of the blood, which Helmont calls *Vital Powers*, is no less wonderful than true, having been myself a witness of this experiment while in South Wales. It was tried upon a body that was maliciously murdered, through occasion of a quarrel over-night at an alehouse. The fellow who was suspected of the murder appeared the next day in public seemingly unconcerned. The Coroner's Jury sat upon the body within twenty-four hours after this notable murder was committed ; when the suspected was suddenly taken into custody, and conveyed away to the same public-house where the inquisition was taken. After some debate, one Dr. Jones desired the suspected to be brought into the room ; which done, he desired the villain to lay his left hand under the wound, which was a deep gash on the neck, and another on the breast ; the villain plainly confessed his guilt by his trepidation ; but as soon as he lightly laid his finger on the body, the blood immediately ran, about six or seven drops, to the admiration of all present. If any one doubts the truth of this narrative, however learned and profound he may think himself, let him call personally upon me, and I will give him such reference, and that truly respectable and fair, as shall convince him of the fact. FRANCIS BARRETT.

reject

reject the magnetifm of the blood, as accounting it among the ridiculous works of Satan.

This I will fay more, to wit, that thofe who walk in their fleep, do, by no other guide than the fpirit of the blood, that is, of the outward man, walk up and down, perform bufinefs, climb walls, and manage things that are otherwife impoffible to thofe that are awake. I fay, by a magical virtue, natural to the more outward man; that Saint Ambrofe, although he was for diftant in his body, yet was vifibly prefent at the funeral folemnities of Saint Martin; yet was he fpiritually prefent at thofe folemnities, in the vifible fpirit of the external man, and no otherwife: for, inafmuch as in that ecftafy which is of the more internal man, many of the faints have feen many and abfent things. This is done without time and place, through the fuperior powers of the foul being collected in unity, and by an intellectual vifion, but not by a vifible prefence; otherwife the foul is not feparated from the body, but in good earneft, or for altogether; neither is it re-connected thereunto, which re-connexion, notwithftanding, is otherwife natural or familiar to the fpirit of the more outward man.

It is not fufficient in fo great a paradox, to have once, or by one fingle reafon, touched at the matter; it is to be further propagated, and we muft explain how a magnetical attraction happens alfo between inanimate things, by a certain perceivance or feeling; not indeed animal or fenfitive, but natural.

Which thing, that it may be the more ferioufly done, it behoves us firft to fhew what Satan can, of his own power, contribute to, and after what manner he can co-operate in the merely wicked and impious actions of witches: for, from thence it will appear unto what caufe every effect may be attributed.

In the next place, what that fpiritual power may be which tends to a far remote object; or what may be the action, paffion, and fkirmifhing between natural fpirits, or what may be the fuperiority of man as to other inferior creatures; and, by confequence, why indeed our unguent, being compounded of human mummies, do thoroughly cure horfes alfo. We will explain the matter in the following chapter.

CHAP. VI.

OF WITCHCRAFT.

LET a witch therefore be granted, who can ſtrongly torment an abſent man by an image of wax, by imprecation or curſing, by enchantment, or alſo by a foregoing touch alone, (for here we ſpeak nothing of Sorceries, becauſe they are thoſe which kill only by poiſon, inaſmuch as every common apothe-cary can imitate thoſe things) that this act is diabolical, no man doubts: however, it is profitable to diſcern how much Satan and how much the witch can contribute hereunto.

The Firſt Suppoſition.

Firſt of all, thou ſhalt take notice, that Satan is the ſworn and irreconcileable enemy of man, and to be ſo accounted by all, unleſs any one had rather have him to be his friend; and therefore he moſt readily procures whatſoever miſ-chief he is able to cauſe or wiſh unto us, and that without doubt and neglect.

The Second Suppoſition.

And then although he be an enemy to witches themſelves, foraſmuch as he is alſo a moſt malicious enemy to all mankind in general; yet, in regard they are his bond-ſlaves, and thoſe of his kingdom, he never, unleſs againſt his will, betrays them, or diſcovers them to judges, &c.

From the former ſuppoſition I conclude, that if Satan were able of himſelf to kill a man who is guilty of deadly ſin, he would never delay it; but he doth not kill him, therefore he cannot.

Notwithſtanding, the witch doth oftentimes kill; hence alſo ſhe can kill the ſame man, no otherwiſe than as a privy murderer at the liberty of his own will ſlays any one with a ſword.

There

There is therefore a certain power of the witch in this action, which belongs not to Satan, and consequently Satan is not the principal efficient and executor of that murder; for otherwise if he were the executioner thereof, he would in nowise stand in need of the witch as his assistant; but he alone had soon taken the greatest part of men out of the way.

Surely most miserable were the condition of mortals who should be subject to such a tyrant, and stand liable to his commands; we have too faithful a God, than that he should subject the work of his own hands to the arbitrary dominion of Satan.

Therefore in this act, there is a certain power plainly proper and natural to the witch which belongs not to Satan.

Moreover, of what nature, extent, and quality that power may be, we must more exactly sift out.

In the first place, it is manifest that it is no corporeal strength of the male sex; for neither doth there concur any strong touching of the extreme parts of the body, and witches are for the most part feeble, impotent, and malicious old women, therefore there must needs be some other power, far superior to a corporeal attempt, yet natural to man.

This power therefore was to be seated in that part wherein we most nearly resemble the image of God; and although all things do also, after some sort, represent that venerable image, yet because man doth most elegantly, properly, and nearly do that, therefore the image of God in man doth far outshine, bear rule over, and command the images of God in all other creatures; for, peradventure, by this prerogative, all things are put under his feet.

Wherefore if God act, *per nutum*, or by a beck, namely by his word, so ought man to act some things only by his beck or will, if he ought to be called his true image: for neither is that new, is that troublesome, is that proper to God alone: for Satan, the most vile abject of creatures, doth also locally move bodies *per nutum*, or by his beck alone, seeing he hath not extremities or corporeal organs, whereby to touch, move, or also to snatch a new body to himself.

That

That privilege therefore ought no lefs to belong to the inward man, as he is a fpirit, if he ought to reprefent the image of God, and that indeed not an idle one ; if we call this faculty magical, and thou being badly inftructed, art terrified at this word, thou mayeft, for me, call it a fpiritual ftrength or effica- cy: for, truly, we are nothing folicitous about names. I always, as imme- diately as I can, caft an eye upon the thing itfelf.

That magical power, therefore, is in the inward man, whether thou, by this etymology, or true word, underftandeft the foul or the vital fpirit thereof, it is now indifferent to us ; fince there is a certain proportion of the internal man to- wards the external in all things, glowing or growing after its own manner, which is an appropriated difpofition, and proportioned property.

Wherefore the power or faculty muft needs be difperfed throughout the whole man ; in the foul, indeed, more vigorous, but in the flefh and blood far more remifs.

C H A P. VII.

OF THE VITAL SPIRIT, &c.

THE vital fpirit in the flefh and blood performs the office of the foul; that is, it is the fame fpirit in the outward man, which, in the feed, forms the whole figure, that magnificent ftructure and perfect delineation of man, and which hath known the ends of things to be done, becaufe it contains them ; and the which, as prefident, accompanies the new framed young, even unto the period of its life ; and the which, although it depart therewith, fome fmacks or fmall quantity, at leaft, thereof remains in a carcafs flain by violence, being as it were moft exactly co-fermented with the fame. But, from a dead carcafs that was extinct of its own accord, and from nature failing, as well the implanted as inflowing fpirit paffed forth at once.

For

For which reason, physicians divide this spirit into the implanted or mummial, and inflowing or acquired spirit, which departs; to wit, with the former life and this influxing spirit they afterwards subdivide into the natural, vital, and animal spirit; but, we likewise, do here comprehend them all at once in one single word.

The soul therefore being wholly a spirit could never move or stir up the vital spirit, (being indeed corporeal,) much less flesh and bones, unless a certain natural power, yet magical and spiritual, did descend from the soul into the spirit and body.

After what sort, I pray, could the corporeal spirit obey the commands of the soul, unless there should be a command from her for moving of the spirit, and afterwards the body?

But against this magical motive faculty thou will forthwith object, that that power is limited within her composed body, and her own natural inn: therefore although we call this soul a magicianness, yet it shall be only a wresting and abuse of the name; for truly the true and superstitious magic draws not its foundation from the soul; seeing this same soul is not able to move, alter, or exite any thing out of its own body.

I answer, that this power, and that natural magic of the soul which she exerciseth not of herself, by virtue of the image of God, doth now lie hid as obscure in man, and as it were lie asleep since the fall or corruption of Adam, and stands in need of stirring up; all which particulars we shall anon in their proper place prove; which same power, how drowsy and as it were drunk soever, it otherwise remains daily in us, yet it is sufficient to perform its offices in its own body.

CHAP.

C H A P. VIII.

OF THE MAGICAL POWER, &c.

THEREFORE the knowledge and power magical, and that faculty in man which acteth only *per nutum*, sleeps since the knowledge of the apple was eaten ; and as long as this knowledge (which is of the flesh and blood, gross and material, belonging to the external man and darkness) flourishes, the more noble magical power is lying dormant.

But because in sleep this outward or sensual knowledge is sometimes dormant, hence it is that our dreams are sometimes prophetical, and God himself is therefore nearer unto man in dreams, through that effect, *viz.* when the more inward magic of the soul being uninterrupted by the flesh, diffuses itself on every side into the understanding ; even as when it sinks itself into the inferior powers thereof it safely leads those who walk in their sleep by moving or conducting them, whither those that were awake could not surmount or climb.

Therefore we establish this point, *viz.* that there is inherent in the soul a certain magical virtue given her by God, naturally proper and belonging to her, in asmuch as we are his image and engravement ; and in this respect she acts also in a peculiar manner, *i. e.* spiritually on an object at a distance, and that more powerfully than by any corporeal assistance ; for seeing the soul is the principal part of the body, therefore all action belonging to her is spiritual, magical, and of the greatest validity.

Which power man is able, by the Art of the Cabala, to excite in himself at his own pleasure, and these, as we have before said, are called Adepts ; who are governed by the Spirit of God.

Thus we have endeavoured to shew that man predominates over all other creatures that are corporeal, and that by his magical faculty he is able to subdue the magical virtues of all other things ; which predominance of man, or the

soul's

soul's natural magic, some have ignorantly attributed solely to *verses*, *charms*, *signs*, *characters*, &c. by which hierarchy or holy dominion inherent in man, those effects, whatever they may be, are wrought, which some (who but too corporeally philosophize) have attributed to the dominion of Satan.

High and sacred is the force of the microcosmical spirit, which, as is evident in pregnant women, stamps upon the young the image and properties of a thing desired, as we have before instanced in a cherry, which, without the trunk of a tree, brings forth a true cherry, that is flesh and blood, enobled with the properties and power of the more inward or real cherry, by the conception of the imagination alone; from whence are two necessary consequences.

First, that all the spirits, and as it were the essences of all things, lie hid in us, and are born and brought forth only by the working, power, and phantasy of the microcosm.

The second is, that the soul, in conceiving, generates a certain idea of the thing conceived; the which, as it before lay hid unknown, like fire in a flint, so by the stirring up of the phantasy there is produced a certain real idea, which is not a naked quality, but something like a substance, hanging in suspence between a body and a spirit, that is the soul.

That middle being is so spiritual, that it is not plainly exempted from a corporeal condition, since the actions of the soul are limited on the body, and the inferior orders of faculties depending upon it, nor yet so corporeal that it may be inclosed by dimensions, the which we have also related to be only proper to a seminal being. This ideal entity, therefore, when it falls out of the invisible and intellectual world of the microcosm, it puts on a body, and then it is first inclosed by the limitation of place and numbers.

The object of the understanding is in itself a naked and pure essence, not an accident, by the consent of practical, that is, mystical divines; therefore this Proteus or transferable essence, the understanding doth, as it were, put on and clothe itself, with this conceived essence.

But because every body, whether external or internal, hath its making in its own proper image, the understanding knows or discerns not, the will loves and wills not, the memory recollects not, but by images or likenesses: the understanding

ſtanding therefore puts on this ſame image of its objeČt ; and becauſe the ſoul is the pure ſimple form of the body, which turns itſelf about to every member, therefore the aČting underſtanding cannot have two images at once, but firſt one and then the other. He, who is wholly the life, created all things and hath ſaid, nothing is to be expeČted as dead out of his hand. Likewiſe nothing can come to our view wherein himſelf is not clearly apparent or preſent ; for it is ſaid, "the ſpirit of the Lord hath filled the whole globe of the earth :" and, again, "that he containeth or comprehendeth all things," therefore there is nothing in being, no creature but what poſſeſſes a certain degree of divine fire and life, yet lying dormant or unexcited; till ſtirred up by the art, power, and operation of man.

CHAP. IX.

OF THE EXCITING OR STIRRING UP THE MAGICAL VIRTUE.

EVERY magical virtue therefore ſtands in need of an excitement, by which a certain ſpiritual vapour is ſtirred up, by reaſon whereof the phantaſy which profoundly ſleeps is awakened, and there begins an aČtion of the corporeal ſpirit, as a medium, which is that of Magnetiſm, and is excited by a foregoing touch.

There is a magical virtue, being as it were abſtraČted from the body, which is wrought by the ſtirring up of the power of the ſoul, from whence there are made moſt potent procreations, and moſt famous impreſſions, and ſtrong effeČts, ſo that nature is on every ſide a magicianneſs, and aČts by her own phantaſy ; and by how much the more ſpiritual her phantaſy is, ſo much the more powerful it is, therefore the denomination of magic is truly proportionable or concordant.

Now

Now the higheft fort of magic is that which is ftirred up from an intellectual conception, and indeed that of the inward man is only to be excited by the Holy Spirit, and by his gift the Cabala ; but that of the external man is ftirred up by a ftrong imagination, by a daily and heightened fpeculation, and, in witches, by the devil.

But the magical virtue of the exhaled fpiritual vapour, or fubtil fpirits fent from the body, which before lay *in potentia*, or by way of poffibility only, is either excited by a more ftrong imagination, the magician making ufe of the blood as a medium, and eftablifhing his kindled entity thereon, or by the afcending phantafy of the weapon falve, the exciterefs of the property lying in the blood ; elfe by a foregoing appointment or difpofition of the blood unto corruption, *viz.* whereby the elements are difpofed unto a feparation, and the effences (which cannot putrify) and the effential phantafies, which lay hid in the properties come forth into action.

The phantafy therefore, of any fubject whatfoever has obtained a ftrong appetite to the fpirit of another thing, for the moving of fome certain thing in place, for the attracting, repelling, or expulfion thereof ; and there and not elfewhere we acknowledge magnetifm as the natural magical endowment of that thing firmly planted in it by God.

There is therefore a certain formal property feparated from fympathetical and abftrufe qualities ; becaufe the motive phantafy of thefe qualities do not directly fly unto a local motion, but only to an alterative motion of the object. Now it is fufficient that (if a man happens to receive many wounds in his body) blood be had only from one of thefe wounds, and from this one the reft are cured alfo, becaufe that blood keeps a concordant harmony with the fpirit of the whole, and draws forth from the fame the offenfive quality communicated, not only to the lips of the wound, but to the whole man, for from one wound only the whole man is liable to grow feverifh.

Therefore the outchafed blood being received on the weapon is introduced into the magnetic unguent.

For then the phantafy of the blood, being otherwife as yet drowfy and flow to action, being ftirred up by the virtue of the magnetic unguent, and there finding the balfamic virtue of it, defires the quality induced into it, to be beftowed on itfelf throughout, and from thence by a fpiritual magnetifm to draw out all the ftrange tincture of the wound, which, feeing it cannot fitly enough effect by it-felf, it implores the aid of the *mofs*, *blood*, *fat*, and *mummy*, which are conjoined together into fuch a balfam, which not but by its own phantafy becomes alfo medicinal, magnetical, and is alfo a tractor of all the ftrange qualities out of the body, whofe frefh blood, abounding with fpirit, is carried unto it, whether it fhall be that of a man or any other living creature. The phantafy therefore is a returner, or reducible and ecftatical, from part of the blood that is frefh and newly brought unto the unguent; but the magnetic attraction began in the blood is perfected by the medicinal virtue of the unguent; not that the unguent draws the infirmity of the wound unto itfelf, but it alters the blood newly brought unto it, in its fpirit, and makes it medicinal, and ftirs up the power thereof: from thence it contracts a certain medicinal virtue, which returns unto its whole body to correct the fpirit of the blood throughout the whole man. Now, to manifeft a great myftery, *viz.* to fhew that in man there is placed a great efficacy whereby he may be able only by his beck, (as we before men-tioned) nod or phantafy, to act out of himfelf, and to imprint a virtue, a certain influence which afterwards perfeveres, or conftantly fubfifts by itfelf, and acts upon objects at a very great diftance; by which only myftery, thofe things which we have fpoken (relative to ideal entity conveyed in a fpiritual fewel, and departing far from home to execute its offices, concerning the magnetifm of all things begotten in the imagination of man, as in that which is proper to every thing, and alfo concerning the magical fuperiority of men over all other bodies,) will plainly and confpicuoufly appear.

CHAP.

C H A P. X.

OF THE MAGICAL VIRTUE OF THE SOUL, AND THE MEDIUMS BY WHICH IT ACTS.

SOMETHING more we will add, before we difmifs the prefent fubject, which is that if a nail, dart, knife, or fword, or any other iron inftrument be thruft into the heart of a horfe, it will bind and withhold the fpirit of a witch, and conjoin it with the mummial fpirit of the horfe, whereby they may be burnt in the fire together, and by that the witch is tormented, as by a fting or burning, by which means fhe may be known fo that fhe who is offenfive to God, and deftructive to mortal men, may be taken away from fociety according to the law of God "thou fhall not fuffer a witch to live ;" for if the work be limited to any outward object, that work the magical foul never attempts without a medium or mean : therefore it makes ufe of the nail, or fword, or knife, or any other thing as aforefaid.

Now this being proved, that man hath a power of acting, *per nutum,* or by his nod, or of moving any object remotely placed ; it has alfo been fufficiently confirmed by the fame natural example, that this efficacy was alfo given unto man by God.

And as every magical faculty lies dormant, and has need of excitement, or ftirring up ; which is always true, if the object whereon it is to act is not nearly difpofed, if its internal phantafy doth not wholly confirm to the impreffion of the agent, or alfo if the patient be equal in ftrength, or fuperior to the agent therein.

But on the contrary, where the object is plainly and nearly difpofed, as fteel is, for the receiving of magnetifm, then the patient without much ftirring up, the alone phantafy of the more outward man being drawn out to the work and bound up to any fuitable mean, yields to the magnetifm.

Therefore we repeat, the magician muft always make ufe of a medium ; for then the words or forms of facraments do always operate, becaufe from

the

the work performed. But the reason why exorcisms, conjurations, charms, incantations, &c. do sometimes fail of their desired effect, is because the un-excited mind, or spirit of the exorcist, renders the words dull or inef-fectual.

Therefore no man can be a happy or successful magician, but him who knows how to stir up the magical virtue of his soul, or can do it practically without science.

And there can be no nearer medium of magnetism, than human blood with human blood.

And no sympathetic remedies, magnetical or attractive, but from the idea or phantasy of the operator impressing upon it a virtue and efficacy from the excited power in his own soul.

And now to bring our Magnetic Treatise to a total conclusion, we have to say, that whoever, through ignorance or obstinacy, will say there is no validity or reason, or reality in the science of magnetism, proves himself unworthy the sacred name of philosopher, because he condemns what he knows nothing at all about.

For those who will give themselves the leisure to examine the truth of those things which we have taught, will not find their expectation deceived, therefore will not condemn.

But whoever should be so superstitious as to attribute a natural effect so created by God, and bestowed on the creature, unto the power and craft of the devil, he filches the honour due to the Omnipotent Creator, and re-proachfully applies the same unto Satan; the which (under favour) will be found to be express idolatry and blasphemy.

" There are three" (as says the Scripture) " who bear record in heaven; the Father, the Word, and the Holy Spirit; and these three are only one."

There are three that bear record on earth; the *blood*, the *spirit*, and the *water*; and these three are only *one*.

We therefore, who have the like humanity, contain blood and spirit of a co-like unity; and the action of the blood is merely spiritual. Therefore, in
Genesis.

Genesis, it is not called by the etymology of *blood,* but is made remarkable by the name of a *red spirit.*

Therefore, let those who would attain knowledge in these things, and be perfect in what we have set before them, constantly meditate and desire that the First Cause and Archetype of all things would graciously and mercifully illuminate their minds; without which, they grope but in darkness and uncertainty, and are subject to the delusions of impure spirits and devils, who are only to be put to flight by putting on the whole armour of God, in whom we all *live, move, breathe,* and have our being.

 END OF MAGNETISM.

THE CABALA;

OR, THE

SECRET MYSTERIES

OF

CEREMONIAL MAGIC

ILLUSTRATED.

SHEWING

THE ART OF CALCULATING BY DIVINE NAMES;

The Rule, Order, and Government of

ANGELS, INTELLIGENCES, AND BLESSED SPIRITS;

Holy Seals, Pentacles, Tables of the Cabala, Divine Numbers, Characters and Letters;
Of Miracles, Prophecy, Dreams, &c. &c. &c.

———————

Embellished and beautified with a vast Number of

RARE FIGURES, PENTACLES, CHARACTERS, &c. &c. &c.

Used in the

CABALISTIC ART.

———

By FRANCIS BARRETT,

STUDENT OF CHEMISTRY, NATURAL AND OCCULT PHILOSOPHY, THE CABALA, &c.

CABALISTICAL MAGIC.

CHAP. I.

OF THE CABALA, &c.

WE shall now turn our pen to the explaining of the high and mysterious secrets of the Cabala, by which only we can know the truth; and likewise how to prepare our mind and spirit for the contemplation of the greatest and best part of magic, which we call intellectual and divine, because it chiefly takes God and the good spirits for its object; and as the cabalistic art opens many and the chiefest mysteries and secrets of ceremonial magic.

But in respect of explaining or publishing those few secrets in the Cabala, which are amongst a few wise men, and communicated by word of mouth only, I hope the student will pardon me if I pass over these in silence, because we are not permitted to divulge some certain things: but this we shall do; we will open all those secrets which are necessary to be known; and by the close reading of which, you shall find out, of your own head, to be both profitable and delightful.

Therefore, all we solicit is, that those who perceive those secrets should keep them together as secrets, and not expose or babble them to the unworthy; but reveal them only to faithful, discreet, and chosen friends. And we would caution you in this beginning, that every magical experiment flies from the public, seeking to be hid, is strengthened and confirmed by silence, but is destroyed by publication; never does any complete effect follow after: likewise all the virtue of thy works will suffer detriment when poured into weak, prating, and incredulous minds; therefore, if thou would be a magi-

F   cian,

cian, and gain fruit from this art, to be secret, and to manifest to none, either thy *work*, or *place*, or *time*, nor thy *desire* or *will*, except it be to a master, or partner, or companion, who should likewise be faithful, discreet, silent, and dignified by nature and education; seeing that even the prating of a companion, his unbelief, doubting, questioning, and, lastly, unworthiness, hinders and disturbs the effect in every operation.

C H A P. II.

WHAT DIGNITY AND PREPARATION IS ESSENTIALLY NECESSARY TO HIM WHO WOULD
BECOME A TRUE MAGICIAN.

IT is fit that we who endeavour to attain so great a height should first study two things : *viz.* First, how we should leave vain and carnal affections, frail sense, and material passions ; Secondly, by what ways and means we may ascend to an intellect pure, and joined with the powers of the celestials, without which we shall never happily ascend to the scrutiny of secret things, and to the power of working wonderful effects, *&c.* Now, if thou art a man perfect in thy understanding, and constantly meditating upon what we have in this book written, and without doubting, believeth, thou shalt be able, by praying, consecrating, deprecating, invocating, *&c.* to attract spiritual and celestial gifts, and to imprint them on whatever things thou shalt please ; and by it to vivify every magical work.

C H A P.

C H A P.   III.

THAT THE KNOWLEDGE OF THE TRUE GOD IS NECESSARY FOR A MAGICIAN.

SEEING that the being and operation of all things depend on the Moſt High God, Creator of all things, and from thence on the other divine powers, to whom alſo is granted a power of faſhioning and creating, not principally indeed, but inſtrumentally, by virtue of the Firſt Great Creator, (for the beginning of every thing is the firſt cauſe; but what is produced by the ſecond cauſe is much more produced by the firſt, which is the producer of the ſecond cauſe, which therefore we call ſecondaries.) It is neceſſary, therefore, that every magician ſhould know that very God, which is the firſt cauſe and creator of all things, and likewiſe the other divine powers, (which we call the ſecond cauſes,) and not to be ignorant of them, and likewiſe what holy rites, ceremonies, &c. are conformable to them; but, above all, we are to worſhip in ſpirit and truth, and place our firm dependance upon that one only God who is the author and promoter of all good things, the Father of all, moſt bountiful and wiſe; the ſacred light of juſtice, and the abſolute and ſole perfection of all nature, and the contriver and wiſdom thereof.

C H A P.   IV.

OF DIVINE EMANATIONS, AND TEN SEPHIROTHS, AND TEN MOST SACRED NAMES OF GOD WHICH RULE THEM, AND THE INTERPRETATION OF THEM.

GOD himſelf, although he is trinity in perſons, yet he is but one only ſimple eſſence; yet we doubt not but that there are in him many divine powers, which emanate or flow from him.

F 2   The

The Cabalifts moft learned in divine things have received the ten principal names of God, as certain divine powers, or, as it were, members of God ; which, by ten numerations, which we call Sephiroth, as it were veftiments, inftruments, or exemplars of the Archetype, have an influence upon all created things, from the higheft to the loweft ; yet by a certain order: for firft and immediately they have influence upon the nine orders of angels and quire of bleffed fouls, and by them into the celeftial fpheres, planets and men ; by the which Sephiroth every thing receiveth power and virtue.

The firft of thefe is the name *Eheia*, the name of the divine effence ; his numeration is called Cether, which is interpreted a crown or diadem, and fignifies the moft fimple effence of the divinity ; and it is called that which the eye feeth not ; and is attributed to God the Father, and hath its influence by the order of feraphims, or Hajoth Hakados, that is, creatures of holinefs ; and then by the *primum mobile*, it beftows the gift of being upon all things, and filleth the whole univerfe, both through the circumference and center ; whofe particular intelligence is called Merattron, that is, the prince of faces, whofe duty it is to bring others to the face of the Prince ; and by him the Lord fpake to Mofes.

The fecond name is Jod, or Tetragrammaton joined with Jod ; his numeration is Hochma, that is, wifdom, and fignifies the divinity full of ideas, and the Firft Begotten ; and is attributed to the Son, and has its influence by the order of cherubins, or that the Hebrews call Orphanim, *i. e.* forms or wheels ; and from thence into the ftarry heavens, where he frames fo many figures as he hath ideas in himfelf, and diftinguifhes the very chaos of the creatures, by a particular intelligence called Raziel, who was the ruler of *Adam*.

The third name is called Tetragrammaton Elohim ; his numeration is named *Prina*, *viz.* providence and underftanding ; and fignifies remiffnefs, quietnefs, the jubilee, penetential converfion, a great trumpet, redemption of the world, and the life of the world to come : it is attributed to the Holy Spirit, and hath his influence by the order of thrones, or which the Hebrews call *Abalim*, that is, great angels, mighty and ftrong ; and from thence, by the fphere of *Saturn*, adminifters form to the unfettled matter, whofe particular

cular intelligence is Zaphkiel, the ruler of Noah, and another intelligence named Jophiel, the ruler of Sem ; and these are the three supreme and highest numerations, as it were, seats of the divine persons, by whose command all things are made ; but are executed by the other seven, which are therefore called numerations framing.

The fourth name is El, whose numeration is *Hesed*, which signifies clemency or goodness ; likewise grace, mercy, piety, mgnificence, the scepter, and right-hand ; and hath its influx by the order of dominations, which the Hebrews call *Hasmalim* ; and so through the sphere of Jupiter fashions the images of bodies, bestowing clemency and pacifying justice on all : his particular intelligence is *Zadkiel*, the ruler of Abraham.

The fifth name is Elohim Gibor, that is, the mighty God, punishing the sins of the wicked ; and his numeration is called Gebusach, which is to say, power, gravity, fortitude, security, judgment, punishing by slaughter and war ; and it is applied to the tribunal of God, the girdle, the sword, the left hand of God ; it is also called Pachad, which is fear ; and hath his influence through the order of powers, which the Hebrews call Seraphim, and from thence through the sphere of Mars, to whom belongs fortitude, war, and affliction. It draweth forth the elements ; and his particular intelligence is *Camael*, the ruler of Samson.

The sixth name is *Eloha*, or a name of four letters joined with *Vaudahat* ; his numeration is Tiphereth, that is, apparel, beauty, glory, pleasure, and signifies the tree of life, and hath his influence through the order of virtues, which the Hebrews call *Malachim*, that is, angels, into the sphere of the sun, giving brightness and life to it, and from thence producing metals ; his particular intelligence is *Raphael*, who was the ruler of *Isaac*, and *Toby* the younger, and the angel *Peliel*, the Ruler of Jacob.

The seventh name is *Tetragrammaton Sabaoth*, or *Adonai Sabaoth*, that is, the God of Hosts ; and his numeration is *Nezah*, that is, truimph and victory : the right column is applied to it, and it signifies the justice and eternity of a revenging God ; it hath its influence through the orders of principalities, whom the Hebrews call *Elohim*, i. e. Gods, into the sphere of *Venus*, gives zeal and

love

love of righteousnefs, and produces vegetables; his intelligence is *Haniel*, and the angel *Cerviel*, the ruler of David.

The eighth is called alfo Elohim Sabaoth, which is likewife the God of Hofts, not of war and juftice, but of piety and agreement, for this name fignifies both, and precedeth his army; the numeration of this is called *Hod*, which is, praife, confeffion, honour and fame; the left column is attributed to it; it hath his influence through the order of the archangels, which the Hebrews call Ben Elohim, that is, the fons of God, into the fphere of Mercury, and gives elegancy, and confonancy of fpeech, and produces living creatures; his intelligence is Michael, who was the ruler of Solomon.

The ninth name is called *Sadai*, that is, Omnipotent, fatisfying all, and *Elhai*, which is the Living God; his numeration is Jefod, that is, foundation, and fignifies a good underftanding, a covenant, redemption and reft; and hath his influence through the order of angels, whom the Hebrews name Cherubim, into the fphere of the moon caufing the increafe and decreafe of all things, and provideth for the genii and keepers of men, and diftributeth them; his intelligence is *Gabriel*, who was the keeper of *Jofeph*, *Jofhua*, and *Daniel*.

The tenth name is *Adonai Melech*, that is, lord and king; his numeration is *Malchuth*, that is, kingdom and empire, and fignifies a church, the temple of God, and a gate; and hath his influence through the order of *Animaftic*, *viz.* of *bleffed fouls*, which, by the Hebrews, is called Iffim, that is, nobles, lords, and princes; they are inferior to the *hierarchies*, and have their influences on the fons of men, and give knowledge and the wonderful underftanding of things, alfo induftry and prophecy; and the foul of the Meffiah is prefident amongft them, or the intelligence Merattron, which is called the firft creature, or the foul of the world, who was the ruler of Mofes.

CHAP.

CHAP V.

OF THE POWER AND VIRTUE OF THE DIVINE NAMES.

GOD himself, though he be one only effence, yet hath divers names, which expound not his divers effences or deities; but certain properties flowing from him; by which names he pours down upon us, and all his creatures, many benefits; ten of thofe names we have above defcribed. The Cabalifts, from a certain text of Exodus, derive feventy-two names, both of the angels and of God, which they call the name of feventy-two letters and Schemhamphores, that is, the expofitory. From thefe therefore, befides thofe which we have reckoned up before, is the name of the divine effence, *Eheia*, אהיה, which Plato tranflates ὤν, from hence they call God τοὅν, others ὤων, that is, the Being. *Hu*, הוא, is another name revealed to Efay, fignifying the abyfs of the godhead, which the Greeks tranflate ταυτὸν, the Latins, himfelf the fame. *Efch*, אש, is another name received from Mofes, which foundeth fire, and is the name of God; *Na*, נא, is to be invocated in perturbations and troubles. There is alfo the name Ja, יה, and the name Elion, עליון, and the name *Macom*, מוקם, the name *Caphu*, כפכ, the name *Innon*, יינון, and the name *Emeth*, אמה, which is interpreted truth, and is the feal of God; and there are two other names, *Zur*, צור, and *Aben*, אבן, both of thefe fignify a folid work, and one of them expreffeth the Father with the Son; and many names we have placed in the fcale of numbers; and many names of God and the angels, are extracted out of the Holy Scriptures by our Cabala, and the Notarian and Gimetrian arts, where many words retracted by certain of their letters, make up one name; or one name difperfed by each of its letters, fignifies or renders more. Sometimes they are gathered from the heads of words, as the the name *Agla*, אגלא, from this verfe of the Holy Scripture, *viz.* אתהגיכר לעולמסארכי, that is, the Mighty God for ever. In like manner the name *Iaia*, איא, from this verfe, *viz.* הוהאלהינו יהוהאהר, that is, God our God is one God; in like manner the name *Java*, אוא, from

this

this verfe, יהי אור ויהי‎אור, that is, let there be light and there was light: in like manner the name *Ararita*, אראריתא, from this verfe, אהרותו ראש יהורו תמורהזואהר אהר ראש, that is, one principal of his unity, one beginning of his individuality, his viciffitude is one thing; and this name *Hacaba*, הקבא, is extracted from this verfe, והקרושכברהוא, the holy and bleffed One; in like manner this name *Jefu*, ישו, is found in the heads of thefe two verfes, *viz*, יביאשלוחילו, that is, until the Meffiah fhall come; and the other verfe, ינון שמות, that is, his name abides till the end. Thus alfo is the name *Amen*, אמנ, extracted from this verfe, ארנימלר נאמן, that is, *the Lord is the faithful King*. Sometimes thefe names are extracted from the ends of words, as the fame Amen from this verfe, לאב והרשעים, that is, *the wicked not fo*; but the letters are tranfpofed: fo, by the final letters of this verfe, לימח שמזמח, that is, *to me what?* or *what is his name?* is found the name Tetragrammaton: in all thefe a letter is put for a word, and a letter extracted from a word, either from the beginning, end, or where you pleafe; and fometimes thefe names are extracted from all the letters, one by one, even as thofe feven-two names of God are extracted from thofe three verfes of Exodus, beginning from thefe three words, יוסע ידאו יש, the firft and the laft verfes being written from the right to the left; but the middle contrariwife, from the left to the right, as we fhall fhew hereafter; and fo fometimes a word is extracted from a word, or a name from a name, by the tranfpofition of letters, as *Meffia*, משיח, from *Ifmah*, ישמח, and *Michael* from *Malachi*, מלאבי; but fometimes by changing the alphabet, which the Cabalifts call *Ziruph*, צירוף; fo from the name *Tetragrammaton*, יהוה, are drawn forth מאפץ, *Maz-Paz*, כוו, *Kuzu*. Sometimes, by reafon of the equality of the numbers, names are changed, as *Merattron*, מטטרון, *pro Sadai*, שדי, for both of them make three hundred and fourteen; fo *Jiai*, ייאי, and *El*, אל, are equal in number, for both make thirty-one; and thefe are the hidden fecrets, concerning which it is moft difficult to judge, or to deliver a perfect fcience; neither can they be underftood or taught in any other language but the Hebrew. Therefore, thefe facred words have not their power in magical operations from themfelves, as they are words, but from the occult divine powers working by them in the mind of thofe who by faith adhere to them.

We

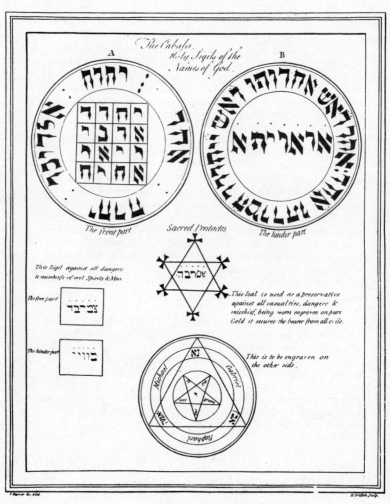

The Cabala.
Holy Sigils of the
Names of God.

A

B

The front part

The hinder part

Sacred Pentacles

This Sigil against all dangers
& mischiefs of evil Spirits & Men

The fore part

The hinder part

This Seal is used as a preservative
against all casualties, dangers &
mischief, being worn engraven on pure
Gold it secures the bearer from all evils.

This is to be engraven on
the other side.

Michael

Gabriel

Raphael

Pub by Lackington Allen & Co.

We will here deliver unto thee a sacred seal, efficacious against any disease of man, or any griefs whatsoever, in whose fore-side are the four-squared names of God, so subordinate to one another in a square, that, from the highest to the lowest, those most holy names or seals of the godhead do arise, whose intention is inscribed in the circumference; but on the backside is inscribed the *seven-lettered name Araritha*, and his interpretation is written about, *viz.* the verse from which it is extracted, even as you may see in the annexed plate, where A represents the former part, B the hinder; but all this must be done in most pure gold, or virgin parchment, pure, clean, and unspotted; also with ink made of the smoke of consecrated wax-lights, or incense and holy water. The operator must be purified and cleansed, and have an infallible hope, a constant faith, and have his mind lifted up to the Most High God, if he would surely obtain this divine power.

Now, against the depredations of evil spirits and men, and what dangers soever, either of journies, waters, enemies, arms, &c. in the same manner as is above said, these characters on the one side מזב, and these on the other עבזמ, which are the beginnings and ends of the five first verses of *Genesis*, and representation of the creation of the world; and, by this ligature, they say that a man shall be free from all mischiefs, if that he firmly believes in God, the Creator of all things.

Now these being done on a small plate of gold, as before described, (will be found to have the effect above mentioned); the figure of which you may likewise see in the annexed plate, fig. C and D, where C shows the former part, and B the hinder.

Now let no one distrust or wonder, that sacred words and divine names applied outwardly, can effect wonderful things, seeing, by them, the Almighty created the heavens and the earth; for there is no name of God amongst us (according to Moses the Egyptian) which is not taken from his works, besides the name Tetragrammaton, which is holy, signifying the substance of the Creator in a pure signification.

CHAP. VI.

OF INTELLIGENCES AND SPIRITS, AND OF THE THREE-FOLD KIND OF THEM, AND OF THEIR
DIFFERENT NAMES, AND OF INFERNAL AND SUBTERRANEAL SPIRITS.

NOW, confequently, we muft difcourfe of intelligences, fpirits, and angels. An intelligence is an intelligible fubftance, free from all grofs and
putrifying mafs of a body, immortal, infenfible, affifting all, having influence over all; and the nature of all intelligences, fpirits, and angels is the
fame. But I call angels here, not thofe whom we ufually call devils, but
fpirits fo called from the propriety of the word, as it were, knowing, underftanding, and wife. But of thefe, according to the tradition of magicians,
there are three kinds; the firft of which we call fuper-celeftial, and minds
altogether feparated from a body, and, as it were, intellectual fpheres worfhipping one only God, as it were, their moft firm and ftable unity or centre.
Wherefore they even call them Gods, by reafon of a certain participation of the
Divinity, for they are always full of God. Thefe are only about God, and
rule not the bodies of the world, neither are they fitted for the government of
inferior things, but infufe the light received from God unto the inferior
orders, and diftribute every one's duty to all of them. The celeftial intelligences do next follow thefe in the fecond order, which they call worldy angels, *viz.* being appointed, befides the divine worfhip for the fpheres of the
world, and for the government of every heaven and ftar; whence they are
divided into fo many orders as there are heavens in the world, and as there
are ftars in the heavens. And they called thefe *Saturnine*, who rule the heaven
of *Saturn*, and *Saturn* himfelf; others *Jovial*, who rule the heaven of
Jupiter, and *Jupiter* himfelf; and in like manner they name different angels, as well for the name as the virtue of the other ftars; and becaufe the
old aftrologers maintained fifty-five motions, therefore they invented fo many
intelligences or angels. They placed alfo in the ftarry heaven angels who
                                                                        might

Fallen Angels. Plate 1.

A Deceiver

Apollyon

Vessels of Iniquity

Belial

Designed by P. Barrett.   Engraved by B. Griffith.

might rule the figns, triplicities, decans, quinaries, degrees and ftars ; for although the fchool of Peripatetics affign one only intelligence to each of the
orbs of the ftars, yet feeing every ftar and fmall part of the heaven hath its
proper and different power and influence, it is neceffary alfo that it have its
ruling intelligence which may confer power and operate ; therefore they have
eftablifhed twelve princes of the angels, who rule the twelve figns of the
zodiac, and thirty-fix who may rule fo many decans, and feventy-two who may
rule fo many quinaries of heaven, and the tongues of men and nations, and four
who may rule the triplicities and elements, and feven governors of the whole
world, according to the feven planets ; and they have given to all of them *names*
and *feals*, which they call *charaƈters*, and ufed them in their invocations, incantations and carvings, defcribing them in the inftruments of their operations,
images, *plates*, *glaffes*, *rings*, *papers*, *wax-lights*, and fuch like. And if at any
time they operated for the fun, they invocated by the name of the fun and
by the names of folar angels, and fo of the reft. Thirdly, they eftablifhed angels as minifters for the difpofing of thofe things which are below, which Origen
called certain invifible powers, to which thofe things which are on earth are
committed to be difpofed of. For fometimes, they being vifible to none do
direƈt our journies and all our bufinefs, are often prefent at battles, and, by
fecret helps, do give the defired fuccefs to their friends ; for, at their pleafure, they can procure profperity, and inflict adverfity. In like manner they
diftribute thefe into more orders, fo as fome are fiery, fome watery, fome aërial,
fome terreftrial ; which four fpecies of angels are computed according to the
four powers of the celeftial fouls, *viz.* the mind, reafon, imagination, and
vivifying and moving nature ; hence the fiery follow the mind of the celeftial fouls, whence they concur to the contemplation of more fublime
things ; but the aërial follow reafon, and favour the rational faculty, and, after a certain manner, feparate it from the fenfitive and vegetative ; therefore
it ferves for an aƈtive life, as the fiery the contemplative ; but the watery
follow the imagination, ferve for a voluptuous life ; the earthly following nature,
favours vegetable nature. Moreover, they diftinguifh alfo this kind of angels
into *faturnine* and *jovial*, according to the names of the ftars and the hea-

vens; farther, some are oriental, some occidental, some meridional, some septentrional. Moreover, there is no part of the world destitute of the proper assistance of these angels, not because they are alone, but because they reign there especially; for they are every where, although some especially operate, and have their influence in this place, some elsewhere; neither truly are these things to be understood as though they were subject to the influence of the stars, but as they have correspondence with the heaven above the world, from whence especially all things are directed, and to which all things ought to be conformable; whence, as these angels are appointed for diverse stars, so also for diverse places and times; not that they are limited to any place or time, neither by -the bodies which they are appointed to govern, but because the Divine Wisdom hath so decreed; therefore they favour more, and patronize those bodies, places, times, stars: so they have called some diurnal, some nocturnal, others meridional. In like manner some are called woodmen, some mountaineers, some fieldmen, some domestics: hence the gods of the woods, country gods, satyrs, familiars, fairies of the fountains, fairies of the woods, nymphs of the sea, the Naïades, Nereïdes, Dryades, Piërides, Hamadryades, Patumides, Hinnides Agapte, Pales, Parcades, Dodonæ, Fanilæ, Levernæ, Parcæ, Muses, Aonides, Castalides, Heliconides, Pegasides, Meonides, Phebiades, Camenæ, the graces, the genii, hobgobblins, and such like; whence the vulgar call them superiors, some the demi-gods and godesses: some of these are so familiar and acquainted with men, that they are even affected with human perturbations; by whose instructions Plato thinks that men do oftentimes wonderful things, even as by the instruction of men; some beasts which are most nigh to us, apes, dogs, elephants, do often strange things above their species; and they who have written the chronicles of the Danes and Norwegians, do testify that spirits of several kinds in those regions are subject to men's commands; moreover, some of these appear corporeal and mortal, whose bodies are begotten and die; yet to be long-lived is the opinion of the Egyptians and Platonists, and especially approved by Proclus, Plutarch also, and Demetrius the philosopher, and Æmilianus the rhetorician, affirm the same; therefore of these

Heads of Evil
Dæmons
Nº 2.

Vessels of Wrath

Theutus

Asmodeus

The Incubus

Designed by F. Barrett.

Engraved by B. Griffith.

thefe fpirits of the third kind, as the opinion of the Platonift is, they report that there are fo many legions as there are ftars in the heaven, and fo many fpirits in every legion as in heaven itfelf ftars : but there are, (as Athanafius delivers,) who think, that the true number of the good fpirits is according to the number of men, ninety-nine parts, according to the parable of the hundred fheep ; others think only nine parts, according to the parable of the ten goats ; others fuppofe the number of the angels equal-with men, becaufe it is written, he that hath appointed the bounds of the people according to the number of the angels of God ; and concerning their number many have written many things ; but the latter theologians, following the mafters of the fentences, *Auftin* and *Gregory*, eafily refolve themfelves, faying, that the number of the good angels tranfcendeth human capacity ; to the which, on the contrary, innumerable unclean fpirits do correfpond, there being fo many in the inferior world as pure fpirits in the fuperior ; and fome divines affirm that they have received this by revelation. Under thefe they place a kind of fpirits fubterraneous or obfcure, which the Platonifts call angels that failed, revengers of wickednefs and ungodlinefs, according to the decree of the divine juftice ; and they call them evil angels and wicked fpirits, becaufe they often annoy and hurt, even of their own accord. Of thefe alfo they reckon more legions ; and, in like manner, diftinguifhing them according to the names of the ftars and elements, and parts of the world, they place over them kings, princes, and rulers ; and the names of them : of thefe, four moft mifchievous kings rule over the other, according to the four parts of the world. Under thefe many more princes of legions govern, and many private officers ; hence the *Gorgones, Statenocte,* the Furies ; hence *Tifiphone, Alecto, Megæra, Cerberus.* They of this kind of fpirits, *Porphyry* fays, inhabit a place nigh the earth, yea within the earth itfelf ; there is no mifchief which they dare not commit ; they have altogether a violent and hurtful nature, therefore they plot, and endeavour violent and fudden mifchiefs ; and when they make incurfions, fometimes they lie hid, and fometimes offer open violence, and are very much delighted in all fuch things done wickedly and mifchievoufly.

CHAP.

CHAP. VII.

OF THE ORDER OF EVIL SPIRITS, AND THEIR FALL, AND DIFFERENT NATURES.

THERE are some of the school of theologians, who distribute the evil
spirits into nine degrees, as contrary to the nine orders of angels. Therefore,
the first of these, which are called false gods, who, usurping the name of God,
would be worshipped for gods, and require sacrifices and adorations; as that
devil who said to Christ, " If thou wilt fall down and worship me, I will give
thee all these things," shewing him all the kingdoms of the world; and the
prince of these is he who said, I will ascend above the height of the clouds,
and will be like to the Most High, who is called Beelzebub, that is, an old god.
In the second place, follows the spirits of lies, of which sort was he who went
forth, and was a lying spirit in the mouth of the prophet of Ahab; and the
prince of these is the serpent Pytho, from whence Apollo is called Pythius, and
that woman a Pythoness, or witch, in Samuel, and the other in the gospel,
who had Pytho in her belly. Therefore, these kind of devils join themselves to
the oracles, and delude men by divinations and predictions, so that they may be
deceived. In the third order, are the vessels of iniquity, which are called vessels
of wrath: these are the inventors of evil things, and all wicked arts; as in Plato,
that devil Theutus, who taught cards and dice; for all wickedness, malice, and
deformity, proceeds from these, of which in *Genesis*, in the benedictions of
Simeon and Levi, Jacob said, " vessels of iniquity are in their habitations, into
their counsel let not my soul come;" which the *Psalmist* calls vessels of death,
Isaiah, vessels of fury; and *Jeremiah*, vessels of wrath; *Ezekiel*, vessels of destroying and slaying; and their prince is Belial, which signifies, without a yoke,
and disobedient, a prevaricator, and an apostate; of whom Paul to the Corinthi-
ans says, " what agreement has Christ with Belial?" Fourthly, follow the revengers of evil, and their prince is Asmodeus, *viz.* causing judgment. After
these, in the fifth place, come the deluders, who imitate miracles, and serve
                                                                    conjurers

Ophis.

The Spirit
Antichrist

F. Barrett Del.   Pub. by Lackington & Allen.   R. Griffith Sculp.

conjurers and witches, and seduce the people by their miracles, as the serpent seduced Eve, and their prince is Satan, of whom it is written in the Revelation, " that he seduces the whole world, doing great signs, and causing fire to descend from heaven in the sight of men ; seducing the inhabitants of the earth by these signs, which are given him to do." Sixthly, the aerial powers offer themselves and join themselves to thunder and lightning, corrupting the air, causing pestilencies, and other evils ; in the number of which are the four angels of whom the the Revelations speak, to whom it is given to hurt the earth and the sea, holding the four winds from the four corners of the earth ; and their prince is called Meririm: he is the meridian devil, a boiling spirit, a devil raging in the south, whom *Paul*, to the *Ephesians*, calls " the prince of the power of the air, and the spirit which works in the children of disobedience." The seventh mansion the furies possess, who are powers of evil, discords, war, and devastation ; whose name in the Revelation is called in Greek, *Apollyon* ; in the Hebrew, *Abaddon*, that is, destroying and wasting. In the eighth place are the accusers or inquisitors, whose prince is Astaroth, that is, a searcher out ; in the Greek language he is called Diabolus, that is, an accuser or calumniator ; which in the Revelation is called the " accuser of the brethren, accusing them night and day before the face of God." Moreover, the tempters and ensnarers have the last place ; one of which is present with every man, which we call the evil genius, and their prince is *Mammon*, which is interpreted covetousness. But we of the Cabala unanimously maintain that evil spirits do wander up and down this inferior world, enraged against, all whom we call devils ; of whom *Austin*, in his first book of the Incarnation of the Word, to *Januarius*, says, concerning the devils and his angels contrary to virtues, the ecclesiastical preachers have taught that there are such things, but what they are, and who they are, he has not clear enough expounded : yet there is this opinion among them, that this devil was an angel, and being made an apostate, persuaded many of the angels to fall with him, who to this day are called his angels. Greece, notwithstanding, thinks not that these are damned, nor that they are all purposely evil ; but that from the creation of the world the dispensation of things is ordained by

this

this means, that the tormenting of sinful souls is made over to them. The other theologians say, that no devil was created evil, but that they were driven and cast out of heaven from the orders of good angels, for their pride; whose fall not only our and the *Hebrew theologians*, but also the *Assyrians*, *Arabians*, *Egyptians*, and *Greeks*, do confirm by their tenets. *Pherycies*, the *Assyrian*, describes the fall of the devils; and *Ophis*, that is, the develish serpent, was the head of that rebelling army; Trismegistus sings the same fall, in his Pimander; and Homer, under the name of Ararus, in his verses, and Plutarch, in his Discourse on Usury, signifies that Empedocles knew that the fall of the devils was in this manner; the devils themselves often confess their fall. They being cast out into this valley of misery, some that are near to us wander up and down in this obscure air; others inhabit lakes, rivers, and seas; others the earth, and terrify earthly things, and invade those who dig wells and metals, cause the gaping of the earth, to strike together the foundations of the mountains, and vex not only men but also other crea-tures; some being content with laughter and delusion only, do contrive rather to weary men than to hurt them; some heightening themselves to the length of a giant's body, and again shrinking themselves down to the smallness of pig-mies, and changing themselves into different forms, to disturb men with vain fear; others study lies and blasphemies, as we read of one in third book of Kings, saying, " I will go forth and be a lying spirit in the mouth of all the prophets of Ahab." But the worst sort of devils are those who lie in wait, and overthrow passengers in their journies, and rejoice in wars and effusion of blood, and afflict men with most cruel stripes: we read of such in *Matthew*, " for fear of whom no man dared pass that way." Moreover, the Scripture reckons up *nocturnal*, *diurnal*, and *meridional* devils; and describes other spirits of wickeness by different names, as we read in *Isaiah* of satyrs, screech-owls, sirens, storks, owls; and in the *Psalms*, of asps, basilisks, lions, dragons; and in the *Gospel*, we read of scorpions, and Mammon, and the prince of this world, and rulers of darkness, of all whom Beelzebub is the prince, whom the Scripture calls the prince of wickedness.

CHAP.

Heads of Evil Damons

Powers of Evil

Astaroth

Abaddon

Mammon

F. Barrett Del.

Pub by Lackington & Allen

R. Griffith Sculp

CHAP. VIII.

OF THE ANNOYANCE OF EVIL SPIRITS, AND THE PRESERVATION WE HAVE FROM
GOOD SPIRITS.

IT is the opinion of divines, that all evil spirits are of that nature, that they hate God as well as man; therefore Divine Providence has set over us more pure spirits, with whom he hath entrusted us, as with shepherds and governors, that they should daily help us, and drive away evil spirits from us, and curb and restrain them, that they should not hurt us, as they would otherwise; as is read in *Tobias*, that *Raphael* did apprehend the demon called *Asmodeus*, and bound him in the wilderness of the Upper Egypt. Of these, Hesiod says, there are 30,000 of Jupiter's immortal spirits living on the earth, who are the keepers of mortal men, who, that they might observe justice and merciful deeds, having clothed themselves with air, go to and fro every where on the earth. For there is no potentate could be safe, nor any woman continue uncorrupted, no man in this vale of ignorance could come to the end appointed to him by God, if good spirits did not secure us, or if evil spirits should be permitted to satisfy the wills of men; as therefore among the good there is a proper keeper or protector deputed to every one, corroborating the spirit of the man to good; so of evil spirits, there is sent forth an enemy ruling over the flesh and desire thereof; and the good spirit fights for us as a preserver against the enemy and flesh, now man, between these contenders is in the middle, and left in the hand of his own counsel to whom he will give victory : we cannot therefore accuse angels, or deny free-will, if they do not bring the nations entrusted to them to the knowledge of the true God and true piety, but suffer them to fall into errors and perverse worship; it is to be imputed to themselves, who have, of their own accord, declined from the right path, adhering to the spirits of error, giving victory to the devil : for it is in the hand of man to adhere to whom he

Book II.   H   pleases,

pleafes, and overcome whom he will; by whom if once the devil be overcome, he is made his fervant, and being overcome, cannot fight any more
with another, as a wafp that has loft his fting.   To which opinion Origen
affents, in his book Periarchon, concluding that the faints fight againft evil
fpirits, and, overcoming, do leffen their army; neither can he that is overcome by any moleft any more.   As therefore there is given to every man a
good fpirit, fo there is given to every man an evil diabolical fpirit, whereof each
feeks an union with our fpirit, and endeavours to attract it to itfelf, and to be
mixed with it, as wine with water; the good indeed, through all good
works conformable to itfelf, change us into angels by uniting us; as it is
written of John the Baptift in Malachi, " behold I fend my angel before
thy face:" of which transmutation and union it is written elfewhere, he that
adheres to God is made one fpirit with him.   An evil fpirit alfo, by evil
works, ftudies to make us conformable to itfelf, and unite us, as *Chrift* fays
of *Judas*, " Have not I chofen twelve, and one of you is a devil?"   And
this is that which *Hermes* fays, when a fpirit hath influence on the foul of man,
he fcatters the feed of his own notion, whence fuch a foul, being fown with
feeds, and full of fury, brings forth thence wonderful things, and whatfoever are the offices of fpirits: for when a good fpirit hath influence on a holy
foul, it doth exalt it to the light of wifdom; but an evil fpirit being tranf-
fufed into a wicked foul, doth ftir it up to theft, to man-flaughter, to luft,
and whatfoever are the offices of evil fpirits.   Good fpirits, as Jamblicus
fays, purge the fouls moft perfectly, and fome beftow upon us other good
things; they being prefent, do give health to the body, virtue to the foul, and
fecurity; what is mortal in us they take away, cherifh heat, and make it
more efficacious to life; and, by an harmony, do always infufe light into an
intelligible mind.   But whether there be many keepers of a man, or one
alone, theologians differ among themfelves: *we* think there are more, the
prophet faying, " he hath given his angels a charge concerning thee, that
they fhould keep thee in all thy ways," which, as Hierome fays, is to be
underftood of any man, as well as of Chrift.   All men, therefore, are governed by the miniftry of different angels, and are brought to any degree
                                                                    of

of virtue, deferts, and dignity, who behave themfelves worthy of them ;
but they who carry themfelves unworthy of them, are depofed and thruft
down, as well by evil fpirits as good fpirits, unto the loweft degree of mifery,
as their evil merits fhall require ; but they that are attributed to the fublimer angels, are preferred before other men ; for angels having the care
of them, exalt them, and fubject others to them by a certain occult
power, which, although neither of them perceive, yet he that is fubjected
feels a certain yoke of prefidency, of which he cannot eafily quit himfelf ;
yea, he fears and reverences that power, which the fuperior angels make to
flow upon inferiors, and with a certain terror bring the inferiors into a fear
of prefidency. This did Homer feem to be fenfible of, when he fays, that
the Mufes begot of Jupiter, did always, as infeparable companions, affift the
kings begot of Jupiter, fpeaking figuratively, who by them were made venerable and magnificent : fo we read that M. Antoninus being formerly joined
in fingular friendfhip with Octavius Auguftus, were accuftomed always to
play together ; but when, as always, Auguftus always went away conqueror, a
certain magician counfelled M. Antoninus thus : " O Anthony, what doft
thou do with that young man ? Shun and avoid him, for although thou art
older than he, and art more fkilful than he, and art better defcended than he,
and hath endured the wars of more emperors, yet thy *Genius* doth much
dread the *Genius* of this young man, and thy fortune flatters his fortune ;
unlefs thou fhalt fhun him, it feems wholly to decline to him." Is not the prince
like other men ? how fhould other men fear and reverence him, unlefs a divine
terror fhould exalt him, and ftriking a fear into others, deprefs them, that they
fhould reverence him as a prince ? Wherefore we muft endeavour, that, being
purified by doing well, and following fublime things, and choofing opportune
times and feafons, we be entrufted or committed to a degree of fublimer and
more potent angels, who taking care of us, we may defervedly be preferred
before others.

H 2   CHAP.

CHAP. IX.

THAT THERE IS A THREEFOLD KEEPER OF MAN, AND FROM WHENCE EACH OF THEM PROCEED.

EVERY man hath a threefold good demon as a proper keeper or pre-server, the one whereof is holy, another of the nativity, and the other of pro-feſſion. The holy demon is one, according to the doctrine of the *Egyptians,* aſſigned to the rational ſoul, not from the ſtars or planets, but from a ſupernatural cauſe—from God himſelf, the preſident of demons, being univerſal and above nature. This directs the life of the ſoul, and does always put good thoughts into the mind, being always active in illuminating us, although we do not always take notice of it; but when we are purified and live peaceably, then it is perceived by us, then it does, as it were, ſpeak with us, and communicates its voice to us, being before ſilent, and ſtudies daily to bring us to a ſacred perfection. So it falls out that ſome profit more in any ſcience, or art, or office, in a leſs time and with little pains, when another takes much pains and ſtudies hard, and all in vain; and although no ſcience, art or virtue, is to be contemned, yet that you may live proſperouſly, carry on thy affairs happily, in the firſt place, know thy good *genius,* and his nature, and what good the celeſtial diſpoſition promiſes thee, and God the diſ-tributer of all theſe, who diſtributes to each as he pleaſes, and follow the be-ginnings of theſe, profeſs theſe, be converſant in that virtue to which the moſt high diſtributer doth elevate and lead thee; who made *Abraham* excel in juſ-tice and clemency, *Iſaac* with fear, *Jacob* with ſtrength, *Moſes* with meekneſs and miracles, *Joſhua* in war, *Phineas* in zeal, *David* in religion and victory, *Solomon* in knowledge and fame, *Peter* in faith, *John* in charity, *Jacob* in devo-tion, *Thomas* in prudence, *Magdalen* in contemplation, *Martha* in officiouſ-neſs. Therefore in what virtue you think you can moſt eaſily be a proficient in, uſe diligence to attain to the height thereof, that you may excel in one,

when

when in many you cannot, but in the rest endeavour to be as great a proficient as you can; but if thou shalt have the overseers of nature and religion agreeable, thou shalt find a double progress of thy nature and profession; but if they shall be disagreeing, follow the better, for thou shalt better perceive at some time a preserver of an excellent profession then of nativity.

CHAP. X.

OF THE TONGUE OF ANGELS, AND OF THEIR SPEAKING AMONGST THEMSELVES AND WITH US.

WE might doubt whether angels or demons, since they are pure spirits, use any vocal speech or tongue among themselves or to us; but that Paul, in some place says, " if I speak with the tongue of men or angels ;"—but what their speech or tongue is, is much doubted by many. For many think that if they use any idiom, it is Hebrew, because that was first of all, and came from heaven, and was before the confusion of languages in Babylon, in which the law was given by God the Father, and the gospel was preached by Christ the Son, and so many oracles were given to the prophets by the Holy Ghost; and seeing all tongues have and do undergo various mutations and corruptions, this alone does always continue inviolated. Moreover, an evident sign of this opinion is, that though this demon and intelligence do use the speech of those nations with whom they do inhabit, yet, to them who understand it, they never speak in any idiom but in this alone, *viz.* Hebrew. But now, how angels speak, it is hid from us, as they themselves are. Now, to us, that we may speak, a tongue is necessary with other instruments; as the jaws, palate, lips, teeth, throat, lungs, the *aspera arteria*, and muscles of the breast, which have the beginning of motion from the soul. But if I speak at a distance to another, he

must

muft ufe a louder voice; but, if near, he whifpers in my ear, as if he fhould be coupled to the hearer, without any noife, as an image in the eye or glafs. So fouls going out of the body, fo angels, fo demons fpeak; and what man does with a fenfible voice, they do by impreffing the conception of the fpeech in thofe to whom they fpeak after a better manner than if they fhould exprefs it in an audible voice. So the Platonift fays, that Socrates perceived his demon by fenfe, indeed, but not of this body, but by the fenfe of the *etherial body* concealed in this; after which manner *Avicen* believes the angels were wont to be feen and heard by the prophets. That inftrument, whatfoever the virtue be, by which one fpirit makes known to another fpirit what things are in his mind, is called by the *apoftle Paul*, the *tongue of angels*. Yet oftentimes they fend forth an audible voice, as they that cried at the afcenfion of the Lord, Ye men of Galilee, why ftand ye here gazing unto the heaven? And in the old law they fpake with divers of the fathers with a fenfible voice; but this never but when they affumed bodies. But with what fenfes thefe fpirits and demons hear our invocations and prayers, and fee our ceremonies, we are altogether ignorant.

For there is a *fpiritual body* of demons every where fenfible by nature, fo that it touches, fees, hears without any medium, and nothing can be an impediment to it; yet they do not perceive after the fame manner as we do, with different organs, but haply as fponges drink in water, fo do they all fenfible things with their body or fome other way unknown to us; neither are all animals endowed with thofe organs, for we know that many want ears, yet we know they perceive a found, but after what manner we know not.

CHAP.

CHAP. XI.

OF THE NAMES OF SPIRITS, AND THEIR VARIOUS IMPOSITION, AND OF THE SPIRITS THAT
ARE SET OVER THE STARS, SIGNS, CORNERS OF THE HEAVEN, AND THE ELEMENTS.

MANY and different are the names of good and bad spirits; but their proper and true names, as those of the stars, are known to God alone, who only numbers the multitude of stars, and calls them by their names, whereof none can be known by us but by divine revelation; very few are expressed to us in sacred writ. But the masters of the Hebrews think, that the names of angels are imposed on them by Adam, according to that which is written, "the Lord brought all things which he had made unto Adam, that he should name them, and as he called any thing, so the name of it was." Hence the Hebrew *Mecubals* think, together with Magicians and Cabalists, that it is in the power of man to impose names upon spirits, but of such a man only who is dignified and elevated to this virtue by some divine gift or sacred authority: but because a name that may express the nature of divinity, or the whole virtue of angelical essences, cannot be made by any human voice, therefore names for the most part are put upon them from their works, signifying some certain office or effect which is required by the quire of spirits; which name then, and not otherwise, obtains efficacy and virtue to draw any spiritual substance from above, or beneath, to make any desired effect.

I have seen and known some writing on virgin parchment the name and seal of some spirit in the hour of the moon, which afterwards he gave to be devoured by a water-frog, and had muttered over some verse; the frog being let go into the water, rains and showers presently followed. I saw also the same man inscribing the name of another spirit with the seal thereof in the hour of Mars, which was given to a crow, who, being let go, after a verse muttered over, there followed from that part of the heaven whither it flew, lightnings, shaking, and horrible thunders, with thick clouds; neither were
those

thofe names of fpirits of an unknown tongue, neither did they fignify any thing elfe but their offices ; of this kind are the names of thofe angels, *Raziel, Gabriel, Michael, Raphael, Haniel,* which is as much as to fay the vifion of God, the virtue of God, the ftrength of God, the medicine of God, the glory of God. In like manner, in the offices of evil demons are read their names, *viz. a player, a deceiver, a dreamer, a fornicator,* and many fuch like. So we receive from many of the ancient fathers of the Hebrews the names of angels fet over the planets and figns ; over *Saturn, Zaphiel* ; over *Jupiter, Zadkiel* ; over *Mars, Camael* ; over the *Sun, Raphael* ; over *Venus, Haniel* ; over *Mercury, Michael* ; over the *Moon, Gabriel.* Thefe are thofe feven fpirits which always ftand before the face of God, to whom is entrufted the difpofing the whole celeftial and terrene kingdoms which are under the moon : for thefe (as the more curious theologians fay) govern all things by a certain viciffitude of hours, days, and years ; as the aftrologers teach concerning the planets which they are fet over, which Mercurius Trifmegiftus calls the feven governors of the world, who, by the heavens as by inftruments, diftribute the influences of all the ftars and figns upon their inferiors. There are fome who afcribe them to the ftars by names fomewhat differing, faying, that over Saturn is fet an intelligence called *Oriphael,* over Jupiter *Zachariel,* over Mars *Zamael,* over the Sun *Michael,* over Venus *Anael,* over Mercury *Raphael,* over the Moon *Gabriel.* And every one of thefe governs the world 354 years and four months ; and the government begins from the intelligence of *Saturn* ; afterwards, in order, the intelligences of *Venus, Jupiter, Mercury, Mars,* the *Moon,* and the *Sun* reigns, and the government returns to the fpirit of Saturn.

Tritemius writ to Maximilian Cæfar a fpecial treatife concerning thefe, which he that will thoroughly examine may from thence draw great knowledge of future times. * Over the twelve figns are fet thefe, *viz.* over Aries, *Malahidael* ; over *Taurus, Afmodel* ; over *Gemini, Ambriel* ; over *Cancer, Muriel* ; over *Leo, Verchiel* ; over *Virgo, Hamaliel* ; over *Libra, Zuriel* ; over *Scorpio, Barchiel* ; over *Sagittarius, Advachiel* ; over *Capricorn, Hanael* ; over *Aquarius, Cambiel* ; over *Pifces, Barchiel.* Of thefe fpirits fet over the planets and figns,

* TRITEMIUS on Spirits.

figns, *John* made mention of in the Revelation, fpeaking of the former in the beginning; and the feven fpirits which are in the prefence of the throne of God, which I find are fet over the feven planets, in the end of the book, where he defcribes the platform of the heavenly city, faying, that on the twelve gates thereof are twelve angels. There are again twenty-eight angels, who rule in the twenty-eight manfions of the moon, whofe names are thefe; *Geniel, Enediel, Anixiel, Azariel, Gabiel, Dirachiel, Scheliel, Amnediel, Barbiel, Ardefiel, Neciel, Abdizuel, Jazèriel, Ergediel, Atliel, Azeruel, Adriel, Egibiel, Amutiel, Kyriel, Bethnael, Geliel, Réquiel, Abrinael, Aziel, Tagriel, Atheniel, Amnixiel.* There are alfo four princes of the angels, which are fet over the four winds, and over the four parts of the world. Michael is placed over the eaft-wind, Raphael over the weft, Gabriel over the north. Nariel, who by fome is called Ariel, is over the fouth. There are alfo affigned to the elements thefe, *viz.* to the air *Cherub,* to the water *Tharfis,* to the earth *Ariel,* to the fire *Seraph.* Now every one of thefe fpirits is a great prince, and has much power and freedom in the dominion of his own planets and figns, and in their times, years, months, days and hours; and in their elements, and parts of the world, and winds. And every one of them rules over many legions; and after the fame manner, among evil fpirits, there are four, who, as moft potent kings, are fet over the reft, according to the four parts of the world, whofe names are thefe, *viz. Urieus,* king of the eaft; *Amaymon,* king of the fouth, *Paymon,* king of the weft; *Egin,* king of the north; which the Hebrew doctors perhaps call more rightly thus, *Samuel, Azazel, Azael,* and *Mahazuel,* under whom many others rule as princes of legions and rulers. Likewife there are innumerable demons of private offices. Moreover the ancient *theologians* of the Greeks reckon up fix demons, which they call *Telchines,* others *Alaftores;* which bearing ill-will to men, take up water out of the river *Styx* with their hands, fprinkle it upon the earth, whence follow calamities, plagues, and famines; and thefe are faid to be *Acteus, Megalezius, Ormenus, Lycus, Nicon, Mimon.* But he that defires to know exactly the diftinct names, offices, places, and times of angels, and evil demons, let him inquire into the book of *Rabbi Simon* of the Temples, and in his book of Lights, and in his treatife of the Greatnefs of Stature,

Book II.   I   and

and in the treatife of the Temples of *Rabbi Ifhmael,* and in almoft all the commentaries of his book of Formation, and he fhall find it written at large concerning them.

C H A P. XII.

THERE are alfo other facred names of good and evil fpirits deputed to each office of much greater efficacy than the former, which the Cabalifts draw from facred writ, according to that art which we teach concerning them ; as alfo certain names of God are drawn forth out of certain places : the general rule of thefe is, that wherefoever any thing of divine effence is expreffed in the Scripture, from that place the name of God may be gathered ; but in what place foever in the Scripture the name of God is found expreffed, then mark what office lies under that name ; wherefoever therefore the Scripture fpeaks of the office or work of any fpirit, good or bad, from thence the name of that fpirit, whether good or bad, may be gathered ; this unalterable rule being obferved, that of good fpirits we receive the names of good fpirits, of evil the names of evil : and let us not confound black with white, nor day with night, nor light with darknefs, which, by thefe verfes as by an example, is manifeft :

" Let them be as duft before the face of the wind ; and let the angel of the Lord fcatter them : let their ways be darknefs and flippery and let the angel of the Lord purfue them."

יהו במוץ ינפל דיות ומאלאף יהוהזדרה
יהדירכם המף והלק לקות ומלאף יהוה דירפם

in the xxxvth Pfalm with the Hebrews, but with us, the xxxivth ; of which the names of thofe angels are drawn, מידאל *Midael,* and מיראל *Miriael,*
of

of the order of warriors; fo of that verfe, " *thou fhalt fet over him the wicked,
and Satan fhall ftand at his right-hand*," out of Pfalm cix. with the Hebrews, but with the Latins, cviii.

חפקר עליו רשע ושטן יאמלאל ימינו

is extracted the name of the evil fpirit *Schii*, ‏שׁעי‎, which fignifies a fpirit
that is a worker of engines.   There is a certain text in Exodus contained
in three verfes, whereof every one is written with feventy-two letters, beginning thus; the firft *Vajifa*, ‏ויסע‎, the fecond *Vajabo*, ‏ויבא‎, the third *Vajot*,
‏ויט‎; which are extended into one line, *viz.* the firft and the third from the
left-hand to the right, but the middle in a contrary order, beginning from
the right to the left, is terminated on the left-hand; then each of the three
letters being fubordinate the one to the other, make one name, which are
feventy-two names, which the Hebrews call *Schembamphoræ*, to which if the
divine name El ‏אל‎ or Jah ‏יה‎ be added, they produce feventy-two trifyllable
names of angels, whereof every one carries the great name of God, as it is
written, " my angel fhall go before thee; obferve him, for my name is in
him."   And thefe are thofe that are fet over the feventy-two celeftial quinaries, and fo many nations and tongues, and joints of man's body, and co-
operate with the feventy-two feniors of the fynagogue, and fo many difciples
of Chrift: and their names, according to the extraction which the Cabalifts
make, are manifeft in the following table, according to the manner which we
have mentioned.

Now there are many other ways of making *Schembamphoræ* out of thofe
verfes; as when all three are written in a right order, one after the other,
from the right to the left, befides thofe which are extracted by the tables of
Ziruph, and the tables of commutations, of which we made mention of before.   Becaufe thefe tables ferve for all names, as divine, fo angelical, we
fhall therefore fubjoin them to this chapter.

Thefe are the feventy-two angels, bearing the name of God, *Schembamphoræ*.

For the tables, &c. fee the annexed Plates, No. 1, 2, 3, 4.

CHAP. XIII.

OF FINDING OUT THE NAMES OF SPIRITS AND GENII, FROM THE DISPOSITION OF THE CELESTIAL BODIES.

THE ancient magicians taught an art of finding out the name of a spirit to any desired effect, drawing it from the disposition of the heavens; as, for example, any celestial harmony being proposed to thee, to make an image or a ring, or any other work to be done under any constellation, if thou wilt find out the spirit that is the ruler of that work the figure of the heaven being erected, cast forth letters in their number and order, from the degree of the ascendant, according to the succession of signs through each degree, by filling the whole circle of the heavens; then those letters which fall into the places of the stars, the aid of which you would use, being according to the number and power of those stars, marked without into number and order, make the name of a good spirit. But if thou wilt do so from the beginning of a degree falling *against* the progress of the signs, the resulting spirit shall be evil. By this art some of the Hebrews and Chaldean masters teach that the nature and name of any genius may be found out; as for example, the degree of the ascendant of any one's nativity being known, and the other corners of the heaven being co-equated, then let that which had the most dignities of planets in those four corners, which the *Arabians* call *Almutez*, be first observed among the rest; and according to that in the second place, that which shall be next to it in the number of dignities, and so in order the rest of them, which obtain any dignity in the aforesaid corners.

This order being used, you may know the true place and degree of them in the heavens, beginning from the degree of the ascendant through each degree, according to the order of signs, to cast twenty-two of the letters of the Hebrews; then what letters shall fall into the places of the aforesaid stars, being marked and disposed according to the order found out above in the stars, and rightly

rightly joined together according to the rules of the Hebrew tongue, make the name of a genius; to which, according to the custom, some *monosyllable* name of Divine Omnipotence, *viz.* El or Jah, is subjoined. But if the casting of the letters be made from an angle of the falling, and against the succession of the signs, and the letters which shall fall in the Nadir (that is the opposite point) of the aforesaid stars be after that order, as are said, joined together, shall make the name of an evil genius.

But the Chaldeans proceed another way, for they take not the Almutez of the angles but the Almutez of the eleventh house, and do all things as has been said. Now they find out an evil genius from the Almutez of the angle of the twelfth house, which they call an evil spirit, casting from the degree of the falling against the progress of the signs.

—————————————

C H A P. XIV.

OF THE CALCULATING ART OF SUCH NAMES BY THE TRADITION OF CABALISTS.

THERE is yet another art of these kind of names, which they call calculatory; and it is made by the following tables, by entering with some sacred, divine, or angelical name, in the column of letters descending, by taking those letters which thou shalt find in the common angles under their stars and signs, which beingr educed into order, the name of a good spirit is made of the nature of that star or sign under which thou didst enter; but if thou shalt enter in the column ascending, by taking the common angles above the stars and signs marked in the lowest line, the name of an evil spirit is made. And these are the names of spirits of any order of heaven ministering, as of good, so of bad, which you may after this manner multiply into nine names of so many orders; inasmuch as you may, by entering with one name, draw forth another of a spirit

of

of a superior order out of the same, as well of a good as a bad one; yet the beginning of this calculation depends upon the names of God; for every word hath a virtue in *magic*, inasmuch as it depends on the word of God, and is thence framed. Therefore we must know that every angelical name must proceed from some primary name of God. Therefore angels are said to bear the name of God, according to that which is written, "because my name is in him;" therefore that the names of good angels may be discerned from the names of bad, there is wont oftentimes to be added some name of Divine Omnipotence, as *El*, or *On*, or *Jah*, or *Jod*, and to be pronounced together with it: and because *Jah* is a name of beneficence, and *Jod* the name of a deity, therefore these two names are put only to the names of angels; but the name *El*, because it imports power and virtue, is therefore added, not only to good but bad spirits; for neither can evil spirits either subsist or do any thing without the virtue of *El*, God. But we must know that common angles of the same star and sign are to be taken, unless entrance be made with a mixt name, as are the names of genii, and those of which it hath been spoken in the preceding chapter, which are made of the dispositions of the heavens, according to the harmony of divers stars. For as often as the table is to be entered with these, the common angle is to be taken under the star or sign of him that enters.

There are moreover some that do so extend those tables that they think also if there be an entrance made with the name of a star, or office, or any desired effect, a demon, whether good or bad, serving to that office or effect may be drawn out; upon the same account they that enter with the proper name of any person can extract the names of the genii under that star which shall appear to be over such a person as they shall, by his physiognomy, or by the passions and inclinations of his mind, and by his profession and fortune, know him to be either *martial*, or *saturnine*, or *solary*, or of the nature of any other star.

And although such kind of primary names have none or little power by their signification, yet such kind of extracted names, and such as are derived from them, are of very great efficacy; as the rays of the sun collected in a hollow glass do most intensely burn, the sun itself being scarce warm.

Now

Cabala.

The Averse Table of Commutations.

F. Barrett Del.

R. Griffith Sculp.

Pub. by Lackington & Allen.

The Cabala.

| Vehuiah | Jeliel | Sitael | Elemiah | Mahasiah | Lelahel | Achaiah | Cahethel | Haziel | Aladiah | Lauiah | Hahaiah | Ieiazel | Mebahel | Hariel | Hakamiah | Loviah | Caliel |

| Leuviah | Pahaliah | Nelchael | Ieiaiel | Melahel | Hahuiah | Nithhaiah | Haaiah | Ierathel | Seehiah | Reiiel | Omael | Lecabel | Vasariah | Iehuiah | Lehahiah | Chavakiah | Menadel |

| Aniel | Haamiah | Rehael | Ihiazel | Hahahel | Michael | Veualiah | Ielahiah | Sealiah | Ariel | Asaliah | Mihael | Vehuel | Daniel | Hahaziah | Imamiah | Nanael | Nithael |

| Mebahiah | Poiel | Nemamiah | Ieilael | Harael | Mizrael | Umabel | Iahhel | Annauel | Mehekiel | Damabiah | Menkiel | Eiael | Habuiah | Rochel | Iibamiah | Haiaiel | Mumiah |

F. Barrett Del.   Pub. by Lackington & Allen.   R. Griffith Sculp.

The Cabala

Table 2.º The Right Table of the Commutations.

Barrett Del.   Pub. by Lackington & Allen   R. Griffith Sculp.

The Cabala.

Table 4 & 5

The Table of the Combinations of Ziruph.

The Rational Table of Ziruph.

Barrett Del.   Pub. by Lackington & Allen.   R. Griffith Sculp.

Now there is an order of letters in those tables under the stars and signs, almost like that which is with the astrologers, of tens, elevens, twelves. Of this calculatory art *Alphonsus Cyprius* once wrote, and also fitted it to Latin characters; but because the letters of every tongue, as we shewed in the first book, have, in their number, order and figure, a celestial and divine original, I shall easily grant this calculation concerning the names of spirits to be made not only by Hebrew letters, but also *Chaldean, Arabick, Egyptian, Greek* and *Latin,* and many others, the tables being rightly made after the imitation of the presidents.

But here it is objected by many that it falls out that in these tables men of a differing nature and fortune do oftentimes, by reason of the sameness of name, obtain the same genius of the same name. We must know therefore that it must not be thought absurd, that the same dæmon may be separated from any one soul, and the same be set over more. Besides, as many men have the same name, so also spirits of divers offices or natures may be noted or marked by one name, and by one and the same seal or character, yet in a different respect; for as the serpent does sometimes typify Christ, and sometimes the devil, so the same names and the same seals may be applied sometimes to the order of a good demon, sometimes of a bad one. Lastly, the very ardent intention of the invocator, by which our intellect is joined to the separated intelligences, is the cause that we have sometimes one spirit, sometimes another, (although called upon under the same name,) made obsequious to us.

See the following Plates for the tables of the calculation of the names of spirits, good and bad, under the presidency of the seven planets, and under the order of the twelve militant signs.

CHAP.

CHAP. XV.

OF THE CHARACTERS AND SEALS OF SPIRITS.

WE muſt now ſpeak of the characters and ſeals of ſpirits. Characters are nothing elſe than certain unknown letters and writings, preſerving the ſecrets of ſpirits and their names from the uſe and reading of prophane men, which the ancients called hieroglyphical, or ſacred letters, becauſe devoted to the ſecrets of God only. They accounted it unlawful to write the myſteries of God with thoſe characters which prophane and vulgar things were wrote. Whence Porphyry ſays, " that the ancients were willing to conceal God and divine virtues, by ſenſible figures and by thoſe things which are viſible, yet ſignifying inviſible things;" as being willing to deliver great myſteries in ſacred letters, and explain them in certain ſymbolical figures; as when they dedicated all round things to the world, the ſun and the moon, hope and fortune; a circle to the heavens, and parts of a circle to the moon; pyramids and obeliſks to the fire, a cylinder to the ſun and earth.——See the plate.

CHAP. XVI.

ANOTHER WAY OF MAKING CHARACTERS, ACCORDING TO THE CABALISTS.

AMONG the Hebrews I find more faſhions of characters, whereof one is moſt ancient, viz. an ancient writing which Moſes and the prophets uſed, the form of which is not raſhly to be diſcovered to any; for thoſe letters which they uſe at this day were inſtituted by Eſdras. There is among them a writing which they call celeſtial, becauſe they ſhew it placed and figured among the ſtars.

The Cabala

The Tables for the calculations of the names of Spirits good & bad & under the presidency of the 7 Planets & 12 militant Sig:

The entrance of the Good Angels

The entrance of the Evil Angels

The entrance of Good Angels

The entrance of Evil Angels

Mysterious Characters of Letters deliver'd by Honorious call'd the Theban Alphabet.

A B C D E F G H I K L M

N O P Q R S T V X Y Z

The Characters of Celestial Writing.

Lamed Caph Jod Theth Cheth Zain Vau He Daleth Gimel Beth Aleph

Tau Shin Res Kuff Zade Pe Ain Samech Nun Mem

The Writing call'd Malachim.

Caph Jod Theth Cheth Zain Vau He Daleth Gimel Beth Aleph

Pesh Kuff Zade Pe Ain Samech Samech Schin Tau Nun Mem Lamed

The Writing call'd Passing the River.

Lamed Caph Jod Theth Cheth Zain Vau He Daleth Gimel Beth Aleph

Tan Schin Resh Kuff Zade Pe Ain Samech Nun Mem

well Del. Pub by Lackington & Allen. R Griffith Sculp

ſtars. There is alſo a writing which they call *Malachim*, or *Melachim*, *i. e.* of angels, or regal; there is alſo another, which they call the paſſing through the river, and the characters and figures of all which you may ſee in the fol-lowing Plates.

There is another manner among the Cabaliſts, formerly held in great eſteem, but now it is ſo common that it is placed among prophane things, *viz.* the twenty-ſeven characters of the Hebrews may be divided into three claſſes, whereof every one contains nine letters. The firſt, *viz.* אבגדההחט which are the ſeals or marks of ſimple numbers and of intellectual things diſtributed into nine orders of angels. The ſecond hath יכלמנסעפצ, the marks of tens and celeſtial things in the nine orbs of the heavens. The third hath the other four letters, with the five final, *viz.* קרשתךםןףץ, which are marks of hundreds, and inferior things, *viz.* four ſimple elements, and five kinds of perfect com-pounds. They do now and then diſtribute theſe three claſſes into nine cham-bers, the firſt is of units, *viz.* intellectual, celeſtial and elemental. The ſecond is of two's, the third of three's, and ſo of the reſt; theſe chambers are framed by the interſection of four parallel lines interſecting themſelves into right angles, as is expreſſed in the following Plate, fig. A.

Out of which, being diſſected into parts, proceed nine particular figures (ſee Plate, fig. B.) which are of the nine chambers, characterizing their letters by that Notariacon, which, if it be of one point, ſhews the firſt letter of that chamber; if of two, the ſecond; if of three, the third letter; as if you would frame the character Michael, מיכאל, that comes forth extended with five figures (for which ſee the Plate C.) which are contracted to three figures, which then are contracted into one, yet the points Notariacon are uſually omitted, and then there comes forth ſuch a character of Michael. See fig. D.

There is yet another faſhion of characters common to almoſt all letters and tongues, and very eaſy, which is by gathering together of letters; as if the name of the angel Michael be given, the characters thereof ſhall be framed according to the fig. E.

BOOK II.   **K**   And

And this fashion among the Arabians is most received; neither is there any writing which is so readily and elegantly joined to itself as the Arabick. You must know that angelical spirits, seeing they are of a pure intellect, and altogether incorporeal, are not marked with any marks or characters, or any other human signs; but we, not otherwise knowing their essence or quality, do, from their *names*, or *works*, or otherwise, devote and consecrate to them figures and marks, by which we cannot any way compel them to us, but by which we rise up to them, as not to be known by such characters and figures; and, first of all, we do set our senses, both inward and outward, upon them; then, by a certain admiration of our reason, we are induced to a religious veneration of them; and then are wrapt with our whole mind into an ecstatical adoration; and then with a wonderful belief, an undoubted hope, and quickening love, calling upon them in spirit and truth by true names and characters, do obtain from them that virtue or power which we desire.

C H A P. XVII.

THERE is another kind of character received by revelation only, which can be found out no another way; the virtue of which characters is from the Deity revealing; of whom there are some secret works breathing out a harmony of some divinity, or they are, as it were, some certain agreements or compacts of a league between us and them. Of this kind there was a sign shewed to *Constantine*, which was this, *in hoc vince*; there was another revealed to *Antiochus* in the figure of a Pentangle, which signifies health; for, being

The Cabala

Fig. A

א יק	בכר	גרלש
דמת	הנך	וסם
וע ז	חפף	טצץ

Fig. B

Fig. C

Fig. D

Fig. F

F The Cabalistic Character of the Spirit Michal as Composed out of the above Tables A B C D

Barrett Del.

Pub. by Lackington & Allen

Kürzfih Sculp

being refolved into letters, it fpeaks the word ὑγίεια, *i. e.* health : in the faith and virtue of which figns, both kings obtained a great victory againft their enemies.   So Judas, who by reafon of that, was afterwards firnamed Macha-beus, being to fight with the Jews againft *Antiochus Eupator*, received from an angel a notable fign, מכבי, in the virtue of which they firft flew 11,000, with an infinite number of elephants, then again 35,000 of their enemies : for that fign did reprefent the name of *Jehovah,* and was a memorable emblem of the name of feventy-two letters by the equality of number ; and the expofition thereof is מי במך באלי כיהוה, *i. e.* who is there among thee ftrong as *Jehovah ?* See Plate, fig. F.

CHAP. XVIII.

OF THE BONDS OF SPIRITS, AND THEIR ADJURATIONS, AND CASTING OUT.

THE bond by which fpirits are bound, befought, or caft out, are three; fome of them are taken from the elemental world, as when we adjure a fpirit by any inferior and natural thing of affinity with or adverfe to them ; inafmuch as we would call up or caft them out, as by fumigations of *flowers, herbs, animals, fnow, ice,* or by *hell, fire,* and *fuch like* ; and thefe alfo are often mixt with divine praifes, and bleffings, and confecrations, as appears in the fong of the Three Children, and in the pfalm, Praife ye the Lord from the heavens, and in the confecration and bleffing of the *pafchal taper:* This bond works upon the fpirits by an apprehenfive virtue, under the account of love or hatred, inafmuch as the fpirits are prefent with, or favour, or abhor any thing that is natural or againft nature, as thefe things themfelves love or hate one another. The fecond bond is taken from the celeftial world, *viz.* when we adjure them by their heaven, by the ftars, by their motions, rays, light, beauty, clearnefs, excellency, fortitude, influence and wonders, and fuch like ; and this bond works

upon

upon spirits by way of admonition and example. It hath also some command, especially upon the ministering spirits, and those who are of the lowest orders. The third bond is from the intellectual and divine world, which is perfected by religion; that is to say, when we swear by the sacraments, miracles, divine names, sacred seals, and other mysteries of religion; wherefore this bond is the highest of all and the strongest, working upon the spirits by command and power; but this is to be observed, that as after the universal Providence there is a particular one, and after the universal soul, particular souls; so, in the first place, we invocate by the superior bonds, and by the names and powers which rule the things, then by the inferior and the things themselves. We must know further, that by these bonds, not only spirits, but also all creatures are bound, as tempests, burnings, floods, plagues, diseases, force of arms, and every animal, by assuming them, either by adjuration or deprecation, or benediction, as in the charming of serpents; besides the natural and celestial, by rehearsing out of the mysteries and religion, the cure of the serpent in terrestrial paradise, the lifting up of the serpent in the wilderness; likewise by assuming that verse of the 91ſt Pſalm, *thou ſhalt walk upon the aſp and the baſiliſk, and ſhalt tread upon the lion and the dragon.*

C H A P. XIX.

BY WHAT MEANS MAGICIANS AND NECROMANCERS CALL FORTH THE SOULS OF THE DEAD.

BY the things which have been already spoken it is manifest, that souls after death do as yet love their body which they left, as those souls do whose bodies want due burial or have left their bodies by violent death, and as yet wander about their carcasses in a troubled and moist spirit, being, as it were, allured by something that hath an affinity with them, the means being known, by which, in times past, they were joined to their bodies, they may be easily called forth

and

and allured by the like vapours, liquors and favours, certain artificial lights being also ufed, fongs, founds, and fuch like, which moves the imaginative and fpiritual harmony of the foul; and facred invocations, and fuch like, as belong to religion, ought not to be nelgected by reafon of the portion of the rational foul which is above nature.

Necromancy has its name becaufe it works on the bodies of the dead, and gives anfwers by the ghofts and apparitions of the dead, and fubterraneous fpirits, alluring them into the carcaffes of the dead, by certain hellifh charms, and infernal invocations, and by deadly facrifices and wicked oblations.

There are two kinds of necromancy: raifing the carcaffes, which is not done without blood; the other fciomancy, in which the calling up of the fhadow only fuffices. To conclude, it works all its experiments by the carcaffes of the flain and their bones and members, and what is from them; for there is in thefe things a fpiritual power friendly to them: therefore they eafily allure the flowing down of wicked fpirits, by reafon of the fimilitude and property of every familiar, by whom the necromancer, ftrengthened by their help, can do much in human and terreftrial things, and kindle unlawful lufts, caufe dreams, difeafes, hatred, and fuch like paffions; to which alfo they can confer the powers of the foul, which as yet being involved in a moift and turbid fpirit, wandering about their caft bodies, can do the fame things that the wicked fpirits commit, feeing therefore they experimentally find, that the wicked and impure fouls violently plucked from their bodies, and of men not expiated, and wanting burial, do ftray about carcaffes, and are drawn to them by affinity. The witches eafily abufe them for effecting witchcraft, alluring thefe unhappy fouls, by the appofition of their body, or by the taking of fome part thereof, and compelling them by their devilifh charms, by entreating them by the deformed carcaffes difperfed through the wide fields, and the wandering fhadows of thofe who want burials, and by the ghofts fent back from *Acheron*, and the guefts of hell, whom untimely death has precipitated into hell, and by the horrible defires of the damned and proud devils, revengers of wickednefs. But he who
could

could reſtore the ſouls truly to their bodies, muſt tfirſt know what is the proper nature of the ſoul from whence it went forth, with how many and how
great degrees of perfection it is repleniſhed, with what intelligence it is
ſtrengthened, by what means diffuſed into the body, by what harmony it ſhall
be compacted with it, what affinity it hath with God, with the intelligences,
with the heavens, elements, and all other things, whoſe image and reſem-
blance it holds. To conclude, by what influences the body may be knit
together again for the raiſing of the dead, requires all theſe things which
belong not to men, but to God only, and to whom he will communicate
them.

<hr>

CHAP. XX.

OF PROPHETICAL DREAMS.

I CALL that a dream which proceeds either from the ſpirit of the phantaſy and intellect united together, or by the illuſtration of the agent intellect above our ſouls, or by the true revelation of ſome divine power in a quiet
and purified mind; for by this our ſoul receives true oracles, and abundantly
yields prophecies to us; for in dreams we ſeem both to aſk queſtions, and
learn to find them out; alſo many doubtful things, many policies, many things
unknown, unwiſhed for, and never attempted by our minds, are manifeſted
to us in dreams: alſo the repreſentation of things unknown, and unknown
places, appear to us; and the images of men, both alive and dead, and of
things to come, are foretold; and alſo things which at any time have happened are revealed, which we know not by any report. And theſe dreams
need not any art of interpretation, as thoſe of which we have before ſpoken,
which belong to divination, not to foreknowledge; and it comes to paſs that
they who ſee dreams, for the moſt part, underſtand them not: for as to ſee
dreams

dreams is from the ftrength of *imagination*, fo to underftand them is frcm the ftrength of the underftanding. They, therefore, whofe intellect being over-whelmed by too much commerce of the flefh is in a dead fleep, or its imaginative or phantaftic power or fpirit is too dull and unpolifhed, that it cannot receive the fpecies and reprefentation which flow from the fuperior intellect; this man, I fay, is altogether unfit for the receiving of dreams and prophefying by them.

Therefore it is neceffary that he who would receive true dreams fhould keep a pure undifturbed, and an undifquieted imaginative fpirit, and fo compofe it that it may be made worthy of the knowledge and government by the mind and underftanding; for fuch a fpirit is moft fit for prophefying, and is a moft cleai glafs of all the images which flow (every where) from all things. When therefore we are found in body, not difturbed in mind, our intellect not dulled by meats and drinks, not fad through poverty, not provoked through luft, not incited by any vice, not ftirred up by wrath or anger, not being irreligioufly and prophanely inclined, not given to levity, not loft in drunkennefs, but chaftely going to bed, fall afleep; then our pure and divine foul, being free from all the evils above recited, and feparated from all hurtful thoughts, and now freed by dreaming, is endowed with this divine fpirit as an inftrument, and doth receive thofe beams and reprefentations which are darted down, as it were, and fhine forth from the Divine Mind into itfelf; and, as it were in a deifying glafs, it does more certain, more clear and efficacioufly behold all things than by the vulgar inquiry of the intellect, and by the difcourfe of reafon. The divine powers inftructing the foul, being invited to their fociety by the opportunity of the nocturnal folitarinefs, neither will that genius be wanting to him when he is awake, which rules all his actions.

Whofoever therefore, by quiet and religious meditation, and by a diet temperate and moderate according to nature, preferves his fpirit pure fhall very much prepare himfelf, and by this means become (in a degree) divine and knowing all things, juftly merits the fame. But whofoever, on the contrary, languifhes with a fantaftic fpirit, he receives not perfpicuous and

distant

diſtant viſions; but even as the divine ſight, by reaſon of its viſion, being weakened and impaired, judges confuſedly and indiſtinctly, ſo alſo when we are overcome with wine and drunkenneſs, then our ſpirit, being oppreſſed with noxious vapours (as a troubled water is apt to appear in various forms) is deceived, and waxes dull; therefore thoſe who would receive oracles by dreams, and thoſe oracles true and certain, I would adviſe him to abſtain one whole day from meat, and three days from wine or any ſtrong liquors, and drink nothing but pure water; for, to ſober and religious minds, the pure ſpirits are adherent, but fly thoſe who are drowned in drunkenneſs and ſurfeiting. Although impure ſpirits do very often adminiſter notable ſecrets to thoſe who are apparently beſotted with wine or liquors; yet all ſuch communications are to be contemned and avoided.

But there are four kinds of true dreams, *viz.* the firſt, *matutine, i. e.* between ſleeping and waking; the ſecond that which one ſees concerning another; the third, that whoſe interpretation is ſhewn to the ſame dreamer in the nocturnal viſion; and, laſtly, the fourth, that which is repeated to the ſame dreamer in the nocturnal viſion.

END OF PART FIRST.

THE

THE PERFECTION AND KEY

OF

THE CABALA,

OR

CEREMONIAL MAGIC.

BOOK II. PART II.

IN this laſt book, which we have made the Perfection and Key of all that
has been written, we have given thee the whole and entire practice of
Ceremonial Magic, ſhewing what is to be done every hour of the day;
ſo that as by reading what we have heretofore written, thou ſhalt contemplate in theory, here thou ſhalt be made perfect by experiment and practice:
for in this Key you may behold, as in a mirror, the diſtinct functions of the
ſpirits, and how they are to be drawn into communication in all places, ſea-
ſons, and times.

This then is to be known, that the names of the intelligent preſidents
of every one of the planets are conſtituted after this manner; that is to ſay,
by collecting together the letters out of the figures of the world from the
riſing of the body of the planet, according to the ſucceſſion of the ſigns
through the ſeveral degrees, and out of the ſeveral degrees, from the aſpects
of the planet himſelf, the calculation being made from the degree of the aſcendant.

Book II.   L   In

In like manner are conftituted the names of the princes of the evil fpirits ; they are taken under all the planets of the prefidents in a retrograde order, the projection being made contrary to the fucceffion of the figns, from the beginning of the feventh houfe. Now the name of the fupreme and higheft intelligence, which many fuppofe to be the foul of the world, is collected out of the four cardinal points of the figure of the world, after the manner already delivered ; and by the oppofite and contrary way is known the name of the great demon or evil fpirit, upon the four cadent angles.

In like manner you fhall underftand the names of the great prefidential fpirits ruling in the air, from the four angles of the fuccedent houfes, fo as to obtain the names of the good fpirits : the calculation is to be made according to the fucceffion of the figns, beginning from the degree of the afcendant, and to attain the names of the evil fpirits by working the contrary way.

You muft alfo obferve, that the names of the evil fpirits are extracted as well from the names of the good fpirits as of the evil : fo, notwithftanding, that if we enter the table with the name of a good fpirit of the fecond order, the name of the evil fhall be extracted from the order of *princes* and *governors*; but if we enter the table with the name of a good fpirit of the third order, or with the name of an evil fpirit, a governor, after what manner foever they are extracted, whether by this table or from a celeftial figure, the names which do proceed from hence fhall be the names of the evil fpirits, the minifters of the inferior order.

It is further to be noted, that as often as we enter this table with the good fpirits of the fecond order, the names extracted are of the fecond order ; and if under them we extract the name of an evil fpirit, he is of the fuperior order of the governors. The fame order is, if we enter with the name of an evil fpirit of the fuperior. If therefore we enter this table with the names of the fpirits of the third order, or with the names of the miniftering fpirits, as well of the good fpirits as of the evil, the names extracted fhall be the names of the miniftering fpirits of the inferior order.

But

But many magicians, men of no small authority, will have the tables of this kind to be extended with *Latin* letters; so that by the same tables also, out of the name of any office or effect, might be found out the name of any spirit, as well good as evil, by the same manner which is above delivered, by taking the name of the office or of the effect in the column of letters, in their own line, under their own star. And of this practice *Trismegistus* is a great author, who delivered this kind of calculation in Egyptian letters: not improperly also may they be referred to the letters of other tongues, for the reason assigned to the signs; for truly he only is extant of all men who have treated concerning the attaining to the names of spirits.

Therefore the *force, secrecy*, and *power*, in what manner the sacred names of spirits are truely and rightly found out, consisteth in the disposing of vowels, which make the name of a spirit, and wherewith is constituted the true name and right word. Now this art is thus perfected and brought to pass. First, we are to take heed to placing the vowels of the letters, which are found by the calculation of the celestial figure, to find the names of the spirits of the second order, presidents and governors: and this, in the good spirits, is thus brought to effect, by considering the stars which do constitute and make the letters, and by placing them according to their order. First, let the degree of the eleventh house be subtracted from the degree of that star which is first in order, and that which remains thereof, let it be projected from the degree of the ascendant; and where the number ends, there is part of the vowel of the first letter.

Begin therefore to calculate the vowels of these letters according to their number and order, and the vowel which falls in the place of the star, which is the first in order, the same vowel is attributed to the first letter; then afterwards thou shalt find the part of the second letter, by subtracting the degree of a star, which is the second in order from the first star; and that which remains cast from the ascendant. And this is the part from which you shall begin the calculation of vowels; and that vowel which falls upon the second star the same is the vowel of the second letter: and so consequently thou mayest search out the vowels of the following letters

by

by always, subtracting the degree of the following star from the degree of the star next preceding and going before. And, likewise, all calculations and numerations in the names of the good spirits ought to be made according to the succession of the signs. And whereas in calculating the names of the evil spirits, the names of the good spirits are taken from the degree of the eleventh house; in these ought to be taken the degree of the twelfth house. And all numerations and calculations may be made with the succession of the signs, by taking the beginning from the degree of the tenth house.

But in all extractions by tables, the vowels are placed after another manner. In the first place, is taken the certain number of letters, making the name itself, and is thus numbered from the beginning of the column of the first letter, or whereupon the name is extracted; and the letter on which this number falleth is referred to the first letter of the name extracted, by taking the distance of the one from the other, according to the order of the alphabet. But the number of that distance is projected from the beginning of that column, and where it ends there is part of the first vowel; from thence thou shalt calculate the vowels themselves, in their own number and order in the same column; and the vowel which shall fall upon the first letter of a name, the same shall be attributed to that name.

Now thou shalt find the following vowels, by taking the distance from the preceding vowel to the following, and so consequently according to the succession of the alphabet; and the number of that distance is to be numbered from the beginning of his own column, and where he shall cease, there is part of the vowel sought after. From thence therefore must you calculate the vowels, as we have above said, and those vowels which shall fall upon your own letters, are to be attributed to them. If therefore any vowel should happen to fall upon a vowel, the former must give place to the latter: and this you are to understand only of the good spirits. In the evil spirits likewise you may proceed in the same way; except only that you make the numerations after a contrary and backward order, contrary to the succession of the alphabet, and contrary to the order of the colums (that is to say) ascending.

The

The name of good angels, and of every man, which we have before taught how to find out, according to that manner, is of no little authority, nor of a mean foundation. But now we will give thee some other ways illustrated with no vain reasons. One whereof is by taking in the nativity the five places of Hylech; which being noted, the characters of the letters are projected in their order and number, beginning from *Aries*, and those letters which fall upon the degrees of the said places, according to their order and dignity disposed and aspected, make the name of an angel.

There is also another way wherein they take *Almutel*, which is the ruling and governing star over the aforesaid five places, and the projection is to be made from the degree of the ascendant; which is done by gathering together the letters falling upon Almutel, which being placed in order, according to their dignity, make the name of an angel. There is likewise another way used, and very much had in observation from the Egyptians, by making calculations from the degree of the ascendant, and by gathering together the letters according to the Almutel of the eleventh house; which house they call a good demon; which being placed according to their dignities, the names of the angels are constituted.

Now the names of the evil angels are known after the like manner, except only that the projections must be performed contrary to the course and order of the succession of the signs; so that in seeking the names of good spirits, we are to calculate from the beginning of *Aries*; contrariwise, in attaining the names of evil, we ought to account from the beginning of *Libra*. And whereas, in the good spirits, we number from the degree of the ascendant; contrariety, in the evil, we must calculate from the degree of the seventh house.

But according to the Egyptians, the name of this angel is collected according to the Almutel of the twelfth house, which they call an evil spirit. Now all those rites, which are elsewhere already by us delivered in this Book, may be made by the characters of any language. In all which (as we have said before) there is a mystical and divine number, order and figure, from whence it comes to pass, that the same spirit may be called by divers names; but others
are

are difcovered from the name of the fpirit himfelf, of the good or evil, by tables formed to this purpofe.

Now thefe celeftial characters do confift of lines and heads. The heads are fix, according to the fix magnitudes of the ftars, whereunto the planets likewife are reduced. The firft magnitude holds a ftar with the fun or a crofs; the fecond, with Jupiter, a circular point; the third, with Saturn, a femicircle, a triangle, either crooked, round, or acute; the fourth, with a Mars, a little ftroke penetrating the line, either fquare, ftraight or oblique; the fifth, with Venus and Mercury, a little ftroke or point with a tail afcending or defending; the fixth, with the moon, a point made black, all which you may fee in the annexed Plate. The heads then being pofited according to the fite of the ftars of the figure of heaven, then the lines are to be drawn out according to the congruency or agreement of their natures. And this you are to underftand of the fixed ftars. But in the erecting of the planets, the lines are drawn out, the heads being pofited according to their courfe and nature among themfelves.—See the Plate, No. 1.

So when a character is to be found, of any celeftial image afcending in any degree or face of a fign, which confifts of ftars of the fame magnitude and nature, then the number of thefe ftars being pofited according to their place and order, the lines are drawn after the fimilitude of the image fignified, as copioufly as the fame can be done.

But the characters which are extracted according to the name of a fpirit are compofed by the table following, by giving to every letter that name which agrees to him out of the table; and although it may appear eafy to thofe that apprehend it, yet there is no fmall difficulty herein; to wit, when the letter of a name falls upon the line of letters or figures, that we may know which figure or which letter is to be taken. And this may thus be known; if a letter falls upon the line of letters; confider of what number this letter may be in the order of the name, as the fecond or the third; then how many letters that name contains, as five or feven; and multiply thefe numbers one after another by themfelves, and treble the product; then caft the whole (being
added

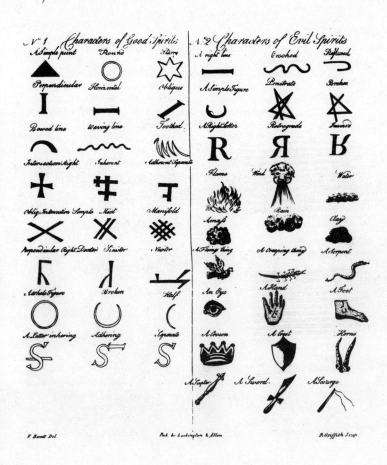

Nº 1 *Characters of Good Spirits*   Nº 2 *Characters of Evil Spirits*

F. Barett Del.   Pub. by Lackington & Allen   R. Griffith Sculp.

added together) from the beginning of the letters according to the succeſſion
of the alphabet; and the letter upon which that number ſhall happen to fall,
ought to be placed for a character of that ſpirit.   But if any letter of a name
fall upon the line of figures, it is thus wrought :   take the number how many
this letter is in the order of the name, and let it be multiplied by the number of
which this letter is in the order of the alphabet; and, being added together,
divide it by nine, and the remainder will ſhew the figure or number to be placed in the character, and this may be put either in a geometrical or arithme-
trical figure of number; which, notwithſtanding, ought not to exceed the
number of nine, or nine angels.—See the Plate, No. 2.

But the characters which are underſtood by the revelations of ſpirits
take their virtue from thence, becauſe they are, as it were, certain hidden
ſeals, making the harmony of ſome divinity : either they are ſigns of a
covenant entered into, and of a promiſed or plighted faith, or of obedience.
And theſe characters cannot by any other means be found out.

Beſides theſe characters there are certain familiar figures and images of
evil ſpirits, under which forms they are wont to appear, and yield obedience to
thoſe who invoke them. And all theſe characters or images may be ſeen in the
conſiderations of each day's buſineſs, according to the courſe of the letters conſtituting the names of ſpirits themſelves; ſo that if in any letter there is found
more than the name of one ſpirit, his image holds the pre-eminence, the
others imparting their own orders; ſo they which are of the firſt order, to them
is attributed the head, the upper part of the body, according to their own
figure; thoſe which are loweſt poſſeſs the thighs and feet; ſo likewiſe the
middle letters do attribute like to themſelves the middle parts of the body, to
give the parts that fit; but if there happen any contrariety, that letter which
is the ſtrongeſt in the number ſhall bear rule; and if they are equal they all
impart equal things.   Moreover if any name ſhall obtain any notable character
or inſtrument out of the table, he ſhall likewiſe have the ſame character in
the image.

We may alſo attain to the knowledge of the dignities of the evil ſpirits,
by the ſame tables of characters and images : for upon whatſoever ſpirit falls

any

any excellent fign or inftrument out of the table of characters, he poffeffes that dignity. As if there fhould be a crown, it fhews a kingly dignity; if a creft or plume, a dukedom; if a horn, a county: if without thefe there be a fcepter, fword, or forked inftrument, it fhews rule and authority. Like-wife out of the table of images you fhall find them who bear the chief kingly dignity: from the crown judge dignity; and from the inftruments, rule and authority.

Laftly, they which bear a human fhape and figure have a greater dig-nity than thofe which appear under the forms and images of beafts. They likewife who ride do excel them which appear on foot. And thus, accord-ing to all their commixtures, you may judge the dignity and excellency of fpirits, one before another. Moreover, you muft underftand that the fpi-rits of the inferior order, of what dignity foever, they are always fubject to the fpirits of the fuperior order; likewife that it is not incongruent for their kings and dukes to be fubject and minifter to the prefidents of the fuperior order.

Of Magic Pentacles and their Composition.

WE now proceed to fpeak of the holy and facred Pentacles and Seals. For thefe pentacles are certain holy figns and characters, preferving us from evil chances and events, helping and affifting us to bind, exterminate, and drive away evil fpirits, alluring the good fpirits, and reconciling them to us. Thefe pentacles confift either of characters of good fpirits of the fuperior order, or of facred pictures of holy letters or revelations, with apt and proper verficles, which are compofed either of geometrical figures and holy names of God, according to the courfe and manner of many of them, or they are compounded of all of them, or many of them mixed. The characters which are ufeful for us to conftitute and make the pentacles are the characters of
the

the good spirits, chiefly of the good spirits of the first and second order, and sometimes of the third order. These kind of characters are especially to be named holy.

Whatsoever characters of this kind are to be instituted, we must draw about him a double circle, wherein we must write the name of his angel; and if we will add some divine name congruent with his spirit and office, it will be of greater force and efficacy; and if we draw about him any angular figure, according to the manner of his numbers that is lawful to be done. But the holy pictures which make the pentacles are they which every where are delivered to us in the prophets and sacred writings, both in the Old and New Testaments; even as the figure of the serpent hanging on the cross, and such like; whereof many may be found in the visions of the prophets, as in *Isaiah, Daniel, Esdras,* and others, and likewise in the revelations of the *Apocalypse.* And we have before spoken of them in our First Part, where we have made mention of holy things, therefore where any picture is posited of any of these holy images, let the circle be drawn round it on each side; wherein let there be written some divine name that is apt and conformed to the effect of that figure, or else there may be written around it some versicle taken out of part of the body of holy Scripture, which may ascertain or deprecate the desired effect.

If a pentacle were to be made to gain a victory, or revenge against one's enemies, as well visible as invisible, the figure may be taken out of the Second Book of the *Maccabees*; that is to say, a hand holding a golden sword drawn, about which let there be written the versicle there contained, to wit, *take the holy sword, the gift of God, wherewith thou shalt slay the adversaries of my people Israel.* Or else there may be written about a versicle of the fifth Psalm; *in this is the strength of thy arm: before thy face there is death*; or some other such like versicle. But if you will write a divine name about the figure, then let some name be taken that signifies fear; a sword, wrath, the revenge of God, or some such like name congruent and agreeing with the effect desired. And if there shall be written any angular figure, let it be taken according to the rule of the numbers, as we have taught where we

BOOK II.   M   have

have treated of numbers, and the like operations. And of this sort there are two pentacles of sublime virtue and great power, very useful and necessary to be used in the consecration of experiments and spirits; one whereof is that in the first chapter of the Apocalypse, to wit, a figure of the majesty of God sitting upon a throne, having in his mouth a two-edged sword, as there is described; about which let there be written, "I am Alpha and Omega, the Beginning and the End, which is, and which was, and which is to come, the Almighty. I am the First and the Last, who am living, and was dead, and behold I live for ever **and ever**; and I have the keys of death and hell." Then there shall be written about it these three versicles:

Munda Deus virtuti tuæ, &c.—*Give commandment, O God, to thy strength; confirm, O God, thy strength in us. Let them be as dust before the face of the wind: and let the angel of the Lord scatter them. Let all their ways be darkness and uncertain: and let the angel of the Lord persecute them.*

Moreover, let there be written about it the ten general names, which are El, Elohim, Elohe, Zebaoth, Elion, Escerchie, Adonay, Jah, Tetragrammaton, Saday.

There is another pentacle, the figure whereof is like *a lamb slain, having seven eyes and seven horns*; *and under his feet a book sealed with seven seals,* as it is in the fifth chapter of the *Apocalypse*. Round about let be written this versicle, *behold the lion hath overcome of the tribe of Judah, the root of David. I will open the book and unloose the seven seals thereof.* And another versicle, *I saw Satan like lightning fall down from heaven. Behold I have given you power to tread upon serpents and scorpions, and over all the power of your enemies, and nothing shall be able to hurt you.* And let there be also written about it the ten general names as aforesaid.

But those pentacles which are thus made of figures and names, let them keep **this** order; for when any figure is posited, conformable to any number, to produce any certain effect or virtue, there must be written thereupon, in all the several angles, some divine name obtaining the force and efficacy of the thing desired; yet so nevertheless, that the name which is of this sort do consist of just so many letters as the figure may constitute a number; or of so

many

many letters of a name, as, joined together among themselves, may make the number of a figure; or by any number which may be divided without any superfluity or diminution. Now such a name being found, whether it be only one name or more, or divers names, it is to be written in all the several angles in the figure; but in the middle of the figure, let the revolution of the name be wholly and totally placed, or at least principally.

We likewise constitute pentacles by making the revolution of some kind of name, in a square table, and by drawing about it a single or double circle, and writing therein some holy versicle competent and befitting this name, or from which that name is extracted. And this is the way of making the pentacles, according to their several distinct forms and fashions, which we may, if we please, either multiply or commix together by course among themselves, to work the greater efficacy, extension and enlargement of force and virtue.

As, if a deprecation would be made for the overthrow and destruction of one's enemies, we are to mind, and call to remembrance how God destroyed the face of the whole earth in the deluge of waters, and the destruction of *Sodom* and *Gomorrah*, by raining down fire and brimstone; likewise, how God over-threw Pharoah and his host in the Red Sea; and to call to mind if any other malediction or curse be found in holy writ. And thus in things of the like sort. So likewise in deprecating and praying against perils and dangers of waters, we ought to call to remembrance the saving of *Noah* in the deluge of waters, the passing of the children of *Israel* through the Red Sea; and also we are to mind how Christ walked on the waters, and how he saved the ship in danger from being cast away by the tempest; and how he commanded the winds and the waves, and they obeyed him; and also, that he drew *Peter* out of the water, being in danger of drowning, and the like. And, lastly, with these we invoke and call upon some certain holy names of God; to wit, such as are significative to accomplish our desire, and accommodated to the desired effect; as if it be to overthrow enemies, we are to invoke and call upon names of *wrath*, *revenge*, *fear*, *justice*, and *fortitude* of God; and if we would avoid and

M 2   escape

efcape any evil or danger, we then call upon the names of mercy, defence, falvation, fortitude, goodnefs, and fuch like names of God. When likewife
we pray to God that he would grant us our defires, we are likewife to inter-
mix therewith the name of fome good fpirit, whether one only, or more,
whofe office it is to execute our defires; and fometimes alfo we require
fome evil fpirit to reftrain or compel, whofe name likewife we intermingle,
and that rightly, efpecially if it be to execute any evil work; as *revenge, punifhment*, or *deftruction*.

Furthermore, if there be any verficle in the Pfalms, or any other part of the
holy Scripture that fhall feem congruent and agreeable to our defire, the fame
is to be mingled with our prayers. Now, after prayer has been made to
God, it is expedient afterwards to make an oration to that executioner, whom,
in our precedent prayer to God, we have defired fhould adminifter to us,
whether one or more, or whether he be an angel, or ftar, or foul, or any of the
noble angels. But this kind of oration ought to be compofed according
to the rules which we have delivered in the former part of our work,
where we have treated of the manner of the compofition of enchantments,
&c.

You may know farther, that thefe kind of bonds have a threefold difference;
for the firft bond is when we conjure by natural things; the fecond is compounded of religious myfteries, by facraments, miracles, and things of this
fort; and the third is conftituted by divine names and holy feals. With
thefe kind of bonds we may bind not only fpirits, but alfo other creatures
whatfoever, as *animals, tempefts, burnings, floods of waters, the force and power
of arms*. Alfo we ufe thefe bonds aforefaid, not only by conjuration, but
fometimes alfo ufing the means of deprecation and benediction. Moreover,
it conduces much to this purpofe to join fome fentence of holy Scripture,
if any fhall be found convenient thereto, as in the conjuration of ferpents, by
commemorating the curfe of the ferpent in the earthly paradife, and the fetting
up the ferpent in the wildernefs; and further, adding that verficle, *thou fhalt
walk upon the afp and the bafilifk*, &c. Superftition is alfo of much preve-
                                                                    lancy

lancy herein, by the tranflation of fome facramental rites, to bind that which we intend to hinder; as, the rites of excommunication, of fepulchres, funerals, buryings, and the like fort.

Of the Confecration of all magical Inftruments and Materials which are ufed in this Art.

THE virtue of confecrations chiefly confifts in two things, *viz.* the power of the perfon confecrating, and the virtue of the prayer by which the confecration is made.

For in the perfon confecrating, there is required firmnefs, conftancy, and holinefs of life; and that the confecrator himfelf fhall, with a firm and undubitable faith, believe the virtue, power, and effect thereof.

Then in the prayer by which the confecration is made it derives its virtue either from divine infpiration, or elfe by compofing it from fundry places in the holy Scriptures, in the commemoration of fome of the wonderful miracles of God, effects, promifes, facraments and facramental things, of which we have abundance in holy writ.

There muft likewife be ufed the invocation of divine names, that are fignificative of the work in hand; likewife a fanctifying and expiation which is wrought by fprinkling with holy water, unctions with holy oil, and odoriferous fuffumigations. Therefore in every confecration there is generally ufed a benediction and confecration of water, earth, oil, fire, and fuffumigations, &c. with confecrated wax-lights or lamps burning; for without lights no confecration is duly performed. You muft therefore particularly obferve this, that when any thing (which we call prophane) is to be ufed, in which there is any defilement or pollution, it muft, firft of all, be purified by an *Exorcifm* compofed folely for that purpofe, which ought to precede the confecration; which

which things being fo made pure are moft apt to receive the influences of the divine virtue. We muft alfo obferve that at the end of any confecration after the prayer is rightly performed, as we have mentioned, the operator ought to blefs the thing confecrated, by breathing out fome fentence with divine virtue and power of the prefent confecration, with a commemoration of his virtue and authority, that fo it may be the more duly performed, and with an earneft and attentive mind. Now I fhall mention here fome examples, that, by thefe, a path may be made to the whole perfection thereof.

The Confecration of WATER.

SO in the confecration of water, we muft commemorate that God has placed the firmament in the midft of the waters, and likewife that God placed the fountain of waters in the earthly paradife, from whence fprang four holy rivers that watered the whole earth ; likewife we are to remember that God caufed the waters to be an inftrument of his juftice in deftroying the giants, by bringing on the deluge which covered the face of the whole earth ; and in the overthrow of the hoft of Pharoah in the Red Sea, and that God led the children of Ifrael through on dry land, and through the midft of the river Jordan, and likewife his marvelloufly drawing water out of the ftony rock in the wildernefs ; and that, at the prayer of Samfon, he caufed water to flow out of the jaw-bone of an afs ; and likewife that God has made water the inftrument of his mercy and falvation for the expiation of original fin ; alfo that Chrift was baptized in the river Jordan, and hath thereby fanctified and cleanfed the waters. Likewife certain divine names are to be invocated which are conformable hereto ; as, that God is a living fountain, living water, the fountain of mercy, and names of the like fort.

Confecration

Confecration of FIRE.

AND likewife, in the confecration of fire, we are to commemorate that God hath created the fire to be an inftrument to execute his juftice, for punifhment, vengeance, and the expiation of fins; alfo, when God comes to judge the world that he will command a conflagration of fire to go before him; likewife we. are to mention that God appeared to Mofes in a burning bufh; and alfo how he went before the children of Ifrael in a pillar of fire; and that nothing can be duly offered, fanctified, or facrificed, without fire; and how that God inftituted fire to be kept in continually in the tabernacle of the covenant; and how miraculoufly he re-kindled the fame, being extinct, and preferved it elfewhere from going out being hidden under the waters; and things of this fort; likewife the names of God are to be called upon which are confonant to this; as we read in the law and prophets, that God is a comfuming fire; and likewife if there is any divine names which fignify fire, as the glory of God, the light of God, the fplendor and brightnefs of God, &c.

The Confecration of OIL.

AND likewife in the confecration of oil and perfumes we are to mention fuch things as are confonant to this purpofe, as of the holy anointing oil, mentioned in Exodus, and divine names fignificant thereunto; fuch as is the name Chrift, which fignifies *anointed*; and whatever myfteries there are relative to oil in the Scriptures, as the two olive-trees diftilling holy oil into the lamps that burn before the face of God, mentioned in Revelations.

Of the Benediction of LIGHTS, LAMPS, WAX, &c.

NOW, the bleffing of the lights, lamps, wax, &c. is taken from the fire, and whatever contains the fubftance of the flame, and whatever fimilitudes are in the myfteries, as the feven candlefticks which burn before the face of God.

Therefore

Therefore we have here given the manner of composing the confecrations, which first of all are neceffary to be ufed in every kind of ceremony, and ought to precede every experiment or work, and without which nothing in magic rites can be duly performed.

In the next place, we will fhew thee the confecration of *places, inftruments,* and the like things.

The Confecration of PLACES, GROUND, CIRCLE, &c.

THEREFORE when you would confecrate any place or circle, you fhould take the prayer of Solomon ufed in the dedication and confecration of the temple; you muft likewife blefs the place by fprinkling with holy water and with fuffumigations, and commemorate in the benediction holy myfteries; fuch as thefe, the fanctification of the throne of God, of Mount Sinai, of the tabernacle of the covenant, of the holy of holies, of the temple of Jerufalem: alfo the fanctification of Mount Golgotha, by the crucifixion of Chrift; the fanctification of the temple of Chrift; of Mount Tabor, by the transfiguration and afcenfion of Chrift, &c. And by invocating all divine names which are fignificant to this; fuch as the place of God, the throne of God, the chair of God, the tabernacle of God, the altar of God, the habitation of God, and the like divine names of this fort, which are to be written about the circle, or place to be confecrated.

And, in the confecration of inftruments, and every other thing that is ufed in this art, you muft proceed after the fame manner, by fprinkling with holy water the fame, by fumigation, by anointing with holy oil, fealing it with fome holy feal, and blefling it with prayer, and by commemorating holy things out of the facred Scriptures, collecting divine names which are agreeable to the things to be confecrated; as for example, in the confecration of the fword we are to remember in the gofpel, "he that hath two coats," &c. and that in the fecond of the Maccabees, it is faid that a fword was divinely and miraculoufly fent to *Judas Maccabeus*; and if there is any thing of the like in the prophets, as "take unto you two-edged fwords," &c. And you fhall

also,

alfo, in the fame manner, confecrate experiments and books, and whatever of the like nature, as writings, pictures, &c. by fprinkling, perfuming, anointing, fealing, bleffing, with holy commemorations, and calling to remembrance the fanctification of myfteries; as the table of the ten commandments, which were delivered to Mofes by God in mount Sinai, the fanctification of the Old and New Teftaments, and likewife of the law, prophets, and Scriptures, which were promulgated by the Holy Ghoft : and again, there are to be mentioned fuch divine names as are convenient to this; as thefe are, viz. the teftament of God, the book of God, the book of life, the knowledge of God, the wifdom of God, and the like. And with fuch kind of rites as thefe is the perfonal confecration performed.

There are befide thefe another rite of confecration of great power and efficacy; and this is one of the kinds of fuperftition, viz. when the rite of confecration or collection of any facrament in the church is transferred to that thing which we would confecrate.

It muft be noted that vows, oblations, and facrifices, have the power of confecration alfo, as well real as perfonal; and they are, as it were, certain conventions between thofe names with which they are made and us who make them, ftrongly cleaving to our defire and wifhed effects, as when we facrifice with certain names, or things; as fumigations, unctions, rings, images, mirrors; and fome things lefs material, as characters, feals, pentacles, enchantments, orations, pictures, Scriptures, of which we have largely fpoken before.

Of the Invocation of EVIL SPIRITS, *and the binding of, and conftraining of them to appear.*

NOW, if thou art defirous of binding any fpirit to a ready obedience to thee, we will fhew you how a certain book may be made by which they may be invoked; and this book is to be confecrated a book of Evil Spirits, ceremonioufly to be compofed in their name and order, whereunto they bind

BOOK II.   N   with

with a certain holy oath, the ready and present obedience of the spirit. This book is therefore to be made of the most pure and clean paper, which is generally called virgin paper; and this book must be inscribed after this manner, *viz.* let there be drawn on the left side of the book the image of the spirit, and on the right side thereof his character, with the oath above it, containing the name of the spirit, his dignity and place, with his office and power. Yet many magicians do compose this book otherwise, omitting the characters and images; but I think that it is much more efficacious not to neglect any thing above mentioned in the forms.

There is likewise to be observed the circumstances of places, times, hours, according to the stars which these spirits are under, and are seen to agree to; with their site, rite, and order, being applied.

Which book being so written, is to be well bound, adorned, garnished, embellished and kept secure, with registers and seals, lest it should happen after the consecration to open in some part not designed, and endanger the operator. And, above all, let this book be kept as pure and reverent as possible; for irreverance of mind, causes it to lose its virtue by pollution and prophanation.

Now this sacred book being thus composed according to the form and manner we have delivered, we are to consecrate it after a two-fold way; the first is, that all and singularly each of the spirits who are written in the book be called to the circle, according to the rites magical, which we have before taught, and place the book which is to be consecrated in a triangle on the outside of the circle; then read, in the presence of the spirits, all the oaths which are contained and written in that book; then the book to be consecrated being already placed without the circle in a triangle there drawn, compel all the spirits to impose their hands where their images and characters are drawn, and to confirm and consecrate the same with a special and common oath. This being done, let the book be shut and preserved as we have spoken before; then licence the spirits to depart according to due rite and magical order.

There

There is another method extant among us of confecrating a general book of fpirits which is more eafy, and of as much efficacy to produce every effect, except that in opening this book, the fpirits do not always appear vifible. And this way is thus: let be made a book of fpirits, as we have before fhewn, but in the end thereof write invocations, bonds, and ftrong conjurations, wherewith every fpirit may be bound; then bind this book between two lamens or tables, and on the infide thereof draw or let be drawn two holy pentacles of the divine Majefty, which we have before fet forth, out of the Apocalypfe. Then let the firft of them be placed in the beginning of the book, and the fecond at the end of the fame.

This book being thus perfected, let it be brought, in a clear and fair night, to a circle prepared in a crofs-way, according to the art which we have before delivered; and there, in the firft place, the book is to be opened, and to be confecrated according to the rites and ways which we have before delivered concerning confecration, which being done, let all the fpirits be called which are written in the book, in their own order and place, conjuring them thrice by the bonds defcribed in the book that they come to that place within the fpace of three days, to affure their obedience and confirm the fame, to the book fo to be confecrated; then let the book be wrapped up in a clean linen cloth, and bury it in the midft of the circle, and ftop the hole fo as it may not be perceived or difcovered: the circle being deftroyed, after you have licened the fpirits, depart before fun-rife; and on the third day, about the middle of the night, return and make the circle anew, and on thy knees make prayer unto God, and give thanks to him; and let a precious perfume be made, open the hole in which you buried your book and take it out, and fo let it be kept, not opening the fame. Then after licenfing the fpirits in their order and deftroying the circle, depart before fun-rife. And this is the laft rite and manner of confecrating, profitable to whatever writings, experiments, &c. that direct the fpirits, placing the fame between two holy lamens or pentacles, as is before mentioned.

But when the operator would work by the book thus confecrated he fhould do it in a fair and clear feafon, when the fpirits are leaft troubled; and let him

turn himfelf towards the region of the fpirits ; then let him open the book under a due regifter, and likewife invoke the fpirits by their oaths there defcribed and confirmed, and by the name of their character and image, to whatever purpofe you defire, and if there be need conjure them by the bonds placed
in the end of the book *. And having attained thy defired effect licenfe them to
depart.

And now we proceed to fpeak of the *Invocation of good as well as bad Spirits.*

The good fpirits may be invocated of us, or by us, divers ways, and they in
fundry fhapes and manners offer themfelves to us, for they openly fpeak to thofe
that watch, and do offer themfelves to our fight, or do infom us by dreams and
by oracle of thofe things which we have a great defire to know. Whoever therefore would call any good fpirit to fpeak or appear in fight, he muft particularly obferve two things ; one whereof is about the *difpofition* of the invocant,
the other concerning thofe things which are outwardly to be adhibited
to the invocation for the conformity of the fpirit to be called.

It is neceffary therefore that the invocant religioufly difpofe himfelf for the
fpace of many days to fuch a myftery, and to conferve himfelf during the
time chafte, abftinent, and to abftract himfelf as much as he can from all manner of foreign and fecular bufinefs ; likewife he fhould obferve fafting, as much
as fhall feem convenient to him, and let him daily, between fun-rifing and
fetting, being clothed in pure white linen, feven times call upon God, and
make a deprecation to the angels to be called and invocated, according to the
rule which we have before taught. Now the number of days of fafting and
preparation is commonly one month, *i. e.* the time of a whole lunation. Now,
in the Cabala, we generally prepare ourfelves forty days before.

Now concerning the place, it muft be chofen clean, pure, clofe, quiet, free
from all manner of noife, and not fubject to any ftranger's fight. This place
muft firft of all be exorcifed and confecrated ; and let there be a table or altar
placed therein, covered with a clean white linen cloth, and fet towards the
eaft : and on each fide thereof place two confecrated wax-lights burning, the

* I have given an example of the book of fpirits, by which you may fee the method in which the
characters, &c, are placed as above defcribed. See the Plate.

flame

flame thereof ought not to go out all these days. In the middle of the altar let there be placed lamens, or the holy paper we have before described, covered with fine linen, which is not to be opened until the end of the days of confecration. You shall also have in readiness a *precious perfume*, and a *pure anointing oil*.——And let them both be kept consecrated. Then set a senfor on the head of the altar, wherein you shalt kindle the *holy fire*, and make a precious perfume every day that you pray.

Now for your habit, you shall have a long garment of white linen, close before and behind, which may come down quite over the feet, and gird yourself about the loins with a girdle. You shall likewise have a veil made of pure white linen on which must be wrote in a gilt lamen, the name *Tetragrammaton*; all which things are to be consecrated and fanctified in order. But you must not go into this holy place till it be first washed and covered with a cloth new and clean, and then you may enter, but with your feet naked and bare; and when you enter therein you shall sprinkle with holy water, then make a perfume upon the altar; and then on thy knees pray before the altar as we have directed.

Now when the time is expired, on the laft day, you shall fast more strictly; and fafting on the day following, at the rising of the sun, enter the holy place, using the ceremonies before spoken of, first by sprinkling thyself, then, making a perfume, you shall sign the cross with holy oil in the forehead, and anoint your eyes, using prayer in all these consecrations. Then, open the lamen and pray before the altar upon your knees; and then an invocation may be made as follows:

An INVOCATION of the GOOD SPIRITS.

IN the name of the bleffed and Holy Trinity, I do desire thee, strong and mighty angels *(here name the spirits you would have appear)* that if it be the divine will of him who is called Tetragrammaton, &c. the holy God, the Father, that thou take upon thee some shape as best becometh thy celestial nature, and appear to us visibly here in this place, and answer our demands, in as far as we shall not transgress the bounds of the divine mercy and goodness,

by

by requesting unlawful knowledge; but that thou wilt graciously shew us what things are most profitable for us to know and do to the glory and honour of his divine Majesty who liveth and reigneth, world without end. *Amen.*

Lord thy will be done on earth as it is in heaven—make clean our hearts within us, and take not thy holy spirit from us. O Lord, by thy name we have called them, suffer them to administer unto us.

And that all things may work together for thy honour and glory, to whom with thee, the Son and blessed Spirit, be ascribed all might, majesty, and dominion, world without end. *Amen.*

The particular Form of the LAMEN.—(For the form of the Lamen see the Plate.)

THE invocation being made, the good angels will appear unto you which you desire, which you shall entertain with a chaste communication, and licence them to depart.

Now the lamen which is used to invoke any good spirit must be made after the following manner : either in metal conformable or in new wax mixed with convenient spices and colours ; or it may be made with pure white paper with convenient colours, and the outward form of it may be either square, circular, or triangular, or of the like sort, according to the rule of the numbers, in which there must be written the divine names, as well general as special. And in the centre of the lamen draw a hexagon or character of six corners, in the middle thereof write the name and character of the star, or of the spirit his governor, to whom the good spirit that is to be called is subject. And about this character let there be placed so many characters of five corners or pentacles as the spirits we would call together at once. But if we should call only one, nevertheless there must be made four pentagons, wherein the name of the spirit or spirits, with their characters, are to be written. Now this lamen ought to be composed when the moon is in her encrease, on those days and hours which agree to the spirit ; and if we take a fortunate planet

therewith,

therewith, it will be the better for the producing the effect : which table or lamen being rightly made in the manner we have fully described, must be consecrated acoording to the rules above delivered.

And this is the way of making the general table or lamen for the invocating of all spirits whatever ; the form whereof you may see in the Plates of pentacles, seals, and lamens.

Nevertheless, we make special tables congruent to every spirit by the rule which we have above spoken concerning holy pentacles.

We will yet declare unto you another rite more easy to perform this thing : let the man who wishes to receive an oracle from a spirit be chaste, pure, and sanctified ; then a place being chosen pure, clean, and covered every where with clean and white linen, on the Lord's-day in the new of the moon, let him enter into that place clothed with white linen ; let him exorcise the place, bless it, and make a circle therein with a consecrated coal ; let there be written in the outer part of the circle the names of the angels ; in the inner part thereof write the mighty names of God ; and let be placed within the circle, at the four parts of the world, the vessels for the perfumes.   Then, being washed and fasting, let him enter the place and pray towards the east this whole Psalm, " Blessed are the undefiled in the way," &c. Psalm cxix.   Then make a fumigation, and deprecate the angels by the said divine names, that they will appear unto you, and reveal or discover that which you so earnestly desire ; and do this continually for six days, washed and fasting.   On the seventh day, being washed and fasting, enter the circle, perfume it, and anoint thyself with holy oil upon the forehead, eyes, and in the palms of both hands, and upon the feet ; then, with bended knees, say the Psalm aforesaid, with divine and angelical names.   Which being said, arise, and walk round the circle from *East* to *West*, until thou shalt be wearied with a giddiness of thy head and brain, then straitway fall down in the circle, where thou mayest rest, and thou wilt be wrapped up in an ecstasy ; and a spirit will appear and inform thee of all things necessary to be known.   We must observe also, that in the circle there ought to be four holy candles
burning

burning at the four parts of the world, which ought not to want light for the space of a week.

And the manner of fasting is this : to abstain from all things having a life of sense, and from those which do proceed from them, let him drink only pure running water; neither is there any food or wine to be taken till the going down of the sun.

Let the perfume and the holy anointing oil be made as is set forth in Exodus, and other holy books of the Bible. It is also to be observed, that as often as he enters the circle he has upon his forehead a golden lamen, upon which there must be written the name *Tetragrammaton*, in the manner we have before mentioned.

Of ORACLES *by* DREAMS.

BUT natural things and their own commixtures do likewise belong unto magicians, and we often use such to receive oracles from a spirit by a dream; which are either by perfumes, unctions, meats, drinks, seals, rings, &c.

Now those who are desirous to receive oracles in or through a dream, let him make himself a ring of the sun or Saturn for this purpose. There are likewise images of dreams, which, being put under the head when he goes to sleep, doth effectually give true dreams of whatever the mind hath before determined or consulted upon, the practice of which is as follows :

Thou shalt make an image of the sun, the figure whereof must be, a man sleeping upon the bosom of an angel, which thou shalt make when Leo ascends, the sun being in the ninth house in Aries ; thou shalt write upon the figure the name of the effect desired, and in the hand of the angel the name of the intelligence of the sun. Let the same image be made in Virgo ascending, Mercury being fortunate in Aries in the ninth ; or Gemini ascending, Mercury being fortunate in the ninth house in Aquarius ; and let

it

it be received with Saturn with a fortunate afpect, and let the name of the
fpirit be written upon it. Let the fame likewife be made in Libra afcending, Venus being received from Mercury in Gemini in the ninth houfe, and
write upon it the angel of Venus. Again, you may make the fame image
Aquarius afcending, Saturn fortunately poffeffing the ninth in his exaltation, which is Libra; and let there be written upon it the angel of
Saturn. The fame may be made Cancer afcending, the moon being received
by Jupiter and Venus in Pifces, and being fortunately placed in the ninth
houfe, and write upon it the fpirit of the moon.

There are likewife made rings of dreams of wonderful efficacy; and there
are rings of the fun and Saturn; and the conftellation of them is when the
fun or Saturn afcend in their exaltations in the ninth, and when the moon
is joined to Saturn in the ninth, and in that fign which was the ninth houfe
of the nativity; and write and engrave upon the rings the name of the fpirit
of the fun or Saturn; and by thefe rules you may know how and by what
means to conftitute more of thyfelf: but know this, that fuch images work
nothing (as they are fimply images) unlefs they are vivified by a fpiritual and
celeftial virtue, and chiefly by the ardent defire and firm intent of the foul of
the operator. But who can give a foul to an image, or make a ftone, or
metal, or clay, or wood, or wax, or paper to live? certainly no man; (for this
arcanum doth not enter into an artift of a ftiff neck,) he only hath it who
tranfcends the progrefs of angels, and comes to the very architype himfelf.

The tables of numbers likewife confer to the receiving of oracles, being
duly formed under their own conftellations. Holy tables and papers likewife
ferve to this effect, being efpecially compofed and confecrated; fuch as the
Almutel of *Solomon*, and the Table of the Revolution of the name *Tetragrammaton*; and thofe things which are of this kind, and written to produce
thefe effects, out of various figures, numbers, holy Scriptures, and pictures,
with infcriptions of the divine names of God and names of holy angels; the
compofition whereof is taken out of diverfe places of the holy Scriptures,
Pfalms, and verficles, and other certain promifes out of the divine revelations
and prophecies.

Book II.   O   To

To the same effect do conduce, likewise, holy prayers and deprecations as well to God as to the blessed angels; the deprecations of which prayers are to be composed, as we have before shewn, according to some religious similitude, making mention of those things which we intend to do; as out of the Old Testament of the dream of Jacob, Joseph, Pharoah, Daniel, and Nebuchadnezzar: if out of the New Testament, of the dream of Joseph; of the three wise men, or magi, of John the evangelist sleeping upon the breast of our Lord; and whatever of the like kind can be found in religion, miracles, and revelation. According to which the deprecation may be composed; if when he goes to sleep it be with a firm intention, and then, without doubt, they will afford a wonderful effect.

Therefore he who is desirous of receiving true oracles by dreams, let him abstain from supper, from drink, and be otherwise well disposed, so his brain will be free from turbulent vapours; let him also have his bed-chamber fair and clean, *exorcised* and *consecrated* if he will; then let him perfume the same with some convenient fumigation, and let him anoint his temples with some unguent efficacious hereunto, and put a ring of dreams upon his finger; then let him take one of the images we have spoken of, or some holy table, or paper, and place the same under his head; then, having made a devout prayer, let him addrefs himself to sleep, meditating upon that thing which he desires to know; so shall he receive a most certain and undoubted oracle by a dream, when the moon goes through that sign which was in the ninth house of his nativity, and also when she goes through the sign of the ninth of the revolution of his nativity, and when she is in the ninth sign from the sign of perfection.

This is the way whereby we may obtain all sciences and arts whatsoever, whether alchemy, magic, or else, suddenly and perfectly with a true illumination of our intellect; although all inferior familiar spirits whatsoever conduce to this effect, and sometimes also evil spirits sensibly inform us intrinsically and extrinsically.

Of

Of the Method of raising EVIL *or* FAMILIAR SPIRITS *by a* CIRCLE ;
likewise the Souls and Shadows of the Dead.

IT is here convenient that we say something about the means used by exor-
cists to raise up what are usually termed evil spirits to the circle, and the
methods of calling up the ghosts or souls of those who have died a violent or
premature death.

Now, if any one would call any evil spirit to the circle, he must first consider and know his nature, and to which of the planets it agrees, and what offices are distributed unto him from the planet. This being known, let there
be sought out a place fit and convenient, and proper for his invocation,
according to the nature of the planet and the quality of the offices of the same
spirit, as near as it can be done ; as if their power be over the sea, rivers or
floods, then let the place be the sea-shore, and so of the rest. Then chuse a
convenient time both for the quality of the air (being serene, quiet, clear and
fitting for the spirits to assume bodies) ; as also of the quality of and nature of
the planet and the spirit, as on his day and time in which he rules ; he may be
fortunate or unfortunate sometimes of the day, and sometimes of the night, as
the stars and spirits do require.

These things being judiciously considered, let the circle be made at the
place elected, as well for the defence of the invocant as the confirmation of the
spirit. And in the circle write the divine general names, and all those
things which do yield defence to us ; and, with them, those divine names
which do rule his planet, and the offices of the spirit himself ; likewise write
therein the names of the good spirits which bear rule in the time you do this,
and are able to bind and constrain that spirit which we intend to call. And
if we will further strengthen and fortify our circle, we may add characters and
pentacles agreeing to the work ; then also, if we will, we may either, within or
without the circle, frame an angular figure with the inscription of such convenient numbers as are congruent amongst themselves to our work, which

are

are to be known according to the manner of numbers and figures delivered in
our first Book.

Further we are to be provided with *lights*, perfumes, unguents, and
medicines, compounded according to the nature of the spirit and planet,
which agree with the spirit by reason of their natural and celestial
virtue.

Then we are to be furnished with holy and consecrated things necessary, not
only for the defence of the invocant and his companions, but also serving
for bonds to bind and constrain the spirits; such as holy papers, lamens,
pictures, pentacles, swords, scepters, garments of convenient colour and
matter.

Then, with all these things provided, let the exorcist and his companions
go into the circle. In the first place, let him consecrate the circle and every
thing he uses; which being done in a solemn and firm manner, with convenient gesture and countenance, let him begin to pray with a loud voice after
the manner following. First, by making an oration or prayer to God, and then
intreating the good spirits; but we should read some prayer, or psalm, or gospel, for our defence in the first place. After those prayers and orations are
said, let him begin to invocate the spirit which he desireth, with a gentle and
loving enchantment to all the coasts of the world, with a commemoration of
his own authority and power. Then rest and look round to see if any spirit
does appear; which if he delays, then let him repeat his invocation, as above
said, until he hath done it three times; and if the spirit is obstinate and will
not appear, then let the invocator begin to *conjure* him with divine power;
but so that all his conjurations and commemorations do agree with the nature
and office of the spirit, and reiterate the same three times, from stronger to
stronger, using contumelies, cursings, punishments, suspension from his power
and office, and the like.

And after these courses are finished, cease; and if the spirit shall appear let
the invocant turn himself towards the spirit, and courteously receive him, and,
earnestly entreating him, let him ask his name, which write down on your
holy paper, and then proceed by asking him whatsoever you will; and if in any
                                                                            thing

thing the fpirit fhall appear to be *obftinate, ambiguous,* or *lying,* let him be bound by convenient conjurations ; and if you doubt any thing, make, without the circle with the confecrated fword, the figure of a triangle or pentagon; and compel the fpirit to enter into it ; and if you receive any promife which you would have confirmed with an oath, ftretch the fword out of the circle, and fwear the fpirit by laying his hand on the fword. Then having obtained of the fpirit that which you defire, or are otherwife contented, licenfe him to de-part with courteous words, giving command that he do no hurt ; and if he will not depart, compel him by powerful conjurations ; and if need require ex-pel him by exorcifms and by making contrary fuffumigations. And when he is departed, go not out of the circle, but make a ftay, and ufe fome prayer giv-ing thanks to God and the good angels ; and alfo praying for your future defence and confervation, which being orderly performed you may depart.

But if your hopes are fruftrated, and no fpirit will appear, yet for this you need not defpair ; but leaving the circle after licenfing to depart (*which muft never be omitted, whether a fpirit appears or not* *,) return at other times, doing as before. And if you think that you have erred in any thing, then you fhall amend by adding or diminifhing ; for the conftancy of repetition encreafes your authority and power, and ftrikes a terror into the fpirits, and compels them to obey.

And often the fpirits do come although they appear not vifible (to caufe terror to him who calls them,) either in the thing which he ufes, or elfe in the operation itfelf. But this kind of licenfing is not given *fimply,* but by a kind of difpenfation, with fufpenfion, until they fhall render themfelves obedient : alfo, without a circle, thefe fpirits may be called to appear, by the way we have delivered in the confecration of a book. But when we intend to execute any effect where an apparition is not needful, then that is to be done, by making and forming that which is to be to us an inftrument ; as whether it be an image, ring, character, table, writing, candle, facrifice, or

---

* They who neglect licenfing the fpirits are in very great danger, becaufe inftances have been known of the operator experiencing fudden death.

any

any thing else; then the name of the spirit is to be written therein with his character, according to the exigency of the experiment, either by writing it with blood, or otherwise using a perfume agreeable to the spirit. Likewise we are often to make orations and prayers to God and the good angels before we invocate any evil spirit, conjuring him by divine power.

In some former parts of our work we have taught how and by what means the soul is joined to the body.

We will in this place inform thee farther, that those souls do still love their relinquished bodies after death, a certain affinity alluring them as it were. Such are the souls of noxious men who have violently relinquished their bodies, and souls wanting a due burial, which still wander in a liquid and turbulent spirit about their dead carcasses; for these souls, by the known means by which they were joined to their bodies, by the like vapours, liquors, and savours, are easily drawn into them.

Hence it is that the souls of the dead are not to be called up without blood or by the application of some part of their relict body.

In the *raising* therefore of these shadows, we are to perfume with new blood the bones of the dead, and with flesh, eggs, milk, honey, and oil, which furnish the soul with a medium apt to receive its body.

It is likewise to be understood, those who are desirous to raise any souls of the dead, ought to select those places wherein these kind of souls are most known to be conversant; or by some alliance alluring the souls into their forsaken *bodies*, or by some kind of affection in times past impressed in them in their life, drawing the souls to certain places, things, or persons; or by the forcible nature of some place fitted and prepared to purge or punish these souls: which places, for the most part, are to be known by the appearance of visions, nightly incursions, and apparitions.

Therefore the places most fitting for these things are church-yards. And better than them are those places devoted to the executions of criminal judgments; and better than these are those places where, of late years, there have been so great and so many public slaughters of men; and that place is still better than those where some dead carcass that came by violent death is

not

not yet expiated, nor was lately buried ; for the expiation of those places is likewise a holy rite duly to be adhibited to the burial of the bodies, and often prohibits the soul returning to its body, and expels the same afar off to the place of judgment.

And from hence it is that the souls of the dead are not easy to be raised up, except it be the souls of them whom we know to be evil, or to have perished by a violent death, and whose bodies do want the rite of due burial.

Now although we have spoken concerning such places of this kind, it will not be safe or commodious to go unto them ; but it is requisite for us to take to whatsoever place is to be chosen some principal relict of the body, and therewith make a perfume in due manner, and to perform other competent rites.

It is also to be known, that because the souls are certain spiritual lights, therefore artificial lights framed out of certain competent things, compounded according to a true rule, with congruent inscriptions of names and seals, do very much avail to the raising up of departed souls. But those things which are now spoken of are not always sufficient to raise up souls, because of an extra-natural portion of understanding and reason, which is above and known only to the heavenly destinies and their powers.

We should therefore allure the said souls by supernatural and celestial powers duly administered, even by those things which do move the very harmony of the soul, as well imaginative as rational and intellectual, such as voices, songs, sounds, enchantments ; and religious things, as prayers, conjurations, exorcisms, and other holy rites, which may commodiously be administered hereunto.

END OF PART SECOND.

A Table, shewing the names of the Angels governing the 7 days of the week, with their Sigils, Planets, Signs, &c.

Sunday	Monday	Tuesday	Wednesday	Thursday	Friday	Saturday
Michaël	Gabriel	Camael	Raphaël	Sachiel	Ana'el	Cassiel
☉ ♌	☽ ♋	♂ ♈ ♏	☿ ♊ ♍	♃ ♐ ♓	♀ ♎ ♉	♄ ♑ ♒
name of the 4.ᵗʰ Heaven	name of the 1.ˢᵗ Heaven	name of the 5.ᵗʰ Heaven	name of the 2.ᵈ Heaven	name of the 6.ᵗʰ Heaven	name of the 3.ᵈ Heaven	Nᵒ Angels ruling above the 6.ᵗʰ Heaven
Machen.	Shamain.	Machon.	Raquie.	Zebul.	Sagun.	

The Book of Spirits

Specimen of the Book of Spirits to [be] made of virgin Vellum.

Saturday ♄ Cassiel. Ruler.

See the Conjuration of Saturday in cerimonial magic.

Cassiel.

Barrett Del.   Pub. by   Lackington & Allen   R. Griffith Sculp.

OF THE

PARTICULAR COMPOSITION

OF THE

MAGICAL CIRCLE;

OF

EXORCISMS, BENEDICTIONS, AND THE CONJURATIONS OF EVERY DAY IN THE WEEK;

AND

THE MANNER OF WORKING DESCRIBED.

BOOK II. PART III.

THE following instructions are the principal and sum total of all we have said, only we have brought it rather into a closer train of experiment and practice than any of the rest; for here you may behold the distinct functions of the spirits; likewise the whole perfection of magical ceremonies is here described, syllable by syllable.

But as the greatest power is attributed to the circles, (for they are certain fortresses,) we will now clearly explain, and shew the composition and figure of a circle.

The Composition of the CIRCLE.—(For the figure of the Circle see the Plate.)

The forms of circles are not always one and the same, but are changed according to the order of spirits that are to be called, their places, times, days, and hours; for in making a circle it ought to be confidered in what time of the year, what day, and what hour, what fpirits you would call, and to what ftar or region they belong, and what functions they have: therefore, to begin, let there be made three circles of the latitude of nine feet, diftant one from another about a hand's breadth. Firft, write in the middle circle *the name of the hour* wherein you do the work; in the fecond place, write *the name of the angel of the hour*; in the third place, the feal of the angel of the hour; fourthly, the name of the angel that rules the day in which you work, and the names of his minifters; in the fifth place, the name of the prefent time; fixthly, the name of the fpirits ruling in that part of time, and their *prefidents*; feventhly, the name of the head of the fign ruling in the time; eighthly, the name of the earth, according to the time of working; ninthly, and for the compleating of the middle circle, write the name of the fun and moon, according to the faid rule of time: for as the times are changed, fo are the names: and in the outer circle let there be drawn, in the four angles, the names of the great prefidential fpirits of the air that day wherein you would do this work, *viz.* the name of the king and his three minifters. Without the circle, in four angles, let *pentagons* be made. In the inner circle write four divine names, with four croffes interpofed: in the middle of the circle, *viz.* towards the eaft let be written Alpha; towards the weft, Omega; and let a crofs divide the middle of the circle.

When the circle is thus finifhed, according to rule, you fhall proceed to confecrate and blefs it, faying,

In the name of the holy, bleffed, and glorious Trinity, proceed we to our work in thefe myfteries to accomplifh that which we defire; we therefore, in the names aforefaid, confecrate this piece of ground for our defence, fo that no fpirit whatfoever fhall be able to break thefe boundaries, neither be able to caufe injury nor detriment to any of us here affembled; but that they may be compelled to ftand before this circle, and anfwer truly our demands, fo far as it pleafeth Him who liveth for ever and ever; and who fays, I am Alpha and Omega, the Beginning and the End, which is, and which was, and which is to come, the Almighty; I am the Firft and the Laft, who am living and was dead; and behold I live
for

Two Holy wax Lights used in the Invocation by the Chrystal

The true size & form of the Chrystal which must be sett in pure Gold & the same names & characters as in the model here given.

Michael
Gabriel
Uriel
Raphael

The magic Circle of a simple construction in which the operator must stand or sit when he uses the Chrystal

The Magic Wand to be used in Invocations by the Chrystal.

Agla

On

Tetragrammaton

write or engrave on the other side
Ego sm Alpha et Omega

Tetragrammaton

ADONAI

Elohim

The Tripod on which the perfumes are put, & may be either held in the hand or sett in the earth.

מיכאל

El, Elohim, Eloha, Eluath, Elion, Eschereie,
Michael
ᚃ
Adonai, Jah, Jehova, Tetragrammaton, Saday, Jod, Eheie.

The Lamen, or Holy Table of the Archangel Michael.

*for ever and ever; and I have the keys of death and hell. Bless, O Lord!
this creature of earth wherein we stand; confirm, O God! thy strength in us, so
that neither the adversary nor any evil thing may cause us to fail, through the
merits of Jesus Christ. Amen.*

It is also to be known that the angels rule the hours in a successive order,
according to the course of the heavens and the planets to which they are subject; so the same spirit which governeth the day rules also the first hour of the
day; the second from this governs the second hour, and so on throughout;
and when seven planets and hours have made their revolution it returns again
to the first which rules the day.   Therefore we shall first speak of the names
of the hours, *viz.*

A TABLE *shewing the* MAGICAL NAMES *of the* HOURS, *both* DAY
and NIGHT.

	Names of Hours of the Day.		Names of Hours of the Night.
1	Yain	1	Beron
2	Janor	2	Barol
3	Nasnia	3	Thami
4	Salla	4	Athar
5	Sadedali	5	Methon
6	Thamur	6	Rana
7	Ourer	7	Netos
8	Thamic	8	Tafrac
9	Neron	9	Saffur
10	Jayon	10	Agle
11	Abai	11	Calerva
12	Natalon	12	Salam

Of the names of the angels and their seals it shall be spoken in their proper
places; but here we will shew the names of the times.

A year

A year therefore is four-fold, and is divided into ſpring, ſummer, autumn, and winter ; the names thereof are theſe :

The ſpring, *Talvi* ; the ſummer, *Caſmaran* ; autumn, *Adarcel* ; winter, *Farlas.*

The ANGELS *of the* SPRING—Caracaſa, Core, Amatiel, Commiſſoros.
The head of the ſign in ſpring is called Spugliguel.
The name of the earth in ſpring, Amadai.
The names of the ſun and moon in ſpring : ſun, Abraym ; moon, Aguſita.

The ANGELS *of the* SUMMER—Gargatel, Tariel, Gaviel.
The head of the ſign of the ſummer, Tubiel.
The name of the earth in ſummer, Feſtativi.
The names of the ſun and moon in ſummer : ſun, Athemay ; moon, Armatus.

The ANGELS *of the* AUTUMN—Tarquam, Guabarel.
The head of the ſign of autumn, Torquaret.
The name of the earth in autumn, Rabinnara.
The names of the ſun and moon in autumn : the ſun, Abragini ; the moon, Mataſignais.

The ANGELS *of the* WINTER—Amabael, Cetarari.
The head of the ſign of winter, Attarib.
The name of the earth in winter, Geremiah.
The names of the ſun and moon in winter : the ſun, Commutoff ; the moon, Affaterim.

Theſe things being known, finiſh the conſecration of the circle by ſaying, " Thou ſhalt purge me with hyſop, O Lord, and I ſhall be clean : thou ſhalt waſh me and I ſhall be whiter than ſnow."

Then ſprinkle the ſame with holy water, and proceed with the benediction of the perfumes.

BENE-

BENEDICTION *of* PERFUMES.

THE God of Abraham, God of Isaac, God of Jacob, bless here the creatures of these kinds, that they may fill up the power and virtue of their odours; so that neither the enemy nor any false imagination may be able to enter into them; through our Lord Jesus Christ, &c. Then sprinkle the same with holy water.

The EXORCISM *of* FIRE *into which the* PERFUMES *are to be put.*

I EXORCISE thee, O thou creature of fire, by the only true God Jehovah, Adonai, Tetragrammaton, that forthwith thou cast away every phantasm from thee, that it shall do no hurt to any one. We beseech thee, O Lord, to bless this creature of fire, and sanctify it, so that it may be blessed to set forth the praise and glory of thy holy name, and that no hurt may be permitted to come to the exorciser or spectators; through our Lord Jesus Christ. *Amen.*

Of the HABIT *of the* EXORCIST.

IT should be made, as we have before described, of fine white linen and clean, and to come round the body loose, but close before and behind

Of the PENTACLE *of* SOLOMON.—(For the fig. see the Plate.)

IT is always necessary to have this pentacle in readiness to bind with, in case the spirits should refuse to be obedient, as they can have no power over the exorcist while provided with and fortified by the pentacle, the virtue of the holy names therein written presiding with wonderful influence over the spirits.

It should be made in the day and hour of Mercury upon parchment made of a kidskin, or virgin, or pure, clean, white paper; and the figures and
letters

letters wrote in pure gold; and it ought to be confecrated and fprinkled (as before often fpoken) with holy water.

When the vefture is put on, it will be convenient to fay the following oration:

An ORATION *when the* HABIT *or* VESTURE *is put on.*

ANOOR, Amacor, Amides, Theodonias, Anitor; by the merits of the angels, O Lord! I will put on the garment of falvation, that this which I defire I may bring to effect, through thee, the moft holy Adonai, whofe kingdom endureth for ever and ever. *Amen.*

The Manner of Working.

LET the moon be increafing and equal, if it can then be conveniently done; but efpecially let her not be combuft, or in Via Combufta, which is between fourteen degrees of Libra and fourteen degrees of Scorpio.

The operator ought to be clean and purified for nine days before he does the work. Let him have ready the perfume appropriated to the day wherein he does the work; and he muft be provided with holy water from a clergyman, or he may make it holy himfelf, by reading over it the confecration of water of baptifm; he muft have a new veffel of earth, with fire, the vefture, and the pentacle; and let all thefe things be rightly and duly confecrated and prepared. Let one of the companions carry the veffel with fire, and the perfumes, and let another bear the book, the garment, and pentacle; and let the operator himfelf carry the fword, over which fhould be faid a prayer of confecration: and on the middle of the fword on one fide let there be engraven *Agla* †, and on the other fide, † *On*, † Tetragrammaton †. And the place being fixed upon where the circle is to be erected, let him draw the lines we have before taught, and fprinkle the fame with holy water, confecrating, &c. &c.

The

The operator ought therefore to be prepared with fasting, chastity, and abstinence, for the space of three days before the day of operation ; and on the day that he would do this work, being clothed with the fore-mentioned vesture, and furnished with *pentacles, perfumes,* a *sword, bible, paper, pen,* and *confecrated ink,* and *all things neceffary hereunto,* let him enter the circle, and call the angels from the four parts of the world which do rule the feven planets, the feven days of the week, colours, and metals, whofe names you will fee in their places ; and, with bended knees, firft let him fay the Paternofter or Lord's Prayer, and then let him invocate the faid angels, faying,

O angeli ! fupradicti eftote adjutores mihi petitioni, & in adjatorum mihi, in meis rebus et petitionibus.

Then call the angels from the four parts of the world that rule the air the fame day in which he makes the experiment ; and, having employed efpecially all the names and fpirits within the circle, fay,

O vos omnes, adjutore atque conteftor, per fedem Adonai, per Hagios, Theos, Ifchyros, Athanatos, Paracletos, Alpha & Omega, & per hæc tria nomina fecreta, Ayla, On, Tetragrammaton, quod hodie debeatis adimplere quod cupio.

Thefe things being performed, let him read the conjuration affigned for the day; but if they fhall be pertinacious or refractory, and will not yield themfelves obedient, neither to the conjuration affigned for the day, nor any of the prayers before made, then ufe the exorcifm following :

A GENERAL EXORCISM *of the* SPIRITS *of the* AIR.

WE being made after the image of God, endued with power from God, and made after his will, do exorcife you, by the moft mighty and powerful name of God, *El,* ftrong and wonderful, *(here name the fpirit which is to appear,)* and we command you by Him who fpoke the word and it was done, and by all the names of God, and by the name Adonai, El, Elohim, Elohe, Zebaoth, Elion, Eferchie, Jah, Tetragrammaton, Sadai, Lord God Moft High: we exorcife you, and powerfully command you that you forthwith appear unto us here before this circle in a fair human fhape, without any deformity

mity or tortuofity; come ye all fuch, becaufe we command you by the name Yaw and Vau, which Adam heard and fpoke; and by the name of God, **Agla,** which Lot heard, and was faved with his family; and by the name **Joth,** which Jacob heard from the angel wreftling with him, and was delivered from the hand of his brother Efau; and by the name Anaphexeton, which Aaron heard and fpoke, and was made wife; and by the name Zebaoth, which Mofes named, and all the rivers were turned into blood; and by the name Eferchie Orifton, which Mofes named, and all the rivers brought forth frogs, and they afcended into the houfes of the Egyptians, deftroying all things; and by the name Elion, which Mofes named, and there was great hail, fuch as had not been fince the beginning of the world; and by the name Adonai, which Mofes named, and there came up locufts, which appeared upon the whole land of Egypt, and devoured all which the hail had left; and by the name Schema Amathia, which Jofhua called upon, and the fun ftayed his courfe; and by the name Alpha and Omega, which Daniel named, and deftroyed Bel and flew the dragon; and in the name Emmanuel, which the three children, Sidrach, Mifach, and Abednego, fung in the midft of the fiery furnace, and were delivered; and by the name Hagios; and by the feal of Adonai; and by Ifchyros, Athanatos, Paracletos; and by thefe three fecret names, Agla, On, Tetragrammaton, I do adjure and conteft you; and by thefe names, and by all the other names of the living and true God, our Lord Almighty, I exorcife and command you, by Him who fpoke the word and it was done, to whom all creatures are obedient; and by the dreadful judgment of God; and by the uncertain fea of glafs, which is before the divine *Majefty,* mighty and powerful; by the four beafts before the throne, having eyes before and behind; and by the fire round about his throne; and by the holy angels of heaven; by the mighty wifdom of God, we do powerfully exorcife you, that you appear here before this circle, to fulfil our will in all things which fhall feem good unto us; by the feal of Baldachia, and by this name Primeumaton, which *Mofes* named, and the earth opened and fwallowed up Corah, Dathan, and Abiram: and in the power of that name Primeumaton, commanding the whole hoft of heaven, we curfe you, and deprive you of your

office,

office, joy, and place, and do bind you in the depth of the bottomless pit, there to remain until the dreadful day of the last judgment; and we bind you into eternal fire, and into the lake of fire and brimstone, unless you forthwith appear before this circle to do our will: therefore, come ye, by these names, Adonai, Zebaoth, Adonai, Amioram; come ye, come ye, come ye, Adonai commandeth; Saday, the most mighty King of Kings, whose power no creature is able to resist, be unto you most dreadful, unless ye obey, and forthwith affably appear before this circle, let miserable ruin and fire unquenchable remain with you; therefore come ye, in the name of Adonai, Zebaoth, Adonai, Amioram; come, come, why stay you? hasten! Adonai, Sadai, the King of Kings commands you: El, Aty, Titcip, Azia, Hin, Jen, Minosel, Achadan Vay, Vaah, Ey, Exe, A, El, El, El, A, Hy, Hau, Hau, Hau, Vau, Vau, Vau, Vau.

A PRAYER *to* GOD, *to be said in the four Parts of the* WORLD *in the* CIRCLE.

AMORULE, Taneha, Latisten, Rabur, Teneba, Latisten, Escha, Aladia, Alpha and Omega, Leyste, Orision, Adonai; O most merciful heavenly Father! have mercy upon me, although a sinner; make appear the arm of thy power in me this day against these obstinate spirits, that I, by thy will, may be made a contemplator of thy divine works, and may be illustrated with all wisdom, to the honour and glory of thy holy name. I humbly beseech thee, that these spirits which I call by thy judgment may be bound and constrained to come and give true and perfect answers to those things which I shall ask of them; and that they may do and declare those things unto us, which by me may be commanded of them, not hurting any creature, neither injuring or terrifying me or my fellows, nor hurting any other creature, and affrighting no man; but let them be obedient to those things which are required of them.

Q   Then

Then, standing in the middle of the circle, stretch out thy hand towards the pentacle, saying, *By the pentacle of Solomon I have called you ; give me a true answer.*

Then follows this ORATION.

BERALANENSIS, Baldachiensis, Paumachia, and Apologià Sedes, by the most mighty kings and powers, and the most powerful princes, genii, Liachidæ, ministers of the Tartarean seat, chief prince of the seat of Apologia, in the ninth legion, I invoke you, and by invocating, conjure you ; and being armed with power from the supreme Majesty, I strongly command you, by Him who spoke and it was done, and to whom all creatures are obedient ; and by this ineffable name, Tetragrammaton Jehovah, which being heard the elements are overthrown, the air is shaken, the sea runneth back, the fire is quenched, the earth trembles, and all the host of the celestials, and terrestrials, and infernals do tremble together, and are troubled and confounded : wherefore, forthwith and without delay, do you come from all parts of the world, and make rational answers unto all things I shall ask of you; and come ye peaceably, visibly and affably now, without delay, manifesting what we desire, being conjured by the name of the living and true God, Helioren, and fulfil our commands, and persist unto the end, and according to our intentions, visibly and affably speaking unto us with a clear voice, intelligible, and without any ambiguity.

Of the APPEARANCE of the SPIRITS.

THESE things being duly performed, there will appear infinite visions, apparitions, phantasms, &c. beating of drums, and the sound of all kinds of musical instruments ; which is done by the spirits, that with the terror they might force some of the companions out of the circle, because they can effect nothing against the exorcist himself: after this you shall see an infinite company

pany

pany of archers, with a great multitude of horrible beasts, which will arrange themselves as if they would devour the companions; nevertheless fear nothing.

Then the exorcist, holding the pentacle in his hand, let him say, Avoid hence these iniquities, by virtue of the banner of God. Then will the spirits be compelled to obey the exorcist, and the company shall see them no more.

Then let the exorcist, stretching out his hand with the pentacle, say, Behold the pentacle of *Solomon*, which I have brought into your presence; behold the person of the exorcist in the middle of the exorcism, who is armed by God, without fear, and well provided, who potently invocateth and calleth you by exorcising; come, therefore, with speed, by the virtue of these names, Aye Saraye, Aye Saraye; defer not to come, by the eternal names of the living and true God, Eloy, Archima, Rabur, and by the pentacle of Solomon here present, which powerfully reigns over you; and by the virtue of the celestial spirits, your lords; and by the person of the exorcist, in the middle of the exorcism: being conjured, make haste and come, and yield obedience to your master, who is called Octinomos. This being performed, immediately there will be hissings in the four parts of the world, and then immediately you shall see great motions; which when you see, say, Why stay you? Wherefore do you delay? What do you? Prepare yourselves to be obedient to your master in the name of the Lord, Bathat or Vachat rushing upon Abrac, Abeor coming upon Aberer.

Then they will immediately come in their proper forms; and when you see them before the circle, shew them the pentacle covered with fine linen; uncover it, and say, Behold your confusion if you refuse to be obedient; and suddenly they will appear in a peaceable form, and will say, Ask what you will, for we are prepared to fulfil all your commands, for the Lord hath subjected us hereunto.

Then let the exorcist say, Welcome spirits, or most noble princes, because I have called you through Him to whom every knee doth bow, both of things in heaven, and things in earth, and things under the earth; in

whose

whofe hands are all the kingdoms of kings, neither is there any able to con-
tradict his Majefty. Wherefore, I bind you, that you remain affable and
vifible before this circle, fo long and fo conftant; neither fhall you depart
without my licence, until you have truly and without any fallacy performed
my will, by virtue of his power who hath fet the fea her bounds, beyond
which it cannot pafs, nor go beyond the law of his providence, *viz.* of
the Moft High God, Lord, and King, who hath created all things. *Amen.*

Then let the exorcift mention what he would have done.

After which fay, In the name of the Father, and of the Son, and of
the Holy Ghoft, go in peace unto your places; peace be between us and you;
be ye ready to come when you are called. (For the figures of the circle,
pentacle, and other inftruments, fee the Plate.)

Now, that you may have an idea of the manner of compofing the circle,
we have given the fcheme of one for the firft hour of the Lord's day, in
fpring.

———————————

Here follow the CONSIDERATIONS *and* CONJURATIONS *for every Day
in the Week; and firft of*

The CONSIDERATIONS, *&c. of* SUNDAY.

(For the figure of the *feals, planets, figns,* names of the angels of the feveral days, and names of the fourth heaven, with the characters and magic
book, fee the Plate.)

THE angels of the Lord's day—*Michael, Dardiel, Huratapel.*

The angels of the air ruling on the Lord's day, *Varcan,* king;—his minifters, *Tus, Andas, Cynabal.*

The wind which the angels of the air are faid to rule, is the north wind.

The angels of the fourth heaven ruling on the Lord's day, which fhould
be called from the four parts of the world, are,—eaft, *Samael, Baciel, Abel,
Gabriel,*

Gabriel, Vionatraba ;—from the weſt, *Anael, Pabel, Uſtael, Burchat, Suceratos, Capabili ;*—from the north, *Aiel, Ariel, vel Aquiel, Maſgabriel, Saphiel, Matuyel ;*—at the ſouth, *Haludiel, Machaſiel, Charſiel, Uriel, Naromiel.*

The perfume of Sunday is *Red Sanders.*

The CONJURATION *for* SUNDAY.

I CONJURE and confirm upon you, ye ſtrong and holy angels of God, in the name *Adonai, Eye, Eye, Eya,* which is he who was, and is, and is to come, *Eye, Abray* ; and in the name *Saday, Cados, Cados,* ſitting on high upon the *cherubin* ; and by the great name of *God* himſelf, ſtrong and powerful, who is exalted above all the heavens ; *Eye, Saraye,* who created the world, the heavens, the earth, the ſea, and all that in them is, in the firſt day, and ſealed them with his holy name Phaa ; and by the name of the angels who rule in the *fourth heaven,* and ſerve before the moſt mighty *Salamia,* an angel great and honourable ; and by the name of his ſtar, which is Sol, and by His ſign, and by the immenſe name of the living *God,* and by all the names aforeſaid, I conjure thee, Michael, O great angel ! who art chief ruler of this day ; and by the name Adonai, the God of Iſrael, I conjure thee, O Michael ! that thou labour for me, and fulfil all my petitions according to my will and deſire in my cauſe and buſineſs.

The ſpirits of the air of the Lord's day are under the north wind ; their nature is to procure gold, gems, carbuncles, diamonds, and rubies, and to cauſe one to obtain favour and benevolence, to diſſolve enmities amongſt men, to raiſe to honours, and to take away infirmities. *They appear,* for the moſt part, in a large, full and great body, ſanguine and groſs, in a gold colour, with the tincture of blood. Their motion is like the lightning of heaven ; the ſign of their becoming viſible is that they move the perſon to ſweat that calls them ; but their particular forms are as follow ; *viz.*

A king, having a ſcepter, riding on a lion.

A king crowned ; a queen with a ſcepter.

A bird ;

A bird; a lion; a cock.

A yellow garment.

A fcepter.

Considerations, &c. of Monday.

(For the angel of Monday, his figil, planet, fign of the planet, and name of the firft heaven, fee the Plate.)

THE angels of Monday—*Gabriel, Michael, Samael.*

The angels of the air ruling Monday, *Arcan,* king;—his minifters, *Bilet, Miffabu, Abubaza.* The wind which thefe are fubject to is the *weft wind.*

The angels of the firft heaven, ruling on Monday, to be called from the four parts of the world. From the eaft, *Gabriel, Madiel, Deamiel, Janak;*—from the weft, *Sachiel, Zaniel, Habiel, Bachanæ, Corobael;*—from the north, *Mael, Uvael, Valnum, Baliel, Balay, Humaftraw;*—from the fouth, —*Curaniel, Dabriel, Darquiel, Hanun, Vetuel.*

The perfume of Monday—*Aloes.*

The Conjuration of Monday.

I CONJURE and confirm upon you, ye ftrong and good angels, in the name *Adonai, Adonai, Adonai, Adonai, Eye, Eye, Eye; Cados, Cados, Cados, Achim, Achim, Ja, Ja,* ftrong *Ja,* who appeared in mount Sinai with the glorification of king *Adonai, Sadai,* Zebaoth, Anathay Ya, Ya, Ya, Maranata, Abim, Jeia, who created the fea, and all lakes and waters, in the fecond day, which are above the heavens and in the earth, and fealed the fea in his high name, and gave it its bounds beyond which it cannot pafs; and by the names of the angels who rule in the *firft legion,* and who ferve *Orphaniel,* a great, precious, and honourable angel, and by the name of his ftar which is Luna, and by all the names aforefaid, I conjure thee, *Gabriel,* who art chief ruler of Monday, the fecond day, that for me thou labour and fulfil, &c.

The

The spirits of the air of Monday are subject to the west wind, which is the wind of the moon; their nature is to give silver and to convey things from place to place; to make horses swift, and to disclose the secrets of persons both present and future.

Their familiar Forms are as follow:

They appear generally of a great and full stature, soft and phlegmatic, of colour like a black, obscure cloud, having a swoln countenance, with eyes red and full of water, a bald head, and teeth like a wild boar; their motion is like an exceeding great tempest of the sea. For their sign there will appear an exceeding great rain, and their particular shapes are,

A king, like an archer, riding upon a doe.

A little boy.

A woman-hunter with a bow and arrows.

A cow; a little doe; a goose.

A green, or silver-coloured garment.

An arrow; a creature with many feet.

Considerations *of* Tuesday.

(For the angel of Tuesday, his sigil, planet, sign governing the planet, and name of the fifth heaven, see the Plate.)

THE angels of the air on Tuesday—*Samael, Satael, Amabiel.*

The angels of the air ruling on Tuesday, *Samax,* king; his Ministers, *Carmax, Ismoli, Paffran.*

The wind to which the said angels are subject is the *east wind.*

The angels of the fifth heaven ruling on Tuesday.—At the east, *Friagne, Guel, Damael, Calzas, Arragon;*---the west, *Lama, Astagna, Lobquin, Soneas, Jazel, Isiael, Irel;*---the north, *Rhaumel, Hyniel, Rayel, Seraphiel, Fraciel, Mathiel;*—the south, *Sacriel, Janiel, Galdel, Osael, Vianuel, Zaliel.*

The perfume of Tuesday---*Pepper.*

The

The CONJURATION of TUESDAY.

I CONJURE and call upon you, ye strong and good angels, in the names Ya, Ya, Ya; He, He, He; Va, Hy, Hy, Ha, Ha, Ha; Va, Va, Va; An, An, An; Aia, Aia, Aia; El, Ay, Elibra, Elohim, Elohim; and by the names of the high God, who hath made the sea and dry land, and by his word hath made the earth, and produced trees, and hath set his seal upon the planets, with his precious, honoured, revered and holy name; and by the name of the angels governing in the fifth house, who are subservient to the great angel Acimoy, who is strong, powerful, and honoured, and by the name of his star which is called *Mars*, I call upon thee, *Samael*, by the names above mentioned, thou great angel! who presides over the day of *Mars*, and by the name Adonai, the living and true God, that you assist me in accomplishing my labours, &c. *(as in the conjuration of Sunday.)*

The spirits of the air on Tuesday are under the east wind; their nature is to bring or cause war, mortality, death, combustions, and to give two-thousand soldiers at a time; to bring death, infirmity or health.

Familiar Forms of the SPIRITS of MARS.

THEY appear in a tall body and choleric, a filthy countenance, of colour brown, swarthy, or red, having horns like harts, and griffins claws, and bellowing like wild bulls. Their motion is like fire burning: their sign thunder and lightning round about the circle.

Their particular shapes are, a king armed, riding on a wolf; a man armed. A woman with a buckler on her thigh.

A she-goat; a horse; a stag.

A red garment; a piece of wool; a cowslip.

CON-

Considerations *of* Wednesday.

(For the angel of Wednefday his figil, &c. &c. fee the Plate.)

THE angels of Wednefday—*Raphael, Meil, Seraphiel.*

The angels of the air ruling on Wednefday, *Mediat,* king; Minifters, *Suquinos, Sallales;* the faid angels of the air are fubject to the *fouth-weft wind.*

The angels of the fecond heaven, governing Wednefday, that are to be called, &c. At the eaft—*Mathlai, Tarmiel, Baraborat*—at the weft, *Jerufcue, Merattron;*—at the north, *Thiel, Rael, Jarihael, Venahel, Velel, Abuiori, Ucirmiel*—at the fouth, *Milliel,. Nelapa, Calvel, vel Laquel.*

The perfume of Wednefday---*Maftic.*

The Conjuration *of* Wednesday.

I CONJURE and call upon you, ye ftrong and holy angels, good and powerful, in a ftrong name of fear and praife, Ja, Adonay, Elohim, Saday, Saday, Saday; Eie, Eie, Eie; Afamie, Afamie; and in the name of Adonay, the God of Ifrael, who hath made the two great lights, and diftinguifhed day from night for the benefit of his creatures; and by the names of all the difcerning angels, governing openly in the fecond houfe before the great angel, *Tetra,* ftrong and powerful; and by the name of his ftar which is *Mercury;* and by the name of his feal, which is that of a powerful and honoured God; and I call upon thee, Raphael, and by the names above mentioned, thou great angel who prefideft over the fourth day: and by the holy name which is written in the front of Aaron, created the moft high prieft, and by the names of all the angels who are conftant in the grace of Chrift, and by the name and place of Ammaluim, that you affift me in my labours, &c. &c.

The fpirits of the air, on Wednefday are fubject to the fouth-weft wind; their nature is to give all forts of metals, to reveal all earthly things paft, pre-

Book II.   R   fent,

sent, and to come ; to pacify judges, to give victory in war, to teach experiments and all sciences decayed, and to change bodies mixt of elements, conditionally, out of one thing into another ; to give health or infirmities, to raise the poor and cast down the rich, to bind or loose spirits, to open locks or bolts.

Such kinds of spirits have the operations of others, but not in their perfect power, but in virtue or knowledge.

Forms of the SPIRITS of MERCURY.

THE spirits of Mercury appear in a body of a middle stature, cold, liquid and moist, fair and of an affable speech, in a human shape and form, like a knight armed, of colour clear and bright.   The motion of them is like silver coloured clouds : for their sign they cause horror and fear to him that calls them.

Their particular shapes are, a king riding upon a bear.

A fair youth ; a woman holding a distaff.

A dog, a she-bear, and a magpye.

A garment of various changeable colours.

A rod, a little staff.

CONSIDERATIONS of THURSDAY.

(For the angel of Thursday, his sigil, &c. see the Plate.)

THE angels of Thursday---*Sachiel, Cassiel, Asasiel.*

The angels of the air of Thursday, *Suth,* king ; Ministers, *Maguth, Gutrix.*

The angels of the air are under the south-wind.—(But because there are no angels of the air to be found above the fifth heaven, therefore, on Thursday, say the prayers following in the four parts of the world :)

At the east—*O Deus magne et excelse et honorate, per infinita secula* ; or, O great and most high God, honoured be thy name, world without end.

At

At the west—O wise, pure, and juft God, of divine clemency, I befeech thee, moft holy Father, that this day I may perfectly underftand and accomplifh my petition, work, and labour; for the honour and glory of thy holy name, who liveft and reigneft, world without end. *Amen.*

At the north—O God, ftrong, mighty, and wonderful, from everlafting to everlafting, grant that this day I bring to effect that which I defire, through our bleffed Lord. *Amen.*

At the fouth—O mighty and moft merciful God, hear my prayers and grant my petition.

The perfume of Thurfday—*Saffron.*

The CONJURATION *of* THURSDAY.

I CONJURE and confirm upon you, ye ftrong and holy angels, by the names Cados, Cados, Cados, Efchereie, Efcherei, Efchereie, Hatim, Ya, ftrong founder of the worlds ; Cantine, Jaym, Janic, Anic, Calbot, Sabbac, Berifay, Alnaym ; and by the name Adonai, who created fifhes and creeping things in the waters, and birds upon the face of the earth, flying towards heaven, in the fifth day ; and by the names of the angels ferving in the fixth hoft before Paftor, a holy angel, and a great and powerful prince and by the name of his ftar, which is Jupiter, and by the name of his feal, and by the name of Adonai, the great God, Creator of all things, and by the name of all the ftars, and by their power and virtue, and by all the the names aforefaid, I conjure thee, Sachiel, a great Angel, who art chief ruler of Thurfday, that for me thou labour, *&c.*

The fpirits of the air of Thurfday are fubject to the fouth wind ; their nature is to procure the love of women, to caufe men to be merry and joyful, to pacify ftrifes and contentions, to appeafe enemies, to heal the difeafed, and to difeafe the whole, and procure loffes, or reftore things loft.

R 2

The

The familiar Forms of the SPIRITS *of* JUPITER.

The appear with a body sanguine and choleric, of a middle stature, with a horrible, fearful motion, but with a mild countenance, and a gentle speech, and of the colour of iron : the motion of them is flashings of lightning, and thunder. For their sign there will appear about the circle men who shall seem to be devoured by lions. Their forms are,

A king, with a sword drawn, riding on a stag.

A man, wearing a mitre, with long raiment.

A maid, with a laurel crown, adorned with flowers.

A bull ; a stag ; a peacock.

An azure garment ; a sword ; a box-tree.

CONSIDERATIONS *of* FRIDAY.

(For the seal planet, and sign governing the planet, and name of the third heaven, see the Plate.)

THE angels of Friday—*Anael, Rachiel, Sachiel.*

The angels of the air ruling on Friday, *Sarabotes,* king ; Ministers, *Amabiel, Aba, Abalidoth, Blaef.* The wind which the angels of the air are subject to is the west wind.

Angels of the third heaven, which are to be called from the four parts of the world, are

At the east, *Setchiel, Chedusitaniel, Cor'at, Tamuel, Tenaciel*;—at the west, *Turiel, Coniel, Babiel, Kadie, Maltiel, Huphaltiel*;—at the north, *Peniel, Penael, Penat, Raphael, Ranie, Doremiel*;—at the south, *Porosa, Sachiel, Chermiel, Samael, Santanael, Famiel.*

The perfume of Friday—*Pepperwort.*

The

The CONJURATION *of* FRIDAY.

I CONJURE and confirm upon you, ye ftrong and holy angels, by the names *On, Hey, Heya, Ja, Je, Saday, Adonai,* and in the name *Sadai,* who created four-footed beafts, and creeping things, and man, in the fixth day, and gave to Adam power over all creatures; wherefore bleffed be the name of the Creator in his place; and by the name of the angels ferving in the third hoft, before Dagiel, a great angel, and a ftrong and powerful prince, and by the name of his ftar, which is Venus, and by his feal which is holy; and by all the names aforefaid, I conjure upon thee, *Anael,* who art the chief ruler this day, that thou labour for me, *&c.*

The fpirits of the air on Friday are fubject to the weft wind; their nature is to give filver, to incite men, and incline them to luxury, to caufe marriages, to allure men to love women, to caufe or take away infirmities, and to do all things which have motion.

Their familiar Shapes.

They appear with a fair body, of middle ftature, with an amiable and pleafant countenance, of colour white or green, their upper parts golden; the motion of them is like a clear ftar. For their fign there will appear naked virgins round the circle, which will ftrive to allure the invocator to dalliance with them : but

Their particular Shapes are,

A king, with a fcepter, riding on a camel.
A naked girl; a fhe-goat.
A camel; a dove.
A white or green garment.
Flowers; the herb favine.

The

The CONSIDERATIONS *of* SATURDAY.

(For feal, &c. &c. fee the Plate.)

THE angels of Saturday--*Caffiel, Machatan, Uriel.*

The angels of the air ruling this day, *Maymon,* king; Minifters, *Abu-malith, Affaibi, Balidet.* The wind they are fubject to, the *fouth wind.*

The fumigation of Saturday is *fulphur.*

There are no angels ruling in the air on Saturday above the fifth heaven, therefore in the four corners of the world, in the circle, ufe thofe orations which are applied to Thurfday.

The CONJURATION *of* SATURDAY.

I CONJURE and confirm upon you, Caphriel, or Caffiel, Machator, and Seraquiel, ftrong and powerful angels; and by the name Adonai, Adonai, Adonai; Eie, Eie, Eie; Acim, Acim, Acim; Cados, Cados; Ima, Ima, Ima; Salay, Ja, Sar, Lord and Maker of the World, who refted on the feventh day; and by him who of his good pleafure gave the fame to be obferved by the children of Ifrael throughout their generations, that they fhould keep and fanctify the fame, to have thereby a good reward in the world to come; and by the names of the *angels* ferving in the feventh hoft, before Booel, a great angel, and powerful prince; and by the name of his ftar, which is Saturn; and by his holy feal, and by the names before fpoken, I conjure upon thee, Caphriel, who art chief ruler of the feventh day, which is the Sabbath, that for me thou labour, &c. &c.

The fpirits of the air on Saturday are fubject to the fouth-weft wind: the nature of them is to fow difcords, hatred, evil thoughts and cogitations, to give leave to kill and murder, and to lame or maim every member.

Their familiar Shapes.

THEY generally appear with a tall, lean, slender body, with an angry countenance, having four faces, one on the back of the head, one in the front, and one on each side, nosed or beaked, likewise there appears a face on each knee of a black shining colour; their motion is the moving of the wind, with a kind of earthquake; their sign is white earth, whiter than snow.

Their particular Shapes are,

* A king, bearded, riding on a dragon.

An old man with a beard.

An old woman leaning on a crutch.

A hog; a dragon; an owl.

A black garment; a hook or sickle.

A juniper tree.

Those are the figures that these spirits usually assume, which are generally terrible at the first coming on of the visions, but as they have only a limited power, beyond which they cannot pass, so the invocator need be under no apprehensions of danger, provided he is well fortified with those things we have directed to be used for his defence, and above all, to have a firm and constant faith in the mercy, wisdom, and goodness of God.

* Those spirits who appear in a kingly form, have a much higher dignity than them who take an inferior shape; and those who appear in a human shape, exceed in authority and power them that come as animals; and again, these latter surpass in dignity them who appear as trees or instruments, and the like: so that you are to judge of the power, government, and authority of spirits by their assuming a more noble and dignified apparition.

END OF THE THIRD PART, AND OF CABALISTICAL AND CEREMONIAL MAGIC.

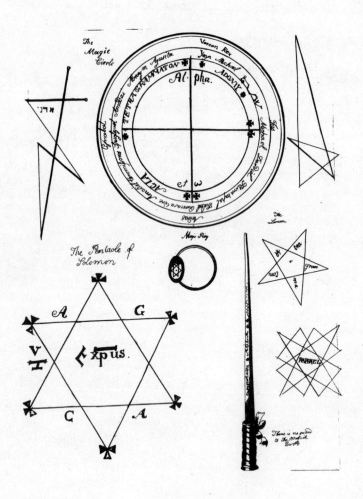

The
Magic
Circle

Varcan Rex

Yayn Michael

TETRAGRAMMATON

Al. pha.

Adonay

The Pentacle of Solomon

A   G

H / V   xpus.

G   A

Magic Ring

The Lamen

RAPHAEL

There is no period to the Magical Circle

THE

MAGIC AND PHILOSOPHY

OF

TRITHEMIUS OF SPANHEIM:

CONTAINING HIS BOOK OF

SECRET THINGS,

AND

DOCTRINE OF SPIRITS:

With many curious and rare Secrets (hitherto not generally known;)

THE ART OF DRAWING SPIRITS INTO CRYSTALS, &c.

With many other Experiments in the Occult Sciences, never yet published in the English Language.

———

TRANSLATED FROM A VALUABLE LATIN MANUSCRIPT,

By FRANCIS BARRETT,

STUDENT OF CHEMISTRY, NATURAL AND OCCULT PHILOSOPHY, THE CABALA, &c.

———

PART IV.

MAGIC AND PHILOSOPHY

OF

TRITHEMIUS OF SPANHEIM.

The Tranſlator's LETTER *to a* FRIEND *of his, a young Student in theſe occult Sciences.*

MY FRIEND,

KNOWING thee to be a curious ſearcher after thoſe ſciences which are out of the common track of ſtudy, (I mean the art of foretelling events, magic, teliſmans, &c.) I am moved ſpiritually to give thee my thoughts upon them, and by theſe ideas here written, to open to thine eye (ſpiritual) as much information as it ſeems neceſſary for thee to know, by which thou mayeſt be led by the hand into the delectable field of nature ; and to give thee ſuch documents as, guided by the ſupreme wiſdom of the Higheſt, thou mayeſt refreſh thy ſoul with a delicious draught of knowledge ; ſo that after recreating thy ſpirit with the uſe of thoſe good gifs which may pleaſe God to beſtow on thee, thou mayeſt be wrapped up into the contemplation of the immenſe wiſdom of that great munificent Being who created thee.

Now, art thou a man, in whoſe ſoul the image of Divinity is ſealed for eternity, think firſt what is thy deſire in the ſearching after theſe myſteries ! Is it wealth, honour, fame, power, might, aggrandizement, and the like ? Perhaps thy heart ſays, All ! all theſe I would gladly crave ! If ſo, this is my anſwer,—ſeek firſt to know thyſelf thoroughly, cleanſe thy heart from all wicked, vain, and rapacious deſires. Thinkeſt thou, oh man ! to attain power *to gratify thy luſts, to enrich thy coffers, to build houſes,* to raiſe thyſelf to the pinnacle of human admiration ; if theſe are thy hopes and deſires, thou haſt reaſon to lament thy being born : all ſuch deſires are immediately from

S 2

the

the devil, I mean that Being whofe engines (*i. e.* myriads of demons) are continually in the act of placing fenfual delights and luxuries before the depraved
minds and hearts of man, and whofe chief bufinefs and property it is to
counteract the benevolent actions and infpiration of thofe bleffed fpirits who
are the inftruments of God our Creator.

Fear God and love thy neighbour; ufe no deceit, fwear not, neither lye;
let all thy actions be fincere. Here, O man! is the grand feal of all earthly
wifdom, the true talifman of human happinefs. When thou fhalt accomplifh this, behold nothing will be impoffible unto thee as far as God permits:
then with all fpeed apply thy mind and heart to attain knowledge and wifdom; with all humility throw thy dependance on God alone, the author of
all things that cannot die.

To know thyfelf is to know God, for it is a fpiritual gift *from God* that
enables a man to know himfelf. This gift but very few poffefs, as may be
daily feen. How many are there toffed about to and fro' upon the perilous fea
of contending paffions, and who are more light than feathers! how many in
this great city who place their chiefeft *good* in debauchery and letchery! See
their *actions, manners,* and *difpofitions*; thefe poor, unfortunate, miferable
wretches, fuch is their fatal magical infatuation and ignorance, that they
think thofe mad who might even attempt to reafon with them on the
vanity and mifery of their fituation. To make myfelf more intelligible, thefe
are what the world calls men of fafhion, a phrafe infignificant enough
when we confider that the univerfal fafhion of this time is vice, and that
fo glaring, that it needs no great intellect to difcover what is daily open to
the view of the obferver. But to you, my friend, I have addreffed thefe
lines; therefore let it not be fuppofed that I am reprehending my friend for
vices which I cannot fuppofe him attached to: for I know thou art a young
man defigned for the receiving of inftruction, in much higher and more
glorious contemplations than thofe fons of earth are capable of, therefore
I have prefented thee with this tranflation which thou didft defire me to
give thee.

                                                                    But

But beware of flattery, felf-love, and covetoufnefs, fo wilt thou thrive ; and be diligent in thy occupation, fo fhall thy body be fed. Idlenefs is offenfive to the Deity, induftry fhall fweeten thy brown bread, and the fruits of it fhall warm thine heart, and infpire thy foul with gratitude to him that blefles thee with *enough :* feek for no more, for it will damn thee ; pray for enough to feed and clothe thy body, but afk no more, leaft thou pine away in heart-rending poverty, and fpend the remainder of thy days in contumely and beggary. For know a thing moft neceffary for thee to know, that if by thy ftudy, by thy art, or any other thing, thou couldft *command* a *million of fpirits,* it fhould not be lawful for thee to wifh to gain riches fuddenly, for the Wifdom Eternal has put forth the fiat ; and it has been faid by him who never fpoke in vain, and who cannot lye, *that man fhall get bread by the fweat of his brow* ; therefore let us not have in view the enriching of ourfelves in worldly goods, by fupernatural means, or by a greedy defiring of what we ought to look upon with eyes of contempt, draw upon us the wrath of God. Rather let us cheerfully rely on, and follow in very deed, fpirit and truth, thefe words of the apoftle, " Seek ye firft the kingdom of God, and all thefe things fhall be added unto you ;" fear not but that God fhall make thy houfehold as a flourifhing tree, and thy wife fhall be as a fruitful vine. Farewell, remember my poor counfel, and be happy. From thy true friend,   F. B.

N. B. To enable thee the better to comprehend this Book, I have drawn out the various figures, of which mention is made in this work, that thou mayeft fee the very exact method of working ; likewife the images of feals, fpirits, and various other rare, and curious inftruments, which are neceffary for thee to know and fee with the eye ; therefore in the conftruction of them thou canft not be liable to error.

Fig. 1. The form of the cryftal for invocating fpirits, with the plate of pure gold in which the cryftal muft be faftened, with the divine characters around.

Fig. 2.

Fig. 2. A magical circle (C D E F), of a fimple conftruction, for the operator to ftand or fit in when he calleth the fpirits.

Fig. 3. The cryftal (A), two filver or other candlefticks (G G,) with the wax tapers burning, and tripod or veffel for the oderiferous fuffumigation.

Fig. 4. A wand of black ebony with golden characters. The characters are explained.

_A_ CAUTION _to the inexperienced in this_ ART, _and a Word of Advice to thofe who would be Adepts._

BROTHER,

IT is neceffary for me to inform thee, that whatever thy defires are in the purfuit of this art, which we call Magic, fo wilt thy connexion and anfwer be. If in the purfuit of revenge, it is but proper thou fhouldeft know that thou wilt, in any of thefe experiments here laid down, draw to thyfelf a revengeful demon, or an infernal furious fpirit, ferving in the principle of the wrath of God ; if worldly riches and aggrandizement, then fhalt thou have an earthial or fiery fpirit, which will delude thee with the riches of the central world ; if fame, or the blaze of glory, then the _fpirits of pride_ will be alloted thee, who will gratify thy inordinate defire of vain glory ; for all thefe offices are there fpirits allotted and will be eager to mix with thy fpirit : it will attract thee to his own nature, and ferve all thy purpofes according to the extent of God's permiffion ; and as thy defires are and from what principle they proceed, fo fhalt thou be anfwered : but if thou defireft to know nothing but for the honour and glory of God, and the help of thy neighbour, and, in great humility, fill thy heart with the love of God, thou fhalt then have a pure fpirit which

will

will grant (by the Lord's permiſſion) thy deſires. Therefore ſeek for that which is good; avoid all evil either in thought, word, or action; pray to God to fill thee with wiſdom, and then thou ſhalt reap an abundant harveſt. There are two ways magically ſet before thee; chuſe which thou wilt, thou ſhalt be ſure of thy reward. Farewel.

London, 1800. F. B.

Of the making of the CRYSTAL *and the Form of Preparation for a* VISION.

PROCURE of a lapidary a good clear pellucid cryſtal, of the bigneſs of a ſmall orange, *i. e.* about one inch and a half in diameter; let it be glo-bular or round each way alike; then, when you have got this cryſtal, fair and clear, without any clouds or ſpecks, get a ſmall plate of pure gold to encom-paſs the cryſtal round one half; let this be fitted on an ivory or ebony pedeſtal, as you may ſee more fully deſcribed in the drawing, (ſee the Plate, fig. 1.) Let there be engraved a circle (A) round the cryſtal with theſe characters around inſide the circle next the cryſtal ⬡ ⬡ ✠ ; afterwards the name " *Tetragrammaton*". On the other ſide of the plate let there be engra-ven " *Michael, Gabriel, Uriel, Raphael*;" which are the four principal angels ruling over the *Sun, Moon, Venus* and *Mercury*; but on the table on which the cryſtal ſtands the following names, characters, &c. muſt be drawn in order.

Firſt, The names of the ſeven planets and angels ruling them, with their ſeals or characters. The names of the four kings of the four corners of the earth. Let them be all written within a double circle, with a triangle on a table; on which place the cryſtal on its pedeſtal: this being done,

thy

thy table is complete (as in the Fig. D,) and fit for the calling of the spirits; after which thou shalt proceed to experiment, thus:

In what time thou wouldest deal with the spirits by the *table* and *cryftal*, thou muft obferve the planetary hour; and whatever planet rules in that hour, the angel governing the planet thou shalt call in the manner following; but, firft, fay this fhort prayer:

"Oh, God! who art the author of all good things, ftrengthen, I befeech thee, thy poor fervant, that he may ftand faft, without fear, through this dealing and work; enlighten, I befeech thee, oh Lord! the dark underftanding of thy creature, fo that his fpiritual eye may be opened to fee and know thy angelic fpirits defcending here in this cryftal: *(Then lay thy hand on the cryftal, faying,)* and thou, oh inanimate creature of God, be fanctified and confecrated, and bleffed to this purpofe, that no evil phantafy may appear in thee; or, if they do gain ingrefs into this creature, they may be conftrained to fpeak intelligibly, and truly, and without the leaft ambiguity, for Chrift's fake. *Amen.* And forafmuch as thy fervant here ftanding before thee, oh, Lord! defires neither evil treafures, nor injury to his neighbour, nor hurt to any living creature, grant him the power of defcrying thofe celeftial fpirits or intelligences, that may appear in this cryftal, and whatever good gifts (whether the power of healing infirmities, or of imbibing wifdom, or difcovering any evil likely to afflict any perfon or family, or any other good gift thou mayeft be pleafed to beftow on me, enable me, by thy wifdom and mercy, to ufe whatever I may receive to the honour of thy holy name. Grant this for thy fon Chrift's fake. *Amen.*"

Then taking your ring and pentacle, put the ring on the little finger of your right hand; hang the pentacle round thy neck; (*Note,* the pentacle may be either wrote on clean virgin parchment, or engraven on a fquare plate of filver and fufpended from thy neck to the breaft), then take your black ebony wand, with the gilt characters on it and trace the circle, (Fig. 7. C D E F,) faying, "In the name of the bleffed Trinity, I confecrate this piece of ground for our defence; fo that no evil fpirit may have power to break thefe bounds prefcribed here, through Jefus Chrift our Lord." *Amen.*

Then

Then place the veſſel for the perfumes between thy circle and the holy table on which the cryſtal ſtands, and, having fire therein, caſt in thy perfumes, ſaying,

" I conjure thee, oh thou creature of fire! by him who created all things both in heaven and earth, and in the ſea, and in every other place whatever, that forthwith thou caſt away every phantaſm from thee, that no hurt whatſoever ſhall be done in any thing. Bleſs, oh Lord, this creature of fire, and ſanctify it that it may be bleſſed, and that they may fill up the power and virtue of their odours; ſo neither the enemy, nor any falſe imagination, may enter into them; through our Lord Jeſus Chriſt. *Amen*."

Now, this being done in the order preſcribed, take out thy little book, which muſt be made about ſeven inches long, of pure white virgin vellum or paper, likewiſe pen and ink muſt be ready to write down the *name*, *character*, and *office*, likewiſe the ſeal or image of whatever ſpirit may appear (for this I muſt tell you that it does not happen that the ſame ſpirit you call will always appear, for you muſt try the ſpirit to know whether he be a pure or impure being, and this thou ſhalt eaſily know by a firm and undoubted faith in God.)

Now the moſt pure and ſimple way of calling the ſpirits or ſpirit is by a ſhort oration to the ſpirit himſelf, which is more effectual and eaſy to perform than compoſing a table of letters; for all celeſtial operations, the more pure and unmixed they are, the more they are agreeable to the celeſtial ſpirits: therefore, after the circle is drawn, the book, perfumes, rod, &c. in readineſs, proceed as follows:

(After noticing the exact hour of the day, and what angel rules that hour, thou ſhalt ſay,)

" In the name of the bleſſed and holy Trinity, I do deſire thee, thou ſtrong and mighty angel *, Michæl, that if it be the divine will of him who is called Tetragrammaton, &c. the Holy God, the Father, that thou take upon thee ſome ſhape as beſt becometh thy celeſtial nature, and appear to us viſibly here in this cryſtal, and anſwer our demands in as far as we ſhall not tranſgreſs the

* Or any other angel or ſpirit.

bounds of the divine mercy and goodnefs, by requefting unlawful knowledge ; but that thou wilt gracioufly fhew us what things are moft profitable for us to know and do, to the glory and honour of his divine Majefty, who liveth and reigneth, world without end. *Amen.*

" Lord, thy will be done on earth, as it is in heaven ;—make clean our hearts within us, and take not thy Holy Spirit from us.

" O Lord, by thy name, we have called him, fuffer him to adminifter unto us. And that all things may work together for thy honour and glory, to whom with thee, the Son, and bleffed Spirit, be afcribed all might, majefty and dominion. *Amen.*"

Note, In thefe dealings, two fhould always be prefent; for often a fpirit is manifeft to one in the cryftal when the other cannot perceive him ; therefore if any fpirit appear, as there moft likely will, to one or both, fay,

" Oh, Lord ! we return thee our hearty and fincere thanks for the hearing of our prayer, and we thank thee for having permitted thy fpirit to appear unto us which we, by thy mercy, will interrogate to our further inftruction, through Chrift. *Amen.*"

Interrog. 1. In the name of the holy and undefiled Spirit, the Father, the begotten Son, and Holy Ghoft, proceeding from both, what is thy true name ?

If the fpirit anfwers, *Michael,* then proceed.

Queft. 2. What is thy office ? 3. What is thy true fign or character ? 4. When are the times moft agreeable to thy nature to hold conference with us ?

Wilt thou fwear by the blood and righteoufnefs of our Lord Jefus Chrift, that thou art truly Michael ?

(Here let him fwear, then write down his feal or character in thy book, and againft it, his office and times to be called, through God's name ; alfo write down any thing he may teach thee, or any refponfes he may make to thy queftions or interrogations, concerning life or death, arts or fciences, or any other thing ;) and then fhalt thou fay,

" Thou

" Thou great and mighty ſpirit, inaſmuch as thou cameſt in peace and in the name of the ever bleſſed and righteous Trinity, ſo in this name thou mayeſt depart and return to us, when we call thee in his name to whom every knee doth bow down. Fare thee well, Michael; peace be between us, through our bleſſed Lord Jeſus Chriſt. *Amen.*"

Then will the ſpirit depart; then ſay, " To God the Father, eternal Spirit, fountain of Light, the Son, and Holy Ghoſt, be all honour and glory, world without end. *Amen.*"

I ſhall here ſet down the Table of the names of Spirits and Planets governing the Hours; ſo thou ſhalt eaſily know by inſpection, what Spirit and Planet governs every Hour of the Day and Night in the Week.

Hours Day.	Angels and Planets ruling SUNDAY.	Angels and Planets ruling MONDAY.	Angels and Planets ruling TUESDAY.	Angels and Planets ruling WEDNESDAY	Angels and Planets ruling THURSDAY.	Angels and Planets ruling FRIDAY.	Angels and Planets ruling SATURDAY.
	Day.	*Day.*	*Day.*	*Day.*	*Day.*	*Day.*	*Day.*
1	☉ Michael	☽ Gabriel	♂ Samael	☿ Raphael	♃ Sachiel	♀ Anael	♄ Caffiel
2	♀ Anael	♄ Caffiel	☉ Michael	☽ Gabriel	♂ Samael	☿ Raphael	♃ Sachiel
3	☿ Raphael	♃ Sachiel	♀ Anael	♄ Caffiel	☉ Michael	☽ Gabriel	♂ Samael
4	☽ Gabriel	♂ Samael	☿ Raphael	♃ Sachiel	♀ Anael	♄ Caffiel	☉ Michael
5	♄ Caffiel	☉ Michael	☽ Gabriel	♂ Samael	☿ Raphael	♃ Sachiel	♀ Anael
6	♃ Sachiel	♀ Anael	♄ Caffiel	☉ Michael	☽ Gabriel	♂ Samael	☿ Raphael
7	♂ Samael	☿ Raphael	♃ Sachiel	♀ Anael	♄ Caffiel	☉ Michael	☽ Gabriel
8	☉ Michael	☽ Gabriel	♂ Samael	☿ Raphael	♃ Sachiel	♀ Anael	♄ Caffiel
9	♀ Anael	♄ Caffiel	☉ Michael	☽ Gabriel	♂ Samael	☿ Raphael	♃ Sachiel
10	☿ Raphael	♃ Sachiel	♀ Anael	♄ Caffiel	☉ Michael	☽ Gabriel	♂ Samael
11	☽ Gabriel	♂ Samael	☿ Raphael	♃ Sachiel	♀ Anael	♄ Caffiel	☉ Michael
12	♄ Caffiel	☉ Michael	☽ Gabriel	♂ Samael	☿ Raphael	♃ Sachiel	♀ Anael
Hours Night	*Night.*	*Night.*	*Night.*	*Night.*	*Night.*	*Night.*	*Night.*
1	♃ Sachael	♀ Anael	♄ Caffiel	☉ Michael	☽ Gabriel	♂ Samael	☿ Raphael
2	♂ Samiel	☿ Raphael	♃ Sachiel	♀ Anael	♄ Caffiel	☉ Michael	☽ Gabriel
3	☉ Michael	☽ Gabriel	♂ Samael	☿ Raphael	♃ Sachiel	♀ Anael	♄ Caffiel
4	♀ Anael	♄ Caffiel	☉ Michael	☽ Gabriel	♂ Samael	☿ Raphael	♃ Sachiel
5	☿ Raphael	♃ Sachiel	♀ Anael	♄ Caffiel	☉ Michael	☽ Gabriel	♂ Samael
6	☽ Gabriel	♂ Samael	☿ Raphael	♃ Sachiel	♀ Anael	♄ Caffiel	☉ Michael
7	♄ Caffiel	☉ Michael	☽ Gabriel	♂ Samael	☿ Raphael	♃ Sachiel	♀ Anael
8	♃ Sachiel	♀ Anael	♄ Caffiel	☉ Michael	☽ Gabriel	♂ Samael	☿ Raphael
9	♂ Samael	☿ Raphael	♃ Sachiel	♀ Anael	♄ Caffiel	☉ Michael	☽ Gabriel
10	☉ Michael	☽ Gabriel	♂ Samael	☿ Raphael	♃ Sachiel	♀ Anael	♄ Caffiel
11	♀ Anael	♄ Caffiel	☉ Michael	☽ Gabriel	♂ Samael	☿ Raphael	♃ Sachiel
12	☿ Raphael	♃ Sachiel	♀ Anael	♄ Caffiel	☉ Michael	☽ Gabriel	♂ Samael

T 2

Note,

Note, The day is divided into twelve equal parts, called Planetary Hours, reckoning from fun-rife to fun-fet, and, again, from the fetting to the rifing; and to find the planetary hour, you need but to divide the natural hours by twelve, and the quotient gives the length of the planetary hours and odd minuets, which shews you how long a spirit bears rule in that day; as Michael governs the first and the eighth hour on Sunday, as does the ☉. After you have the length of the first hour, you have only to look in the Table, as if it be the fourth hour, on Sunday, you fee in the Table that the ☽ and Gabriel rules; and fo for the reft it being fo plain and eafy you cannot err.

THE CONCLUSION OF THE MAGUS.

ADVERTISEMENT.

THE Author of this Work refpectfully informs thofe who are curious in the ftudies of Art and Nature, efpe-cially of Natural and Occult Philofophy, Chemiftry, Aftrology, &c. &c. that, having been indefatigable in his refearches into thofe fublime Sciences, of which he has treated at large in this Book, that he gives private inftructions and lectures upon any of the above-mentioned Sciences ; in the courfe of which he will difcover many curious and rare experiments. Thofe who become Students will be initiated into the choiceft operations of Natu-ral Philofophy, Natural Magic, the Cabala, Chemiftry, the Talifmanic Art, Hermetic Philofophy, Aftrology, Phyfiognomy, &c. &c. Likewife they will acquire the knowledge of the Rites, Myfteries, Ceremonies, and Principles of the ancient Philofophers, Magi, Cabalifts, Adepts, &c.—The purpofe of this School (which will confift of no greater number than Twelve Students) being to inveftigate the hidden treafures of Nature ; to bring the Mind to a contemplation of the Eternal Wifdom ; to promote the difcovery of whatever may conduce to the perfection of Man ; the alleviating the miferies and calamities of this life, both in refpect of ourfelves and others ; the ftudy of morality and religion here, in order to fecure to ourfelves felicity hereafter ; and, finally, the promulgation of whatever, may conduce to the general happinefs and welfare of mankind.—— Thofe who feel themfelves thoroughly difpofed to enter upon fuch a courfe of ftudies, as is above recited, with the fame principles of philanthropy with which the Author invites the lovers of philofophy and wifdom, to incor-porate themfelves in fo felect, permanent, and defirable a fociety, may fpeak with the Author upon the fubject, at any time between the hours of Eleven and Two o'clock, at 99 Norton Street, Mary-le-Bonne.

Letters (poft paid) upon any fubject treated of in this Book, will be duly anfwered, with the neceffary in-formation.

BIOGRAPHIA ANTIQUA;

OR,

AN ACCOUNT OF THE LIVES AND WRITINGS

OF THE ANCIENT AND MODERN

MAGI, CABALISTS, AND PHILOSOPHERS,

DISCOVERING THE

PRINCIPLES AND TENETS OF THE FIRST FOUNDERS

OF THE

MAGICAL AND OCCULT SCIENCES:

WHEREIN THE MYSTERIES OF THE PYTHAGORIANS, GYMNOSOPHISTS, EGYPTIANS, BRAGMANNI,
BABYLONIANS, PERSIANS, ETHIOPIANS, CHALDEANS, &c. ARE DISCOVERED:

Including a particular and interesting Account of

ZOROASTER, THE SON OF OROMASIUS,

THE FIRST INSTITUTOR OF PHILOSOPHY BY FIRE, AND MAGIC;

LIKEWISE OF

HERMES TRISMEGISTUS, THE EGYPTIAN,

And other Philosophers, famous for their Learning, Piety, and Wisdom.

TO WHICH IS ADDED,

A SHORT ESSAY,

Proving that the First Christians were Magicians, who foretold, acknowleged, and worshipped

THE SAVIOUR OF THE WORLD,

AND

FIRST FOUNDER OF THE CHRISTIAN RELIGION.

BIOGRAPHIA ANTIQUA.

ZOROASTER, THE SON OF OROMASIUS,

FIRST INSTITUTOR OF PHILOSOPHY BY FIRE, AND MAGIC.

Z OROASTER, the fon of Oromafius, flourifhed in the reign of Darius, the fucceffor of Cambyfes. * All authors are full of variations in their accounts of this famous perfon, fome making him of a much later date than others; however, we fhall give what we have collected from thofe who appear moft authentic, not omitting the traditional hiftory extant amongft the Magi, with which our readers may compare the feveral ftories of biographers, and accept that account which fhall feem to them the moft rational.   Zoroafter, king of the Bactrians, was vanquifhed by Ninus, and paffed for the inventor of magic †.   Eufebius places this victory of Ninus in the feventh year of Abraham:

* The Author regrets, that, notwithftanding his laborious refearches to obtain an authentic and fatisfactory account of Zoroafter to prefent to his readers; that a few generals, and not particulars, can only be given : indeed, the moft ferious and refpectable hiftorians differ fo widely in their accounts of him, that nothing certain can from thence be deduced : however, we have above recited feveral anthorities to which we have annexed various notes and commentations.

† *Paffed for the inventor of magic.*—It is to be noted that he was the inventor of it, and the firft of the magi. Juftin informs us that this victory was the laft of Ninus ; that Zoroafter philofophized moft judicioufly upon the nature and influences of the ftars, and on the principles of the univerfe. Thomas Stanleius, Hift. of Philof. Orientalis, lib. I. cap. iii. informs us, that Zoroafter, according to Eufebius, was cotemporary with Semiramis ; but it is certain, according to Eufebius, that he was vanquifhed by king Ninus. Arnobius, lib. I. pa. m. 5. fays, " Anciently the Affyrians and Bactrians, " the former under the conduct of Ninus, and the latter under Zoroafter, fought againft each other, " not only with men and weapons, but alfo by the help of magic, and the fecret difcipline of the " Chaldeans." Hermippus, who has wrote cautioufly on every thing relative to magic, and explained twenty thoufand verfes compofed by Zoroafter, relates, that one Azonaces initiated

him

Abraham; now several authors make Zoroaster appear much earlier. It has been reported that Zoroaster laughed on the same day he was born, and that he

him into this art, and that he lived 5,000 years before the Trojan war. St. Augustin and Orosius have followed the tradition mentioned by Justin. Apuleius, in his Catalogue of all the most famous Magicians of Antiquity, with great justice places Zoroaster in the first rank, and proves him the most ancient of all: " *Magicarum artium fuisse perhibetur inventor Zoroastres.*" Augustin. de Civitat. Dei, lib. 21. cap. xiv. Eudoxus, who esteemed the art of magic to be accounted the noblest and most useful of all worldly knowledge, relates that Zoroaster lived six thousand years before the death of Plato. Note, that the same thing is affirmed by Aristotle. Agathias, who lived in the reign of Justinian, informs us, that, according to the Persians of that time, Zoroaster and Hystaspes were cotemporary; but they do not say whether this Hystaspes was father to Darius or any other. Sir John Marsham positively decides that he was the father of Darius; and grounds his opinion on this, that one of the elogies engraven on the tomb makes him the instructor of the Magi; and that the same historian who makes Hystaspes excel in magic, calls him the father of Darius. Ammianus Marcellinus, lib. 23, pag. m. 324, says, " After the time of Zoroaster, reigned Hystaspes, a very prudent king, and the " father of Darius. This prince, having boldly penetrated into the remotest parts of the Upper India, " came at length to a solitary forest, where there dwelt, in silent and awful tranquility, the Brachmans. " In this peaceful solitude they instructed him in the knowledge of the earth's motion, likewise of the " stars; and from them he learned the pure and sacred rites of religion. Part of this knowledge he " communicated to the Magi, which, together with the art of predicting future events, they delivered " down to posterity, each in his own family. The great number of men who have descended from " these families, ever since that age down to the present, have all been set apart for cultivating the " knowledge of the Gods." But Ammianus Mercellinus was wrong in saying, that this father of Da-rius was a king; and no doubt he committed this blunder by having read in general that one king Hystaspes was a great magician, and thought there was no other Hystaspes than the father of Darius. But it is beyond dispute, that one Hystaspes, older than the foundation of Rome, and a great prophet, is mentioned by authors. " Hystaspes also, the most ancient king of the Medes, and from whom the river " Hystaspes derives its name, is the most admirable of them all; for, under the interpretation of the pro-" phecy of a boy, he informed posterity that the Roman empire, nay, even the Roman name, should be " utterly destroyed; and this he predicted a long time before the establishment of that colony of Trojans," Lactant. lib. VII. cap. xv. pag. m. 492. Justin Martyr informs us, that he predicted the general con-flagration of all perishable things, Justin Apolog. ii. pag. 66. It is affirmed that Pythagoras was Zo-roaster's disciple, under the reign of Cambyses, the son of Cyrus: the words of Apuleius inform us of the fact. Some say that Pythagoras having been made a slave in Egypt, was transported into Persia; others will have him transported into Babylon, and there instructed by Zoroaster the Babylonian, whom they distinguish from the Persian. We find no less than five Zoroasters mentioned in history: to these five may be added a sixth, mentioned by Apuleius. This Zoroaster lived in Babylon at the time Py-thagoras was brought thither by Cambyses. The same writer calls him " the chief interpreter of all divine mysteries," and says that Pythagoras was chiefly instructed by him. He appears to be the same
with

he was the only one to whom this happened, and that the palpitation of his brain was so strong as to repulse the hand, it being laid to his head, which they say was a presage of his future knowledge and wisdom. It is added, that he passed twenty years in the deserts, and there eat nothing but a sort of cheese which was never the worse for age; that the love of wisdom and justice obliged him to retire from the world to a mountain, where he lived in solitude; but when he come down from thence there fell a celestial fire upon it, which perpetually burned; that the king of Persia, accompanied with the greatest lords of his court, approached it for the purpose of putting up prayers to God; that Zoroaster came out from these flames unhurt; that he comforted and encouraged the Persians, and offered sacrifices for them to God; that, afterwards, he did not live indifferently with all sorts of men, but only those who were born for truth, and who were capable of the true knowledge of God, which kind of people are called among the Persians, Magi; that he desired his end might be this, viz. to be struck with thunder, and consumed by celestial fire; and that he requested the Persians to collect his ashes, after he was consumed in this manner, and to preserve and venerate them as a pledge of the preservation of their monarchy; that they for a length of time paid great veneration to the relics of Zoroaster, but at length, neglecting them, their monarchy fell to ruin and decay*. The Chronicle of Alexandria adds, that having held this discourse

---

with Zabratus, by whom Diogenes affirms Pythagoras was purged from all his former filth, and instructed in what is essentially necessary for good men to know, viz. God, nature, and philosophy : he is also the same with Nazaratus, the Assyrian, whom Alexander, in his book of the Pythagorical symbols, affirms to have taught Pythagoras. The same person Suidas calls Zares, Cyrillus, Zaranes, and Plutarch, Zarates.

* According to the tradition of the Magi, we shall explain this fabulous and figurative description of Zoroaster's end. The truth is, he enjoined the Persians rigidly to persevere in the laws he had framed, and the doctrine he had been at the labour to establish, which was, to live in the practice of moral virtue, to avoid all species of luxury, to promote the liberal sciences, to govern all their actions with prudence and integrity, and to meet misfortune with resolution, and to encounter it with philosophy, and to endure the unavoidable calamities of life with fortitude : these, his disciplines, he left as a precious relic among them; which while they strictly adhered to, they need be under no apprehension of tyranny and

U   oppression :

difcourfe with them he invoked Orion, and was confumed by celeftial fire. Many will have it that Ham was the Zoroafter of the eaftern nations, and the inventor of magic. Mr. Bochart refutes this falfity. Cedrenus obferves that Zoroafter, who became fo famous for wifdom among the Perfians, was defcended from Belus: this imports that he was defcended from Nimrod. Some authors have taken him for Nimrod; others for Affur or Japhet. The ancient Perfians believe that Zoroafter was before Mofes *. Some maintain he was the prophet Ezekiel, and it cannot be denied that they ground their opinions on the agreement of numerous particulars which belong to the one, and are related of the other. George Hornius foolifhly imagines that he was the falfe prophet Balaam. Huetius fhews that he was the Mofes of the Jews, and mentions an infinite number of particulars in which the accounts we have of Mofes agree with the ftories related of Zoroafter.—How near all or any of thefe come to the probability of truth will appear in the fequel, where we have given the moft probable and rational account of him, as far as we have been able to trace, from the tradition of the Magi, which we prefer before the confufed and partial accounts vulgarly extant. They who believe that Zoroafter pro-

oppreffion :—thefe they collected, and for fome fpace of time religioufly followed the precepts of this great philofopher: at length, human frailty and vice, corrupting their manners, caufed them to relax from their duties, upon which their empire fell into ruin and decay. The idolatry falfely imputed to this wife man, *viz.* his inftituting the worfhipping of fire, is thus to be interpreted.—Under the celeftial fymbol of fire was meant truth :—truth he afcribed purely as the great and wonderful attribute of the Godhead, which he acknowledged and worfhipped, to wit, one only God, the eternal fire of wifdom and everlafting truth, juftice, and mercy !—His magic was the ftudy of the religious worfhip of that Eternal Being. After Zoroafter, there were four perfons chofen to educate the fucceffor of the king of Perfia. They chofe the wifeft, the moft juft, the moft temperate, and the braveft man that could be found. The wifeft man (*viz.* one of the Magi), inftructed him in Zoroafter's magic, the juft in government, the brave in war, and the temperate in focial virtue and temperance. Now obferve, that Zoroafter is called the fon of Oromafius, and that Oromafius is the name given by Zoroafter and his diciples to the good God, and this title was really beftowed upon him by the Perfians; therefore, according to Plato, this Perfian Magus, on account of his uncommon learning, religion, and wifdom, was, in an allegorical or figurative manner, called the fon of God, or the fon of wifdom, truth, &c.

* Some Magi affirm that he is the fame with Abraham, and frequently call him Ibrahim Zerdafcht, which is, Abraham the friend of fire.

feffed

feffed and taught a diabolical magic * are certainly in the wrong; the magic he taught (of which we fhall fpeak more anon) was only the ftudy of the divine nature, and of religious worfhip.   Some have prefumed that Zoroafter was the promulgator of a doctrine of two principles†, or two co-eternal caufes, one of good

* The preceding note fully explains thofe erroneous relations of the wifdom of the Magi. Thofe who defire to fee a great many paffages which teftify that the magic of the Perfians, inftituted by Zoroafter, was the ftudy of religion, virtue, and wifdom, let them refer to *Briffonius de Regno Perfarum,* lib. ii.p. 178, & feq. edit. Commel. 1595 ; likewife Jul. Cæfar, Bullengerus Eclog. ad Arnobium, p. 346, & feq.   Nor are we ignorant that Gabriel Naude hath moft learnedly and folidly juftified our Zoroafter againft the ignorant imputations of necromancy, black art, &c.

† It has been much contended by philofophers whether Zoroafter was the firft fuggefter of this doctrine of the two principles: the one called by the Magi, Oromafes the *good,* and Arimanius the *evil* principle. It is certain Zoroafter afferted the one, *viz.* that of the good, or an effential uncreated felf-exiftent principle, the caufe of all good, called by him Oromafus, meaning a good God, &c.   In refpect of the other principle, Arimanius, we muft, before we decide either for or againft Zoroafter, confider the nature of the thing in its moft impartial fenfe.

Thofe who ever read Mr. Bernard's Journal (*Nouvelles de la Republique des Lettres, Feb.* 1701, *and March* 1701, *Art. iii. L i.*) needs not be informed that the Hiftoria Religionis veterum Perfarum, publifhed by Dr. Hyde (profeffor of the oriental languages in the univerfity of Oxford) at Oxford, in the year 1700, 4to, is one of the moft excellent pieces that could poffibly be written on fuch a fubject.   The idea which the learned journalift hath given of this performance is fufficient to convince us that it contains a very curious erudition, and profound difcuffions, which difcover many rare and uncommon particulars of a country which we fcarce knew any thing of before. But to come to the point: Dr. Hyde affirms, that the ancient Perfians acknowledge no more than one uncreated principle, which was the good principle; or, in one word, God: and that they looked upon the evil principle as a created being. One of the names, or attributes, which they gave to God, was Hormizda ; and they called the evil principle, Ahariman; and this is the original of the two Greek words, Ωρμυζδης and Αρειμανιος ; one of which was the name of the good, and the other of the evil, principle, as we have feen above, in a paffage of Plutarch. The Perfians affirmed that Abraham was the firft founder of their religion. Zoroafter afterwards made fome alterations in it ; but it is faid he made no manner of change with relation to the doctrine of one fole uncreated principle, but that the only innovation in this particular was the giving the name of Light to the good principle, and that of Darknefs to the evil one.

From a mifconftruction put upon the doctrine of the Magi, fome confiderable mifreports of their tenets have been propagated : I think none more curious than the following—"That a war arofe betwixt the army of light and that of darknefs, which at laft ended in an accommodation, of which the angels were mediators, and the conditions were that the inferior world fhould be wholly left to the government of Arimanius for the fpace of 7000 years, after which it fhould be reftored to light. Before the peace, Arimanius had exterminated all the inhabitants of the world. Light had called men to its affiftance while

U 2   they

good, the other of evil things. Of this doctrine Plutarch takes notice: he says, " that Zoroaster the magician, who is said to have lived five thousand years " before the Trojan war, called the good God, Oromazes, and the evil, Arima- " nius, &c. &c." See *Plut. de Iside & Osiride, page* 369.

Dr. Hyde, in his excellent treatise on the religion of the ancient Persians, cites some authors who clear him on this head. We shall examine whether they deserve credit. It is affirmed that he was no idolater, either with respect to the worship of fire, or that of Mithra *. What appears least uncertain, amongst

they were yet but spirits; which it did, either to draw them out of Arimanius' territories, or in order to give them bodies to engage against this enemy. They accepted the bodies and the fight, on condition they should be assisted by the light, and should at last overcome Arimanius. The resurrection shall come when he shall be vanquished. This they conclude was the cause of the mixture, and shall be the cause of the deliverance. The Greeks were not ignorant that Zoroaster taught a future resurrection.

* The ancient Persian Magi never did divine honours to the sun or any of the stars. They maintain they do not adore the sun, but direct themselves towards it when they pray to God. It has been found amongst Zoroaster's secret precepts, that we ought to salute the sun, but not that we should adore him with religious worship. He proves that their ceremonies might very justly pass for civil honours, and to this purpose he makes some exceeding curious observations. He applies to the fire what he says of the sun. The bowings and prostrations of the Persians before the holy fire were not a religious observation, but only a civil one. The same thing must be attributed to their reported worship of fire, which, as I have said above, they kept in their *Pyres* in imitation of the Jews. For though they paid a certain reverence to the fire, and that by prostration, yet this was not a religious, only a civil, worship; as it is from the force of custom that the eastern people prostrate themselves before any great man; (so they might with as much propriety be said to adore or worship him.) Believe me we ought to be the last to censure the eastern people with such gross idolatry as has been represented. The Persians, who have always been devoted to the highest study of wisdom, performed their duties in life for the honour of their God; and, although unenlightened and Barbarians, lived as men, and not as irrational creatures: whereas we, who know our duty so well, yet practise it so ill: for I may truly say, that notwithstanding the great benefits we derive from the divine precepts of Christianity, yet I believe it will be found an incontrovertible fact that man to man is a serpent, a few individuals excepted. But to return to our subject: It was the ancient custom to fall prostrate to angels, as being the messengers and representatives of God. Besides, there are many examples of this kind of worship, not only in the Old, but New Testament, where the women who had been converted to the true faith, upon seeing the angels at the sepulchre of Christ, fell with their faces to the ground and worshipped. Yet they well knew that it was not God they saw, but his angels, as appears from their own confession—" we have seen a vision of angels." Therefore they are wrongfully called *Idolaters* and worshippers of fire, for Zoroaster was the instrument of their continuation in the true faith. He was a man who had the knowledge of the true God, whom he peculiarly

amongſt ſo many things that are related of him is, that he was the introducer of a new religion into Perſia, and that he did it about the reign of Darius the ſucceſſor of Cambyſes: he is ſtill in great veneration among thoſe Perſians who are not of the Mahometan religion, but ſtill retain the ancient worſhip of their country. They call him Zardhuſt, and ſeveral believe that he came from China, and relate many miraculous things on that head. Several authors affirm, that all the books publiſhed hitherto under Zoroaſter's name, ſome of which are yet extant, are ſuppoſititious. Dr. Hyde diſſents from this opinion. *Suidas* affirms, that there were extant four books of Zoroaſter: the firſt, " Of Nature," a book of the Virtues of precious Stones, called de Gemmis; and five books of Aſtrology and Aſtronomy, " Prædictiones ex Inſpectione Stellarum." It is very likely that what Pliny relates, as quoted from Zoroaſter, was taken from thoſe books, *Plin.* lib. xviii, cap. 24. Euſebius recites a paſſage which contains a magnificent deſcription of God, and gives it as the very words of Zoroaſter in his ſacred commentary on the Perſian rites. Clemens Alexandrinus ſays, that the followers of Prodicus boaſted of having the ſecrets or ſecret books of Zoroaſter. But moſt likely he meant that they boaſted of having the ſecret books of Pythagoras. They were printed, together with the verſes of the Sybils at Amſterdam, in the year 1689, according to Opſopæus's edition, Oracula Magica Zoroaſtris, cum Scholiis Plethonis & Pſelli.

peculiarly worſhipped in a natural cave, in which he placed ſeveral ſymbols repreſenting the world; Mithra, repreſenting the ſun, filled the maſter's place. But it was not Mithra, but the true God, that he adored: and, laſtly, as he was a true philoſopher, a profound alchemiſt, greatly informed in all the arts of the mathematics, ſtrict and auſtere in his religion, he ſtruck the Perſians with an admiration of him, and by theſe means made them attentive to his doctrine. The ſum of all is, that he lived in a cave, dedicated to the ſervice of God, and the ſtudy of all natural and ſupernatural knowledge; that he was divinely illuminated, knew the courſes of the ſtars, and the occult and common properties of all compounded and earthly things; that by fire and Geometry (*i. e.* by Chemiſtry and the Mathematics) he inveſtigated, proved, and demonſtrated, the truth and purity, or elſe the fugacity and vileneſs, of all things knowable in this mortal ſtate of humanity. So that the fame, ſagacity, wiſdom, and virtue of Zoroaſter induced ſome certain men wickedly and fraudulently to impoſe upon the unwary ſome falſe magical oracles, and diabolical inventions, written in Greek and Latin, &c. as the genuine works of the divine and illuſtrious Zoroaſter.

HERMES,

HERMES, SURNAMED TRISMEGISTUS,

OR THE

THRICE GREATEST INTELLIGENCER.

H ERMES Trifmegiftus, (who was the author of the divine Pymander and
      fome other books,) lived fome time before Mofes. He received the
name of Trifmegiftus, or Mercurius ter Maximus, *i. e.* thrice greateft Intelligencer, becaufe he was the firft intelligencer who communicated celeftial
and divine knowledge to mankind by writing.

He was reported to have been king of Egypt : without doubt he was an
Egyptian ; nay, if you believe the Jews, even their Mofes ; and for the juf-
tification of this they urge, 1ft, His being well fkilled in *chemiftry* ; nay, the
firft who communicated that art to the fons of men ; 2dly, They urge the
philofophic work, viz. of rendering gold medicinal, or, finally, of the art of
making *aurum potabile* ; and, thirdly, of teaching the *Cabala*, which they fay
was fhewn him by God on Mount Sinai : for all this is confeffed to be originally written in Hebrew, which he would not have done had he not been an
Hebrew, but rather in his vernacular tongue. But whether he was Mofes
or not *, it is certain he was an Egyptian, even as Mofes himfelf alfo was ;
and therefore for the age he lived in, we fhall not fall fhort of the time if we
conclude he flourifhed much about the time of Mofes ; and if he really was
not the identical Mofes, affirmed to be fo by many, it is more than probable
that he was king of Egypt ; for being chief philofopher, he was, according

* The Cabalifts of the Hebrews affirm that Mofes was this Hermes ; and although meek, yet was a
man poffeffed of the moft ferious gravity, and a profound fpeculator in chemiftry and divine magic ;
that he, by divine infpiration on the mount, became acquainted with the knowledge of all the natural
and fecret operations of nature ; that he taught the tranfmutation of metals *per Cabala, i. e.* by oral
tradition, to the Jews.

to

to the Egyptian custom, initiated into the mysteries of priesthood, and from thence to the chief governor or king.

He was called Ter Maximus, as having a perfect knowledge of all things contained in the world (as his *Aureus*, or *Golden Tractate*, and his *Divine Pymander* shews,) which things he divided into three kingdoms, *viz.* animal, vegetable, and mineral; in the knowledge and comprehension of which three he excelled and transmitted to posterity, in *enigmas* and *symbols*, the profound secrets of nature; likewise a true description of the *Philosopher's Quintessence*, or *Universal Elixir*, which he made as the receptacle of all celestial and terrestrial virtues. The *Great Secret* of the philosophers he discoursed on, which was found engraven upon a Smaragdine table, in the valley of Ebron.

Johannes Functius, in his Chronology says, he lived in the time of Moses, twenty-one years before the law was given in the wilderness. Suidas seems to confirm it by saying, " Credo Mercurium Trismegistum sapientem Egyp- " tium floruisse ante Pharaonem." But this of Suidas may be applied to several ages, for that Pharaoh was the general name of their kings; or pos- sibly it might be intended before the name of Pharaoh was given to their kings, which, if so *, he makes Trismegistus to exist 400 years before Moses, yea, before Abraham's descent into Egypt. There is no doubt but that he possessed the great secret of the philosophic work; and if God ever appeared in man, he appeared in him, as is evident both from his books and his Py- mander; in which works he has communicated the sum of the abyss, and the divine knowledge to all posterity; by which he has demonstrated himself to have been not only an inspired divine, but also a deep philosopher, obtaining his wisdom from God and heavenly things, and not from man.

* According to the best authorities to be taken, Hermes Trismegistus lived in the time of Pharaoh, Israel's tyrant and oppressor, and was not the same with Moses who opposed Jannes and Jambres.

APPOL-

APPOLLONIUS of TYANA,

WITH SOME ACCOUNT OF HIS

REMARKABLE MIRACLES, PROPHECIES, VISIONS, RELATIONS, &c. &c.

APPOLLONIUS Tyanæus, was one of the moſt extraordinary perſons that ever appeared in the world. He was born at Tyana in Cappadocia, towards the beginning of the firſt century. At ſixteen years of age he became a rigid diſciple of Pythagoras, renouncing *wine, fleſh,* and *women,* wearing no ſhoes, and letting his hair and beard grow long, and cloathing himſelf only in linen: ſoon after he became a reformer, and fixed his abode in a temple of Æſculapius, where many ſick perſons reſorted to be cured by him. Being come to age, he gave part of his eſtate to his eldeſt brother, and diſtributed another part to his poor relations, and kept back only a very ſmall ſhare to himſelf. He lived ſix years without ſpeaking a word, notwithſtanding during this ſilence he quelled ſeveral ſeditions in Cecilia and Pamphilia; that which he put a ſtop to at *Aſpenda* was the moſt difficult of all to appeaſe, becauſe the buſineſs was to make thoſe hearken to reaſon whom famine had driven to revolt: the cauſe of this commotion was, ſome rich men having monopolized all the corn, occaſioned an extraordinary ſcarcity in the city. *Appollonius* ſtopped this popular commotion, without ſpeaking a word to the enraged multitude: Appollonius had no occaſion for words; his Pythagoric ſilence did all that the fineſt figures of oratory could effect. He travelled much, profeſſed himſelf a legiſlator; underſtood all languages, without having learned them: he had the ſurpriſing faculty of knowing what was tranſacted at an immenſe diſtance, and at the time the Emperor Domitian was ſtabbed, Appollonius being at a vaſt diſtance, and ſtanding in the market-place of the city, exclaimed, " Strike! ſtrike!—'tis done, the tyrant

is

is no more." He underſtood the language of birds; he condemned dancing, and other diverſions of that ſort; he recommended charity and piety; he travelled almoſt over all the countries of the world; and he died at a very great age. His life has been fully related by Philoſtratus; but it contains ſo many fabulous relations that we do not pretend to introduce them in this place. There are many who have very readily oppoſed the miracles of this man to thoſe of Chriſt, and drew a parallel between them. It cannot be denied that this philoſopher received very great honours, both during his life and after his death; and that his reputation continued long after paganiſm. He wrote four books of Judicial Aſtrology, and a Treatiſe on Sacrifices, ſhewing what was to be offered to the Deity.

' We muſt not omit a circumſtance which tends to the honour of this ve-
' nerable perſon. It is related that *Aurelius* had come to a reſolution, and
' had publickly declared his intentions, to demoliſh the city of *Tyana*; but
' that *Appollonius of Tyana*, an ancient philoſopher, of great renown and au-
' thority, a true friend of the gods, and himſelf honoured as a deity, appear-
' ed to him in his uſual form as he retired into his tent, and addreſſed him
' thus:—" *Aurelian*, if you deſire to be victorious, think no more of the
" deſtruction of my fellow-citizens!—*Aurelian*, if you deſire to rule, abſtain
" from the blood of the innocent!—*Aurelian*, if you will conquer, be mer-
" ciful!" Aurelian being acquainted with the features of this ancient phi-
' loſopher, having ſeen his image in ſeveral temples, he vowed to erect a
' temple and ſtatues to him; and therefore altered his reſolution of ſacking
' *Tyana*. This account we have from men of credit, and have met with it
' in books in the Olpian library; and we are the more inclined to believe
' it on account of the dignity of *Appollonius*; for was there ever any thing
' among men more holy, venerable, noble, and divine than *Appollonius*?
' He reſtored life to the dead; he did and ſpoke many things beyond hu-
' man reach; which whoever would be informed of, may meet with many
' accounts of them in the Greek hiſtories of his life.' See *Vopiſcus in Aurelian*, cap. 24.

X   Laſtly,

Lastly, the inhabitants of *Tyana* built a temple to their *Appollonius* after his death ; his statue was erected in several temples : the Emperor *Adrian* collected as many of his writings as he possibly could, and kept them very select, in his superb palace at *Antium*, with a rare but small book of this philosopher's, concerning the *Oracle of Trophonius*. This little book was to be seen at *Antium* during the life of Philostratus ; nor did any curiosity whatever render this small town so famous as did this rare and extraordinary book of Appollonius.

It is reported that a wise prince of the Indians, well skilled in magic, made seven rings of the seven planets, which he bestowed upon Appollonius, one of which he wore every day ; by which he always màintained the health and vigour of his youth, and lived to a very advanced age. His life was translated from the Greek of *Philostratus* into French, by *Blaise de Vignere*, with a very ample commentary by *Artus Thomas*, Lord of *Embry*, a *Parisian* ; and some time since there has been made an English translation of his life, which was condemned, prohibited, and anathematized without reason.

PETRUS

PETRUS DE ABANO, OR PETER OF APONA,

DOCTOR OF PHILOSOPHY AND PHYSIC, &c. &c. &c.

PETRUS APONENSIS, or APONUS, one of the most famous philosophers
and physicians of his time, was born A. D. 1250, in a village, situated four
miles from *Padua*. He studied a long time at *Paris*, where he was promoted
to the degrees of Doctor in philosophy and physic, in the practice of which he
was very successful, but his fees remarkably high. *Gabriel Naude*, in his
Antiquitate Scholæ Medicæ Parisienfis, gives the following account of him:
" Let us next produce Peter de Apona, or Peter de Abano, called the
" Reconciler, on account of the famous book which he published during
" his residence in your university *."—It is certain that physic lay buried in
" Italy, scarce known to any one, uncultivated and unadorned, till its tutelar
" genius, a villager of *Apona*, destined to free Italy from its barbarism and
" ignorance, as Camillus once freed *Rome* from the siege of the *Gauls*, made
" diligent enquiry in what part of the world polite literature was most happily
" cultivated, philosophy most subtilly handled, and physic taught with the
" greatest solidity and purity; and being assured that *Paris* alone laid claim to
" this honour, thither he presently flies; giving himself up wholly to her tutelage,
" he applied himself diligently to the mysteries of philosophy and medicine; ob-
" tained a degree and the laurel in both; and afterwards taught them both with
" great applause: and after a stay of many years, loaden with the wealth acquired
" among you, and, after having become the most famous philosopher, astrologer,
" physician, and mathematician of his time, returns to his own country, where,

---

* *Naude* takes notice of this in a speech in which he extols the ancient glory of the university of
Paris. We have above, recited his words at length, because they incidentally inform us, that Peter de
Abano composed that great work at Paris which procured him the apellation of the *Reconciler*.

X 2

" in the opinion of the judicious *Scardeon,* he was the firſt reſtorer of true
" philoſophy and phyſic.   Gratitude, therefore, calls upon you to acknowledge
" your obligations due to *Michæl Angelus Blondus,* a phyſician of *Rome,* who
" in the laſt century undertaking to publiſh the *Conciliationes Phyſiognomicæ*
" of your *Aponenſian* doctor, and finding they had been compoſed at *Paris,*
" and in your univerſity, choſe to publiſh them in the name, and under the
" patronage, of your ſociety."   'Tis ſaid, that he was ſuſpected of magic*,
and

---

* *Naude,* in his *Apology for great Men accuſed of Magic,* ſays, " The general opinion of almoſt all
" authors is, that he was the greateſt magician of his time ; that by means of ſeven ſpirits, familiar, which
" he kept incloſed in chryſtal, he had acquired the knowledge of the ſeven liberal arts, and that he had
" the art of cauſing the money he had made uſe of to return again into his pocket. He was accuſed of
" magic in the eightieth year of his age, and that dying in the year 1305, before his trial was over, he
" was condemned (as *Caſtellan* reports) to the fire ; and that a bundle of ſtraw, or oſier, repreſenting his
" perſon, was publicly burnt at Padua ; that by ſo rigorous an example, and by the fear of incurring a
" like penalty, they might ſuppreſs the reading of three books which he had compoſed on this ſubject :
" the firſt of which is the noted *Heptameron,* or *Magical Elements of Peter de Abano, Philoſopher,* now extant,
" and printed at the end of *Agrippa's* works ; the ſecond, that which Trithemius calls *Elucidarium*
" *Necromanticum Petri de Abano* ; and a third, called, by the ſame author, *Liber experimentorum mirabilium*
" *de Annulis ſecundem,* 28 *Manſiom Lunæ.*" Now it is to be noted, that Naude lays no ſtreſs upon theſe
ſeeming ſtrong proofs ; he refutes them by immediately after affirming, that *Peter* of *Apona* was a man
of prodigious penetration and learning, living in an age of darkneſs which cauſed every thing out of
the vulgar track to be ſuſpected as diabolical, eſpecially as he was very much given to ſtudy, and
acquainted with the harmony of the celeſtial bodies and the proportions of nature, and addicted to
curious and divinatory ſcience. " He was one (ſays he) who appeared as a prodigy of learning amidſt
" the ignorance of that age, and who, beſides his ſkill in languages and phyſic, had carried his enquiries
" ſo far into the occult ſciences of abſtruſe and hidden nature, that, after having given moſt ample
" proofs, by his writings concerning phyſiognomy, geomancy, and chiromancy, what he was able to
" perform in each of theſe, he quitted them all together with his youthful curioſity to addict himſelf
" wholly to the ſtudy of philoſophy, phyſic, and aſtrology ; which ſtudies proved ſo advantageous to
" him, that, not to ſpeak of the two firſt, which introduced him to all the popes and ſovereign pontiffs
" of his time, and acquired him the reputation which at preſent he enjoys among learned men, it
" is certain that he was a great maſter in the latter, which appears, not only by the aſtronomical figures
" which he cauſed to be painted in the great hall of the palace at *Padua,* and the tranſlations he made
" of the books of the moſt learned *Rabbi Abraham Aben Exra,* added to thoſe which he himſelf compoſed
" on *critical days,* and the improvement of aſtronomy, but by the teſtimony of the renowned mathema-
" tician *Regio Montanus,* who made a fine panegyric on him, in quality of an aſtrologer, in the oration
" which he delivered publicly at *Padua* when he explained there the book of *Alfraganus.*" Now, many
reſpectable authors are of opinion that it was not on the ſcore of magic that the Inquiſition ſentenced
him

and perfecuted on that account by the Inquifition: and it is probable that, if he had lived to the end of his trial, he would have fuffered in perfon what he was fentenced to fuffer in effigy after his death. His apologifts obferve, that his body, being privately taken out of his grave by his friends, efcaped the vigilance of the Inquifitors, who would have condemned it to be burnt. He was removed from place to place, and at laft depofited in *St. Auguftin's Church*, without Epitaph, or any other mark of honour. His accufers afcribed inconfiftent opinions to him; they charged him with being a magician, and yet with denying the exiftence of fpirits. He had fuch an antipathy to milk, that the very feeing any one take it made him vomit. He died in the year 1316* in the fixty-fixth year of his age.. One of his principal books was the Conciliator, already mentioned.

him to death, but becaufe he endeavoured to account for the wonderful effeAs in nature by the *influences of the celeftial bodies*, not attributing them to *angels* or *dæmons* ; fo that herefy, inftead of magic, feems to have been the ground of his falling under the tyranny of the fage fathers of the Roman Cotholic faith, as being one who *oppofed* the doXrine of fpiritual beings.

* If this be true as we read in *Tomafini*, in *Elog. Vilor. Illuftr. p. 22*, *Naude* muft be miftaken where he fays, that " Peter Aponus being accufed at the age of 80 years, died A. D. 1305." *Freberus* affirms the fame upon the authority of *Bernardin Scardeon*. *Gefner* is miftaken in making Peter Aponus flourifh in the year 1320. Konig has copied this error. But Father Rapin is much more grofsly miftaken than any of them when he places him in the fixteenth century, faying, " *Peter of Apona*, a phyfician of *Padua*, " who flourifhed under Clement VII, debauched his imagination fo far by reading the *Arabian* philofo- " phers, and by too much ftudying the aftrology of Alfraganus, that he was put into the Inquifition " upon the fufpicion of magic, &c." See *Rapin Reflex. fur la Philofophiæ, n. 28, p. 363. Voffius* has followed *Gefner*, and makes an obfervation worthy to be confidered. He fays, that *Peter of Apona* fent his book, *De Medicina Omnimoda*, to pope *John* XXII, who was eleXed in the year 1316, and held the *Pontifical Chair* feventeen years. By this we know the age of this phyfician. But if the year 1316 was that of his death, the conclufion is unjuft ; neither does it clear *Voffius* of an error.

APULEIUS,

APULEIUS,

THE PLATONIC PHILOSOPHER.

LUCIUS APULEIUS, a Platonic philosopher, publicly known by the famous work of the *Golden Afs*, lived in the second century under the Antonines. He was a native of *Madaura*, a *Roman* colony in *Africa*; his family was confiderable; he had been well educated, and poffeffed a graceful exterior; he had wit and learning; but was fufpected of magic. He ftudied firft at *Carthage*, then at *Athens*, and afterwards at *Rome*, where he acquired the Latin tongue without any affiftance. An infatiable curiofity to know every thing induced him to make feveral voyages, and enter himfelf into feveral religious fraternities. He would fee the bottom of their myfteries. He fpent almoft all his eftate in travelling; infomuch, that being returned to *Rome*, and having a defire to dedicate himfelf to the fervice of *Ofiris*, he lacked money to defray the expence of the ceremonies of his reception, he was obliged to make money of his clothes to complete the neceffary fum : after this, he gained his living by pleading; and, as he was eloquent and fubtle, he did not want caufes, fome of which were very confiderable. But he improved his fortunes much more by a lucky marriage than by pleading. A widow, whofe name was Pudentilla, neither young nor fair, but who had a good eftate, thought him worth her notice. He was not coy, nor was he folicitous to keep his fine perfon, his wit, his neatnefs, and his eloquence, for fome young girl; he married this rich widow chearfully (and with the moft becoming philofophy overcame all turbulent paffions, which might draw him into the fnares of beauty,) at a country houfe near Oëa, a maritime town of Africa. This marriage drew upon him a troublefome law-fuit. The relations of this lady's two fons urged that he had made ufe of art magic to poffefs himfelf of her

person

pſon and money; they accuſed him of being worſe than a magician, *viz.*
a wizard, before *Claudius Maximus*, Proconſul of *Africa*. He defended himſelf
with great vigour *. His apology, which he delivered before the judges,
furniſhes

* Beſides the accuſation of magic, they reproached him with his beauty, his fine hair, his teeth, and
his looking-glaſs. To the two firſt particulars he anſwered he was ſorry their accuſation was falſe.——
" How do I wiſh," replied he, " that theſe heavy accuſations of beauty, fine hair, &c. were juſt! I
" ſhould, without difficulty, reply, as *Paris* in *Homer* does to Hector,.

> ————— nor thou deſpiſe the charms
> With which a lover golden Venus arms.
> Soft moving ſpeech, and pleaſing outward ſhew,
> No wiſh can gain them, but the Gods beſtow.
>
> POPE.

" Thus would I reply to the charge of beauty. Beſides that, even philoſophers are allowed to be of
" a liberal aſpect; that *Pythagoras*, the firſt of philoſophers, was the handſomeſt man of his time; and
" *Zeno*—but, as I obſerved, I am far from pretending to this apology; ſince, beſides that nature has
" beſtowed but a very moderate degree of beauty on me, my continual application to ſtudy wears off
" every bodily grace, and impairs my conſtitution. My hair, which I am falſely accuſed of curling
" and dreſſing by way of ornament, is, as you ſee, far from being beautiful and delicate: on the contrary,
" it is perplexed and entangled like a bundle of flocks or tow, and ſo knotty through long neglect of
" combing, and even of diſentangling, as never to be reduced to order." As to the third particular,
he did not deny his having ſent a very exquiſite powder for the teeth to a friend, together with ſome
verſes, containing an exact deſcription of the effects of the powder. He alledged that *all*, but eſpecially
thoſe who ſpake in public, ought to be particularly careful to keep their mouths clean. This was a
fine field for defence, and for turning his adverſary into ridicule; though, in all probability, he had
given occaſion enough for cenſure by too great an affectation of diſtinguiſhing himſelf from other learned
men. Obſerve with how much eaſe ſome cauſes are defended, although the defendant be a little in the
wrong. " I obſerved that ſome could ſcarce forbear laughing when our orator angrily accuſed me of
" keeping my mouth clean, and pronounced the word tooth-powder with as much indignation as any one
" ever pronounced the word poiſon. But, ſurely, it is not beneath a philoſopher to ſtudy cleanlineſs,
" and to let no part of the body be foul, or of an ill ſavour, eſpecially the mouth, the uſe of which is
" the moſt frequent and conſpicuous, whether a man converſes with another, or ſpeaks in public, or ſays
" his prayers in a temple. For ſpeech is previous to every action of a man, and, as an excellent poet
" ſays, proceeds from the Wall of the Teeth."

We may make the ſame obſervation upon the laſt head of his accuſation. It is no crime in a doctor
of what faculty ſoever, to have a looking-glaſs; but if he conſults it too often in dreſſing himſelf, he is
juſtly liable to cenſure. Morality in *Apuleius*'s time was much ſtricter than at preſent as to external
behaviour, for he durſt not avow his making uſe of his looking-glaſs. He maintains that he *might* do
it,

furnifhes us with examples of the moſt ſhameful artifices that the villainy of an impudent calumniator is capable of putting in practice *. Apuleius was extremely laborious, and compoſed ſeveral books, ſome in verſe and others in proſe, of which but a ſmall part has reſiſted the injuries of time. He delighted in making public ſpeeches, in which he gained the applauſe of all his hearers. When they heard him at Oëa, the audience cried out with one voice, that he

ir, and proves it by ſeveral philoſophical reaſons, which, to ſay the truth, are much more ingenious than judiciouſly applied ; but he denies that he ever conſulted his looking-glaſs ; for he ſays, alluding to this ludicrous accuſation, " Next follows the long and bitter harangue about the looking-glaſs ; in which, " ſo heinous is the crime, that *Pudens* almoſt burſt himſelf with bawling out—' A philoſopher to have " a looking-glaſs!'—Suppoſe I ſhould confeſs that I have, that you may not believe there is really ſome- " thing in your objection, if I ſhould deny it ; it does not follow from hence that I muſt neceſſarily " make a practice of dreſſing myſelf at it. In many things I want the poſſeſſion but enjoy the uſe of " them. Now, if neither to have a thing be a proof that it is made uſe of, nor the want of it of the " contrary, and as I am not blamed for poſſeſſing, but for making uſe of, a looking-glaſs, it is incum- " bent upon him to prove farther at what time, and in what place, and in the preſence of whom, I made " uſe of it ; ſince you determine it to be a greater crime in a *philoſopher* to ſee a looking-glaſs, than for " the *profane* to behold the attire of *Ceres*."

* I ſhall inſtance one to ſhew that in all ages the ſpirit of calumny has put men upon forging proofs by falſe extracts from what a perſon has ſaid or written. To convict Apuleius of practiſing magic, his accuſers alledge a letter which his wife had wrote during the time he paid his *devoirs* to her, and affirmed that ſhe had confeſſed, in *this letter*, that Apuleius was a *wizard*, and had actually bewitched her. It was no hard matter to make the court believe that ſhe had written ſo, for they only read a few words of her letter, detached from what preceded or followed, and no one preſſed them to read the whole. At laſt, Apuleius covered them with confuſion by reciting the whole paſſage from his wife's letter. It appeared that far from complaining of Apuleius, ſhe juſtified him, and artfully ridiculed his accuſers. Theſe are his words : you will find that preciſely the ſame terms may either condemn or juſtify *Apuleius*, according as they are taken with or without what precedes them. " Being inclined to marry, for the " reaſons which I have mentioned, you yourſelf perſuaded me to make choice of this man, being fond of " him, and being deſirous, by my means, to make him one of the family. But now, at the inſtigation of " wicked men, *Apuleius* muſt be informed againſt as a magician (or wizard), and I, forſooth, am enchanted " by him. I certainly love him : come to me before my reaſon fails me." He aggravates this kind of fraud as it deſerves ; his words deſerve to be engraved in letters of gold, to deter (if poſſible) all calumniators from practiſing the like cheats. He ſays, " There are many things which, produced " alone, may ſeem liable to calumny. Any *diſcourſe* may furniſh matter of accuſation, if what is con- " nected with foregoing words be robbed of its introduction ; if ſome things be ſuppreſſed at pleaſure, " and if what is ſpoken by way of reproach to others, for inventing a calumny, be pronounced by the " reader as an aſſertion of the truth of it."

ought

ought to be honoured with the freedom of the city. Those of Carthage heard him favourably, and erected a statue in honour of him. Several other cities did him the same honour. It is said that his wife held the candle to him whilst he studied; but this is not to be taken literally; it is rather a figure of Gallic eloquence in Sidonis Apollinaris, *Legentibus meditantibusque candelas & candelabra tenuerunt.* Several critics have published notes on Apuleius: witness *Phillipus Beraldus,* who published very large notes on the *Golden Ass,* at *Venice,* in folio, ann. 1504, which were reprinted in 8vo, at Paris, and at several other places. *Godescalk Stewichius, Peter Colvius, John Wiewer,* &c. have written on all the works of *Apuleius. Precius* published the *Golden Ass,* and the Apology, separately, with a great many observations. The annotations of *Casaubon,* and those of *Scipio Gentilis,* on the Apology, are very scarce, and much valued: the first appeared in the year 1594, and the latter in 1607. The *Golden Ass* may be considered (as Bayle says) as a continued satire on the disorders which the pseudo-magicians, priests, pandars, and thieves filled the world with at that time. This observation occurs in Fleuri's annotations. A person who would take the pains, and had the requisite qualifications, might draw up a very curious and instructive commentary on this romance, and might inform the world of several things which the preceeding commentaries have never touched upon. There are some very obscene passages in this book of Apuleius. It is generally believed that this author has inserted some curious episodes in it of his own invention; and amongst others, that of *Psyche. Horum certe noster itæ imitator fuit, ut è suo penu enumerabilia protulerit, atque inter cætera venustissimum illud Psyches,* Ἐπισόδιον. This episode furnished *Moliere* with matter for an excellent Dramatic Piece, and *M. de la Fontaine* for a fine Romance.

Y   ARISTOTLE,

ARISTOTLE,

THE PERIPATETIC.

ARISTOTLE, commonly called the Prince of Philosophers, or the Philosopher, by way of excellence, was the founder of a sect which surpassed, and at
length even swallowed up all the rest. Not but that it has had reverse of fortune
in its turn ; especially in the seventeenth century, in which it has been violently
shaken, though the Catholic divines on the one side, and the Protestant on
the other, have run (as to the quenching of fire) to its relief, and fortified
themselves so strongly, by the secular arm, against the New Philosophy, that
it is not like to lose its dominion. Mr. *Moreri* met with so many good
materials in a work of father Rapin, that he has given a very large article of
Aristotle, enough to dispense with any assistance. Accordingly, I design not
to enlarge upon it as far as the subject might allow, but shall content myself
with observing some of the errors which I have collected concerning this
philosopher. It is not certain that *Aristotle* practised pharmacy in *Athens*
while he was a disciple of *Plato*, nor is it more certain that he did not. Very
little credit ought to be given to a current tradition that he learnt several
things of a *Jew*, and much less to a story of his pretended conversion to
Judaism. They who pretend that he was born a *Jew*, are much more grossly
mistaken : the wrong pointing of a certain passage occasioned this mistake.
They are deceived who say that he was a disciple of *Socrates* for three years,
for *Socrates* died 15 years before *Aristotle* was born. *Aristotle*'s behaviour
towards his master *Plato* is variously related : some will have it that, through
prodigious vanity and ingratitude, he set up altar against altar : that is, he
erected a school in *Athens* during *Plato*'s life, and in opposition to him : others
say that he did not set up for a professor till after his master's death. We are
told

told some things concerning his amours which are not altogether to his advantage. It was pretended that his conjugal affection was idolatrous, and that, if he had not retired from *Athens*, the process for irreligion, which the priests had commenced against him, would have been attended with the same consequences as that against *Socrates*. Though he deserved very great praise, yet it is certain that most of the errors concerning him are to be found in the extravagant commendations which have been heaped upon him: as, for example, is it not a downright falsehood to say, *that if Aristotle spoke in his natural philosophy like a man, he spoke in his moral philosophy like a God; and that it is a question in his moral philosophy whether he partakes more of the lawyer than of the priest; more of the priest than of the prophet; more of the prophet than of the God?* Cardinal *Pallavicini* scrupled not in some measure to affirm that, if it had not been for *Aristotle*, the church would have wanted some of its articles of faith. The Christians are not the only people who have authorized his philosophy; the *Mahometans* are little less prejudiced in its favour; and we are told, that to this day, notwithstanding the ignorance which reigns among them, they have schools for this sect. It will be an everlasting subject of wonder, to persons who know what philosophy is, to find that *Aristotle's* authority was so much respected in the schools, for several ages, that when a disputant quoted a passage from this philosopher, he who maintained the *thesis* durst not say *transeat*, but must either deny the passage, or explain it in his own way. It is in this manner we treat the Holy Scriptures in the divinity schools. The parliaments which have proscribed all other philosophy but that of *Aristotle*, are more excusable than the doctors: for whether the members of parliament were really persuaded that this philosophy was the best of any, or was not, the public good might induce them to prohibit new opinions, lest the academical divisions should extend their malignant influence to the disturbance of the tranquillity of the state. What is most astonishing to wise men is, that the professors should be so strongly prejudiced in favour of *Aristotle's philosophy*. Had this prepossession been confined to his poetry and rhetoric, it had been less wonderful: but they were fond of the weakest

of

of his works; I mean his Logic, and Natural Philosophy *. This juftice,
however, muft be done to the blindeft of his followers, that they have deferted
him where he clafhes with Chriftianity: and this he did in points of the
greateft confequence, fince he maintained the eternity of the world, and did
not believe that providence extended itself to fublunary beings. As to the
immortality of the foul, it is not certainly known whether he acknowledged
it or not †. In the year 1647, the famous capuchin, *Valerian Magni*, publifhed a work concerning the Atheifm of *Ariftotle*. About one hundred and
thirty years before, *Marc Anthony Venerius* publifhed a fyftem of philofophy,
in which he difcovered feveral inconfiftencies between *Ariftotle's* doctrine, and
the truths of religion. Campanella maintained the fame in his book *de Re-
ductione ad Religionem*, which was approved at *Rome* in the year 1630. It was
not long fince maintained in *Holland*, in the prefaces to fome books, that the
doctrine of this philofopher differed but little from Spinozifm. In the mean
time, if fome Peripatetics may be believed, he was not ignorant of the myftery
of the Trinity. He made a very good end, and enjoys eternal happinefs.
He compofed a great number of books; a great part of which is come down
to us. It is true fome critics raife a thoufand fcruples about them. He was
extremely honoured in his own city, and there were not wanting heretics who
worfhipped *his* image with that of *Chrift*. There is extant fome book which
mentions, that, before the Reformation, there were churches in *Germany* in

---

* To be convinced of the weaknefs of thefe works, we need only read *Gaffendus* in his *Exercitationes
Paradoxicæ adverfus Ariftoteleos*. He fays enough there againft *Ariftotle's* philofophy in general, to convince every unprejudiced reader that it is very defective; but he particularly ruins this philofopher's
Logic. He was preparing, likewife, a criticifm on his Natural Philofophy, his Metaphyfics, and Ethics,
in the fame way; when, being alarmed at the formidable indignation of the *peripatetic* party againft him,
he chofe rather to drop his work, than expofe himfelf to their vexatious perfecutions. In *Ariftotle's*
Logic and Natural Philofophy, there are many things which difcover the elevation and profundity
of his genius.

† *Pomponatius* and *Niphus* had a great quarrel on this fubject. The firft maintained, that the immortality
of the foul was inconfiftent with *Ariftotle's* principles: the latter undertook to defend the contrary. See
the difcourfe of *la Mothe le Vayer* on the Immortality of the Soul, and *Bodin*, in page 15 of Pref.
to *Dæmonomania*.

which

which *Ariſtotle*'s Ethics were read every *Sunday* morning to the people inſtead of the Goſpel. There are but few inſtances of zeal for religion which have not been ſhewn for the *Peripatetic* philoſophy. *Paul de Foix*, famous for his embaſſies and his learning, would not ſee *Francis Patricius* at *Ferrara*, becauſe he was informed that that learned man taught a philoſophy different from the *Peripatetic*. This was treating the enemies of *Ariſtotle* as *zealots* treat *heretics*. After all, it is no wonder that the *Peripatetic* philoſophy, as it has been taught for ſeveral centuries, found ſo many protectors; or that the intereſts of it are believed to be inſeparable from thoſe of theology: for it accuſtoms the mind to acquieſce without evidence. This union of intereſts may be eſteemed as a pledge to the *Peripatetics* of the immortality of their ſect, and an argument to abate the hopes of the new philoſophers.—Conſidering, withal, that there are ſome doctrines of Ariſtotle which the moderns have rejected, and which muſt, ſooner or later, be adopted again. The Proteſtant divines have very much altered their conduct, if it is true, as we are told, that the firſt reformers clamoured ſo loud againſt the *Peripatetic* philoſophy. The kind of death, which in ſome reſpects does much honour to the memory of *Ariſtotle*, is, that which ſome have reported, *viz.* that his vexation at not being able to diſcover the cauſe of the flux and reflux of the *Eurippus* occaſioned the diſtemper of which he died. Some ſay, that being retired into the iſland of *Eubæa*, to avoid a proceſs againſt him for irreligion, he poiſoned himſelf: but why ſhould he quit *Athens* to free himſelf from perſecution this way? HESYCHIUS affirms, not only that ſentence of death was pronounced againſt him for an hymn which he made in honour of his father-in-law, but alſo that he ſwallowed aconite in execution of this ſentence. If this were true, it would have been mentioned by more authors.

The number of ancient and modern writers who have exerciſed their pens on *Ariſtotle*, either in commenting on, or tranſlating, him, is endleſs. A catalogue of them is to be met with in ſome of the editions of his works, but not a complete one. See a treatiſe of father Labbé, entitled *Ariſtotelis & Platonis Græcorum Interpretum, typis hactenus editorum brevis conſpectus*; *A ſhort view of the Greek interpreters of Ariſtotle and Plato hitherto publiſhed*; printed

printed at *Paris* in the year 1657 in 4to. Mr. *Teissier* names four authors who have composed the life of *Aristotle*; *Ammonius, Guarini of Verona, John James Beurerus*, and *Leonard Aretin*. He forgot *Jerome Gemusæus*, physician and professor of philosophy at *Bazil*, author of a book, *De Vita Aristotelis, et ejus Operum Censura.—The Life of Aristotle, and a Critique on his Works.*

PETER BAYLE.

ARTEMIDORUS of EPHESUS,

THE

SOMNABULIST, or DREAMER.

A RTEMIDORUS (who wrote so largely upon Dreams) was a native of *Ephesus*. He lived under *Antonius Pius*, as he informs us himself, where he says, he knew an Athlete, who having dreamt that he had lost his sight, obtained the prize in the games which that Emperor ordered to be celebrated. No author has ever taken more pains upon so useful a subject than *Artemidorus* has done. He bought up all that had been written upon the subject of dreams, which amounted to several volumes, but he spent many years in travelling to collect them, as well as the different opinions of all the learned who were then living. He kept a continual correspondence with those in the towns and assemblies of Greece, in Italy, and in the most populous islands; and he collected every where all the dreams he could hear of, and the events they had. He despised the censure of those grave and supercilious persons, who treat all pretenders to predictions as sharpers, or impostors, and without regarding the censures of these *Catos*, he frequented those diviners many years. In a word, he devoted all his time and thoughts to the science of dreams. He

thought

thought that his great labour in making so many collections, &c. had enabled him to warrant his interpretations by reason and experience, but unfortunately he ever fixed upon the most trifling and frivolous subjects, such as almost every one is dreaming of: there is no dream which *Artemidorus* has explained, but will bear a quite different interpretation, with the same probability, and with at least as natural resemblances, as those on which that interpreter proceeds. I say nothing of the injury done to *intelligences*, to whose direction we must necessarily impute our dreams if we expect to find in them any presage of futurity *. *Artemidorus* took great pains to instruct his son in the same science, as appears by the two books which he dedicated to him. So eager a pursuit after these studies is the less to be wondered at, when we consider that he believed himself under the inspiration of *Apollo*. He dedicated his three first

* We find in Artemidorus some of the most trifling incidents in dreams noted by him to presage very extraordinary things; such, as if any one dreams of his nose, or his teeth, or such like trifling subjects, such particular events they must denote.—Now, as we cannot attribute a true and significant dream to any other cause than the celestial *intelligences*, or an *evil dæmon*, or else to the soul itself (which possesses an inherent prophetic virtue, as we have fully treated of in our *Second Book of Magic, where we have spoken of prophetic dreams*). I say from which of these causes a dream proceeds, we must ascribe but a very deficient portion of knowledge to either of them, if we do not allow them capable of giving better and plainer information respecting any calamity or change of fortune or circumstances, than by dreaming of one's nose itching, or a tooth falling out, and a hundred other toys like these.—I say, such modes of dictating to us a fore-knowledge of events to happen, cannot but be unworthy of their wisdom, subtilty, or power, and if they cannot instruct us by better signs, how great is their ignorance, and if they will not, how great is their malice? therefore, all such trifling dreams are to be altogether rejected as vain and insignificant, for we must remember that "*a dream comes through the multitude of business*," and often otherwise ; but such dreams as we are to notice, and draw predictions of future accidents and events, are those where the dream is altogether consistent, not depending upon any prior discourse, accidents, or other like circumstances ; likewise, that the person who would wish to dream true dreams, should so dispose himself as to become a fit recipient of the heavenly powers, but this is only to be done by a temperate and frugal diet, a mind bent on sublime contemplations, a religious desire of being informed of any misfortune, accident, or event, which might introduce misery, poverty, or distraction of mind ; so as when we know it, to deprecate the same by prayer to the divine wisdom, that he would be pleased to divert the evil impending, or to enable us to meet the same with fortitude, and endure it with patience till the will of the Deity is accomplished. These are the things which we ought to be desirous to receive information of by *dream, vision*, or the like, and of which many are often truly forewarned, and thereby foretell things to come, also presage of the death of certain friends ; all which I know by experience to be true and probable.

books

books to one *Caffius Maximus*, and the other two to his fon.—They were printed in *Greek* at *Venice* in the year 1518. In the year 1603 *Rigaultius* publifhed them at *Paris* in *Greek* and *Latin*, with notes. The Latin tranfla-tion he made ufe of was that publifhed by *John Cornarius* at *Bazil*, in the year 1539. *Artemidorus* wrote a treatife of *augury*, and another upon *chiro-mancy*; but we have no remains of them. *Tertullian* has not taken notice of him in that paffage, where he quotes feveral *onirocritic* authors; but *Lucian* does not forget him, though he names but two writers of this clafs.

BABYLONIANS.

UNDER this article of *Babylonians* we fhall juft give the reader a general fketch of the antiquity of occult learning among the Chaldeans of *Ba-bylon*, fo famous for their fpeculations in aftrology. *Diodorus Siculus* informs us, that the inhabitants of Babylon affert, that their city was very ancient; for they counted four hundred and feventy-three thoufand years, from the firft obfervations of their aftrologers to the coming of *Alexander*. Others fay, that the *Babylonians* boafted of having preferved in their archives the obferva-tions which their aftrologers had made on nativities for the fpace of four hundred and feventy thoufand years; from hence we ought to correct a paf-fage of *Pliny*, which fome authors make ufe of improperly, either to confute the antiquity of Babylon, or for other purpofes. Ariftotle knew without doubt that the *Babylonians* boafted of having a feries of aftronomical obfer-vations comprehending a prodigious number of centuries. He was defirous to inform himfelf of the truth of this by means of *Califthenes*, who was in Alexander's retinue, but found a great miftake in the account; for it is pre-tended, that *Callifthenes* affured him that the aftronomical obfervations he had

feen

feen in *Babylon*, comprehended no more than 1903 years. *Simplicius* reports this, and borrows it from *Porphyry*. If *Califthenes* has computed right, it muft be agreed, that after the deluge men made very great hafte to become aftrologers; for according to the Hebrew Bible there is but two thoufand years * to be found from the flood to the death of *Alexander*. There is reafon to queftion what *Simplicius* reports, and it is remarkable that all the ancient authors, who have afcribed the building of *Babylon* to *Semiramis*, have no authority than that of *Ctefias*, whofe hiftories abounded in fables. And, therefore, we fee that *Berofus* blames the *Greek* writers for affirming, that *Semiramis* built *Babylon*, and adorned it with the moft beautiful ftructures. The fupplement to *Moreri* quotes *Quintus Curtius*, in relation to the immodefty of the *Babylonian* women †, who proftituted their bodies to ftrangers for money, under the idea of performing their devotions required by Venus. Obferve, that thefe fums were afterwards applied to religious ufes.

* *Epigenus* tells us, that amongft the Babylonians there were celeftial obfervations for four hundred and feventy thoufand years, infcribed on pillars or tables of bricks. *Berofus* and *Critodemus*, who make the leaft of it, fay four hundred and ninety years.

† This lafcivious ceremony was very ancient. *Jeremiah*'s letter inferted in the book of *Baruch* touches fomething on it, but in an obfcure manner, and wants a commentary taken out of *Herodotus*. Jeremiah's text runs thus:—" The women alfo with cords about them fat in the ways—but if any of " them, drawn by fome that paffeth by, lie with him, fhe reproacheth her fellow, that fhe was not " thought as worthy as herfelf, nor her cord broken."—Herodotus informs us, that there was a law in *Babylon* which obliged all the women of the country to feat themfelves near the temple of *Venus*, and there to wait an opportunity of copulating with a ftranger, &c. &c.

Z   THE

THE LIFE

OF

HENRY CORNELIUS AGRIPPA, Knight,

DOCTOR OF BOTH LAWS, COUNSELLOR TO CHARLES V. EMPEROR OF GERMANY, AND

JUDGE OF THE PREROGATIVE COURT.

HENRY CORNELIUS AGRIPPA, a very learned man and a magician*, flourished in the sixteenth century. He was born at *Cologne* on the 14th of *September*, 1486. He descended from a noble and ancient family of Nettesheim in Belgia; desiring to walk in the steps of his ancestors, who for many generations had been employed by the princes of the house of *Austria*, he entered early into the service of the Emperor *Maximilian*. He had at first the employ of Secretary; but as he was equally qualified for the *sword* as the *pen*, he afterwards turned soldier, and served the Emperor seven years in his *Italian* army. He signalized himself on several occasions, and as a reward of his brave actions he was created *knight* in the field. He wished to add the academical honours to the military, he therefore commenced doctor of laws and physic. He was a man possessed of a very wonderful genius, and from his youth applied his mind to learning, and by his great natural talents he obtained great knowledge in almost all arts and sciences. He was a diligent searcher into the mysteries of nature, and was early in search of the philosopher's stone; and it appears that he had been recommended to some princes

* As he himself asserts in his preface to his three books of Occult Philosophy and Magic, where he says, " who am indeed a magician," applying the word magic to sublime and good sciences, not to prophane and devilish arts. *Paul Jovius*, *Thevet*, and *Martin del Rio*, accuse him not of *magic*, *(because we cannot apply that to necromantic arts)* but the *black art*; but we shall shew in some of the following notes, their grounds on which this accusation of *Agrippa* is founded, and examine how far their information will justify their calumny against this author.

as

as mafter of the art of alchymy *, and very fit for the grand projection. He had a very extenfive knowledge of things in general, as likewife in the learned languages. He was pupil to *Trithemius*, who wrote upon the nature, miniftry, and offices of intelligences and fpirits. He was of an unfettled temper, and often changed his fituation, and was fo unfortunate as to draw upon himfelf the indignation of the Popifh clergy by his writings. We find by his letters that he had been in *France* before the year 1507, that he travelled into *Spain* in the year 1508, and was at *Dole* in the year 1509. He read public lectures there, which engaged him in a conteft with the *Cordelier Catilinet*. The monks in thofe times fufpected whatever they did not underftand, of herefy and error; how then could they fuffer *Agrippa* to explain the myfterious works of *Reuchlinus de Verbo Mirifico* with impunity? It was the fub- ject of the lectures which he read at *Dole* in 1509 with great reputation. To ingratiate himfelf the better with *Margaret of Auftria*, governefs of the *Auftrian Netherlands*, he compofed at that time a treatife on the excellency of women; but the perfecution he fuffered from the monks prevented him from publifhing it; he gave up the caufe, and came into *England*, where he wrote on *St. Paul*'s Epiftles, although he had another very private affair upon his hands. Being returned to *Cologne*, he read public lectures there on the queftions of the divinity, which are called *Quodlibetales*; after which he went to the Emperor *Maximilian*'s army in *Italy*, and continued there till Cardinal *de Sainte Croix* fent for him to *Pifa*. *Agrippa* would have difplayed his abilities there in quality of theologift of the council, if that affembly had continued. This would not have been the way to pleafe the Court of *Rome*, or to deferve the obliging letter he received from *Leo X*, and from whence we may conclude, that he altered his opinion. From that time he taught divinity publicly at *Pavia*, and at *Turin*. He likewife read lectures on *Mercurius Trifmegiftus* at *Pavia*, in the year 1515. He had a wife who was

* We have no authority to fay, that ever he was in poffeffion of the *great fecret* of tranfmutation, neither can we gather any fuch information from his writings; the only circumftance relative to this is what himfelf fays in occult philofophy, *that he had made gold, but no more than that out of which the foul was extracted.*

Z 2   handfome

handfome and accomplifhed, by whom he had one fon; he loft her in 1521; he married again an accomplifhed lady at Geneva in the year 1522, of whom he gives a very good character; by this wife he had three children, two fons and one daughter, who died. It appears by the fecond book of his letters, that his friends endeavoured in feveral places to procure him fome honourable fettlement, either at *Grenoble, Geneva, Avignon,* or *Metz.* He preferred the poft which was of-fered him in this laft city; and I find that in the year 1518 he was chofen by the lords of *Metz* to be their advocate, fyndic, and orator. The perfecutions which the monks raifed againft him, as well on account of his having re-futed the common opinion concerning the three hufbands of *St. Anne,* as be-caufe he had protected a country-woman, who was accufed of withcraft, made him leave the city of *Metz.* The ftory is as follows :—A country-woman, who was accufed of withcraft, was propofed (by the *Dominican, Nicholas Sa-vini,* Inquifitor of the Faith at *Metz*) to be put to the torture, upon a mere prejudice, grounded on her being the daughter of a witch, who had been burnt. Agrippa immediately took up the cudgels, and did what he could to prevent fo irregular a proceeding, but could not prevent the woman from being put to the *queftion*; however, he was the inftrument of proving her innocence. Her accufers were condemned in a fine. The penalty was too mild, and far from a retaliation. This country-woman was of *Vapey,* a town fituated near the gates of *Metz,* and belonging to the chapter of the cathedral. There ap-peared in *Meffin,* who was the principal accufer of this woman, fuch fordid paffions, and fuch a total ignorance of literature and philofophy, that *Agrippa,* in his letter of June 2, 1519, treats the town of Metz as—" *The ftep-mother of learning and virtue.*" This fatyrical reflexion of Agrippa's might give rife to the proverb—" *Metz,* the covetous, and ftep-mother of arts and fciences.''—What induced him to treat of the monogamy of *St. Anne* was his feeing, that *James Faber Stapulenfis,* his friend, was pulled to pieces by the preachers of *Metz,* for having maintained that opinion. *Agrippa* retired to *Cologne,* his native city, in the year 1520, willingly forfaking a city, which the feditious inquifitors had made an enemy to learning and true merit. It is indeed the fate of all cities where fuch perfons grow powerful of what-ever foever religion they are of. He again left his own city in the year 1521, and went to *Geneva*, but his fortunes did not much improve there, for he complained that he was not rich enough to make a journey to *Chamberi* to folicit the pension, which he was led to expect from the Duke of *Savoy*. This expectation came to nothing, upon which *Agrippa* went from *Geneva* to *Fribourg* in *Switzerland* in the year 1523, to practife physic there as he had done at *Geneva*. The year following he went to *Lyons*, and obtained a pension from *Francis I*. He was in the service of that prince's mother in quality of her physician, but made no great improvement of his fortune there; neither did he follow that princefs when she departed from *Lyons* in the month of *August*, 1525, to conduct her daughter to the frontiers of *Spain*. He danced attendance at *Lyons* for some time to employ the interest of his friends in vain, to obtain the payment of his pension; and before he received it he had the vexation to be informed, that he was struck out of the lift. The cause of this disgrace was, that having received orders from his mistrefs to enquire by the rules of astrology what turn the affairs of *France* would take, he expreffed his disapprobation too freely, that the princefs should employ him in such a vain curiofity, instead of making use of his abilities in more important affairs. The lady took this lesson very ill, but she was highly incensed when she heard that *Agrippa* had, by the *Rules of Astrology*, the *Cabala*, or some other art, predicted new triumphs to the conftable of *Bourbon**.—*Agrippa* finding himself

* See Agrippa's words in his 29th Epift. lib. iv. p. 854, which are as follow :—"I wrote to the " *Senechal*, defiring him to advife her not to misapply my abilities any longer in fo unworthy an art; " that I might for the future avoid thefe follies, fince I had it in my power to be of fervice to her by " much happier ftudies." But the greateft misfortune was, that "*this unworthy art*," and "thefe follies," as he called them, predicted fuccefs to the oppofite party, as you may judge by his own words.—" I re- " member I told the *Senefchal* in a letter, that in cafting the conftable of *Bourbon*'s nativity, I plainly " discovered that he would this year likewife gain the victory over your armies."—They who are acquainted with the hiftory of thefe times, muft fee plainly that Agrippa could not pay his court worfe to Francis I. than by promifing good fuccefs to the conftable. From that time Agrippa was looked upon as a *Bourbonift* : to filence this reproach he reprefented the fervice he had done to *France*, by diffuading 4000 foot foldiers from following the Emperor's party, and by engaging them in the fervice of *Francis I*. He alledged the refufal of the great advantages which were promifed him when he left *Fribourg*, if he would enter into the conftable's fervice. It appears by the 4th and 6th Letter of Book V. that he held a ftrict

himself difcarded, murmured, ftormed, threatened, and wrote; but, however, he was obliged to look out for another fettlement. He caft his eyes
on the *Netherlands*, and having after long waiting obtained the neceffary
paffes, he arrived at *Antwerp* in the month of *July*, 1528. One of the
caufes of thefe delays was the rough proceeding of the Duke of *Vendôme*,
who inftead of figning the pafs for *Agrippa* tore it up, faying, that "he
would not fign any paffport for a conjuror." In the year 1529 the King of
England fent *Agrippa* a kind invitation to come into his territories, and at the
fame time he was invited by the Emperor's chancellor, by an *Italian* marquifs,
and by *Margaret* of *Auftria*, governefs of the *Netherlands*. He accepted the
offers of the latter, and was made hiftoriographer to the Emperor, a poft
procured him by that princefs. He publifhed by way of prelude, *The Hiftory
of the Government of Charles V.* and foon after he was obliged to compofe
that princefs's funeral oration, whofe death was in fome manner the life of
our *Agrippa*; for fhe had been ftrangely prejudiced againft him: the fame
ill office was done him with his Imperial Majefty. His treatife of *the Vanity
of the Sciences*, which he caufed to be printed in 1530, terribly exafperated his
enemies. That which he publifhed foon after at *Antwerp*, viz. *of the Occult
Philofophy*, afforded them a ftill farther pretence to défame him. It was
fortunate for him that Cardinal *Campegius*, the Pope's legate, and Cardinal *De
la Mark*, Bifhop of *Liege*, were his advocates; but, however, their good offices could not procure him his penfion as hiftoriographer, nor prevent his
being imprifoned at *Bruffels*, in the year 1531, but he was foon releafed.
The following year he made a vifit to the Archbifhop of Cologne, to whom
he had dedicated his *Occult Philofophy*, and from whom he had received
a very obliging letter. The fear of his creditors, with whom he was much
embarraffed on account of his falary being ftopped, made him ftay longer
in the country of *Cologne* than he defired. He ftrenuoufly oppofed the
inquifitors, who had put a ftop to the printing of his *Occult Philofophy*,

a ftrict correfpondence with that prince in 1527. He advifed and counfelled, yet refufed to go and join
him, and promifed him victory. He affured him that the walls of Rome would fall down upon the firft
attack; yet he omitted informing him of one point, and that was, that the conftable would be killed
there.

when

when he was publiſhing a new edition of it corrected, and augmented
at Cologne.—See the xxvith, and the following Letters of the viith Book.
In ſpite of them the impreſſion was finiſhed, which is that of the year 1533.
He continued at *Bonn* till the year 1535, and was then deſirous of returning
to *Lyons*. He was impriſoned in *France* for ſomething he had ſaid againſt the
mother of Francis I. but was releaſed at the requeſt of certain perſons, and went
Grenoble, where he died the ſame year, 1535. Some ſay, that he died in the
hoſpital (but this is mere malice, for his enemies reported every thing that envy
could ſuggeſt to depreciate his worth and character). *He died at the houſe of the
Receiver General of the province of* Dauphiny, *whoſe ſon was* firſt preſident *of
Grenoble*. Mr. *Allard*, at p. 4, *of the Bibliotheque of Dauphiné*, ſays, that *Agrippa*
died at *Grenoble, in the houſe which belonged to the family of* Ferrand *in Clerk's
Street, and was then in the poſſeſſion of the preſident* Vachon *; and that he was
buried in the convent of the* Dominicans. He lived always in the *Roman* communion, therefore it ought not to have been ſaid that he was a Lutheran *.
Burnet in his hiſtory of the Reformation aſſerts, that *Agrippa* wrote in favour
of the divorce of King *Henry* VIII. But if we look into *Agrippa*'s letters we
ſhall find that he was againſt it, as well in them as likewiſe in his declamation on
the vanity of the ſciences, where he ſays—" I am informed there is a certain
" king, at this time o'day, who thinks it lawful for him to divorce a wife to
" whom he has been married theſe twenty years, and to eſpouſe an harlot."
In reſpect of the charge of magic diabolical being preferred againſt him by
Martin del Rio and others who confidently aſſerted, that *Agrippa* paid his way
at inns, &c. with pieces of horn, caſting an illuſion over the ſenſes, whereby thoſe who received them took them for real money ; together with the ſtory
of the boarder at *Louvain*, who, in *Agrippa*'s abſence, raiſed the devil in his ſtudy,
and thereby loſt his life ; and *Agrippa*'s coming home, and ſeeing the ſpirits
dancing at the top of the houſe, his commanding one of them into the dead
body, and ſending it to drop down at the market-place : all theſe ſtories, aſſerted

* *Agrippa, in his Apolog. cap.* 19. ſpeaks in lofty terms of *Luther*, and with ſuch contempt of the ad-
verſaries of that reformer, that it is plain from hence *Sixtus Sienenſis* affirmed that *Agrippa* was a Lutheran.

by

by *Martin del Rio*, are too ridiculous to be believed by men of fenfe or fcience, they being no way probable even if he had dealt in the Black Art.—As to magic, in the fenfe it is underftood by us, there is no doubt of his being a proficient in it, witnefs his three books of Occult Philofophy; to fay nothing here of the fourth, which we have good authority to fay was never wrote by *Agrippa*, as we fhall fhew prefently, where we fhall treat of the hiftory of his *Occult Philofophy*.—In a word, to fum up the character of Agrippa we muft do him the juftice to acknowledge, that notwithftanding his impetuous temper which occafioned him many broils, yet from the letters which he wrote to feveral of his moft intimate friends, without any apparent defign of printing them, he was a man ufed to religious reflexions, and the practice of Chriftianity; that he was well verfed in many of the chiefeft and moft fecret operations of nature, *viz*. the fciences of natural and celeftial magic; that he certainly performed ftrange things (in the vulgar eye) by the application of *actives* to *paffives*, as which of us cannot? that he was an expert *aftrologer, phyfician*, and *mathematician*, by which, as well as by magic, he foretold many uncommon things, and performed many admirable operations. *John Wierus*, who was his domeftic, has given feveral curious and interefting anecdotes, which throw great light upon the myfterious character of *Agrippa*, and ferve to free him from the fcandalous imputation of his being a profeffor of the BLACK ART. Now, becaufe *Agrippa* continued whole weeks in his ftudy, and yet was acquainted with almoft every tranfaction in feveral countries of the world, many filly people gave out, that a black dog which *Agrippa* kept was an evil fpirit, by whofe means he had all this information, and which communicated the *enemies' pofts, number, defigns, &c*. to his mafter; this is *Paul Jovius*'s account, by which you may fee on what fort of reports he founded his opinions of this great man. We wonder that *Gabriel Naudé* had not the precaution to object to the accufers of *Agrippa*, the great number of hiftorical falfehoods of which they (his accufers) ftand convicted. *Naudé* fuppofes that the monks and others of the ecclefiaftical order did not think of crying down the *Occult Philofophy* till a long time after it was publifhed; he affirms that they exclaimed againft that work, only in revenge for the injuries

they

they believed they had received in that of the *Vanity of the Sciences.* 'Tis true, this latter book gave great offence to many. The monks, the members of the universities, the preachers, and the divines, saw themselves drawn to the life in it. *Agrippa* was of too warm a complexion. *" The least taste of his book* (of the Vanity of the Sciences) *convinced me that he was an author of a fiery genius, extensive reading, and great memory; but sometimes more copious than choice in his subject, and writing in a disturbed, rather than in a composed, style."* He lashes vice, and commends virtue, every where, and in every person: but there are some with whom nothing but panegyric will go down. *See* ERASMI Epist. *lib.* xxvii. *p.* 1083.

Let us now, in a few words, and for the conclusion of this article, describe the history of the *Occult Philosophy. Agrippa* composed this work in his younger days; and shewed it to the Abbot *Trithemius,* whose pupil he had been. Trithemius was charmed with it, as appears by the letter which he wrote to him on the 8th of *April,* 1510; but he advises him to communicate it only to those whom he could confide in. However, several manuscript copies of it were dispersed almost all over *Europe.* It is not necessary to observe that most of them were faulty, which never fails to happen in the like cases. They were preparing to print it from one of these bad copies; which made the author resolve to publish it himself, with the additions and alterations with which he had embellished it, after having shewed it to the Abbot *Trithemius. Melchior Adam* was mistaken in asserting that *Agrippa,* in his more advanced years, having corrected and enlarged this work, shewed it to the Abbot *Trithemius.* He had refuted his *Occult Philosophy* in his *Vanity of the Sciences,* and yet he published it to prevent others from printing a faulty and mutilated edition. He obtained the approbation of the doctors of divinity, and some other persons, whom the Emperor's council appointed to examine it.

" This book has been lately examined and approved by certain prelates of the
" church, and doctors, thoroughly versed both in sacred and profane literature;
" and by commissaries particularly deputed for that purpose by CÆSAR's *council;*
" after which, it was admitted by the whole council, and licensed by the authentic

A a   *diploma*

" *diploma of his Imperial Majesty, and the stamp of the* CÆSAREAN *Eagle in*
" *red wax; and was afterwards publicly printed and sold at* ANTWERP, *and*
" *then at* PARIS, *without any opposition*."

After the death of *Agrippa* a *Fourth Book* was added to it by another hand.
Jo. Wierus de Magis, cap. 5. p. 108, says, " *To these* (books of Magic)
" *may very justly be added, a work lately published, and ascribed to my late*
" *honoured host and preceptor,* HENRY CORNELIUS AGRIPPA, *who has been*
" *dead more than forty years; whence I conclude it is unjustly inscribed to his*
" *manes, under the title of* THE FOURTH BOOK OF THE OCCULT PHILOSOPHY,
" OR OF MAGICAL CEREMONIES, *which pretends likewise to be a Key to the*
" *three former books of the* OCCULT PHILOSOPHY, *and all kinds of Magical*
" *Operations*." Thus John Wierus expresses himself. There is an edition
in folio of the *Occult Philosophy,* in 1533, without the place where it was
printed. The privilege of *Charles* V. is prefixed to it, dated from *Mechlin,*
the 12th of *January,* 1529. We have already mentioned the chief works of
Agrippa. It will be sufficient to add, that he wrote *A Commentary on the Art
of Raimundus Lullius,* and *A Dissertation on the Original of Sin,* wherein he
teaches that the fall of our first parents proceeded from their unchaste love.
He promised a work against the *Dominicans,* which would have pleased many
persons both within and without the pale of the church of *Rome*.* He held
some uncommon opinions, and never any Protestant spoke more forcibly against
the impudence of the Legendaries, than he did. We must not forget the Key
of his *Occult Philosophy,* which he kept only for his friends of the first rank,
and explained it in a manner, which differs but little from the speculations of
our Quietists. Now many suppose that the 4th book of the *Occult Philosophy*
is the Key which Agrippa mentions in his letters to have reserved to himself;
but it may be answered, with great shew of probability, that he amused the

* " In the treatise I am composing of the vices and erroneous opinions of the *Dominicans,* in which
" I shall expose to the whole world their vicious practices, such as the sacrament often infected with
" poison—numberless pretended miracles—kings and princes taken off with poison—cities and states
" betrayed—the populace seduced—heresies avowed—and the rest of the deeds of these heroes and their
" enormous crimes." See AGRIPPA *Opera,* T. ii. p. 1037.

world

world with this Key to cause himself to be courted by the curious. *James Gohory* and *Vigenere* say, that he pretended to be master of the Practice of the Mirror of *Pythagoras*, and the secret of extracting the spirit of gold from its body, in order to convert silver and copper into fine gold. But he explains what he means by this Key, where he says, in the Epist. 19. lib. v. " *This is that true and occult philosophy of the wonders of nature. The key thereof is the understanding: for the higher we carry our knowledge, the more sublime are our attainments in virtue, and we perform the greatest things with more ease and effect.*" Agrippa makes mention of this Key in two letters which he wrote to a religious who addicted himself to the study of the *Occult Sciences, viz. Aurelius de Aquapendente Austin,* friar, where he says, " *What surprising accounts we meet with, and how great writings there are made of the invincible power of the* Magic Art, *of the prodigious images of* Astrologers, *of the amazing transmutations of* Alchymists, *and of that blessed stone by which,* MIDAS-*like, all metals are transmuted into gold: all which are found to be vain, fictitious, and false, as often as they are practised literally.*" Yet he says, " Such things are delivered and writ by great and grave philosophers, whose traditions who dare say are false? Nay, it were impious to think them lies : only there is another meaning than what is writ with the bare letters. We must not, *be adds,* look for the principle of these grand operations without ourselves: it is an internal spirit within us, which can very well perform whatsoever the monstrous *Mathematicians,* the prodigious *Magicians,* the wonderful *Alchymists,* and the bewitching *Necromancers,* can effect."

> Nos habitat, non tartara ; sed nec sidera cœli,
> Spiritus in nobis qui viget, illa facit.
>
> *See* AGRIPPA *Epist. dat. Lyons, Sept.* 24, 1727.

Note. Agrippa's three books of Magic, with the fourth, were translated into English, and published in London in the year 1651. But they are now become so scarce, as very rarely to be met with, and are sold at a very high price by the booksellers.

A a 2   ALBERTUS

ALBERTUS MAGNUS.

ALBERTUS MAGNUS, a *Dominican*, bifhop of *Ratifbon*, and one of the
moft famous doctors of the XIII century, was born at *Lawingen*, on the
Danube, in *Suabia*, in the year 1193, or 1205. *Moreri*'s dictionary gives us
an account of the feveral employs which were conferred upon him, and the
fuccefs of his lectures in feveral towns.   It is likewife faid, that he practifed
midwifery, and that he was in fearch of the *Philofopher's Stone* ; that he was
a famous *Magician*, and that he had formed a machine in the fhape of a man,
which ferved him for an oracle, and explained all the difficulties which he
propofed to it.   I can eafily be induced to believe that, as he underftood the
mathematics, &c. he made a head, which, by the help of fome fpirits, might
form certain articulate founds.   Though he was well qualified to be the inventor of artillery, there is reafon to believe, that they who afcribed the invention of it to him are miftaken.   It is faid that he had naturally a very dull
wit, and that he was upon the point of leaving the cloifter, becaufe he defpaired
of attaining what his friar's habit required of him, but that the Holy Virgin
appeared to him, and afked him in which he would chufe to excel, in philofophy or divinity ; that he made choice of philofophy, and that the Holy
Virgin told him he fhould furpafs all men of his time in that fcience, but that,
as a punifhment for not chufing divinity, he fhould, before his death, relapfe
into his former ftupidity.   They add, that, after this apparition, he fhewed a
prodigious deal of fenfe, and fo improved in all the fciences, that he quickly
furpaffed his preceptors ; but that, three years before his death, he forgot in
an inftant all that he knew: and that, being at a ftand in the middle of a
lecture on divinity at *Cologne*, and endeavouring in vain to recal his ideas, he
                                                                          was

was fenfible that it was the accomplifhment of the prediction. Whence arofe the faying, that he was miraculoufly converted from an afs into a philofopher, and, afterwards, from a philofopher into an afs. Our Albertus was a very little man *, and, after living eighty-feven years, died in the year of our redemption, 1280, at *Cologne*, on the 15th of November; his body was laid in the middle quire of the convent of the *Dominicans*, and his entrails were carried to *Ratifbon*; his body was yet entire in the time of the *Emperor Charles V.* and was taken up by his command, and afterwards replaced in its firft monument. He wrote fuch à vaft number of books, that they amount to twenty-ne volumes in folio, in the edition of *Lyons*, 1651.

ROGER BACON,
COMMONLY CALLED

FRIAR BACON.

ROGER BACON, an Englifhman, and a *Francifcan* friar, lived in the XIII century. He was a great *Aftrologer*, *Chymift*, *Mathematician*, and *Magician*. There runs a tradition in Englifh annals, that this friar made a brazen head, under the rifing of the planet Saturn, which fpake with a man's voice, and gave refponfes to all his queftions. *Francis Picus* fays, " that he read " in a book wrote by Bacon, that a man might foretel things to come by means " of the mirror *Almuchefi*, compofed according to the rules of perfpective; pro-" vided he made ufe of it under a good conftellation, and firft brought his body " into an even and temperate ftate by chymiftry." This is agreeable to what *John Picus* has maintained, that *Bacon* gave himfelf only to the ftudy of *Natural Magic*. This friar fent feveral inftruments of his own invention to pope Clement IV. Several of his books have been publifhed (but they are now very

* When he came before the Pope, after ftanding fome time in his prefence, his Holinefs defired him to rife, thinking he had been kneeling.

fcarce,)

scarce,) *viz. Specula Mathematica & Perspectiva, Speculum Alchymiæ, De Mira-bili Potestate Artis & Naturæ, Epistolæ, cum Notis, &c.* In all probability he did not perform any thing by any compact with devils, but has only ascribed to things a surprising efficacy which they could not naturally have. He was well versed in judicial astrology. His Speculum Astrologiæ was condemned by *Gerson* and *Agrippa. Francis Picus* and many others have condemned it only because the author maintains in it, *that, with submission to better judgments, books of magic ought to be carefully preserved, because the time draws near that, for certain causes not there specified, they must necessarily be perused and made use of on some occasions.* *Naude* adds, " that *Bacon* was so much addicted to judicial astrology, that *Henry de Hassia, William* of *Paris,* and *Nicholas Oresmius,* were obliged to inveigh sharply against his writings." *Bacon* was fellow of *Brazen-nose* college in *Oxford* in the year 1226. He was beyond all compeer the glory of the age he lived in, and may perhaps stand in competition with the greatest that have appeared since. It is wonderful, considering the age wherein he lived, how he came by such a depth of knowledge on all subjects. His treatises are composed with that elegancy, concisenefs, and strength, and abound with such just and exquisite observations on nature, that, among the whole line of chymists, we do not know one that can pretend to contend with him. The reputation of his uncommon learning still survives in *England.* His cell is shewn at *Oxford* to this day; and there is a tradition, that it will fall whenever a greater man than *Bacon* shall enter within it. He wrote many treatises; amongst which, such as are yet extant have beauties enough to make us sensible of the great loss of the rest. What relates to chymistry are two small pieces, wrote at *Oxford,* which are now in print, and the manu-scripts to be seen in the public library at *Leiden*; having been carried thither among *Vossius's* manuscripts from *England.* In these treatises he clearly shews how imperfect metals may be ripened into perfect ones. He entirely adopts *Geber's* notion, that mercury is the common basis of all metals, and sulphur the cement; and shews that it is by a gradual depuration of the mercurial matter by sublimation, and the accession of a subtle sulphur by fire, that nature makes her gold; and that, if during the process, any other third matter happen to

intervene,

intervene, befides the mercury and fulphur, fome bafe metal arifes: fo that, if we by imitating her operations ripen lead, we might eafily change it into good gold.

Several of *Bacon*'s operations have been compared with the experiments of Monfieur *Homberg*, made by that curious prince the duke of *Orleans*; by which it has been found that *Bacon* has defcribed fome of the very things which *Homberg* publifhed as his own difcoveries. For inftance, *Bacon* teaches exprefsly, that if a pure fulphur be united with mercury, it will commence gold: on which very principle, Monfieur *Homberg* has made various experiments for the production of gold, defcribed in the *Memoires de l' Academ. Royale des Sciences*. His other phyfical writings fhew no lefs genius and force of mind. In a treatife* *Of the fecret Works of Nature*, he fhews that a perfon who was perfectly acquainted with the manner nature obferves in her operations, would not only be able to rival, but to furpafs nature herfelf.

This author's works are printed in 8vo and 12mo, under the title of *Frater Rogerius Baco de Secretis Artis & Naturæ*, but they are become very rare. From a repeated perufal of them we may perceive that *Bacon* was no ftranger to many of the capital difcoveries of the prefent and paft ages. Gunpowder he certainly knew; thunder and lightning, he tells us, may be produced by art; and that fulphur, nitre, and charcoal, which when feparate have no fenfible effect, when mingled together in a due proportion, and clofely confined, yield a horrible crack. A more precife defcription of gunpowder cannot be given with words: and yet a Jefuit, *Barthol. Schwartz*, fome ages afterwards, has had the honour of the difcovery. He likewife mentions a fort of inextinguifh-able fire, prepared by art, which indicates he knew fomething of phofphorus. And that he had a notion of the rarefaction of the air, and the ftructure of the air-pump, is paft contradiction. A chariot, he obferves, might be framed on the principles of mechanics, which, being fuftained on very large globes, fpeci-fically lighter than common air, would carry a man aloft through the atmofphere; this proves that he likewife had a competent idea of aeroftation.

* De Secretis Naturæ Operibus.

There

There are many curious speculations in this noble author, which will raise the admiration of the reader: but none of them will affect him with so much wonder, as to see a person of the most sublime merit fall a sacrifice to the wanton zeal of infatuated bigots. See BOERHAAVE's *Chym. p.* 18.

RAYMOND LULLY,

A FAMOUS ALCHYMIST.

RAYMOND LULLY, or *Raymon Lull*, comes the next in order. He was born in the island of *Majorca*, in the year 1225, of a family of the first distinction, though he did not assume his chymical character till towards the latter part of his life.

Upon his applying himself to chymistry, he soon began to preach another sort of doctrine; insomuch that, speaking of that art, he says it is only to be acquired by dint of experiment and practice, and cannot be conveyed to the understanding by idle words and sounds. He is the first author I can find, who considers alchymy expressly with a view to the universal medicine: but after him it became a popular pursuit, and the libraries were full of writings in that vein.

Lully, himself, beside what he wrote in the scholastic way, has a good many volumes wrote after his conversion: 'tis difficult to say how many; for it was a common practice with his disciples and followers to usher in their perform-ances under their master's name. " I have perused (*says Boerhaave*) the best
" part of his works, and find them, beyond expectation, excellent: insomuch,
" that I have been almost tempted to doubt whether they could be the work
" of that age, so full are they of the experiments and observations which
" occur in our later writers, that either the books must be supposititious, or else
                                                                    " the

" the ancient chymifts muft have been acquainted with a world of things which
" pafs for the difcoveries of modern practice.   He gives very plain intimations
" of phofphorus, which he calls the *Veftal Fire*, the *Offa Helmontii*, &c. and
" yet it is certain he wrote 200 years before either *Helmont*, or my Lord
" *Bacon*."

He travelled into *Mauritania*, where he is fuppofed to have firft met with
chymiftry, and to have imbibed the principles of his art from the writings of
Geber: which opinion is countenanced by the conformity obfervable between
the two.   The *Spanifh* authors afcribe the occafion of his journey to an amour:
he had fallen in love, it feems, with a maiden of that country, who obftinately
refufed his addreffes.   Upon enquiring into the reafon, fhe fhewed him a can-
cered breaft.   *Lully*, like a generous gallant, immediately refolved on a voyage
to *Mauritania*, where *Geber* had lived, to feek fome relief for his miftrefs.   He
ended his days in *Africa*; where, after having taken up the quality of miffion-
ary, and preaching the gofpel among the infidels, he was ftoned to death *.

* The hiftory of this eminent adept is very confufed. *Mutius*, an author, is exprefs, that that good man,
being wholly intent upon religion, never applied himfelf either to chymiftry or the philofopher's-ftone :
and yet we have various accounts of his making gold.   Among a variety of authors, *Gregory of Thouloufe*
afferts that " *Lully offered* EDWARD III. *king of England, a fupply of fix millions to make war againft the
Infidels.*"   Befides manufcripts, the following printed pieces bear *Lully's* name, *viz.   The Theory of the
Philofopher's Stone: The Practife: The Tranfmutation of Metals: The Codicil: The Vade-Mecum: The
Book of Experiments: The Explanation of his Teftament: The Abridgements, or Accufations: and The Power
of Riches*.

GEORGE RIPLEY.

———

GEORGE RIPLEY, an *Englishman* by nation, and by profession a canon or monk of *Britlingthon*. His writings were all very good in their kind, being wrote exactly in the style of *Bacon*, only more allegorical. As he was no phyfician, he does not meddle with any thing of the preparations of that kind; but treats much of the cure of metals, which in his language is the purification and maturation thereof. He rigorously pursued *Geber's* and *Bacon's* principles, and maintained, for inftance, with new evidence, that mercury is the universal matter of all metals; that this set over the fire, with the pureft fulphur, will become gold, but that if either of them be fick or leprous, *i. e.* infected with any impurity, inftead of gold, fome other metal will be produced. He adds, that as mercury and fulphur are fufficient for the making of all metals: fo of thefe may an univerfal medicine, or metal, be produced for curing of all the fick; which fome miftakenly underftood of an univerfal metal, efficacious in all the difeafes of the human body.

———

JOHN, and ISAAC HOLLANDUS.

———

THEY were two brothers, both of them of great parts and ingenuity, and wrote on the dry topics of chymiftry. They lived in the 13th century, but this is not affured. The whole art of *enamelling* is their invention, as is alfo, that of *colouring glafs*, and precious ftones, by application of thin metal plates.

plates. Their writings are in the form of procefses, and they defcribe all their operations to the moft minute circumftances. The treatife of *enamelling* is efteemed the greateft and moft finifhed part of their works: whatever relates to the fufion, feparation, and preparation of metals, is here delivered. They write excellently of *diftillation, fermentation, putrefaction,* and their effects; and feem to have underftood, at leaft, as much of thefe matters as any of the moderns have done. They furnifh a great many experiments on human blood; which *Van Helmont* and Mr. *Boyle* have fince taken for new difcoveries. I have a very large work in folio, under their name, of the conftruction of chymical furnaces and inftruments. Their writings are as eafily purchafed, as they are worthy of perufal, on account of valuable fecrets in them, which may pave the way for greater difcoveries. See BOERHAAVE, p. 21.

PHILIPPUS

PHILIPPUS AUREOLUS THEOPHRASTUS PARACELSUS BOMBAST DE HOENHEYM,

THE PRINCE OF PHYSICIANS AND PHILOSOPHERS BY FIRE;
GRAND PARADOXICAL PHYSICIAN;
THE TRISMEGISTUS OF SWITZERLAND;
FIRST REFORMER OF CHYMICAL PHILOSOPHY;
ADEPT IN ALCHYMY, CABALA, AND MAGIC;
NATURE'S FAITHFUL SECRETARY;
MASTER OF THE ELIXIR OF LIFE AND THE PHILOSOPHER'S STONE;

AND THE

GREAT MONARCH OF CHYMICAL SECRETS;

Now living in his Tomb, whither he retired difgufted with the Vices and Follies of Mankind, fupporting
himfelf with his own

QUINTESSENTIA VITÆ.

PARACELSUS was born, as he himfelf writes, in the year 1494, in a village in *Switzerland* called Hoenheym (q. d. *ab alto nido*) two miles diftant
from *Zurich*. His father was a natural fon of a great mafter of the *Teutonic*
order, and had been brought up to medicine, which he practifed accordingly in
that obfcure corner. He was mafter of an excellent and copious library, and
is faid to have become eminent in his art; fo that *Paracelfus* always fpeaks of
him with the higheft deference, and calls him *laudatiſſimus medicus in eo vico.*
Of fuch a father did *Paracelfus* receive his firft difcipline. After a little
courfe of ftudy at home he was committed to the care of *Trithemius*, the celebrated abbot of *Spanheim*, who had the character of an adept himfelf, and
wrote of the *Cabala*, being at that time a reputed *magician*. Here he chiefly
learnt languages and letters; after which he was removed to *Sigifmund
Fugger* to learn medicine, furgery, and chymiftry; all thefe mafters, efpecially
                                                                        the

the laft, *Paracelfus*, ever fpeaks of with great veneration; fo that he was not altogether fo rude and unpolifhed as is generally imagined. Thus much we learn from his own writings, and efpecially the preface to his *Leffer Surgery*, where he defends himfelf againft his accufers. At twenty years of age he undertook a journey through *Germany* and *Hungary*, vifiting all the mines of principal note, and contracting an acquaintance with the miners and workmen, by which means he learnt every thing relative to metals, and the art thereof: in this enquiry he fhewed an uncommon affiduity and refolution. He gives us an account of the many dangers he had run from earthquakes, falls of ftones, floods of water, cataracts, exhalations, damps, heat, hunger, and thirft; and every where takes occafion to infift on the value of an art acquired on fuch hard terms. The fame inclination carried him as far as *Mufcovy*, where as he was in queft of mines near the frontiers of *Tartary* he was taken prifoner by that people, and carried before the great *Cham*; during his captivity there he learnt various fecrets, till, upon the Cham's fending an embaffy to the Grand Signior, with his own fon at the head of it, *Paracelfus* was fent along with him in quality of companion. On this occafion he came to *Conftantinople* in the twenty-eighth year of his age, and was there taught the fecret of the *philofopher's ftone* by a generous *Arabian*, who made him this noble prefent, as he calls it, *Azoth*. This incident we have from *Helmont* only; for *Paracelfus* himfelf, who is ample enough on his other travels, fays nothing of his captivity. At his return from *Turkey* he practifed as a furgeon in the Imperial army, and performed many excellent cures therein; indeed, it cannot be denied but that he was excellent in that art, of which his *great furgery*, printed in folio, will ever be a ftanding monument. At his return to his native country he affumed the title of *utriufque medicinæ doctor*, or doctor both of external and internal medicine or furgery; and grew famous in both, performing far beyond what the practice of that time could pretend to; and no wonder, for medicine was then in a poor condition; the practice and the very language was all *Galenical* and *Arabic*; nothing was inculcated but *Ariftotle*, *Galen*, and the *Arabs*; Hippocrates was not read; nay, there was no edition of his writings, and fcarce was he ever mentioned. Their theory

consisted

confifted in the knowledge of the four degrees, the temperaments, &c. and their whole practice was confined to venefection, purgation, vomiting, clyf-mata, &c. Now, in this age a new difeafe had broke out, and fpread itfelf over Europe, viz. the venereal diforder; the common Galenic medicines had here proved altogether ineffectual; bleeding, purging, and cleanfing medicines were vain; and the phyficians were at their wit's end. Jac Carpus, a cele-brated anatomift and furgeon at Bologne, had alone been mafter of the cure, which was by mercury adminiftered to raife a falivation; he had attained this fecret in his travels through Spain and Italy, and practifed it for fome years, and with fuch fuccefs and applaufe, that it is incredible what immenfe riches this one noftrum brought him (it is faid upon good authority, that in one year he cleared fix thoufand piftoles) he acknowledged himfelf, that he did not know the end of his own wealth; for the captains, merchants, governors, commanders, &c. who had brought that filthy difeafe from America, were very well content to give him what fums he pleafed to afk to free them from it.—Paracelfus about this time having likewife learnt the properties of mercury, and moft likely from Carpus, who undertook the fame cure but in a very different manner; for whereas Carpus did all by falivation—Paracelfus making up his preparation in pills attained his ends in a gentler manner. By this he informs us he cured the itch, leprofy, ulcers, Naples difeafe, and even gout, all which diforders wore incurable on the foot of popular practice, and thus was the great bafis laid for all his future fame and fortune.

Paracelfus, thus furnifhed with arts, and arrived at a degree of eminence beyond any of his brothers in the profeffion, was invited by the curators of the univerfity of Bazil to the chair of profeffor of medicine and philofophy in that univerfity. The art of printing was now a new thing, the tafte for learning and arts was warm *, and the magiftracy of Bazil were very induf-

* We feel ourfelves happy in being able to fay, that the tafte for learning and arts (notwithftanding the follies of the age) was never more prevalent than in the prefent time; the year 1801 commences an age of flourifhing fcience, in which even our females feem to wifh to bear a part—inftance, a lady of quality, who went in her carriage the other day to Fofter-lane, Cheapfide, and bought a portable blackfmith's forge for her private amufement; her perfon was ftrong and athletic, and very fit for the manual practice of handling iron, and working other metallic experiments.

trious

trious in procuring profeffors of reputation from all parts of the world. They had already got *Defid. Erafmus*, profeffor of *theology*, and *J. Oporinus* profeffor of the Greek tongue; and now in 1527 *Paracelfus* was affociated in the 33d year of his age. Upon his firft entrance into that province, having to make a public fpeech before the univerfity, he pofted up a very elegant advertife-ment over the doors inviting every body to his doctrine. At his firft lecture he ordered a brafs veffel to be brought into the middle of the fchool, where after he had caft in fulphur and nitre, in a very folemn manner he burnt the books of *Galen* and *Avicenna*, alledging that he had held a difpute with them in the gates of hell, and had fairly routed and overcome them. And hence he proclaimed, that the phyficians fhould all follow him; and no longer ftyle themfelves *Galenifts*; but *Paracelfifts*.—" Know," fays he, " phyficians, my cap has more learning in it than all your heads, my beard has more experience than your whole academies: Greeks, Latins, French, Germans, Italians, I will be your king."

While he was here profeffor he read his book *De Tartaro, de Gradibus*, and *De Compofitionibus*, in public lectures, to which he added a *commentary* on the book *De Gradibus*; all thefe he afterwards printed at *Bazil* for the ufe of his difciples; fo that thefe muft be allowed for genuine writings; about the fame time he wrote *De Calculo*, which performance *Helmont* fpeaks of with high approbation.

Notwithftanding his being profeffor in fo learned an univerfity, he un-derftood but a very little *Latin*; his long travels, and application to bufinefs, and difufe of the language, had very much difqualified him for writing or fpeaking therein; and his natural warmth rendered him very un-fit for teaching at all. Hence, though his auditors and difciples were at firft very numerous, yet they very much fell off, and left him preaching to the walls. —In the mean time he abandoned himfelf to drinking at certain feafons; *Oporinus*, who was always near him, has the good nature to fay, he was never fober; but that he tippled on from morning to night, and from night to morn-ing, in a continual round. At length he foon became weary of his profeffor-fhip, and after three years continuance therein relinquifhed it, faying, that

no

no language befides the *German* was proper to reveal the fecrets of chymiftry in.

After this he again betook himfelf to an itinerant life, travelling and drinking, and living altogether at inns and taverns, continually flufhed with liquor, and yet working many admirable cures in his way. In this manner he paffed four years from the 43d to the 47th year of his life, when he died at an inn at *Saltzburg*, at the fign of the White Horfe, on a bench in the chimney-corner. *Oporinus* relates, that after he had put on any new thing, it never came off his back till he had worn it into rags ; he adds, that notwithftanding his excefs in point of drinking, he was never addicted to venery.—But there is this reafon for it : when he was a child, being neglected by his nurfe, a *hag* gelded him in a place where three ways met, and fo made a eunuch of him ; accordingly in his writings he omits no opportunity of railing againft women.—Such is the life of Paracelfus ; fuch is the immortal man, who fick of life retired into a corner of the world, and there fupports himfelf with his own *Quinteffence of Life*.

In his life time he only publifhed three or four books, but after his death he grew prodigioufly voluminous, fcarce a year paffing but one book or other was publifhed under his name, faid to be found in fome old wall, ceiling, or the like. All the works publifhed under his name were printed together at *Strafburg* in the year 1603, in three volumes *folio*, and again in 1616. *J. Oporinus*, that excellent profeffor and printer, before named, who conftantly attended *Paracelfus* for three years as his menial fervant, in hopes of learning fome of his fecrets, who publifhed the works of *Vefalius*, and is fuppofed to have put them in that elegant language wherein they now appear : this *Oporinus*, in an epiftle to *Monavius* concerning the life of *Paracelfus*, profeffes himfelf furprized to find fo many works of his mafter ; for, that in all the time he was with him he never wrote a word himfelf, nor ever took pen in hand, but forced *Oporinus* to write what he dictated ; and *Oporinus* wondered much, how fuch coherent words and difcourfe which might even become the wifeft perfons, fhould come from the mouth of a drunken man. His work

called

called *Archidoxa Medicinæ*, as containing the principles and maxims of the art, nine books of which were published at first ; and the author in the prolegomena to them, speaks thus :—" *I intended to have published my ten books of*
" Archidoxa ; *but finding mankind unworthy of such a treasure as the tenth,*
" *I keep it close in my* occiput, *and have firmly resolved never to bring it thence,*
" *till you have all abjured* ARISTOTLE, AVICEN, *and* GALEN, *and have sworn*
" *allegiance to* PARACELSUS *alone.*"

However, the book did at length get abroad, though by what means is not known ; it is undoubtedly an excellent piece, and may be ranked among the principal productions in the way of chymistry, that have ever appeared ; whether or no it be *Paracelsus's* we cannot affirm, but there is one thing speaks in its behalf, *viz.* it contains a great many things which have since been trumped up for great *nostrums* ; and *Van Helmont's* Lithonthriptic and Alcahest are apparently taken from hence ; among the genuine writings of *Paracelsus* are likewise reckoned, that *De Ortu Rerum Naturalium, De Transformatione Rerum Naturalium,* and *De Vita Rerum Naturalium.* The rest are spurious or very doubtful, particularly his theological works.

The great fame and success of this man, which many attribute to his possessing an *universal medicine* may be accounted for from other principles. It is certain he was well acquainted with the use and virtue of *opium*, which the *Galenists* of those times all rejected as cold in the fourth degree. *Oporinus* relates, that he made up certain little pills of the colour, figure, and size of mouse-turds, which were nothing but *opium.* These he called by a barbarous sort of name, his *laudanum* ; *q. d.* laudable medicine ; he always carried them with him, and prescribed them in dysenteries, and all cases attended with intense pains, anxieties, deliriums, and obstinate wakings ; but to be alone possessed of the use of so extraordinary and noble a medicament as *opium*, was sufficient to make him famous.

Another grand remedy with Paracelsus was *turbith mineral*; this is first mentioned in his *Clein Spital Boeck,* or *Chirurgia Minor*, where he gives the preparation.—In respect of the philosopher's stone *Oporinus* says, he often wondered to see him one day without a farthing in his pocket, and the next

C c

day

day, full of money; that he took nothing with him when he went abroad. He adds, that he would often borrow money of his companions, the carmen and porters, and pay it again in twenty-four hours with extravagant interest, and yet from what fund nobody but himself knew. In the *Theatrum Alchemiæ* he mentions a treasure, hid under a certain tree; and from such like grounds they supposed him to possess the art of making gold; but it was hard if such noble nostrums as he possessed would not subsist him without the *lapis philosophorum*.

JOHN RUDOLPH GLAUBER.

J. R. GLAUBER, a celebrated chymist of *Amsterdam*, accounted the *Paracelsus* of his time: he had travelled much and by that means attained to a great many secrets. He wrote above thirty tracts, in some of which he acted the physician; in others, the adept; and in others, the metallist. He principally excelled in the last capacity, and alchymy.

He was a person of easy and genteel address, and, beyond dispute, well versed in chymistry: being author of the salt, still used in the shops, called *Sal Glauberi*; as also of all the salts, by oil of vitriol, &c. He is noted for extolling his arcanæ and preparations, and is reported to have traded unfairly with his secrets: the best of them he would sell, at excessive rates, to chymists and others, and would afterwards re-sell them, or make them public, to increase his fame; whence he was continually at variance with them.

The principal of his writings are *De Furnis*, and *De Metallis*, which, though wrote in *Dutch*, have been translated into *Latin* and *English*. It was *Glauber* who shewed, before the States of *Holland*, that there is gold contained in sand; and made an experiment thereof to their entire satisfaction: but so

much

much lead, fire, and labour, being employed in procuring it, that the art would not pay charges *. However he plainly demonstrated, that there is no earth, sand, sulphur, or salt, or other matter, but what contains gold in a greater or less quantity. In short, he possessed a great many secrets, which are at this time in the hands of some of our modern chymists.

DOCTOR DEE, AND SIR EDWARD KELLY.

DOCTOR JOHN DEE, and SIR EDWARD KELLY, knight, being professed associates, their story is best delivered together. They have some title to the philosopher's stone in common fame. *Dee*, besides his being deep in chymistry, was very well versed in mathematics, particularly geometry and astrology: but Sir *Edward Kelly* appears to have been the leading man in alchymy. In some of *Dee*'s books are found short memoirs of the events of his operations: as, *Donum Dei*, five ounces. And in another place, " *This day* " Edward Kelly *discovered the grand secret to me, fit nomen Domini benedictum.*" *Ashmole* says, absolutely, they were masters of the powder of projection, and, with a piece not bigger than the smallest grain of sand, turned an ounce and a quarter of mercury into pure gold: but here is an equivoque; for granting them possessed of the powder of projection, it does not appear they had the secret of making it. The story is, that they found a considerable quantity of it in the ruins of *Glastonbury Abbey*, with which they performed many notable transmutations for the satisfaction of several persons. *Kelly*, in particular, is said to have given away rings of gold wire to the tune of 4000l. at the

* It has been asserted by several eminent chymists, that it might be performed to advantage, as the process is very simple, and takes up but little time : all that is requisite is silver, sand, and litharge.

C c 2   marriage

marriage of his servant maid. And a piece of a brass warming-pan being cut out by order of queen *Elizabeth*, and sent to them when abroad, was returned pure gold. Likewise *Dee* made a present to the landgrave of *Hesse* of twelve *Hungarian* horses, which could never be expected from a man of his circumstances without some extraordinary means.

In the year 1591 they went into *Germany*, and settled some time at *Trebona*, in *Bohemia*; the design of which journey is very mysterious. Some say their design was to visit the alchymists of these countries, in order to get some light into the art of making the powder. Accordingly they travelled through *Poland*, &c. in quest thereof, and, some say, attained it; others say, not. Others, again, will make them sent by the queen as spies, and that alchymy was only a pretence, or means, to bring them into confidence with the people. But what will give most light upon this subject, is a book, now extant, wrote by *Dee*, entitled *Dee's Conferences with Spirits*, but some conjecture it to be with *Trithemius*'s mere Cryptography; which light Doctor *Hook* takes it in. However, this book is truly curious in respect of the many magical operations there displayed, it being wrote journal-fashion by the Doctor's own hand, and relates circumstantially the conferences he held with some spirits (either good or bad) in company with Sir *Edward Kelly*.

They were no sooner gone out of *England*, than *Dee*'s library was opened by the queen's order, and 4000 books, and 700 choice manuscripts, were taken away on pretence of his being a conjuror. That princess soon after used means to bring him back again, which a quarrel with *Kelly* happening to promote, he returned in 1596, and in 1598 was made warden of *Manchester* college, where he died *.

Some very curious manuscripts, with the chrystal he used to invoke the spirits into, are at this time carefully laid up in the *British Museum* †.

---

* Authors differ very much in respect of the place where Doctor *Dee* resigned his life: it appears from the most eminent historians that he died at his house at *Mortlake*.

† Although *Dee*'s manuscripts, and his Magic Chrystal, are to be seen at the Museum, there are six or seven individuals in *London* who assert they have the stone in their possession; thereby wishing to deceive the credulous, and to tempt them to a purchase at an enormous price.

As

As for Sir *Edward Kelly*, the Emperor, fufpecting he had the fecret of the philofophers in his poffeffion, clapped him up in prifon, in hopes to become a fharer in the profits of tranfmutation: however, *Kelly* defeated his intentions. After having been twice imprifoned, the laft time he was fhut up endeavouring to make his efcape by means of the fheets of his bed tied together, they happened to flip the knots, and fo let him fall, by which he broke his leg, and foon after loft his life.

THE CONCLUSION.

HAVING collected the moft interefting and curious accounts of the lives of thofe great men, fo famous for their fpeculations in philofophic learning, we draw to a conclufion; having only to add, that we have fufficiently difcovered in this biographical fketch whatfoever was neceffary to prove the authenticity of *Our Art*, which we have delivered faithfully and impartially, noting, at the fame time, the various opinions of different men at different ages; likewife, we have taken fufficient trouble to explain what is meant by the word *Magic*, and to clear up the term from the imputation of any diabolical affociation with evil fpirits, &c. Alfo, how nearly it is allied to our religious duties, we refer the reader to the annotations under the article *Zoroafter*, where we have fpoke of the *Magi*, or wife men, proving the firft who adored Chrift were actually magicians. It is enough that we have fpoke of the principal characters renowned in paft ages for their laborious inquifition into the labyrinth of occult and natural philofophy; there are many other philofophers ftanding upon ancient and modern record. A copious and general biography falls not within the limits of our work. We have introduced fome characters (applicable to the fubject before us) moft diftinguifhed for occult learning; of which kind of fcience, whether by a particular influence of planetary configuration, which may have directed and impelled my mind and intellects to the obfervation and ftudy of nature, and her fimple operations, as well as to the more occult, I leave to the judgment of the aftrologers, to whofe infpection I fubmit a figure
of

of my nativity, which I fhall annex to a fketch of my own hiftory, which I
mean to make the fubject of a future publication, including a vaft number of
curious experiments in occult and chymical operations, which have fell either
under my own obfervation, or have been tranfmitted to me from others. In
refpect of the aftrologic art, (as we have already obferved) it has fuch an
affinity with talifmanic experiments, &c. that no one can bring any work to a
complete effect without a due knowledge and obfervation of the qualities and
effects of the conftellations (which occafioned us to give it the title of the Con-
ftellatory Art;) likewife, a man muft be well acquainted with the nature,
qualities, and effects, of the four elements, and of the animal, vegetable,
and mineral kingdoms; which knowledge cannot better be obtained than by
chymical experience, for it does, as I may fay, unlock the fecret chambers of
nature, and introduces the ftudent into a world of knowledge, which could not
be attained but by chymical analyzation, whereby we decompound mixt
bodies, and reduce them to their fimple natures, and come to a thorough
acquaintance with thofe powerful and active principles, caufing the wonderful
tranfmutations of one compound body into another of a different fpecies, as is
to be feen in the courfe of our operations upon falts and metals, giving us clear
and comprehenfive ideas of the principles of life or generation, and putrefaction
or death.

Finally, to conclude, we are chiefly to confider one thing to be attained as
the ground of perfection in the reft: *i. e.* The great *Firft Caufe*, the *Eternal
Wifdom*, to know the Creator by the contemplation of the creature. This is
the grand fecret of the philofophers, and the mafter-key to all fciences both
human and divine, for without this we are ftill wandering in a labyrinth of per-
plexity and errors, of darknefs and obfcurity: for this is the fum and perfection
of all learning, to live in the fear of God, and in love and charity with all men.

FINIS.

W. Blackader, Printer,
30, Tooke's Court, Chancery Lane.